Sally Booth

WAITING

D0095612

BOOKS BY VINCENT CRAPANZANO

The Fifth World of Forster Bennett

*The Hamadsha: An Esssay on
Moroccan Ethnopsychiatry*

Case Studies in Spirit Possession
(co-editor with V. Garrison)

Tuhami: A Portrait of a Moroccan

Waiting: The Whites of South Africa

WAITING

THE WHITES OF SOUTH AFRICA

Vincent Crapanzano

Vintage Books
A Division of Random House
New York

First Vintage Books Edition, April 1986

Copyright © 1985, 1986 by Vincent Crapanzano

All rights reserved under International and Pan-American Copyright Conventions.
Published in the United States by Random House, Inc., New York, and
simultaneously in Canada by Random House of Canada Limited, Toronto.
Originally published by Random House, Inc., in 1985.

Portions of this book have appeared in
The New Yorker.

Library of Congress Cataloging-in-Publication Data

Crapanzano, Vincent, 1939–
Waiting: The Whites of South Africa.

Reprint. Originally published: New York: Random
House, 1985. With new epilogue.
Bibliography:
Includes index.
1. Whites—South Africa—Case Studies. I. Title.
DT764.W47C73   1986   305.8'034/068   85-40871
ISBN 0-394-74326-1 (pbk.)

Manufactured in the United States of America

Cover photograph by Sarah Webb Barrel/Sygma.

FOR
TESGEMARIAM ABEBE
AND
RUDOLPH SCHMIDT,
WHO DIED

ACKNOWLEDGMENTS

There are a great many people in the United States, Europe, and South Africa whom I should like to thank. To protect the identity of the people with whom I worked in South Africa, I have chosen not to name them. I have decided, therefore, not to name the Europeans and Americans who have also helped me with my research. They will all understand, I am sure. My research was supported by grants from the Wenner-Gren Foundation for Anthropological Research, the Rockefeller Foundation, and the City University of New York BSC-CUNY Research Award Program.

All personal and place names have been changed to protect the identity of those with whom I worked in South Africa. Other changes have also been made to protect their identity.

CONTENTS

INTRODUCTION

Waiting is about the effects of domination on everyday life—not the everyday life of people who suffer domination but of people who dominate. It treats a minority, the whites of South Africa, who make up roughly 16 percent of the population of the country, and who systematically control the fate of the remaining 84 percent. It is not about the sources of economic, political, and military power or of their display; rather, it is about the discourse of people who are privileged by that power and, paradoxically, in their privilege victims of it. My concern is with social entrapment—with the way in which a people's understanding of themselves, their world, their past, and their future limits their possibility. Potentially, there is a tragic dimension to entrapment, but tragedy demands a kind of consciousness that is generally lacking in white South Africa. In that South Africa what could have been tragedy is often little more than a tale of self-indulgence, cowardice, and bad faith.

Insofar as possible, I have allowed the white South Africans with whom I lived and worked as an anthropologist to tell their own stories in *Waiting*. I have accompanied those stories with my own —my observations, explications, and interpretations. I have tried to re-create something of the cacophony of my—the—South African experience. In structure, *Waiting* came to me to resemble a novel —novels, as the Russian literary critic Mikhail Bakhtine observed,[1] are in essence plurivocal. This plurivocality, the cacophony, the baroque quality, if you will, of social reality is often sacrificed in ethnographic and sociological description to a theoretically inspired classicism. I do not mean to deny the "classical" dimension of social life, its symmetry, its simplicity, and its consistency. I do mean to call attention to the fact that symmetry, simplicity, and consistency are often lost to the social actor through the baroque texture of his everyday life.

Loss, of course, is not without moral implications. At least, this is the case in South Africa, where the discourse of whites describing themselves and their world is weighed with their rationalizations. It carries its own contradictions. It asserts at once privilege, domination, hierarchy, and a common, egalitarian fellowship of men and women in Christ. "Race" is the primary category through which the contradictions are mediated, but other categories, figures, and images play a role. These include "biological inheritance," "evolution," "blood," "culture," "background," "education," "mentality," "intelligence," "personality," "God's will," "the Tower of Babel," and "the unequal distribution of grace." They all figure in the talk of the average white South African and enable him at times, though not always, to avoid the moral implications of his discourse.

The people in *Waiting* come mainly from a little village north of Cape Town. They are English- and Afrikaans-speaking white South Africans who live in ease—some in considerable luxury—in one of the oldest European settlements on the African continent. In many respects they are unique; indeed, they pride themselves on uniqueness. But their discourse is similar to that of other white South Africans. They may speak a dialect, as it were, but their "dialect" is not incomprehensible to the rest of South Africa—or, in many respects, to Europeans and Americans.

The Republic of South Africa is about three times the size of California, and it has a population, including the population of the homelands, of about 28.6 million people,[2] which is broken down in South Africa's official racial classification into four groups.* There

---

*In this book, I have followed the common usage of the whites with whom I worked. "Whites" or "Europeans" refers to Caucasians and people like the Japanese, so-called honorary whites, who have all the rights and privileges of the whites. "English" usually refers to English-speaking white South Africans. "Coloureds," occasionally "Browns" (Afrikaans *bruins*), designates people of mixed descent. "Hottentots" and "Bushmen" are sometimes included in popular usage. "Asians"

are 20.7 million Africans, or Blacks; 2.6 million Coloureds, or people of mixed descent; 800,000 Asians; and 4.5 million whites. Sixty percent of the whites are Afrikaners (descendants of seventeenth-century Dutch, German, and Huguenot settlers), and the rest are English-speaking. There is considerable hostility between the two groups. The present government and bureaucracy are almost entirely in the hands of the Afrikaners. Until recently, the English-speaking whites—including about 130,000 Jews—had virtual control of the private economic sector. The Asians, whose ancestors were indentured laborers brought to South Africa in the last decades of the nineteenth century and the first decades of the twentieth, are almost entirely Indian. Seventy percent are Hindu, 20 percent Muslim, and 8 percent Christian. Their principal languages are Urdu and Gujarati. Most of them live in the province of Natal. The Coloureds, who live principally in the Cape Province, are the descendants of whites and of slaves imported from Madagascar, tropical Africa, and Southeast Asia, and local Khoikhoi (Hottentots) and San (Bushmen). Most speak Afrikaans and are members of the Dutch Reformed Church.* They have almost no ties with traditional African cultures. The Black population, over two thirds of which is rural, can be divided into four ethnolinguistic groups: the Nguni, the largest, which includes the Xhosa, the Zulu, the Swazi, and the Ndebele; the Sotho, the second largest; the Venda; and the Tsonga. There are important cultural and linguistic differences between these groups, differences that are stressed by the South African government in its divide-and-rule policy, but are attenuated by a common opposition to the present Nationalist government. About two thirds of the Blacks are nominally Christian. They are by far the poorest people in the country.

South Africa occupies a semiarid plateau, separated from a narrow coastal strip by a long escarpment. Twenty-one percent of the coun-

---

or "Indians" is used for the descendants of Indian and Chinese indentured laborers. "Blacks" refers to the Bantu populations of the country. "Africans" and the derogatory terms "Bantus" and "kaffirs" are used by some whites. I have not adopted the convention of some authors of referring to "non-whites" as "Blacks" and to the Bantu peoples as "Africans." This was not common usage in the Cape. My use of these racial terms should in no way be construed as an acceptance of them. They are, to use the anthropological jargon, "native categories."

*About 70,000 of them, known as Cape Malays, are Muslims and in some ways are treated as a separate group.

try gets less than eight inches of rain a year and another 47 percent between eight and twenty-four inches. Droughts, as in the last few years, are frequent. There are no navigable rivers, few forests, and the animal life that greeted the first European settlers has been pushed back into the most marginal areas. The climate is mild—people in Cape Town like to say they have a Mediterranean climate—the soil is often rich, and the country has immense mineral resources, seventy of them exploitable. Gold—the country's main source of foreign income—and diamonds are the most important of these resources, but there are also rich deposits of copper, iron, manganese, asbestos, coal, silver, beryllium, antimony, uranium, tin, vanadium, chrome, and platinum in the country. As far as anyone knows, there is no oil in South Africa, although some off-shore finds have recently been made south of Mossel Bay.

With such vast mineral resources, a high level of industrial development, and a very considerable agricultural potential, South Africa is an important economic power. Its gross national product accounts for over 20 percent of the GNP of the entire African continent. South Africa produces 90 percent of the continent's steel and generates as much electricity as the rest of Africa together. (Its recoverable coal reserves can supply more energy—a total of 1,300 trillion megajoules—than Saudi Arabia's oil reserves, which can produce about 1,000 trillion megajoules.) The country has advanced communication and transportation systems—more telephones and automobiles than the rest of Africa. It not only feeds itself but exports food to other countries in Africa and to Europe. Its ports are important links in international trade. The United States, Great Britain, West Germany, France, and Japan account for almost two thirds of South Africa's trade. (The United States has replaced Great Britain as South Africa's biggest trading partner; in 1981 2.7 billion rand* of American goods were sold in South Africa and 1.3 billion rand of South African products were sold in the United States.) South Africa has recently increased its trade with Israel, South Korea, Taiwan, and several South American countries. In 1982 its exports to other African countries were worth 926 million rand, and its imports were valued at 329 million rand. Foreign investment in

---

*The rand is the official South African currency. At the time of my research, the value of the rand ranged from about $1.30, the first year, to $0.90 the second year. On November 5, 1984, it was valued at $0.56.

US. Investmts.

South Africa has been shrinking in real terms over the past few years, but since the Reagan administration began its policy of "constructive engagement," United States investments there have increased—by 13 percent in 1982. Foreign investment totaled 32.5 billion rand (or 46 percent of South Africa's gross domestic product) in 1981. Sixty-eight percent of this investment was accounted for by Western Europe, with Great Britain contributing the most. United States direct investment that year was 2.8 billion rand. The South Africa government itself controls 47 percent of South Africa's fixed capital stock and contributes 26 percent of the country's gross domestic product. Many of the largest industries, the parastatals, are owned and run by the government. (ARMSCOR, an arms development and production corporation, is one, and ISCOR, an iron and steel company, is another). South Africa's military is modern, disciplined, and, despite an international arms blockade, well equipped.

South Africa is a parliamentary democracy with a racially limited franchise. Afrikaners have dominated the government since 1948, and despite the recent creation of largely symbolic Coloured and Asian parliaments (but no Black parliament), political control of the country remains in the hands of the whites. In fact, the white executive president now has near-dictatorial powers. At the time of my research in 1980 and 1981, there were four main legal white parties: the far-right Herstigte Nasionale Party (HNP), whose membership is almost entirely Afrikaner; the governing right-wing National Party (NP); the New Republic Party (NRP), essentially a conservative English party, though called centrist; and the "liberal," largely English-speaking Progressive Federal Party (PFP), usually referred to as the Progs. In February 1983, an Afrikaner cabinet minister named Andries Treurnicht defected from the National Party in protest against the creation of a tricameral parliament and started a fifth party, the Conservative Party (CP). Since Treurnicht's defection, the National Party has been strengthened by some English conservatives. It is too soon to judge the Conservative Party's influence, or the influence that Coloured and Asian parties will have in the new government. Most Coloureds and Asians boycotted their first elections in August of 1984. Blacks, of course, have no power.

South Africa has four provinces: the Cape of Good Hope Province, which is the largest; the Transvaal; the Orange Free State; and Natal, which is the smallest. Pretoria is the administrative capital;

Cape Town, the legislative. The Appellate Division of the Supreme Court, the highest court in the republic, sits in Bloemfontein, in the Orange Free State. (The law is Roman-Dutch.) South West Africa, or Namibia, which was a German colony mandated to South Africa by the League of Nations after World War I, is still administered by South Africa, although the United Nations has ordered that it be granted complete independence. It is an area of considerable— and continual—fighting. South Africa also includes ten homelands, or Bantustans, of varying constitutional status and political integrity. Essentially a continuation of an African "reserve" system, instituted under the Union in 1913 and amended in 1936, these homelands are crude categories meant to control the influx of Blacks into "white" South Africa. They "solve" the Black problem by declaring Blacks to be citizens of homelands, in which supposedly they have full political rights and responsibilities. Apart from Blacks who were born in a white urban area or who have lived there legally for the last fifteen years or who are dependent on someone in one of these categories, Blacks can only be employed in white urban areas on a contractual basis and do not have the right to bring their families with them. The homelands have to accommodate 36 percent of the total South African population (52 percent of the Black population), with only 13 percent of the country's land.* The land they do have is generally poor; the governments are corrupt. In 1980 they produced 3.4 percent of South Africa's total gross domestic product. The homelands have been especially hard-hit by the recent drought. Poverty is acute and relieved only by remittances from contract workers and by limited South African government transfer payments. (The proportion of destitute families—families without any income, land, or cattle—rose from 5 percent in 1960 to 13 percent in 1980.) According to a recent report,[3] 80 percent of the homeland population—roughly 8 million people—live below a stringently defined poverty level, and despite the fact that South Africa is considered an upper-middle-income country by the World Bank, it ranks forty-seventh in life expectancy at birth and sixty-fourth in infant mortality out of 117 non-Soviet-bloc countries. In real terms,

---

*Homeland populations have more than doubled in the last twenty years—largely from natural increase but also from the forced removal of Blacks from white areas. The percentage of Blacks living in white rural areas fell from 35 percent in 1950 to 21 percent in 1980.

over 50,000 children die each year of hunger in South Africa—
almost all of them children of color and most living in the homelands. Only one of the homelands—the tiny Qwaqwa, with a population of about 50,000—consists of a single, contiguous territory.
The other nine homelands are scattered over 200 separate areas.
Four of the homelands—Transkei, Bophuthatswana, Venda, and
Ciskei—have been granted "independence" by the South African
government. None of them have been recognized as "independent"
by anybody else. All polls indicate that the Black population of
South Africa would prefer a single multiracial democratic South
Africa to any of the "homeland" alternatives. Chief Gatsha Buthelezi of KwaZulu, one of South Africa's most important leaders,
and Enos Mebuzu of KaNgwane, the Swazi homeland, have been
most vocal in refusing "independence" for their homelands. Tens
of thousands of Africans have been arrested for illegally entering
"white" South Africa from their homelands.

The homelands are one of the many monstrous creations of apartheid. Since the Nationalists came to power in 1948, they have elaborated a body of often contradictory, easily manipulated, certainly
discriminatory laws, regulations, and agencies that serve to maintain
baasskap ("bossdom"), or white supremacy.[4] Based on previous laws
and regulations, crudely rationalized by a romantic-nationalistic
philosophy of separate development, or apartheid—"apartheid"
means "separateness" in Afrikaans—these laws, regulations, and
agencies systematically determine a person's rights and privileges on
the basis of his or her racial classification. Apologists for apartheid
insist that the Population Registration Act of 1950, the cornerstone
of apartheid, which assigns every person to a racial group, is a law
of differentiation and not of discrimination, since all South Africans,
whites as well as non-whites, are classified.* They argue that by
permitting each group to develop "in its own time and in accordance with its own predispositions," apartheid provides the only
realistic basis for a truly plural society. They sometimes support
their argument by reference to the Tower of Babel, a sign, they say,

---

*Similar arguments have been advanced for other "cornerstones" of apartheid: the
Prohibition of Mixed Marriages Act of 1949, which forbids marriages between
Europeans and non-Europeans; the Immorality Acts of 1950 and 1957, which outlaw
sexual relations between whites and non-whites; the Group Areas Act of 1950,
revised in 1957 and 1966, which provides the basis for residential and business
segregation; and various acts concerning freedom of person, speech, and assembly.

of God's desire to preserve a pluriracial, pluricultural, polyglot world. (White South Africans, especially Afrikaners, often substitute culture and language for race.) They attribute many of the world's problems to racial mixture—to ignoring God's "commandment" to respect separate identities. Many of them are messianic and actually see in apartheid a new social order that, according to God's will, will eventually spread to free the world of its serious social problems.

The most blatantly discriminatory policy in the country is the government's refusal to give the vote to Blacks and, until recently, to the Coloureds and Asians. But there are many more discriminatory practices, and they affect the everyday life of non-whites. The Black Areas Consolidation Act of 1945, the misnamed Black Abolition of Passes and Co-ordination of Documents Act of 1952, and the Black Labour Act of 1964 all restrict the movement of Africans. Unlike whites, Coloureds, and Asians, all Blacks are required to carry a reference book, or pass, with them. A policeman can demand to see that pass at any time and for any reason. A Black without a pass is open to arrest and return to his or her homeland. Other legislation, symbolized by the SLEGS BLANKES or WHITES ONLY signs, limits access to restaurants, railway cars, buses, taxis, beaches, elevators, movie houses . . . Although no legislation specifically forbids integrated sports, most sports are in fact segregated. Schools, universities, and hospitals are segregated. (Facilities are, of course, much poorer for non-whites than for whites.) Other legislation—most notably the Internal Security Act of 1976 (based on the Suppression of Communism Act of 1950), the Sabotage Act of 1962, and the Terrorism Act of 1967, which restrict the civil liberties of all South Africans by permitting arbitrary banning and detention, by restricting the freedom of speech and information, and by limiting association and assembly—serves mainly to reinforce the most discriminatory policies of apartheid. These policies are complemented by illegal pressures, threats, harassment, sabotage, and personal violence.

Opposition to apartheid tends to be fragmented and disorganized, and it is often symbolic. This is in part the result of government strong-arm tactics. The African National Congress (ANC), the oldest and most popular opposition movement in South Africa, the Pan-Africanist Congress (PAC), and many other opposition groups are banned. Interracial associations that can be construed as political in intent are illegal. Important Black leaders, such as Nelson Mandela, Walter Sisulu, and Govan Mbeki of the ANC, are in jail; others, such as Steve Biko, have died in jail or have been killed; and thousands more have been summarily arrested, detained without trial, harassed, and banned. White anti-apartheid activists have also been arrested, detained, harassed and banned.* In February 1982, Neil Aggett, a union organizer, died in the custody of the security police. Ruth First, a longtime opponent of apartheid, was killed by a letter bomb in Mozambique in 1982. Joe Gqabi, the chief ANC representative in Zimbabwe, was assassinated there in 1981. ANC headquarters in Lesotho, Mozambique, and Swaziland have been raided repeatedly by South African soldiers over the last few years, and these raids, as well as economic pressure, have forced South Africa's neighbors to clamp down on the ANC in their territories.[5]

In part, too, the fragmented character of the opposition has to do with the different interests of whites, Coloureds, Asians, and Africans. Among Blacks, tribal differences play a role, but presumably not as great a role as the government would have it. (Differences are, of course, accentuated by the homeland policy.) There are also important differences in political and ideological sophistication between urban and rural Blacks and across generations. There is internal conflict in the ANC and between the ANC and other Black organizations, such as Chief Gatsha Buthelezi's Zulu-based Inkatha, which is the largest Black movement in South Africa today.[6] Although some Coloureds and Asians identify ideologically with the Africans, many are afraid of becoming objects of Black rage if and when the Blacks come to power. They think, for example, of the Indians—Ugandan Asians—who were brutally forced out of Uganda in 1972 by Idi Amin Dada. And—despite the courage and obvious dedication of a lot of anti-apartheid whites—their opposition is often tempered by the fear of losing privilege, of possible

---

*According to *The Economist* (March 17, 1984), between 750 and 800 people were in detention. The minister of justice, Kobie Coetsee, reported in February 1984 that 385 people (15 whites, 5 Coloureds, 2 Asians, and 363 Blacks) were serving sentences for acts against state security. As a result of pressure from the United States, the number of banned was reduced in June 1983 from 66 to 12. As of March 1, 1984, 56 people have died in detention since 1963, when the detention laws first went into effect. Since the riots that broke out after the elections for Coloured and Asian members of parliament in August 1984, there has been a dramatic increase in the number of people detained and arrested. According to the *New York Times* (November 8, 1984), between January 1 and November 1, 1984, over 1,000 people were detained and another 2,000 arrested.

violence in the event of a Black takeover, of government harassment, or of the "communists" they see behind the ANC and other Black organizations.* Politically, whites against apartheid are represented by the Progressive Federal Party, and the Progs are very much an "opposition" party, with a poorly articulated platform and very little real power. There are also a number of white organizations in the United Democratic Front (UDF), which was established in January 1983 to oppose the Botha government's constitutional reforms. A sort of umbrella group, representing some 575 organizations, UDF has been able to maintain thus far its multiracial character. Its fundamental aim is to do away with the group areas and the homelands in order to create a united democratic South Africa. It is opposed by some Black groups, and of course by many whites.

Despite the constant talk of change, of imminent bloodbath, of takeover and revolution, despite protests, boycotts, strikes, and acts of terrorism—the bombing of the SASOL coal-to-gas conversion plant in the spring of 1980, the bombing of the Koeberg nuclear power station in the winter of 1982, the bombing of Air Force headquarters in Pretoria in the fall of 1983—and despite the changes in South Africa's parliamentary system, it is my impression that South Africa today is caught in a deadened time of waiting. For most whites, waiting is compounded by fear; for most Blacks, however great their poverty or despair, waiting is illuminated by hope, by a belief that time is on their side. For the Coloureds and Asians, there is both fear *and* hope in waiting. What is clear to me—after many months in South Africa and many more months thinking and writing about South Africa—is that in the very ordinary act of waiting, particularly of waiting in fear, men and women lose what John Keats (in an obviously different context) called *negative capability,* the capability of so negating their identity as to be imaginatively open to the complex and never very certain reality around them. Instead, they close off; they create a kind of psychological apartheid, an apartness that in the case of South Africa is institutionally reinforced. In such circumstances there can be no real recognition of the other—no real appreciation of *his* subjectivity. He becomes at once a menial object to be manipulated and a mythic object to be feared. He cannot be counted in his humanity.

*Many whites have an unrealistic fear of communism—a fear that is encouraged by the government.

THE PEOPLE OF WYNDAL

CELIA, an English-speaking member of the Christian Renewal and one-time Satan worshiper.

PETER COOKE, an English farmer and former businessman.
  DONNA, his wife.

THE DOMINEE, Wyndal's white Dutch Reformed minister.

CAROLINE DU PLESSIS, an Afrikaner who suffers from cancer.

BARBARA ENDICOTT, a young English-speaking member of the Renewal.

CATHERINE FOX, a Jewish woman who retired to Wyndal.

JACK FREELING, an English farmer.
  CONSTANCE, his wife.
  IDA, his sixteen-year-old daughter.
  TONY, his fourteen-year-old son.

DORA HERTZOG, an Afrikaner farmer's daughter and a member of the commandoes.

ALBERT JORDAAN, a Coloured assistant priest in the Anglican Church.

DOMINEE PIETER KOTZE, a young liberal minister in the Dutch Reformed Mission Church.

HUGO MALAN, a farmer of Anglo-Afrikaner origin and former engineer.
  PEGGY, his wife.

DOMINEE RUDY MALHERBE, a Renewal preacher and an expert on the Illuminati.

IRENE PRINSLOO, an Afrikaner woman.
  KOBUS, her husband, a lawyer.
  TOMMY, her son, a farmer.
  MARGOT, her daughter-in-law.

CAROL REID, a retired English secretary.
  DUNCAN, her husband, a retired accountant.

GLEN ROSS, an Afrikaner farmer of Scottish origin, a former bookkeeper.

BEATRIX ROUSSOUW, an Afrikaner and Wyndal's unofficial historian.

OM MAX, her husband, a farmer.

ANDRE, her son, a farmer and a Renewal leader.

TAMARA, her English daughter-in-law.

DR. JAKOBUS STEYN, an Afrikaner and Wyndal's doctor.

HENNIE VAN DER MERWE, an Anglican priest of Afrikaner descent.

ROSE, his wife, an English piano teacher.

ZACHARY, his son, a stage designer in Johannesburg.

DAVID, his son, a preacher.

PIET VAN ROOYEN, an Afrikaner hardware-store owner and Renewal leader.

ANNEMARIE, his wife.

PIET VILJOEN, an Afrikaner builder.

RUTH VISSER, an Afrikaner café manager.

WAITING

I

THE
VALLEY

The church—I always think of it as Hennie's church—lies east of
Wyndal in a field that is surrounded by vineyards and fruit trees.
It was built just after Union by an English farmer who, some say,
felt the need to commemorate his presence, an Englishman's presence, among a people who considered him, as well as the other
English whom he drew into the area, an enemy. He was an adventurer, the third son of a textile merchant from the Midlands, who
had managed to learn something about fruit farming in the American South and then as a volunteer in the Anglo-Boer War had
discovered the beauty and richness, the possibility, of the Cape. He
vowed to return if he survived the war, and return he did, on the
same ship as one of those great gold magnates from the Rand whom
he inspired, some say, conned, into buying up as many farms as he
could from the poor Dutch farmers who had been ruined by
drought and the great phylloxera epidemic of the last decades of the
nineteenth century. The textile merchant's son served as the mag-
nate's agent and bought up the farms with a vengeance that is still
not forgotten by the old Afrikaners of the region, who vowed never
to let an Englishman buy a farm there again. And then, as if to prove
his own imperial worth, he managed somehow to keep the best
farms for himself and a group of cronies from the Natal who were
rather more interested in playing cricket than in farming. The farms
were grape and fruit farms, and unlike the sugar plantations of the

Natal—lazy man's farms as the people of the Cape call them, not, I suspect, without a tinge of jealousy—they required work. On the plantations you had only to sit back on your stoep and drink your rum, your cane, and watch the sugar cane grow like weeds and the Zulu boys hack it down and carry it to the crusher. Here, in the Cape, you had to tend your vines and trees and make sure your Coloured boys, and their women, did not botch them up when they had a *dop*, a tot, too many. The farms that the Englishman bought up failed or, rather, had to be reorganized into a sort of cooperative, and the cricket players left, but the church, named after the Englishman's name-day saint, remained.

The church is not a beautiful church, particularly now that its thatched roof has been replaced by one of corrugated metal, painted black. It keeps the church drier, and colder, in the winter and renders it a cauldron in the summer, but the parish had no money either to rethatch the church or to insulate it properly. Hennie, a practical man, says that Christ knows neither heat nor cold. He grew up under a tin roof in the northern Cape and came to know Christ under a tin roof in Rhodesia. His white parishioners say there would have been money enough had the archbishop sent them a proper Anglican priest and not one of those charismatics, and an Afrikaner at that, who might just as well have been a Baptist. By this they mean they would have given enough money to rethatch the roof had Hennie devoted a little more attention to them and a little less to his Coloured parishioners.

Hennie's white parishioners are also offended by his manner and looks. He is not a distinguished-looking man and certainly does not give the impression of being a man of the cloth even in a country where almost everyone—that is, almost everyone white—calls his priest by his first name. He usually dresses in old black trousers that are shiny with age and in a soft, well-washed checked shirt. When he preaches, his surplice is always wrinkled and never quite white. He is a rough sort of man, with a severe limp, in his late fifties, always a bit out of place, always a bit awkward, never appearing quite clean (though he is in fact always well scrubbed). He is short, broad-shouldered, hollow-cheeked, thin-lipped, and pockmarked. (He had a very serious case of chicken pox just after his father died when he was thirteen and scratched the pocks until they bled.) A shock of silver-blond hair falls across his brow, giving him at times a rather boyish, almost mischievous look. His eyes are slate-blue and not particularly powerful, even when he looks deeply into yours. He is a patient man and kindly, but one has the impression, at least I have the impression, that much of his patience and kindliness are the result of tremendous self-discipline. He is, in any event, stubborn and uses his faith to bully those around him. He knows he is a character and makes full use of this in handling others. "He is a strange mixture of a man," another priest said. "He does not have much upstairs. He is a totally impossible priest, and yet the spirit has enabled him to convert and heal thousands." He is often just slightly off-key in his conversation, and I always had the impression that though he thought he knew what I was after, he did not really understand me or my task.

The parish house, Hennie's house, is a clumsy imitation, on a small scale, of the traditional H-shaped Cape Dutch house. The architect whom the Englishman engaged to build his church clearly had no idea of the domestic needs of a priest of a small parish and his family. Rose, Hennie's wife, has tried to make the house as comfortable as possible with the few pieces of furniture, mostly beds and chests of drawers, that she thought worth bringing down from Rhodesia and then up from Port Elizabeth, where Hennie was last assigned. Most of the furniture comes from one of those chain stores that give enormous credit to their customers and provide them with a wide range of contemporary lounge furniture and bedroom suites: walnut veneer on plywood with foam-rubber cushions and pillows covered in bright flowery synthetic fabrics. The walls are almost bare. In the lounge, as South Africans call the living room, Rose has hung a patchwork tapestry of Christ's Resurrection that was made for her as a farewell gift in their last Rhodesian parish. Over the mantel she has hung a faded watercolor of violets and gentians that she picked up in the Parade, a sort of flea market, in Cape Town. It reminded her of a poem she had written when she was a schoolgirl in Kimberley. Her piano stands untouched in one corner. She was once an exceptional pianist, but can no longer play, she says, because of her arthritis. I have seen her rub her knuckles as if to remind herself of the pain as she looks wistfully at the instrument.

The church and the parish house were placed without much concern for the landscape, on a poor piece of rocky land that the Englishman felt he could spare without much loss. (The grave diggers complain that the earth is so rocky they can't dig their graves deep enough.) Yet somehow the architect managed to re-create the domestic, the intimate, the hallowed space of an English close in a land and climate that are far removed from those of rural England. No grass grows—only clumps of weeds; but in the spring, after the winter rains, the close is covered with white and yellow flowers, and the pollen is so thick that the dirt track that leads from the church up to Hennie's house is often a bright yellow. Behind the house there are a few fruit trees, apple and peach, which give some shade to a vegetable garden that Rose has faithfully tended since her arrival in the parish about five years before. The garden had been neglected by their predecessor.

The little Anglican church stands like a guardhouse at the entrance to the valley, but until a few years ago, almost no one except an occasional English teacher at the local school went to it. The white parishioners were scattered in the plains to the east, and although it was open to people of all races (the Anglican Church has taken a strong stand against apartheid), few Coloureds and no Blacks—there are very few Blacks in the region—attended. They preferred to go to a smaller church that they themselves built, with the help of another farmer, nearer to where they lived, mainly because the priests that preceded Hennie were English or English-speaking South Africans and could not conduct services in Afrikaans, the language the Coloureds speak in the rural areas of the Cape. Hennie of course changed all that.

Before the arrival of the English, nearly everyone in Wyndal attended the Dutch Reformed church. The Afrikaners went to the large cream-colored church, with an enormous, almost majestic, steeple, on the village green. Built a little over a hundred years ago, after the old village church burned down, it has recently been restored. Its highly polished pews and elaborate, thronelike pulpit that still smell of varnish seem to conflict with its stark dimensions and its puritanical spirit. The church, the church hall, and the minister's house are the geographical center of the village, and until the English began moving in a few years earlier, were the center of village life as well.

The Coloureds—they are not permitted to attend services in the white Dutch Reformed church—go to the sprawling Dutch Reformed Mission church, which, as in so many Cape villages, is a source of some embarrassment to the white community, more to the rural administration, because it is located in the white section of Wyndal and not in the squalid Coloured village, a giant eyesore to the north that was legislated into existence shortly after the Afrikaners' National Party came to power in 1948 and began to engineer apartheid. There are, theoretically, plans to build a new church for the Coloureds in their own village, but no one really takes them seriously, and the radical white minister in the Mission church has done everything in his power to discourage the project.

Wyndal lies sparkling white in the center of the valley. It consists of the village green and a few streets that run parallel to the valley walls. They are named after such Afrikaner heroes as the Boer generals Botha and De Wet, the Great Trek leader Piet Retief, and Dirkie Uys, the fourteen-year-old boy who preferred to die alongside his father during a Zulu war than flee. On the main street are a few shops, a garage, a bank in the Cape Dutch style, a farmer's cooperative—a sort of supermarket—the town hall, and Harry's and two other cafés. (A café in South Africa is a small grocery store where one can also buy sandwiches, cold drinks, and other takeout foods. Food and drinks are not served on the premises.) Harry's, once owned by a Jew, whose father, a *smous*, or peddler, made good, is now run by a dark-skinned Portuguese refugee from Mozambique who is resented by Wyndal's "better" Coloureds—school teachers mostly—because he is classified as white and has all the privileges of a white man. The farm workers prefer his café because he gives credit easily. He himself is bitter because his wife has to drive their two daughters about 500 kilometers a week to and from the nearest English "medium" school. The English in the village who send their children to the school have never asked her to join their car pool, or lift club, as it is called.

The village school, on the corner of De Wet and Malan Street, is officially a dual medium school, that is, a school offering instruction in both English and Afrikaans. But, in fact, there has not been a "proper" English teacher at the school since the early sixties. The school buildings are enormous for a village as small as Wyndal. It once had a hostel for several hundred children attached to it, but this was closed down a few years ago. Although there has been some talk of making it into a conference center, and at least one enterprising villager has thought of making it into a hotel, for now it stands empty.

Through standard four (sixth grade) Coloured children go to school in their own village, where several barracks were quickly constructed after apartheid. Only one of these has electricity. The old Coloured school next to the Mission church in the white village —a sturdy building built by the church in the thirties—is still used for students in standards five and six, the highest standards to which the local Coloured school goes. The headmaster and the minister at the Mission church insist that these older children must have a full day of school if they are to go on to high school, and yet the school is on shifts because there are not enough classrooms for all the students. The school secretary has to use the stock room as her office.

There is a second bank, the Volkskas, an Afrikaner bank, on the green, and a tea shop, which also sells pottery, fancy candles, tie-dyed kerchiefs, and other handicrafts made by the younger genera-tion of village women. The doctor and the dentist have converted an old house on Epernaystraat into a small medical center. The pharmacy is just across the street. The houses on the green are large, but many of the small houses on Dirkie Uys Street, which are among the oldest in Wyndal, some dating back to the beginning of the last century, have now been carefully restored by retired couples from Cape Town and farmers who have either sold their farms to the new English residents or have given them to their sons to farm. Many of these houses once belonged to Coloured families, until they were dispossessed and forced to move into the Coloured village. Taking advantage of the situation at the time, whites bought up the houses and made a killing. Several contemporary houses, Mediterra-nean villas painted bright yellow or pale green, with sweeping outside staircases and patios over their three-car garages, have been built by the doctor, the dentist, a semiretired accountant, and a banker—all Afrikaners, the English are quick to remind you—on a knoll just behind the green. Without regard to the demands of the landscape or to the subtleties of Cape Dutch architecture, they stand like monuments to the new-found wealth and status of the Afri-kaner. The English prefer the more traditional Cape houses.

It is difficult to estimate the population of the valley, for it does not form a political unit for which there is a census. Some inhabi-tants think of the valley as ending at Hennie's church; others, at a farm just before the church; and still others extend it beyond the church by several kilometers. The white village has a population of just over 1,000, while the population of the Coloured village is a little more than double that. The majority of whites, many of them retired, are over thirty-five; the majority of Coloureds are children.

Aside from the villagers, there are also the farmers and their laborers. In the official census, the farms are included in a larger rural district. According to Beatrix Roussouw, the valley's unofficial historian, there are just over 120 farms in the valley, partitions of the dozen original farms that the Dutch East India Company granted to French Huguenots who had sought refuge in Holland after the revocation of the Edict of Nantes in 1685. The farms have a white population of between 500 and 600 and a Coloured population that is probably close to 3,000. Some farms have as many as twenty Coloured families living on them, and others have only one or two families. There are a few Black contract laborers from the Transkei as well. Before the Group Areas Act of 1950, which set up special residential zones for different racial groups, there had been a small Black population that lived in a clearing in the woods at the entrance to the village. There were not enough of them for a township of their own, Beatrix Roussouw says, so one Saturday they were rounded up and moved to the nearest town that had a Black location, that is, a district officially set aside for Blacks. "They are happier now living with their own kind," she insists even though she has never talked to any of them, either before or after their move. Some farmers also make use of prison labor, but with the increase in the cost of fuel, they are beginning to find it cheaper to hire permanent or day laborers than to drive the prisoners eighty kilometers to and from the prison each day.

The farms surround the village on all sides. The older ones consist of a main house and a small second house, the *junkerhuis*, as it used to be called, to which the boys of the family moved when they reached adolescence. Today, these second houses on the Afrikaner farms are often inhabited by the married son who will take over the farm upon his father's death or retirement.

The main house is almost always an elegant white single-storied H-shaped building made of stucco on brick, with a bow-shaped gable, a sort of flourish, often decorated with a scroll, over its main facade—a remnant of the baroque that otherwise seems forgotten in the rectilinear puritanism of Afrikaner farm life. (One also finds remnants of the baroque in the engravings that illustrate some of the old family Bibles. Salome, naked angels, and Rubenesque Goliaths are simply not "seen" by today's farmers.) Most of these old farmhouses have been carefully restored and have a well-polished look about them. Though only a few still have thatched roofs, several have their original wine cellars (always aboveground in South Africa), which are now used as packing sheds, and at least one has an original "slave bell," which is still rung in the mornings to summon the farmhands. Its stand is freshly painted each year.

The English have been particularly careful to preserve the original character of the old houses, furnishing them with yellowwood stinkwood pieces along with deep couches and armchairs upholstered in bright chintzes. The Afrikaners are more eclectic, combining original Cape Dutch pieces with Victorian chairs and settees. They prefer yellow or red silk upholstery when they can afford it. Their walls are covered with old family portraits and Victorian watercolors. Several of the English have collected South African oils —mainly scenes that seem to occupy a muddy space between the impressionists and the expressionists. There are few books in any of the houses, and the television set usually occupies a privileged place in the lounge or den.

Within a few hundred meters of the main house are the workers' quarters: crude squat white two- or three-room houses with corrugated metal roofs. Although some of the farmers have put in concrete floors, electricity, and running water, many of the workers' houses still have hard earthen floors that turn to mud during the winter rains, no electricity, and no running water. They are usually furnished in a dispirited and desultory way with farm castoffs—a rickety old kitchen table, an iron bedstead or two, a stuffed chair bursting at the seams, a warped chest, brightly painted and peeling —which are as frequently purchased from a neighbor or from the used furniture shop on Kerkstraat as they are gifts from the farmer himself. A few of the better-off laborers have bought veneered wardrobes and beds from one of the modern buy-on-credit furniture shops in the hypermarket, a giant shopping center, near Cape Town.

The farmhouses are surrounded by green lawns, flagstone patios, bright beds of flowers—a turbulent mix of irises and proteas (South Africa's national flower), roses and aloes (the symbol of a stubborn, desiccated survival in Athol Fugard's play, *A Lesson from Aloes*), geraniums and bougainvillea, poinsettias, and bird-of-paradise flowers, to name only a few—and groves of exotic trees, such as jacarandas, kumquats, frangipani, Cape lilacs, cinnamon trees, cypresses, magnolias, wild olives, and poplars imported from Europe, North and South America, Australia, the Pacific islands, and farther north in Africa. Occasionally there is an allée of oaks, a legacy of a seventeenth-century Dutch governor's passion for planting oaks. The *werwe*, or farmyards, of several of the oldest farms are still enclosed by high white stucco walls, which give the places an almost Moorish look. The workers' houses have no gardens and are rarely shaded by trees.

Beyond the gardens are the vineyards and the orchards of apples, pears, plums, and peaches, which, given the new, more productive trellis method of cultivation, have lost much of their beauty, and fields in which a horse or two or some milch cows graze. Higher up the mountains are the dams, manmade ponds, which collect the winter rains and provide water for irrigation and drinking. A few farmers have stocked the larger ones with fish and ducks. The ponds are often surrounded by willows, reeds, and poplars, and at dusk, as the mountains become two-dimensional, their deep brown water reflects the valley walls and the fiery orange glow of the setting sun. It is the time when farmers walk their dogs.

The vineyards and orchards are in transition. Some farmers are switching from grapes to the more lucrative pears and plums. (In 1979 the gross income from the traditional white grapes grown in the area was about 5,000 rand per hectare; from pears and plums, depending on the variety, it ranged between 12,000 and 18,000 rand.)* Others, generally those with the most capital, are upgrading their grapes in the hope of bottling their own wine. The South African government has set up experimental farms and various advisory boards to help the farmers modernize their farms; with drip irrigation, trellis planting, and the careful use of fertilizers and weed killers, production can be dramatically increased. (Using the Australian teturia system of trellises, for example, a farmer can plant as many as 2,000 peach trees per hectare—traditionally he planted only about 400—and thereby increase his production of canning peaches from less than 30 tons per hectare to over 100 tons.)

One or two of the farms in the valley, owned by wealthy businessmen from Johannesburg—Johannesburg businessmen are proverbi-

---

*In 1982 and 1983 the valley farmers suffered severe losses with the collapse of the international fruit market. According to one farmer, the yield for white grapes per hectare now ranges between 3,000 and 3,600 rand; for pears, between 12,000 and 16,000 rand; and for plums, between 7,500 and 10,000 rand. Several farmers have been forced to sell, and other who have the capital are switching to estate-bottled wines.

ally wealthy to the Cape farmer—has been fully developed, but the majority are still in the early phases of development. There are several reasons for this. For one, despite long-term farm loans at minimum rates, various tax breaks, and other financial incentives, the modernization of a vineyard or fruit farm still requires considerable capital outlay. One farmer estimated that it cost him in 1979 over 5,000 rand per hectare just to put in drip irrigation.* For another, it takes time to modernize a fruit farm—plum trees begin to produce in three years, and pear trees, in six. For yet another, many farmers have been reluctant to rush their improvements. The fruit market is considered to be a luxury market and is subject to great oscillations in price, not only because of economic conditions abroad—most of the fruit produced in the valley is exported to England and northern Europe—and competition from other countries—Greece, for example, for peaches—but also because of changes in fashion. And, of course, there is always the unspoken threat of a boycott or, worse still, a change in status quo.

Serious development began only in the mid-seventies, when wealthy English, mainly from Durban, who were afraid to buy farms in the Natal because of their possible incorporation into KwaZulu, the Zulu homeland that the Nationalist government has been trying to create for more than twenty years now, started to move to Wyndal, as well as Rhodesians, locally called "when we's" because they always talk about "when we were" in Rhodesia (never Zimbabwe), and white farmers who were forced, or felt themselves forced, to leave Zambia, Kenya, and Malawi. Unlike the local Afrikaners, they had the capital not only to purchase farms at a price earnings multiple that was considered suicidal by the local farmers but also to make improvements. Most of the farms they purchased needed to be completely rehauled, irrigated, and replanted. After a time, with increased production and generally inflationary conditions, the price the English had paid for the farms and the cost of improvements no longer seemed so outrageous to the local farmers, and those that had sufficient capital or credit, especially if their sons had studied agriculture at Stellenbosch University, as many of them had, also began to improve their farms. Some who did not have sufficient capital were unable to carry through their improvements and found themselves forced to sell or live under the burden of heavy debt. Of course, those who had neither capital nor credit have

---

*Estimates in 1984 were 10,000 rand per hectare.

been gradually selling, but a few of the most conservative farmers, whose tenacity Beatrix Roussouw never ceases to praise, hold on to their farms and their traditional methods of cultivation. Their children have at least the pleasure of watching the farms increase in value. An underdeveloped farm that sold well in 1975 for 50,000 rand now sells, with capital improvements of 100,000 rand, for 450,000 rand or more if it has a fine old Cape Dutch house on it.*

The improvement in earnings is of course dependent on cheap labor. With the exception of Hugo Malan, a very Anglicized Afrikaner who had a lucrative engineering firm in Pietermaritzburg before he came to the valley, none of the farmers has talked of mechanized farming. Fruit growing and grape farming are labor-intensive in South Africa, and although there is some seasonal labor (mainly the farmhands' wives and daughters), most farmers prefer a permanent labor force even if it costs them a bit more each year. Wages have in fact increased dramatically if looked at from a percentage point of view, though hardly if looked at in absolute terms. In 1975 the average farm laborer was paid 5.50 rand (roughly 6 dollars) a week plus a wine allowance and provided with, the farmers are quick to remind you, free housing, free firewood, and free uniforms. The English farmers virtually doubled wages within a year or two of their arrival (causing rather less resentment among the Afrikaner families than I, at least, would have expected), and today the average laborer receives between 25 and 30 rand a week, no wine or only a bottle on payday, and of course free housing, free firewood, and free uniforms. (There are, however, farmers in the valley, some of those most admired by Beatrix Roussouw, who pay their workers 12 rand a week.) Some exceptionally good workers are paid as much as 38 rand a week; women, who serve as pickers or work in gardens or as maids, are paid about half as much as men.†
Most farmers give bonuses of 50 to 100 rand to their workers at the

*Since my research in 1980 and 1981, the price of houses in South Africa soared, but it collapsed by as much as 40 percent in 1984. Farm prices in the valley have, however, held their own because, as one farmer put it, "we are still in a desirable location, far from all that trouble up north." He was referring to the 1984 riots. Those farmers who plan to sell are holding on until the South African economy improves.

†The average laborer received between 15 and 20 rand a week at the time of my research. Some were paid as little as 7 rand; the best were paid 38 rand. Given inflation, the worker in Wyndal is no better off than he was three years ago. Some say that he is worse off.

end of the season and drive them to the hypermarket, where they can make major purchases. Others have recently taken to giving monthly bonuses on an award system. A worker from a church or caught in a fight receives no bonus.

The workers walk everywhere: to the fields, to visit friends and relatives at other farms, to the liquor store for Coloureds behind the Berg Hotel (an excuse really for selling liquor since no one has spent a night there in years), to the shops in the village on Saturdays (when the village belongs to the Coloureds since the whites do all their shopping on weekdays to avoid them), to church on Sundays and every evening during Pentecostal services. They walk for miles, and only occasionally, as if to confirm the futility of their gesture, do they try to hail a passing *bakkie*, as the South Africans call a pickup truck; unless they are recognized, they will not be given a ride. Their children, barefoot in summer and winter alike, never seem to walk. They are always running, to and from school, to and from the nearest café for a loaf of bread or, if they are lucky, a piece of candy. What I have found most saddening and yet hopeful is that as they run they smile even at the hardened drivers of the white Mercedes, who have learned not to see them and their smiles.

The farmers never run or walk. They are always behind the wheel of a car or *bakkie*. As one English woman put it, "All our friends have white Mercedes."

The valley is isolated, not just for the workers, who must spend almost ten percent of their weekly salary to take the bus to the nearest town, but for the whites as well. The whites do shop in the town, but they rarely go to Cape Town. They complain about the cost of fuel and the cheeky manners of the Cape Town Coloureds and thereby justify their immobility and their isolation. They preserve, too, what a visitor from Johannesburg once called "a serene unawareness" of the terror and degradation that surrounds them.

Wyndal looks stubbornly European, a sort of restless cross between a Norman orchard and a Burgundian vineyard, a Dutch village and an Alpine valley, especially when the mountaintops are covered with snow. From the air it seems like a green oasis, bright white houses lost in the middle of the deeply crevassed, gray-granite mountains that lie to the north of Cape Town. These mountains are dangerous, alien, and savage. Each year hikers are lost in them, and some die of the cold before they are discovered, or of a snakebite. Until a few years ago the valley was protected by a leopard whose presence kept the baboons from wrecking the farmers' trellises, but a forester killed the leopard and now the farmers are forced to set baboon traps to protect their fields. The baboons soon learn to avoid the traps, and the farmers are obliged to invent new ones. One farmer caught a baboon, sprayed it white with paint, and chained it in the middle of his pear orchard in the hope that it, a *white* baboon, would scare away the black baboons, but it did not.

From the valley floor, particularly on gray wintry days, the mountains are an oppressive presence: a giant bulwark, itself dangerous, forming a cul de sac and affording but illusory protection from that which lurks beyond. The old Afrikaners who first settled in Wyndal tried to humanize the mountains by finding the contours of men and animals in their summits. The Coloureds insist that they are filled with spooks, and they try never to venture into them, especially at night. For me the mountains were a constant reminder that despite its declared Europeanness, the valley is very much an African valley.

2

WAITING

Ruth Visser

"There is one thing about the shop—you come in contact with people," Ruth Visser said. Ruth, a handsome woman in her mid-thirties, manages one of Wyndal's three cafés. Her husband works in a garage. She was one of the first villagers I met and proved to be one of the most open-minded. In the morning her counters are piled with loaves of white and brown bread, which are usually sold out by midafternoon. Her shelves are stacked with staples. There is flour, sugar, soap powder—usually in the smallest containers possible, for the Coloured and occasional Black workers. And there is an odd assortment of specialties—Ruth calls them "luxuries"—which whites are apt to run out of when the Cooperative is closed. Ruth is assisted by two Coloured girls, whom she calls "dear" and "darling" interchangeably. She pays them well by village standards, 16 rand a week, and she is proud of this. "The café gives us a little extra," she says. "We've not put anything away, but working here, I forget my troubles and worries. It is not like sitting home all day with nothing to do."

"When you are in close contact with the *volk*"—Ruth was referring to the Coloureds—"you develop a sympathy for them. You come to understand them. I worked in a big department store for years. It was impersonal. I didn't understand the *volk*. Here we get to know one another. If other people could get as close, there would be fewer problems in this country. The *volk* respond immediately to friendliness. The problem is with the youngsters. It is hard to get close to them. You feel an immediate tension, a *spanning*. I feel it most on weekends. My husband is in the store then, and the young men are hostile to him. I suppose it is better with women.

"My parents came here from the Karoo.* There the white man is king. Here the *volk* move about at ease. They have their little houses. There they must always say 'madame' and 'master.' The white man never takes the Black man's feelings into account. They give them a caning if they don't behave. Here my help uses all the same facilities I do. We discuss everything together. In small shops this is possible. In big ones, like the Co-op, it isn't. They give credit only to whites. With the Coloureds it's strictly cash. The Coloureds all come to us because we give them credit. We try to cater to everyone. We have all kinds of specialties, and we also sell things in small quantities. We turn over between eleven and twelve thousand rand a month.

"I don't hesitate to give the Coloureds credit. They always pay me back. With whites it's different. There have been those who left me with a debt of a few hundred rand. What am I to do? Go to the law? It is expensive and takes time. Many of the Coloureds here get old-age or disability pensions from the government. They cash their checks in the post office and come here to pay off their debt. Our government takes good care of them. No one in the village goes hungry, although there are some very poor people.

"Most of the workers do their shopping once a week, on payday, Fridays. By Thursday, they have used up their food and have no money. Well, I cut up some of the bread into half-loaves. They can manage on half a loaf of bread for a day. And then they can usually get hold of some fruit. Most of them, ninety-five percent of them, live from day to day. They never put anything away. They can't.

*Ruth is referring here to the Great Karoo, the larger of two extensive plateaus in the Cape Province. "Karoo" comes from a Khoisan (Hottentot) word meaning "dry" or "barren." The Karoo is in fact a parched plain, like that of the American Southwest, punctuated occasionally by eerie hillocks or mounds of rocks called *kopjes*. Although the soil is rich, little grows in the Karoo except stunted bushes, such as mimosa, wild pomegranates, and wax heath, which burst into vivid colors —yellows, purples, and greens—when it rains. Most of its inhabitants are conservative Afrikaner sheep farmers. The people of Wyndal consider them "raw."

They simply don't have enough to put away. Men get paid twelve to fifteen rand a week, and women about eight. Families pool their money, and that is how they manage. They get their houses free, and sometimes electricity, and there is the local clinic, where they can get lactogen for their babies for half price. The sister [nurse] there helps them with family planning. The pills or shots are free, and the sister keeps very careful track of them. If they don't come in for a shot, she'll go out to the farms to find them. Small families are better. They can live better that way. In the big families there is stone throwing, rape, robbery. They have to rob to survive.

"The old people"—Ruth was referring to the Afrikaners—"don't understand this. They are very conservative. They'll never change. They'll sit in the shadow of their ox wagons until they die. I see this with my own mother and father. They are always humiliating the Coloureds. I try to raise my children to see the *volk* as humans, with feelings. I teach them to respect them and treat them kindly. Sometimes my thirteen-year-old daughter is whistled at. I tell her not to be bothered, that it is normal. My children love the Coloured woman who takes care of them. They tell her all their secrets, the eldest about her boyfriends, things I don't even know. Sometimes she tells me what the children have said. That is how I know. She is like their mother. They can talk their hearts out to her, and she will understand because she has children of her own. We have to give, and then they will give too. Of course, there are criminals, but you find them in all walks of life and in all races. The whites who are unemployed always have a parent who can give them a bit of money. The Coloureds have no one.

"Here I know the whole community. I know whom I can give credit to and who will steal from me. The most honest of all are the Bantu. They are even more honest than I am. Truck drivers—they're mostly from the Transkei—stop here, and sometimes I'm alone, but I'm not afraid of them. Their wives and kids are in the Transkei. You can't blame them if they look at you. We just can't have their entire families here. They are hard workers and are under a lot of pressure. They send their money home. People are very poor in the Transkei, and if the drivers lose their jobs, they'll have nothing . . .

"I don't like cities. I get scared there. It is all so closed in. People are impersonal. Here if you are in a spot, people will help you. In the city everyone is lost. Here you feel secure.

"Ah, you ask me about the future. I don't like to think about it.

Everything could have been all right. Things should have been done earlier. When I think about the future, I get scared. We are all acting out of fear, and so we are not doing the right thing. We didn't pay enough attention in the past, and now no one knows what to do."

Ruth Visser is one of the few villagers who gives me a sense of Wyndal as a working whole. Most of the villagers, including the other shopkeepers, have only a partial, a fragmented, a curiously static picture of the valley. Its inhabitants are divided into groups that seem at times to share only a common geography. It is not that the people are separated by the animosities that occur so often in small communities, though such animosities exist in Wyndal and divide the community as elsewhere. It is of another division that I write here: the apartheid understood not just in its legal sense but in a broader social and epistemological sense. Wyndal is riven by classification. Its inhabitants are separated not only into the "official" white, Coloured, and Black races—there are no Asians in the valley—but ethnically as well and in terms of class and age. "Race" and "ethnicity" are not negotiable categories as they are, say, in Brazil or Morocco, but essential ones. One is white, Coloured, or Black. One is Afrikaner, English, German, Jewish, Dutch, or Portuguese. One is Malay, Indian, Chinese, Japanese, a Zulu, a Mosotho, or a Xhosa. One may even be a Marais, a du Plessís, a Cook, or a Maxwell. Such classifications, at least the racial and the ethnic ones, describe one's essential being. They permit exquisitely mechanical stereotyping and promiscuous generalization; they prescribe social behavior and determine an often terrifying social distance; they provide the basis for apartheid understood in its narrower legal sense.

"The Blacks are barbarians, uncivilized, raw," one Afrikaner woman in Wyndal told me. "They can become professors and doctors, but there is always something lacking. Just a few days ago a Black man who had been educated in Europe said that he found something lacking in his own people. It was on TV. It is in the blood. Give a Black a drink, even an educated one—well, the same is true of common whites—he will drink until morning and behave in a barbaric manner. It is a question of breeding and background. My son is in the permanent forces, in South West Africa. He says, 'You can take a Black man from the bush but you can't take the bush from the Black man.' "

South Africa's apartheid, understood, as here, in its broadest sense, is an extreme case of the Western predisposition to classify and categorize just about everything in essentialist terms. In this view, once an object or being is classified, it is forever that object or being. It has an identity. It partakes of a particular essence. It is subject to certain regularities, which are understood as rules or laws of nature, and has its own place within a particular picture of the universe, rather like a piece in a jigsaw puzzle. Essentialist classification is static. Any change in identity, in essence, in regularity, or in place poses a problem; indeed, it threatens the classificatory system itself. Such change must be accounted for in terms of "transformations," "evolution," "growth," or "conversion," which are somehow compatible with the classificatory system itself. Or, as in the case of human society, where we have at least some control or the illusion of control, we try to interdict changes that risk toppling the classificatory system. We legalize them out of existence. We deny them. When applied to human beings, essentialist thought precludes that small space of freedom that is at the heart of our humanity and enables us to engage in a vital manner with those about us. Racism is, of course, one of the most blatant and potentially evil forms of essentialist thought, but often its critical consideration masks other classifications that have the same epistemological roots and permit the same social and psychological tyranny. When we isolate racism, we risk the perpetuation of the *status quo* by letting one weasel category substitute for another. This is clear in South Africa, where many of the more "enlightened" whites no longer talk about "race" but about "culture," "ethnicity," "class," or "character," while still making the same social discriminations. It is true in the United States as well, where for many "the culture of poverty" refers essentially to Blacks and Hispanics as racist terms did and still do.

Although racist and other essentialist social categories—when they exist—enter the rhetoric of domination and subordination in hierarchical societies, they are not as freely manipulated by the dominant, the possessors of power, status, and wealth, as is popularly thought. In the popular imagination, the dominant—"the establishment," "capitalists," "imperialists," "the upper classes," "the rich"—are often cast as though they were immune from social, cultural, and psychological constraint. How often is "the imperialist" characterized as a ruthless exploiter without conscience! If he were only that, he would have been far more successful in his exploitations. Such a view fails, of course, to recognize the constraints on the dominant. To be dominant in a system is not to dominate the system. Both the dominant and the dominated are equally caught in it.[1] One has the advantage; the other does not.

When I first came to Cape Town, I stayed in a little hotel that was managed by a student at the university. Like most South Africans with whom I talked, he was interested in my research and gave me his view of South Africa whenever he could. One day he told me that to understand South Africa I must realize that the whites are as terrorized by the system as the people of color. He could have been simply quoting Henri Lefebvre[2] had he not motioned with his chin to a little man in an ill-fitting gray suit who checked into the hotel shortly after I did and seemed to take a self-consciously distant interest in me. I got the manager's message—and I came to understand something about South African society. Fear is pervasive. "We are all acting out of fear," Ruth Visser says. It is not, however, the fear of little men in ill-fitting gray suits that terrorizes the whites. Most of them have little or no contact with such men. Nor is it the fear of change: the loss of power, status, and wealth, "the good life" as many South Africans put it. It is, I believe, a much more primordial fear that comes from the absence of any possibility of a vital relationship with most of the people around one. It is an unspoken, pervasive fear that has its source in the apartheid and that maintains the apartheid in all its virulence. It is a fear that informs much, though by no means all, that I heard in South Africa and report here.

I do not in fact know if the little man in the ill-fitting gray suit was a member of the Special Branch assigned to keep an eye on me. He may very well have been. He left the hotel when I did and returned when I did a few weeks later. I did not see him in the interim, and after my second visit to the hotel, I never saw him again. But he became for me in those weeks a focus of suspicion and terror. He was later replaced by other focuses of terror. Forced by "the laws of the land," as several English acquaintances referred to apartheid, and by the research permission granted me to work only with whites, I came to share something of the whites' fear of those others with whom they cannot vitally engage. It is difficult to explain the relief I felt when I left South Africa, for Botswana after my first stay and for Swaziland after my second. I experienced an immense opening up: a joy at the possibility of contact even in societies I did not understand and in languages I did not speak.

At times during the months I spent in Wyndal I had the impression that I was living in a tiny society surrounded by servicing ghosts. There was, I assume, some curiosity—and some knowledge —about me among the Coloureds and the few Blacks in the valley, but there was no real, vital contact between us. Although I was an American, a foreigner, I was still a white living among whites, and that whiteness, I must assume, determined the range of permissible responses. Emotional invisibility was preferred or, on those occasions when I did talk with people of color, I elicited a stereotypic response: an initial mistrust followed by a flattened keening, a stream of uncomprehending complaint, a kind of angry victimized dignity, a longing for release, and a feeling—at least among the most religious Coloureds, so strong is their Calvinism—of being on trial. The Blacks of the valley kept quiet and showed greater confidence. Like the other whites, I was inordinately terrified of Friday and Saturday night drunks.

"I'm not afraid of the Coloureds," another Wyndal woman, also an Afrikaner, said stubbornly. "I sleep with my windows open. When the Coloureds are in trouble, they go to the whites. They're like children. We are like parents. I'm not afraid of educated Coloureds. The schoolmaster here is a fine man. I've had tea with him, but I wouldn't go to bed with him. And I'm not afraid of the farmhands. It's the half-educated ones—the troublemakers—who scare me. The Bantus are different. They are not loyal the way the Coloureds are. They are always fighting one another. One of them, a truck driver, shouted to my father, 'Get out of the way, you white Boer!' They're becoming so cheeky. They don't know their place anymore."

I had come to South Africa to study the effect of domination on the dominating. I had discovered that even in their research on domination most anthropologists had never bothered to study the dominant. They had only studied the dominated and from that perspective described the structure of domination. As often as not they shared the popular view of the dominant (despite their own dominant position at least in contrast to the people they studied) and tended to confuse dominance within a system with the domination of the system. The dominant became precut figures in some ideological argument or other: ruthless exploiters, say, motivated only by the desire for material gain and devoid, rather like the psychopath, of conscience. Most often missed were the pathos and the terror, however indulgent, of the hotel manager and others like him. Pathos, terror, guilt, the joy of power and acquisition, the weight of responsibility and the resentment of such responsibility, feelings of solitude, misunderstanding, and un-understanding, to name only a few of the dispositions and predispositions of the dominant, have to be understood if any understanding of domination is to be achieved.

Ideally I should have worked with both the dominant and the dominated in South Africa, but, as I have noted, this was legally precluded. It was also practically precluded because had I spent much time with non-whites, many whites would have grown suspicious and would not have talked to me. The reverse is probably true, too. I do not know. I do know that had I spent too much time with non-whites, I could have endangered their lives. My study is inevitably skewed, but that is, I believe, revealing.

I did not come to South Africa as a neutral observer. I came morally and politically outraged at the brute, unmediated legislation of human inferiority. I was filled with horror by tales of arbitrary banning, detention and imprisonment, torture, forced suicide, and murder, of violent dispossession, banishment, and the splitting of families, that are familiar to anyone who reads the newspapers. I had an almost mythic image of the perpetrators of this inhumanity. I was horrified by the depths to which humans will sink to preserve their trivial privilege and disgusted by the accommodations that others, outsiders, make with such humans to preserve their privilege. I indulged myself in my horror and disgust and learned later that my indulgence was itself a symptom of the "system." I met many white South Africans who were equally horrified and disgusted. Paradoxically, their horror and disgust rendered their life in South Africa tolerable. It gave them the certainty that they were different. Tales of banning, detention and imprisonment, torture, forced suicide, and murder, of dispossession, banishment, and the breaking up of families, were common. They appeared daily—as scandals in the English-language press, with caution in the Black and Coloured press, and with moralistic pretension in the Afrikaans press. They were talked up, especially in the cities where in "liberal" circles they produced a sort of hysterical heat. They were loudly denied in conservative circles, or somehow justified, and as such acknowledged. They were a sort of living folklore, genre tales really, which, like tales of war and terrorism, render the unsayable sayable, and, thereby, if not less real, then at least more manageable.

I also came to South Africa cynical. (I learned during the Vietnam War that a highly pitched cynicism requires periodic shock, outrage, and horror.) I had read the papers. I had lived in the Third World. I had visited countries under totalitarian, authoritarian, terroristic rule. One of my friends, perhaps my closest ever, was forced to suicide by an army of liberation. Others were arbitrarily imprisoned and tortured. Still others live in constant, chafing apprehension. I think of one in particular who lives curled up in a corner of a squalid hut—his wings plucked, as one of my colleagues put it—waiting for inevitable arrest because a tenure-seeking American academic had the courtesy to thank him for the help he had given in a "perfectly harmless" book that now lies unread on the back shelves of a few hundred college libraries. I had spent months in shanty towns, in expensive countries, with people who earn less in a year than I have spent on taxis in a week. So I could cast myself as a cynic. I had read; I had heard, I had witnessed, from a distance.

And I met many white South Africans, some living abroad, who shared my cynicism. Some—mainly Afrikaners, but also English—were driven by their cynicism. Others—mainly English, but also Afrikaners—were pained by their cynicism, as if it somehow betrayed their humanity. Tales of the Third World, of Black Africa in particular, of the abuse of human beings, of postcolonial deterioration, of dilapidated farms and roads, of rusting trucks and cars, of inhuman medical treatment, of bribery and corruption, of dramatic decreases in the productivity of agriculture and the output of mines, all spiced with incidents of violence (rape, murder, torture) and ignorance (the by-now proverbial Zairean *douanier* who kicks off his shoes as he pokes through your bags because he is not used to wearing them), were common. They too were a living folklore, genre tales that legitimated what South African whites like to call "pragmatism." They also permitted, in those who were more sensitive, pain, nostalgia for the good old days, and a feeling of not being understood by the rest of the world. After all, what other Europeans have had to live in such close contact with people of such alien and exotic ways as the Zulu, the Xhosa, and the Basotho?

I experienced moral claustrophobia throughout my stay in South Africa. I tried to bracket off my outrage, my cynical pretense, and my sadness in order to be as "objective" as possible. (One South African friend pointed out that those feelings and, for that matter, the desire to be objective are part of the South African picture and should not be easily dismissed.) I learned that it is possible to have a certain sympathy even for people whose values one finds reprehensible. I was, and I am still, confused by this. The very first person I interviewed in South Africa was a stenographer of middling intelligence who had left Johannesburg only once: to visit Durban after being jilted. There, on the rebound I imagine, she met her future husband, a factory foreman, who courted her for two years before they finally married. They live in a tiny three-room house with their two children: one is feebleminded and the other, her mother dreams, will be a ballet dancer. The stenographer believes in apartheid.

I came to Wyndal on the recommendation of several South Africans who lived in the United States. I had decided on the Cape because I wanted to work with middle- and upper-class whites who were considered by South African standards "liberal," "subtle," and, as the Afrikaners of Wyndal would put it, "cultured." I did not want to produce another caricature of the *verkrampte*—the reactionary—Afrikaner of the Transvaal or the Free State, or of the "colonial" English of Natal whose "Zulu boys" serve them in white tunics with red sashes. I was in fact less interested in English-speaking white South Africans *per se* or in the Afrikaners than in the relationship between them.

Wyndal impressed me from the start as an excellent place to study the relationship between the two dominant white populations. Traditionally a very Afrikaner community, it was now a favored spot for wealthy English farmers and retired businessmen. Here, the English and the Afrikaners were forced into contact in a small, well-defined community. Wyndal was not a typical community (do such communities exist?), although several of my English acquaintances there insisted that it was a microcosm of South Africa. Others insisted that it was so unique that no reasonable generalization about South Africa could be made from it. Both views were, I believe, exaggerated. What in fact interested me about Wyndal was precisely its uniqueness. It would highlight what was taken for granted elsewhere. (Most South African farming towns are exclusively Afrikaner or, more rarely, exclusively English.) Wyndal's population was diverse enough to cover a wide range of white attitudes and values. It was close enough to Cape Town to be cosmopolitan in orientation. The recent arrival of the English dramatized the tensions between the two white groups. Although I regret that there were not more Blacks and that there were no Asians, my concern was not with the "perfectly balanced village" but with the discourse of domination. Wyndal would provide the locus, and the occasion, for this discourse.

I had noticed that in the literature on white South Africa there was a marked tendency to treat Afrikaners—"the white tribe of Africa," the BBC calls them—as the subject of study. The English seemed to slip away in these studies; often, particularly in studies by foreigners, they were the lens through which the Afrikaner was seen. The Afrikaner seemed content to be the subject of study. As such, his identity was affirmed. The relationship between the two groups was usually discussed in historical terms.

There was, in any event, a marked asymmetry in the way the two groups presented themselves to foreigners, and this was certainly true of the Afrikaners and English in Wyndal, meeting me. I always introduced myself as an American social anthropologist who had come to South Africa to study the nature of stereotyping. Once I had explained myself to the Afrikaners, they began, without exception, to recount their history, the way they had been wronged by the English, and how they were misunderstood today. Often they concluded by attacking Kurt Waldheim's understanding of South West Africa and Jimmy Carter's human-rights policy. They were usually apologetic about the latter, as though they were attacking me personally. (I should note that on my second trip to South Africa, after Ronald Reagan's election, the attitude of most whites changed dramatically: At last the United States had a president who understood them!) Once the Afrikaners had presented themselves and their victimization, they were almost always eager to participate in my research. They were very much the subject of their discourse, and they used themselves to transform me into a sort of emissary come to tell the world that they had been misunderstood.

The English response was quite different. They usually interrupted my introduction, cast themselves as informal colleagues, and began to describe the Afrikaners. When I tried to turn the conversation to the English themselves, they would begin to talk about the Coloureds, the Zulu, the Xhosa, anyone who might be of such captivating interest that I would spare them the embarrassment of scrutiny, of being the "objects" of research. With time, however, I was able to learn a lot about them, though never in as composed a manner as with the Afrikaners. They also tended to cast me as their emissary.

Despite their very different styles, then, both white groups were united in their desire to make me into a *porte-parole* to whites outside South Africa. It was this desire that governed many of my encounters with them and is in part responsible for the sociologically descriptive tenor of much of what they had to say to me.

It would be a mistake, though, to dismiss the sociological descriptions of the people I interviewed as the result only of their desire to explain their society to me so that I could explain it to the world. White South Africans seem always to be talking about their country, its problems, and its image abroad. It is *their* subject. Few, if any, of the "new" countries of the world have produced as large a self-descriptive literature. Few have developed, and legislated, as complete a self-descriptive language. Self-description is, like rugby, a national pastime. As it occurs among South African whites, it is repetitive, mythic, closed in on itself—a series of variations on a single theme or a small group of related themes. It is morally and politically charged. It gives a frozen and ultimately unrealistic picture of social reality that requires confirmation and reconfirmation through endless repetition. One has only to read the daily editorials in both the English-language and the Afrikaans press to appreciate this repetition. South African newspapers, I should add, devote little space to international news, and most of the news reported from abroad either relates to South Africa or is made to relate to it.

White South Africa's sociological language poses a serious problem to the Western observer. To use Malinowski's word for the function of myth, it "charters" a particular picture of social reality.[3] How does one objectively describe a social reality that is indigenously described, and legislated, in terms that approximate those of the observer? This may at first seem an epistemological problem of little relevance to the prevailing conditions in South Africa, but it is, in my view, a serious problem. By employing the same social categories as the South African white, the outside observer slips into the white's self-description—a description that is determined by self-interest. He risks losing the distance necessary to evaluate the effects of his own social position on his sociological understanding. As Pierre Bourdieu puts it: "It is when he does not know how to introduce that objectifying, hence critical, distance, that the sociologist justifies those who see in him a sort of terrorist inquisitor available for all the actions of a symbolic police."[4] In the South African case one can easily delete the word "symbolic." The observer replicates the whites' social discriminations and legitimates them. He implicates himself in *their* self-interest. Each time I use one of the racist terms—"white," "Coloured," "Asian," or "Black"—or refer to "Afrikaners" or "English," I am participating in a particular self-interested constitution of social reality, which I find morally reprehensible and which does not, in any event, do justice to the human reality it purports to describe. I am forced to think that reality, and I am not alone. It is thought by the whites of whatever persuasion and by the peoples of color as well. Such is the power of legislation. Such is the power of language. "A whole mythology is deposited in our language," Wittgenstein says.[5] We can replace "mythology" with "sociology," "psychology," and "anthropology" and not betray his observation.

The problem of language is central to the South African experience. Language, there, is a kind of sabotage observes Jane Kramer, writing anonymously in the *New York Review of Books*.

> White or Black or Coloured, English-speaking or Afrikaans-speaking or speaking any one of a dozen native languages, one starts, even in the best of faith, in bad faith. The languages of South Africa have been consonant with race and caste, owner and worker, citizen and servant, for so long that language itself—the language one speaks and writes—is a weapon there, quite apart from those details of identity and ideology with which it happens to coincide. Words smother, sacrifices to apartheid, in the closed context of the expectations they arouse. They can sanction such perverse exaggerations, such profound contempt, that anyone who wants to write in South Africa is left with the home truth that language has lost its metaphoric flexibility and assumed, instead, a kind of brute synecdochic power. By now, to write in South Africa is by definition political.[6]

And, in a very real sense, so is to talk. It is also, as Jane Kramer notes, "to suffer the constraints of responsibility": to have always to take the world seriously. There is humor among South African whites —frivolous humor, hackneyed humor, little entertainments—but there is little, if any, irony, for there is no vantage point outside the word-given reality in which the white South African finds himself.

There are some, to be sure, who have sought escape through self-descriptions that are cast in some ideology or other. Some vulgar Marxists have, for example, attempted to understand South African social reality in terms of class struggle. They have all too facilely substituted for a South African social category another, for "Blacks," say, "lumpen proletariat." Others, like Nadine Gordimer, have looked to more sophisticated languages: poetic languages ("I live at 6,000 feet in a society whirling, stamping, swaying with the force of revolutionary change," Gordimer writes in the *New York Review of Books*. "The vision is heady; the image of the demonic dance is accurate, not romantic: an image of actions springing from emotions, knocking deliberation aside. The city is Johannesburg, the country South Africa, and the time the last years of the colonial era in Africa"[7]); philosophical languages ("The state of interregnum is a state of Hegel's disintegrated consciousness, of contradictions"). Gordimer allies herself here with a New York intelligentsia of the liberal left, with a suburbanized version of the Frankfurtschule, and also in a kind of identity play with East European émigré writers —Milan Kundera, Czesław Miłocz, and even the nineteenth-century Russian Alexander Herzen. Somehow the moral burden of South Africa slips away only to return, after passing through all these pretentious defiles, in lighter form. My point here is not to criticize Gordimer—I appreciate her dilemma and agree with much of what she says—but I point here to the tyranny of language that offers no escape, no metaphorical flexibility, no possibility of transcendence. "I was born into a language of hierarchy, of distance and perspective," the deranged heroine of J. M. Coetzee's brilliant novel *In the Heart of the Country* says. "It was my father-tongue. I do not say it is the language my heart wants to speak, I feel too much the pathos of its distances, but it is all we have. I can believe there is a language lovers speak but cannot imagine how it goes. I have no words left to exchange whose value I trust."[8] Earlier in the novel Coetzee's nameless heroine, expressive somehow of the madness of white South Africa, overhears her father "exchanging forbidden words" with a Coloured servant he is seducing, and she, the heroine, says, "There are few enough words true, rock-hard enough to build a life on, and these he is destroying." He cannot create a private language; she observes, "Whatever they may say to each other, even in the closest dead of night, they say in common words, unless they gibber like apes."[9] How, she asks, can she speak to Hendrik, once her father has corrupted her language? Hendrik is a Coloured servant who will one day take her violently but with her consent.

With varying degrees of self-conscious concern, the people of Wyndal also suffered this tyranny of language. Some, like Hennie, and the many others engaged in a religious renewal, sought to escape through a transcendental religious language; others, like Hennie's son Zachary, through Oriental mysticisms and pointillist word games; and still others, like Hugo Malan, through an unbending rationalism that verged in its rationality on the irrational. Some sought escape through travel and talk about travel; others, through projects of departure. Most repeated the dried-out models and parallels they read about in the newspapers and heard on television and the radio.

The Afrikaners often appear to take what they read about in the newspapers or hear from those in authority as Gospel. Their orientation is fundamentalist. It is borne by their language. "*Taal*," the Afrikaner word for "language," does not readily translate into English. Rather, like the German "*Sprache*," "*taal*" carries with it an entire cultural assumption that the English "language" does not. "Language" is understood in a more instrumental fashion. (I am writing here of the ideology—the symbolism—of language and the way that ideology and symbolism affect the attitudes a people take toward their language.) *Taal* gives the Afrikaners their identity. It is a product of a historical struggle. It is its speakers' culture, their *kultuur*. (*Kultuur* refers less to the creative arts in Afrikaner usage than to the traditional forms of Afrikaner life—forms that have to be preserved from outside interference and pollution.) *Taal* cannot in its implication be separated from its speakers' religion, from their politics, their tradition, their land, and their communality—their *gemeenskap*. It attests to their particularity, their nationhood, and their distinction. It gives them an intimate sense of social and cultural unity, which they call *gemeenlikheidsgevoel*. Derived from Dutch, a European language, Afrikaans is very much a language of Africa. The Afrikaner poet N. P. van Wyk Louw wrote in 1959: "Afrikaans is the language that links western Europe and Africa; it draws its strength from these two sources; it forms a bridge between the enlightened West and magical Africa."[10]

In fact, unlike South African English, which differs only slightly from the English of England, Afrikaans offers no bridge, overseas or to Africa. It is spoken by sixty percent of South Africa's white population, by most of the Cape Coloureds, and by some Indians and Blacks. It is spoken nowhere else in the world except by a few thousand Afrikaners who emigrated to Argentina after the Anglo-Boer War and live there in relative isolation. It is said to be closest

to Flemish and it can be understood only with difficulty by the
Dutch, who treat it with considerable derision. It has nothing in
common with any of the African languages spoken in southern
Africa. When van Wyk Louw writes about its African inspiration,
he refers to the environment, *land en landskap*, and not to the
indigenous languages of Africa.

> But what we should not lose sight of is that the change in environ-
> ment has shaped and fashioned the young, newly evolving language.
> It has caused new words, new images, and new concepts to come into
> being; old words and concepts to be adapted and in many cases to
> disappear; every feature [*riffel*] of the new world to be reflected in its
> scope.[11]

The poet concludes that Afrikaans is able to depict South Africa as
no other European language can.

The development of Afrikaans is closely tied to the development
of Afrikaner nationalism. Although Dutch was the official language
of the Cape settlement, a simplified vernacular quickly evolved and
was well established by the middle of the eighteenth century.[12] It
seems to have been little influenced by the native languages of
Africa, the Malay-Portuguese *lingua franca* of the slaves, or by the
French of the early Huguenot settlers;[13] in fact, the Dutch authorities did their best to discourage French. The new Cape Dutch
reflected the hierarchy between master and slave, and white and
non-white, and the egalitarian relationship among whites. A man of
color was referred to as a *jong* and not a *man*—a word reserved for
whites; a woman of color, as *meid* and not *vrou*. Blacks in general
were called *skepsels*, creatures.[14] It remained a spoken language until
the last quarter of the nineteenth century, when a group of language
nationalists in Paarl started the Afrikaans Language Movement and
the first Afrikaans newspaper, *Di Patriot*. Their aim was to establish
Afrikaans as a *kultuurtaal*, a language into which the Bible could be
legitimately translated. (Dutch had been the language of the Bible
and the sermon.)

The Paarl group and its followers in the Genootskap van Regte
Afrikaners (Society of True Afrikaners), which was founded in 1875
to promote the rights of Afrikaans speakers, had to struggle not only
against English, which had been the official language of the Cape
since the arrival of the British at the beginning of the nineteenth

century, but also against the many Afrikaners who feared that the translation of the Bible from High Dutch into a mere *kombuistaal*, a kitchen language, was blasphemous. (Other Afrikaners considered Afrikaans a "barbarous mixture" incapable of replacing Dutch—a rich and fully developed language.[15]) Hennie's father, years later, would not let his sons read the new Afrikaans Bible until he had compared it word for word with his own Dutch Bible.

The linguistic nationalism of the Paarl group was spurred by the Anglo-Boer War, and the misdirected Anglicization policy of Sir Alfred Milner, the British high commissioner in South Africa and former governor of the Cape Colony who had led England into war with the Boer republics.* It was also fired by a group of fervent poets—Eugene Marais, Jan Celliers, Totius (J. D. du Toit), and C. Louis Leipoldt—whose task van Wyk Louw claimed was "the spiritual transfiguration of the war" so that the Afrikaners "could again become men, with human value and evaluations."[16] "By articulating and universalizing the Afrikaner fate," T. Dunbar Moodie observes in his study of Afrikaner nationalism, "this new Afrikaans literature helped to formulate a clear consciousness of national identity."[17] This identity, I would insist, is founded ultimately on a wound, a feeling of having been victimized.[18] One of these early poets, Totius, writes of a thorn tree, symbolic of the Afrikaners, crushed by a wagon, the British, which gradually grows upright again.

Ook het die loop van jare
die wonde weggewis—
net een plek bly 'n teken
wat onuitwisbaar is.

Die wonde word gesond weer
as jare kom en gaan,
maar daardie merk word groter
en groei maar aldeur aan.[19]

In course of time the hurt-marks
fade where the wheels had lunged

*The authoritarian and arbitrary governor of the Cape, Lord Charles Somerset, had pursued a similar policy with disastrous results during the first years of British occupation.

only one place endures
that cannot be expunged.

The wounds grew healed and healthy,
with years that come and go,
but that one scar grew greater
and does not cease to grow.[20]

The poem is entitled *Vergewe en vergeet*—"Forgive and Forget."

Reaction to defeat and Anglicization led to the growth of an intense, romantic nationalism that could not be divorced from the language question. "The language of the conqueror in the mouth of the conquered is the language of slaves," the ex-president of the Orange Free State said after the Anglo-Boer War.[21] Reaction also led to the foundation of an alternate Christian National school system, financed (though poorly at the time) by the Dutch Reformed Church, to protect Afrikaner children from Milner's English schools—a Christian National school system whose philosophy continues to influence South Africa's educational policy—and to such "cultural" organizations as the notorious Broederbond, whose political influence is still tremendous today.* Notions of linguistic pu-

---

*The Afrikaner Broederbond is a secret society founded in 1918 to promote Afrikaner nationalism and culture. P. J. Meyer, one-time chairman of the Broederbond, wrote in 1966: "The main purpose of this cultural movement was to purify Afrikaans nationalism of all elements by which it could destroy itself and to build it on a Christian-Protestant basis, with (as a yardstick) the legal principles of the Holy Writ, the guidelines of our Christian national tradition and the demands of the time in which we live, in all spheres of life to full independence and maturity." (Quoted in de Villiers, "Afrikaner Nationalism," p. 395.)

The Broederbond has been held responsible by its opponents for all sorts of ills in South Africa. It is frequently given an omnipotence of mythic proportions, and has been the subject of a good deal of sensationalist literature. There is little question of its tremendous influence in South African business and politics. There are over 12,000 members who belong to more than 800 cells that spread systematically across the country. There is a general council, an executive council of "Twelve Apostles," and a "Trinity," which is headed by a "Supreme Chief." All of South Africa's prime ministers since 1948 have been members of the organization. All the heads of the Afrikaans universities in 1978 and all the Afrikaner cabinet ministers in 1980 were members. Almost all the Nationalist members of Parliament, as well as leading businessmen, clergymen, professors, lawyers, bankers, and policemen, are members (Bunting; Moodie; Wilkins and Strydom; Serfontein).

The Wyndal farmers talk a lot about it and speculate about who in the valley belongs to it. A few younger Afrikaner farmers speak bitterly about the Broeder-

rity, as Jordaan points out, are closely related to those of racial purity.[22] With Union in 1910, Dutch became one of the two official languages of South Africa. In 1925 Afrikaans was finally recognized as such, and in the sixties, after South Africa became a republic, the Afrikaans Language Monument, a towering concrete and granite hyperbole, was constructed on a mountain overlooking Paarl to commemorate the "wonder" (so the tourist brochure states) of Afrikaner cultural and political growth. Carved into the walkway that leads to it are the words of the National Party's first prime minister and one of the architects of apartheid, Daniel F. Malan: *"Dit is ons erns"* ("This is our earnest, our seriousness, our gravity").

The English of Wyndal joke about the language monument, just as other English-speaking South Africans do. They talk about an American visitor who told his Afrikaner guide that he thought monuments were only for the dead. Some of the men note its phallic shape and talk derisively about the Afrikaners' limp sexuality, their bluff, their need for "monuments." The English are, in fact, offended by the language monument. It represents their loss of political power, their victimization by Afrikaner Nationalists, and their feelings of exclusion. It also represents, I believe, inarticulate feelings of disunity, fragmentation, and the absence of a focused national identity. The English worry about their identity. At a conference held Afrikaner-style at the opening of the 1820 Settlers National Monument in Grahamstown, a monument commemorating the first organized English emigration to southern Africa, the English participants referred again and again to the absence of unity among the English as though it were somehow a fault. Denis Worrall wrote:

> English South Africans, it seems, have little more in common than the language they speak in their homes, and their out-group status in relation to Afrikaners—something which, when measured in terms of communal objectives, a sense of history (or more specifically, of progress in history), and sense of communal responsibility and leadership, had profoundly important implications. This is what Patrick Duncan meant way back in 1909 when he commented: "The Boers whatever

---

bond because, I have been led to believe, they have not been asked to join. Several of the English farmers make fun of one very conservative man in particular because he is not a member and would like to be one. They say he is too fanatical for the *bond*.

their differences may be are in the last resort solidly fenced round by
national and racial feelings. The others have about as much cohesive
principle as chaff on a windy day."[23]

André de Villiers, the editor of the conference papers, spoke of the
fundamental problem of English identity and went on to talk of
their partnership (despite their reverence for the rule of law) "in the
erection of a social system characterized by segregation in the name
of race and state," their bewilderment at the loss of political power,
the erosion of their economic preeminence, and the frustration of
producing a "vigorous literature" that is largely banned in their own
country.[24]

The "vague communion," as one South African described South
African English identity, cannot measure up to the Afrikaners'
monolithic nationalism. The English do not have a composed tradition, a secure world picture, and an articulate ideology. They do not
even have a language that they can claim roots them in southern
Africa. They have no language monuments, no museums (the 1820
Settlers Monument notwithstanding), to commemorate their past,
to which they can make *in alle erns*, in all earnest, cultural pilgrimages. They have no *interpretation* of history.[25] They do not share
the Afrikaners' self-conscious mythology or the communal fear and
outrage of the Blacks, Coloureds, and Asians. They are left only to
comment. "If Afrikaans is the language of intimate family histories
put to terrorizing public use," Jane Kramer writes, "the language
of theological time and explanation, of spiritual claustrophobia in
vast spaces, of cycles of land and season and crops and calvings and
fixed, ordained station, the language of the trek and the end of
exploration and the beginning of a dream about land for a people
who now can neither leave that land nor inherit it, then English, for
white South Africa, is the language that is to explicate that madness
and that dream. It is the language of commentary and judgment, of
an imperial vision trying to engage itself, of worldly, liberal values
trapped in domestic irrelevance."[26] It is, I would add, a language of
irony that precluded a vantage point for such irony.

English immigration to South Africa began shortly after the second British occupation of the Cape in 1806. (There were at the time
about 23,000 whites, mostly Afrikaans-speaking, in South Africa.[27])
Although there were several organized schemes of immigration
from Britain, the 1820 settlers to the eastern Cape and the Byrne

Byrne settlers of 1848–1849 to Natal being the most notable,* they were never as successful as those organized by Edward Gibbon Wakefield to Australia and New Zealand. Immigration was in fact gradual and on a much smaller scale than to the United States and Canada. Unlike the seventeenth-century Dutch and Huguenot settlers, the English immigrants were imbued with the nineteenth-century colonial spirit. Most of them—urban craftsmen and white-collar workers—settled in towns and cities.[28] The discovery of diamonds in Kimberley in 1870 and gold in the Transvaal in the 1880s spurred immigration. Between 1860 and 1890 the English-speaking population of South Africa increased more than fourfold, and the Afrikaner population, two-and-a-half-fold. By Union in 1910, there were just over a half million English in South Africa, forty percent of whom had been born in Great Britain, and 673,000 Afrikaners, most of whom traced their families back to seventeenth-century Dutch, German, and Huguenot settlers.[29] The continuous pattern of English immigration, coupled with the colonial and then the Commonwealth status of South Africa, created enduring ties between the English South Africans and England that the Afrikaners did not have with Europe, from which they had been more or less cut off since the end of the seventeenth century.

English South African identity was, and still is, certainly in Wyndal, more international than that of the Afrikaners. The nationalism of the English was never as strong, even during Cecil Rhodes's time, when, perhaps, it was at its strongest, never as articulate, and never as enmeshed in a sense of personhood as is the Afrikaners'. Essentially an upward-aspiring urban population subject to the class and other social distinctions of city life, possessed of a strongly materialistic *laissez-faire* individualism, predisposed, at least today, to dream of far off sanctuaries, the English South Africans "have seldom been able to demonstrate strength through unity."[30] Since Union they have had to come to terms with their minority status even within the "enfranchised nation." They live in what Schlemmer calls

*Joseph Byrne, a British adventurer and speculator, took advantage of the economic crisis in Great Britain in the late 1840s and devised a scheme through which he stood to make enormous profit by promoting immigration to Natal. Although his scheme failed miserably and he eventually went bankrupt, over 3,000 men, women, and children arrived in Natal from England between 1849 and 1851 to occupy poor lands with inadequate water. For details, see Hattersley.

"comfortable political suffocation."[31] They complain about their political impotence, but in the area around Wyndal they have made no real organized political effort. They sit in complacent horror. Their politics (the Nationalists in their ranks notwithstanding) is that of an opposition, and for many, given the powerlessness of the opposition in South Africa today, it makes little difference if their opposition is given institutional form or not.

Opposition is more than political. It is existential. It is a matter of style. It is consuming. It is oriented to the other: to the Afrikaner. Just as the Afrikaners appear to measure themselves against the English, so the English respond to the Afrikaners.[32] They are not, however, as ready to admit it. They may in fact be more alienated from the Afrikaner than the Afrikaners are from them.[33] The two prominent white groups are caught in an asymmetrical play of identity. Through the rejection of the other, through opposition to the other, they affirm the significance of the other. They acknowledge, up to a point, the other's outlook, his notion of identity, of the person, of language, religion, and party, of tradition and culture, and they question their own outlook, their notions of identity, person, language, religion, and party, their tradition and culture, in the other's terms. Social psychological studies have shown that the English are more conscious of their identity when they live, as in Wyndal, in close proximity to Afrikaners.[34]

The English South Africans are, for example, conscious of their language in a way that the Australians and Canadians are not. They stress correct pronunciation and usage. I have heard several Wyndal English dismiss the possibility of emigrating to Australia because they did not want to expose their children, and themselves, to a language as rough and styleless as Australian English. Sometimes they identify their English with Great Britain, and at other times they stress its uniqueness, its specifically South African character. There is a dictionary of South African English. Their attitude toward their language is symptomatic of a fissure in their identity. They do not respond to it as easily as the English of Great Britain do or as self-consciously as the Afrikaners do to Afrikaans. They vacillate between two positions and lose the possibility of a position of their own.

All the concern about the absence of unity among the English South Africans implies that there is a virtue in national or ethnic unity. It is very much a product of apartheid thinking, in which the group, determinant in some very essential way of its members, is given priority over the individual. It is my impression (and here I can only speak impressionistically) that the Afrikaners' notion of the person is different from that of the English, who, insofar as they respond to it, are influenced by it. (The Afrikaners, armed with an elaborate ideology and a determined politics, are probably less responsive to the English notion.) The Afrikaner notion of personhood is "fuller" than that of the English. It cuts into the group. Identity comes through group membership. The "person" is encrusted, to speak figuratively, with national, racial, and ethnic affiliation, with party membership, religious belief, and cultural tradition. It is historically, and not simply biographically, determined. The "person" is bounded, however, as is the group, evaluated in terms of purity, and defined against a potentially dangerous other. Too intimate contact with this other can destroy its boundaries, pollute it, and render it fluid and out of control. Personhood must be preserved, as must the group. It must withstand. It may even require sacrifices that are morally compromising. It is assumed that other whites, different as they are, have analogous notions of the person. Throughout my stay in South Africa, Afrikaners I knew would always apologize when they felt they had slighted my country, my beliefs, or my culture—as though they had somehow attacked my person. They assumed an uncritical allegiance that I did not, and would not, have.

English notions of the person were closer to my own. The English did at times respond to the Afrikaner notions and grow self-critical, the way they did when they spoke of their failure to unify. Certainly the Wyndal English, despite marked class differences, were united by common sentiment and group loyalty. Many of them, for example, preferred to have their cars repaired by an inferior mechanic who happened to be English than by a very competent Afrikaner mechanic. Many drove miles out of their way to buy inferior meat from an English butcher. Or, if they did use the local butcher, they apologized for it. They talked about the need to develop ties with the village Afrikaners. When they entertained one another, they put up with differences in taste, background, belief, culture, politics, and morality, and with tactlessness that no Englishman of similar background living in England would have tolerated. The Afrikaners also kept their distance.

What I found extraordinary about the identity play of the two white groups was the insignificance of non-whites. They simply did not enter the self-constituting discourse of the whites, although their potential threat to the whites' "way of life" (not their personhood) was certainly acknowledged. I cannot, of course, speak of all of South Africa, but it is my impression (and here again I must speak impressionistically) that the Blacks, Coloureds, and Asians were not "significant others" from whose standpoint the white could look reflectively at himself and discover, so to speak, his identity.* They were too different—and too distant. Here, I believe, we must take account of the ontological, or perhaps more accurately the psycho-ontological, dimensions of apartheid. It is more than a political stance. It is more than a response to a particular economic arrangement. It is an ontology that affects the very being of its adherents. Apartheid is the product of an essentialist racism in which people of color are considered to be *quintessentially* different from whites and cannot, as such, enter in any meaningful way into the formation of white identity. They—the "Blacks," "Coloureds," "Asians," "kaffirs," "Browns"—are a "lower race," "childlike," "prolific," "raw," "primitive," "savage," "uncivilized," "of the bush." This difference is preserved through distance. Apartheid precludes any contact with people of different races that might undermine the assumption of essential difference. Interracial residence, marriage, sexual relations, political gatherings, sports, entertainment (in the dark of the cinema, at bars and nightclubs, at the beach), toilets, elevators, waiting in line (at the post office, for example), traveling on buses and trains, eating—in short, any situation in which bodily contact between members of different races is possible—have been precluded.† Bodily contact is considered polluting. ("They are try-

---

*Occasionally an Afrikaner would draw a parallel between the situation of his people, say, in the thirties and the situation of the Coloureds today, but the parallel was quickly—symptomatically—dismissed. Similar parallels drawn by the English were, in my opinion, rhetorical. They concerned the Afrikaners and the non-whites—never the English themselves.

†There have been some changes in recent years. There are, for example, no longer separate windows for whites and Blacks at most post offices. Courts are not segregated, and segregation on trains has been relaxed somewhat. In some areas, taxis are no longer restricted to a single race. Some museums, theaters, civic halls, and libraries (but not the library and civic hall in Wyndal) have been opened to a multiracial public. The South African government has stopped enforcing apartheid in sports, and now sports associations can integrate. The South African Cricket Union insists that its clubs be open to all races and has even expelled a Transvaal

ing to create some sort of system," Hennie's son Zachary says, "to keep the unwashed away.") It is considered dangerous. Fear of assault, rape, and murder is widespread. (Violence is at some level always a demand for bodily recognition.) The body of the other simply cannot be acknowledged. It covers social, spiritual, and intellectual attributes.

To illustrate my point, let me cite two examples—one ideological, and the other psychological. They will highlight less dramatic examples in the chapters to come.

1. Toward the end of my first stay in Wyndal, an old Afrikaner couple invited my family to dinner. They were very distressed by their children, then in their thirties, who had joined a Baptist church. One of the children, Marliese, tried to convert my ten-year-old daughter that evening. When Marliese's father saw this, he called my daughter over and, to my surprise, told her not to pay any attention to what Marliese said. "Don't believe those people," he said. "They think every word in the Bible is true. You can't, because then you wouldn't be able to explain how the Black man got here. They come from baboons. That's what evolution has taught us, and the Bible doesn't say anything about evolution. God created the white man in a day. *That*, the Bible tells us. It took evolution to create the Black man."

2. Linda, a six-year-old girl who had always been a model child, began to act wildly in school, to hit other children, to spit at the teacher, and to defecate in the classroom. Linda's mother, an English South African, took Linda to a child analyst, one of the very few in South Africa. She could not account for her daughter's sudden change in behavior. Nothing unusual had happened in her life. After several months of play therapy—Linda would not speak to the analyst, a woman—it became clear that she was markedly hostile to

---

club that refused to admit non-whites. Soccer, a predominantly Black sport in South Africa, is organized along segregationist lines, but clubs are even owned by Blacks. Rugby, now dominated by Afrikaners, is the least integrated of South Africa's three major team sports. Ironically, the Springboks, South Africa's rugby team, competes internationally while its cricket and soccer teams are boycotted. By 1982, seventy-three hotels, mostly expensive, were declared "international" and could receive non-white guests. A few restaurants have also been granted "international" status. Like many of the integrated theaters, these "international" hotels and restaurants have been boycotted by politically conscious Blacks, who recognize the tokenism of this "integration."

her mother, symbolized by a white doll. Her hostility alternated with suffocating affection. The analyst asked Linda's mother about the nanny and learned, to her astonishment, that the nanny had been fired about a week before Linda began acting up in school. (Linda apparently had been very attached to her nanny, a Zulu woman.) The mother had never bothered to explain the nanny's sudden departure to her daughter and had not thought it significant enough to tell the analyst. Of course, the analyst also had not thought it significant enough to ask about Linda's nanny.

Both of these examples are extreme. They are facilitated by South Africa's racial discourse and reveal the conceptual and emotional implications of that discourse. Blacks, Coloureds, and Asians for many whites are little more than pawns in their identity play.* It is this status that is perhaps most undermining of the non-whites. The failure to give conceptual and emotional as well as legal and political recognition to South Africa's majority population morally cripples the white South African. It accounts for the curiously static picture most of the whites in Wyndal have of the valley, indeed, of South Africa. There is no vibrancy in their relationship to non-whites. The Blacks, the Coloureds, and the Asians are at most the subject of the whites' frozen discourse, of their timeless representations. They are opaque, and their opacity is deemed unworthy of

---

*Although many factors can be held responsible for treating people of color as pawns—fear among them—it is noteworthy that many whites, certainly most of those I interviewed, had had Coloured or Black nannies. Most adults had only dim memories of their nannies and did not know what had happened to them. (This would probably not be the case on isolated farms where there was a resident Black population.) "She must have gone back to her people" was a typical reply when I asked where the nanny was. They were often cold—forcedly indifferent. I take this coldness to be a reaction to the frequent abrupt dismissal of the nanny or her devaluation as the child becomes racially conscious. Often the first, most intimate emotional and bodily contact a child has, among the English and perhaps, to a lesser extent, among the Afrikaners, is with a person of color. (The Afrikaner father's beating of his son has to be understood in this context.) From my daughter, who was ten and played with both English and Afrikaner children in Wyndal, I discovered that children of her age had a rich repertoire of stories of how Coloureds and Blacks would attack them, beat them up, rape them, or kill them. Although some of those stories were probably inspired by a recent murder of a white farmer in a nearby town, they also seemed to be a reaction to the "abandonment" by or the "denigration" of the nanny. Several whites told me that when they were old, they would be taken care of by a Coloured or Black nurse. They did not want to show their physical weakness to a white person.

clarification. They stand there, as Hugo Malan's wife, Peggy, put it, "in implacable silence." In their opacity, in their implacable silence, they are unknown and unknowable agents of change, threats to the whites' way of life, bearers of projected fear. In this they have power. Wittingly or unwittingly, the whites wait for something, anything, to happen. They are caught in the peculiar, the paralytic, time of waiting.

It was during my second winter in Wyndal that I came to appreciate the significance of waiting. A friend, whom I will call Carl, came to visit me. He had left South Africa to teach in the United States. He had known Wyndal and the family with which I was living and had, in his self-imposed exile, come to picture them romantically. He was, I imagine, filled with a nostalgia turned sour on encountering its object once again—"in reality"—filled with disappointment, with regret, with anger, at the way things had gone wrong in a country of such extraordinary potential, with feelings of powerlessness, frustration, and rage, and with all this guilt that comes from departure experienced at once as abandonment and liberation. His past was here; his future was there, in America. He was caught now in a present that was both here and there and neither here nor there. Carl had come with a friend, an American who had never been to South Africa before and was experiencing all the confusion of a first visit. Our hosts were warm and friendly and excited, truly excited, to see us, three friends, together on their farm. We spent a delightful evening, and then when all the delight had been expressed, when all the gossip had been said, and when all the jokes had been told, the conversation turned inevitably to South Africa and its future. Carl looked down at his coffee cup. I will never forget the anguish on his face. The next evening, in a steakhouse in Cape Town—I do not remember the exact context—Carl suddenly said with great passion, "I left South Africa because I couldn't stand the waiting any longer for something, anything, to happen."

Waiting for something, anything, to happen. That was the moment my understanding began to crystallize. I had come to South Africa with a special interest in the experience of time. In my previous research, in Morocco, I had been particularly concerned with how one used the past to make sense of the present.[35] In South Africa, where the future, at least for the whites, is problematic, I was interested not only in the rhetoric of the past but in the rhetoric of the future.

Waiting for something, anything, to happen was a constant preoccupation in the stories I had been hearing, the newspapers I was
receiving, and in the literature I was reading. It was also one of the
principal preoccupations in my own fieldwork—a far greater preoccupation, I can say in retrospect, than in my previous research in
Morocco or with the Navaho Indians. How often the subjective
experience of fieldwork parallels the experience of those one studies.

I do not mean to suggest that the whites with whom I talked were
overwhelmed by waiting. For the most part, white South Africans
live what in their terms would be perfectly ordinary, realistic, middle-class lives filled with the pleasures and pains, the joys and sor-
rows, the delights and worries, the concerns, of such lives.

And yet I find that the experience of waiting provides a thematic
unity to what I heard, observed, and read. (It certainly resonated
with those South African whites I talked to about it.) "Waiting"
seems to have the right tone. To talk about *dread, angst, guilt,* or
being overwhelmed, all of which are components of the experience
of waiting, adds a metaphysical dimension, a melodramatic tension,
to the very ordinary experience I am trying to describe. Such terms
"elevate" the experience. They give it importance. They permit a
sort of moral indulgence, a taking comfort, in it. Symptoms of the
ordinary, they mask the ordinary. It is precisely this masking that
has to be avoided. Waiting—the South African experience—must
be appreciated in all of its banality. Therein lies its pity—and its
humanity.

The life of those white South Africans with whom I talked (and
I see no reason to assume that they are very different in this from
other white South Africans) impressed me as somehow truncated.
I found signs of anxiety, helplessness, vulnerability, and rage that
were not very far from the surface. Their experience was not open-
ended, expansive, and adventurous. It did not elicit optimism and
positive excitement. It was limited. Their present seemed devoid of
the vitality that I associate with leading a fulfilling life. It seemed
mechanical, numb, and muted. *Dead* would be an exaggeration. It
was infused with uncertainty or at times what appeared to me to be
a compensatory overcertainty, a stubborn and harsh pragmatism.
The white South African was often ready, too ready, to lose himself
in the swirl of everyday life, in an unmitigated materialism that I
personally found to be without style and élan, certainly without
imagination, or in a genteel way of life that had little to do with the
present.

For many of Wyndal's English, but for some of its Afrikaners as well, farm life provided an escape from concerns that were often frenetically felt in the cities, where the sense of waiting was more acute. They seemed at times to be acting a part in some nineteenth-century rural drama. Concern for the past, particularly strong among the Afrikaners, seemed to compensate for something that was lacking in the present, indeed, in the future. Paul Kruger, the old president of the Transvaal, sent a last message to his people from his deathbed in Clarens, Switzerland: "Look to the past for all it contains which is fine and noble. Let that then be the measure of your ideal; and let your future be the endeavour to realize it."[36] I often had the impression that by recuperating the past, the Afrikaner, and to a lesser extent the English South Africans, hoped, as if by magic, to claim a present and proclaim a future that was somehow lost to them in waiting.

Waiting means to be oriented in time in a special way. It is directed toward the future—not an expansive future, however, but a constricted one that closes in on the present. In waiting, the present is always secondary to the future. It is held in expectation. It is filled with suspense. It is a sort of holding action—a lingering. (In its extreme forms waiting can lead to paralysis.) In waiting, the present loses its focus in the now. The world in its immediacy slips away; it is derealized. It is without élan, vitality, creative force. It is numb, muted, dead. Its only meaning lies in the future—in the arrival or the non-arrival of the object of waiting.

Waiting is always waiting for something. It is an anticipation of something to come—something that is not on hand but will, perhaps, be on hand in the future. It is marked by contingency—the perhaps—and all the anxiety that comes with the experience of contingency. It is a passive activity. We can never actively seek the object of waiting. We can, to be sure, do what we can to ensure its arrival if we desire it or to prevent its arrival if we do not desire it, but ultimately its arrival or non-arrival is beyond our control.

Waiting produces in us feelings of powerlessness, helplessness, and vulnerability—infantile feelings—and all the rage that these feelings evoke. We seek release from these feelings, from the tension and suspense of waiting, from the anxiety of contingency, in many, often magical ways. We tell stories. We lose ourselves in the swirl of everyday activity. We pretend to ourselves that we are indifferent to the object of waiting. We rehearse its arrival, as my friend Carl has observed. He sees much of what the South African does as a rehearsal for the day of reckoning. We pray. We affirm our faith in a transcendent power, a god, a spirit, manifest destiny, that will look after us. We make pilgrimages to holy places and leave offerings and votives to those who will intercede for us. We go to magicians and soothsayers. We invent our own magic, personal taboos, and idiosyncratic rituals. We see omens everywhere. We render the object of waiting itself into an omen, a sign of favor or disfavor. Waiting becomes a moral allegory—a private purgatory in which our moral and psychic fiber is tested, our virtue is rewarded, and our vice is punished. We are expiated through waiting. We learn from it. We become disciplined, hardened, stoical.

The past gives us security when we are waiting. We know "from past experience" that in all likelihood what we are waiting for will or will not come. Our expectations become "realistic." We are able to take waiting in stride—devote ourselves to other things. Still, despite experience, we know that past experience offers no guarantee of the future. It is always possible that the sun will not set tonight or rise tomorrow. We insist that there is meaning, order, purpose, in the past. "It is history," we say. In the West, at least, history is still understood subjectively in broad theological terms; teleologically, eschatologically, as a meaningful coming from and a purposeful going to. (It is colored by notions of expiation and salvation.) There is in waiting always this backward glance, this seeking security in the experience of the past, this taking solace in history, which devitalizes the here and now. We linger because we know from past experience that we can do nothing. We linger because we know that "the forces of history" will have their way.

Waiting is infused with desire. In its positive modality, it is directed toward something that is desired: It is longing. In its negative modality, it is directed toward something that is not desired: It is dread. (Given the ambivalence of human desire, waiting is mostly a longing and a dread. Did not Kierkegaard call dread "a sympathetic antipathy and an antipathetic sympathy"?[37]) Waiting's desire is magical since there is nothing in pure waiting that we can do but wait, have faith, hope for the best, as the saying goes, and prepare for the worst. Hope is the field of desire in waiting. It is where desire is given free play. Such play may be terrifying—the full possibility of desire is always terrifying—and must be limited. It is limited by conscience, which restricts its range, and by faith, which narrows the perception of its possibility.

From Kierkegaard, Freud, and Heidegger we have learned to distinguish fear from anxiety. Like waiting, they both have intentional structures. The object of fear is specific. We are afraid of snakes, war, that man over there. We are afraid there will be a depression, a communist takeover, a failure in the electric system. "The man who is afraid, the nervous man," Heidegger observes, "is always bound by the thing he is afraid of or by the state in which he finds himself."[38] He is "uncertain" in his relations to other things. The object of anxiety, angst, is always uncertain. For Freud it is hidden, repressed, not immediately available to consciousness. For Heidegger anxiety reveals Nothingness. "The fact that when we are caught in the uncanniness of dread [*Angst*] we often try to break the empty silence by words spoken at random only proves the presence of Nothing." We feel something uncanny. We are struck dumb. We are in a "retreat from something, though it is not so much a flight as a spell-bound [*bebannt*] peace."[39] For Freud anxiety is an undesirable state; for Heidegger, at least in its "authentic" form, it is desirable insofar as it reveals the human situation. Given the intentional structure of anxiety, we are predisposed to give anxiety a specific object—to transform it into fear. Through such symbolic projections we alleviate our anxiety but not without cost. We risk entering a world in which "reality" has been sacrificed to "psychic need."

In English we do not distinguish between waiting for something concrete and waiting for something, anything, to happen. The two forms of waiting are related to fear and anxiety. In waiting for something concrete the object of the intentional act of waiting is, like the object of fear, specific. It may be longed for or dreaded. It colors the present and determines the uses we make of the past. In waiting for something, anything, to happen the object of the intentional act of waiting, like the object of anxiety, is not given. It may be hidden, repressed, unavailable to consciousness or it may be simply unknowable. Such waiting is terrible. Like anxiety, it is frequently given a symbolic object. We transform it into a waiting for something specific, which is often expressed in abstract terms. We wait for war, the end of the world, death. Or through an act of disciplined optimism we await eternal peace, the Second Coming, life after death. With the postulation of such symbolic objects, we may reduce the anxiety, the terror, of just waiting for something, anything, to happen, but we risk, here too, sacrificing "reality" to "psychic need."

Nadine Gordimer says that the "historical coordinates" in South Africa "don't fit life any longer."[40] "It is not for nothing," she adds, "that I chose as an epigraph for my most lately written novel a quotation from Gramsci: 'The old is dying, and the new cannot be born; in this interregnum there arise a great diversity of morbid symptoms.' " There is indeed "a great diversity of morbid symptoms" in South Africa today—they are evident in much of what follows—but I would caution against overplaying the *morbidity*. For we in Europe and America have elaborated a marvelous pathology that enables us to declare much of what is a question of morality a matter of disease and eschew thereby our own responsibility and perhaps even something of ourselves. We are fascinated by South Africa. Do we see something of ourselves there, in that haply distant land? Many South African whites say we do and resent our judgment. They are, they say, nothing more than self-judgments cast on the other. "What angers me," one man said, "is that you see in me your own underbelly." I resented their observations, their all too facile analogies, and I still do, but I must also admit that there is some truth in them. It is this truth that we must recognize even if it is but a sign of our own weakness when confronted with an otherness that likes to bully itself into our conscience. "Otherness is a powerful factor of distraction," Michel Tournier, the author of *Vendredi ou les limbes du Pacifique*, says, "not only because it continually disturbs us and wrenches us from our intellectual thinking but also because the very possibility of its occurrence casts a hazy glow on a universe of objects that are situated at the edge of our attention but can at any moment become its center."[41] Insofar as anthropology is the science of otherness, as the French like to say, we must recognize not only an intellectual mission but a moral one as well. We must recognize in our investigations of otherness an investigation of our own possibility.

3

THE PAST

Hennie

"One of the events that most affected our lives was the Anglo-Boer War," Hennie told me the first time I met him. "My dad and twenty-two pals started a little army up in the north and pinned down ten thousand British troops. They ambushed them in a valley, and when the fighting was over, there were rows and rows of crosses. My dad and his men knew the country; they knew the valley; and they knew the farmers who lived in the area. The farmers were all on their side. Their fathers and grandfathers had trekked —many of them had died on the trek—and now they were not about to give up what their fathers and grandfathers had died for. My dad and his pals were finally captured. They never really had a chance —they were so outnumbered. My dad spent the last six months of the war in a British jail. When he was about to be released, the commanding officer said, 'Let's forgive and forget, Mr. van der Merwe.' My dad looked at him for a long time and finally said, 'Forgive, I can. Christ taught us to forgive. Forget, I can't. It's history.' And that's what he told us, his three sons.

"When my eldest brother went off to varsity, my dad told him, 'You grew up in an Afrikaans area. You have learned to hate the English, but they are here to stay. My job was to shoot them. Your job is to live with them.' He made my brother go to an English-

speaking university. He wouldn't let him go to an Afrikaans university. He wouldn't pay his fees. 'You speak Afrikaans, and now you
must speak English. They are the languages of South Africa,' he
said. He was a level-headed sort of man—a realist. He knew where
the future lay. He would say, 'The past is the past. You must live
for tomorrow—and not relive yesterday.'

"I suppose there is an awful lot to be found in history, and we
can learn an awful lot from it, but trying to relive the past is futile.
With the Afrikaner a lot of this has to do with the little kid looking
back and seeing the English interfering with our system: abolishing
slavery in 1834, giving the land the people fought for back to the
Xhosa, putting our women and children in concentration camps
and burning down our houses in the Anglo-Boer War . . . But we're
still trying to get the British out of our blood. We can't do anything
about what happened. We've got to live now and plan a future for
our children, but instead we live our past over and over again. A
little while ago, there was a program on television, the *Springbok
Saga*, about our glorious rugby tradition. Well, you know that
tradition is so young that a lot of the very early Springboks are still
alive! Whenever things get a bit rough for us, we look to the past.
We're out of international rugby* now, and so we create a glorious
tradition and watch it on television. It may be traumatic to face up
to the present, but that's all we can do, really."

Hennie's "really" was midway between a question and an affirma-
tion. I was not used to his manner of speaking. He spoke English
fluently, without much of an accent, but his speech rhythm and his
rhetorical associations were very different from those of the English-
speaking South Africans with whom I had spoken. He seemed, at
times brutally, oblivious to the niceties of language that are so dear
to them. He jumped from subject to subject; he punctuated his
discourse with "you knows," which I have deleted, or with a peculiar, highly nasalized laugh, a friendly laugh, which drew his listeners into one of his perceptions or insights. On reflection these
seemed simple and banal, but in Hennie's presence they always
seemed significant. He spoke in parables, simple epiphanic tales,
which he could never bring to an elegant conclusion but which,
with the aid of his laugh, were not without a certain eloquence.

*Hennie was talking just before the Springboks re-entered international rugby,
with the arrival of the British Lions in South Africa in 1980.

Though he had a good sense of humor, he was not a humorist, nor was he particularly ironic. He took reality too seriously for that, and when he expressed something in a manner that I took to be ironic, I soon found that I had misunderstood him; for what I took to be his irony were simply unconventional juxtapositions of perceptions and ideas that produced a nervousness—a challenge to his faith that had to be overcome through a reaffirmation of his, of man's, burden less to understand than to love.

There is nothing unusual about Hennie's bringing up the Anglo-Boer War. Nearly every South African with whom I spoke brought it up during our first conversation to explain something or other about South African culture, society, or character. History (at least in those cultures that, like the white South African's, take stock in it) always provides a rich repertoire of symbols for offering an explanation of why things are the way they are and why human beings do as they do. It offers a version of the past that pretends to truth and claims responsibility for the present and even the future. It is precisely this truth, this facticity, the stubbornness, if you will, of the "facts of history," that permit us to take solace in it, fatalistically even, and to eschew thereby, as the existentialists would have it, responsibility for ourselves and for the world in which we live. Frequently one historical event becomes *the* summary event.

The second Anglo-Boer War* is such an event. Milner's "little Armageddon," as it was called, is a condensed symbol of the white South Africans with whom I talked. It describes the hostility that existed—and still exists—between South Africa's two great white populations. It describes the bitterness, the frustration, the sense of having been wronged, the defeat of the Afrikaner. It describes the outrage of the Afrikaners at having been made into lower-caste citizens and having their cultural heritage, their language, ignored, denied, or eliminated. It also describes the arrogant shame of the

---

*The first Anglo-Boer War began in the Transvaal in December 1880 over the British armed seizure of Piet Bezuidenhout's wagon, which had been attacked by the court because Bezuidenhout refused to pay taxes. The Transvaalers resented the British annexation of their country in 1877 and were seeking an excuse for war. They roundly defeated the British at Majuba on February 27, 1881, and the Transvaal was granted qualified independence in August 1881. Although the war of 1880–1881 was never brought up in any of my interviews, some authorities, like René de Villiers, argue that it gave "form and content to the nationalism latent in the Afrikaner people" ("Afrikaner Nationalism," p. 366).

British, their sense of being enmeshed in a conflict that sullies them, their imperial aspiration and its demise, a threatened sense of superiority, and their victory in a war in which it makes little sense to talk about victory.

The October war of 1899, which was to be won by Christmas (so the British thought), in fact lasted until June 1902. Twenty-two thousand of the 450,000 imperial and colonial soldiers who fought in South Africa found their graves there. Over 400,000 British horses, mules, and donkeys were lost. Seven thousand Boer commandoes were killed. There were just over 87,000 of them. More than 28,000 Boer women and children died in British concentration camps. Several million Boer cattle, horses, and sheep were killed or looted. Tens of thousands of farms were razed in a ruthless scorched-earth policy. Twelve thousand Africans were killed: the servants and retainers to the Boers. Over 100,000 Africans were held by the British in special camps.[1] We know little of what they thought about the white man's war, but several of the Blacks with whom I talked about it just snickered at what they regarded, I am sure, as the white man's folly.

Dr. Jakobus Steyn

"There has always been a lack of understanding between the English and the Afrikaners. Oh, I suppose we get on better than we did a few years ago, but you mustn't forget that in 1900, only eighty years ago, there was a war between us. I don't think we have ever done the things to the Blacks that the English did to us."

Dr. Jakobus Steyn sounded pained and angered, as if some recent hurt had been aggravated. I had asked him whether or not he thought the relations between the English and the Afrikaners were improving.

Dr. Steyn is an outsider to the valley. He was born in a little town in the Free State just north of one of Britain's most notorious concentration camps, studied medicine in Cape Town and then in England, and bought a practice in Wyndal about twenty years ago. "I had visited Wyndal for the first time when I was a student in Cape Town. I had some friends here. I was taken with the richness of the place, the green, and the mountains. In the Free State, everything was always brown, a dusty brown, except after the rains. That was magical. Suddenly everything turned green. We call it the *opslag*. Here I had to get used to the mountains. Back in the Free State you could see all the way to the horizon. Now I'm used to it. It's a smaller world here, and older."

Dr. Steyn is one of Wyndal's most *verkrampte*—reactionary— inhabitants. He votes for the National Party, as do most of the other Afrikaners in the valley, but he would prefer to vote for the Her- stigte Nasionale Party, the HNP, which is well to the right of the Nats, as the Nationalists are called, were there a local candidate. He is rather more vociferous in his politics than other Afrikaners in the valley, who frequently prefer a discreet silence.

Though as a physician he is respected, Dr. Steyn has never been fully accepted by the old Huguenot families. The English, who know him better than they know the other Afrikaners because of his impeccable English, treat him a little like a museum piece. He is their specimen *verkrampte*. When I arrived in the valley, they urged me to see him. "Then, you will understand the true Afrikaans mentality," they would say and laugh. "Let him tell you about the concentration camps. He really believes that the British fed glass to the women and children. You know that they actually show you the ground glass and the fishhooks that we were supposed to have fed to the Boers at the Vrouemonument,* near Bloemfontein."

"Even when I was a young man, during the war, at university," Dr. Steyn continued, "I was forced to stand at attention at the cinema when they played 'God Save the King.' I was forced to stand up! I, an Afrikaner, who was brought up not to like the English. They did things to us that you may forgive but you don't forget. Over twenty-six thousand of our women and children died in their concentration camps. We were a small nation, and that is a lot of women and children. They just put them in tents, without food, without adequate medical treatment. It is cold in the north. The winters are freezing. Twenty-six thousand people just don't die of broken hearts.

"From the earliest of times there was a difference between the

---

*The Vrouemonument, or National Woman's Monument, which was unveiled December 16, 1913, is dedicated to the "26,370 women and children who died in the concentration camps and to other women and children who perished as a result of the War of 1899–1902." On one of its panels, under the caption "For freedom, *volk*, and fatherland," women and children are seen entering a concentration camp, clutching a few miserable possessions; on another, a child dies at its mother's side.

English and the Afrikaners. And after the war, it was the English, more or less, who ruled the country. We felt, I suppose, as the Coloureds feel today. We had to battle to prove ourselves. The result is that there is still a grudge. I personally don't have a grudge. Still I remember these things. I tell my kids about the war. I take them to visit the concentration camps. I am proud to show them how our people suffered.

"My grandfather was deported to Ceylon, and my grandmother was in one of the camps. She survived. She told me stories. She used to sit in front of the old faceless grandfather clock—the British troops had stolen its mechanism. At least they didn't chop it up for firewood. I have that clock now, and I keep it in the lounge. You will have to see it one day. I have never had it repaired. It is our memory.

"My grandmother would tell me how women and children who slept next to her—whose warmth and life she felt—would be dead when she woke up in the morning. There were days that they were given nothing to eat. The milk of nursing mothers ran dry. There was no medicine, no doctors, no sanitation. In the summers the camps would smell so bad . . ."

Dr. Steyn's voice was choked with rage. He peered at me from across his desk, asking himself, I imagined, who I really was, and then slowly, in a more controlled voice, he went on to tell me about the ground glass that was fed to the women and children.

"We must remember these things. Our relations may be improving but there will always be a feeling between us—a feeling like that between the British and the Germans. They don't like each other very much. I think that is normal! They fought a war, and that was not so long ago. The problem in South Africa is that the English, unlike the Dutch and the French, have become a nation unto themselves. The English, as you know, have always been poor immigrants. They always want to preserve their identity, as Englishmen. What makes me mad is when a bloke shows me the Union Jack and says that it is his flag, when he thinks of 'God Save the Queen' as his anthem, and when he talks about going home to England although he has never even been there. These things worry me. I don't like it. My ancestors came over from Holland, but I don't think of Holland as my home. I am a South African, and I am proud of that.

"We're all South Africans now, and we should intermingle. But the English in Wyndal don't even send their children to our local school. Language and school count a lot for them. They think they speak the language of the world and ask themselves why they should break their backs learning a minor language like Afrikaans. I was raised never to speak English, but then I had to, first at varsity and then in England. My children do not speak English as well as I would like them to speak it. I suppose the correct thing would be to send them to English schools. But over my dead body. If they go to English schools, they will lose all pride in being an Afrikaner. It will undermine them. They will be taught that there is no difference between us. They will learn about the English way of living. They'll come home and ask why we always talk about the Boer War. It's just politics, they will say, and we should forget about it. But do the English themselves forget about Waterloo? Or the Irish about the Battle of the Boyne? We the Afrikaner nation are the only people in the world who have to look around before we start talking about our past.

"My father was a boy during the Boer War. He never talked much about it. He had to try to live off the farm. There was very little there. The English had taken everything off the veld. He spent much of his time trying to escape from the English. Imagine a little boy of ten trying to escape from them.

"Our farm was one of the first to be taken. We were just over the border. They weren't burning down farms yet, but they took everything. They took our horse, but the horse ran away from them and returned to us. They came and got it again, and again the horse came back to our farm. What is a farm without a horse? This time my grandmother wrapped blankets around its hooves and hid it in an outhouse, so when the British came back, they didn't find it. Then when they came to take my grandmother away, my father ran off with the horse and spent the rest of the war living off the veld, hunting birds. I think that if there is one thing the English would take back if they could it's the Boer War.

"People in the Transvaal and the Free State are more conscious of the war than people here in the Cape. Most here didn't join in the war. There were of course a few who did, and some of them died. But most of them couldn't—they were watched, and it was hundreds of miles to the front. We would have liked them all to have fought. If they could have cleared Cape Town harbor, we would have had a better chance. But then again, we didn't have concentration camps. We captured a lot of British soldiers, but we just took their clothes and guns and told them to go. The next day we would be fighting them again. You can't win a war that way.

"I think some of the people here are ashamed of the fact that their parents or grandparents didn't fight. They must ask themselves sometimes why they didn't fight. They make excuses. Who would want to find fault with one's father or grandfather? Who would want to admit that his ancestor did something that he is not proud of?"

Carol Reid

"You have to understand men like Dr. Steyn if you are ever to understand our problems," Carol Reid says. Carol and her husband, Duncan, retired to the valley four years earlier. She was a secretary in Durban, and Duncan was an accountant for a large shipping firm. "He's a typical Afrikaner. He's from the Free State, I believe, but they are just like him in the Transvaal. They're different here. They're more subdued. They're beginning to accept us. I don't think we'd ever be accepted up north.

"I lived in the eastern Transvaal for five years before I married Duncan. It was the loneliest time in my life, but I got to know the Afrikaans mentality. They talk about the trek and the 1900 war and the Zulu wars and the suffering of the Afrikaans people as though no one else has ever suffered.

"I was a young girl then, living alone, and not once in the five years I lived there was I invited to an Afrikaans home. I was the outsider, the enemy, I suppose. They have never forgiven us for winning the Boer War, and I don't think they ever will. It runs in their blood. You can't understand them without understanding the war. It has given them an inferiority complex. They don't like us. They blame us for their problems. They don't consider us true South Africans. They say we always call England home. That makes me mad.

"I was brought up in Durban. It is very English, very colonial. And it is true that some of the English there still refer to England as home, but there are not many who do. My parents were born in England. My father, who came out to South Africa during the Boer War, was a policeman—I never told anyone *that* in the Transvaal.

I was raised in a typical Victorian home, and my mother used to tell me about England. I have a strong feeling for England, but I have never been there and I do not consider England my home. I am a South African, and my children are South African. I love my country, and I used to be proud of it. It is my country too.

"It is these *verkrampte* who are leading South Africa to disaster. I have nothing against Dr. Steyn personally. He is a good doctor, and I have gone to him. But it is men of his background, I mean, who hold his values, who will be the death of us. They can't forget. We have nothing to be proud of. The Boer War was a shameful war. My father used to tell my brothers about it, and they would tell me. (He was very Victorian and wouldn't talk to me about such things.) They always talk about the women and the children who died in the concentration camps, twenty-six thousand of them. That was a terrible thing. But they never talk about the thousands of British soldiers who died here. I suppose I am being unfair. You shouldn't compare a soldier's death to the death of a woman or a child. But they make me so mad."

Om Max and Beatrix Roussouw

The Wyndal Afrikaners do talk about the war, and with emotion, too, but they are not as obsessed by it as Dr. Steyn. Om Max Roussouw, Beatrix's husband, says that Dr. Steyn's attitude is typical of the Free Staters and the Transvaalers, whom Om Max does not much like. He says that they are responsible for South Africa's troubles, and on several occasions he joked about an independent Cape Province. "We are the oldest part of South Africa. We are more cultured, and of course we do not have the same problems that they do up north. We have the Coloureds. We know them, and we can live with them. The Blacks are different. I don't know them. I don't understand them. We could get along just fine without them."

I was not altogether certain whether Om Max's "them" referred to the Blacks or the Free Staters and the Transvaalers.

"I am against apartheid. I mean the word 'apartheid.' That word has caused our problems. The English think it means 'apart-hate.' Apartheid is natural. It means 'separateness.' I always say, birds of a feather flock together. There was no need to name it. You have apartheid in the United States. They have it in Europe. You wouldn't invite your maid to dinner. You wouldn't be comfortable, and she wouldn't be comfortable. You have separate lives. That is all apartheid means. But here in South Africa we have to name everything. That is our problem. We give you the word, and then you can criticize us . . .

"You have to understand these Transvaalers. They are much more direct than we are. When they have something on their mind, they say it, whatever it is. And then afterward they regret it, but they will never take it back. That is the way they are. They are cattle and sheep farmers up there. We are fruit farmers. That is the difference. A fruit farmer has to be more subtle. It is a different way of thinking. It's like the Coloureds. They make good workers on our farms, but you can't make a good worker out of a Xhosa or a Zulu. They understand cattle. They don't understand fruit."

Beatrix is more reticent about the Transvaalers and the Free Staters than her husband. She does not like to criticize *any* Afrikaner in front of me, even those who, like Dr. Steyn, do not come from the valley. Beatrix is proud to be an Afrikaner, particularly of Huguenot ancestry. Her front rooms are filled with family portraits: stern-faced women in black dresses and white *kappies*, or bonnets, and white-bearded gentlemen, also in black, with even sterner faces. I remember in particular the eyes of one old man. They were slate-gray, experienced, harsh, judgmental, and yet somehow in that wrinkled face warm and slightly bemused. He was Beatrix's great-granduncle and was called the King of the Valley. He had been the lawyer, banker, local postmaster, and owner of Wyndal's only store until the railroad came to town just after Union. He lived through the war, was angered by the British but not enough to encourage his sons to fight against them, and generally saw the Transvaalers as following a course that could only lead to disaster.

When I first asked Beatrix about her family, the du Plessis', she began by giving me the name of the French farmer, no traceable relative, who built the farm her great-grandfather bought in the middle of the last century. He is a sort of eponymous ancestor for her: a link to the land her father, her father's father and his father tilled. She knows nothing about him but his name and the name of the little village near La Rochelle from which he is said to have come.

Beatrix has been preparing her genealogy, and Om Max's too, for several years now. She has a book that shows how all the du Plessis' are related to one another, and she has driven all the way to the Huguenot museum in Franschhoek to ask the archivist there for help. Her younger sister, who is married to an engineer in Pretoria and has attended meetings of the Huguenot Society twice, once in France and once in Canada, has written to the society for help. Unfortunately, an old family Bible and a family tree, prepared by a traveling artist in the nineteenth century, were lost in a fire when Beatrix was a little girl.

Om Max's family tree does hang prominently in the dining room to the right of the mantel. It is written in a bold, golden script—the Roussouw name is spelled three different ways—and is surrounded by a floral design that is awkwardly connected to the roots of the tree and its uppermost branches. It is rather crude in comparison to some of the more fanciful ones that one finds on some Wyndal farms —with their faded angels (clearly copied from the engravings in old home Bibles) and intricate Victorian floral designs that weave in and out of the tree itself and are connected to the flourishes under the ancestral names. When her research is completed, Beatrix plans to send the information to a printer in Cape Town who specializes in designing family trees. She says she will copy his design in petit point and give it to the wife of her eldest grandson. He is only nine, but Beatrix is worried about the loss of family tradition, of *gesinsoor- lewering.* "It is important to have a close and—how shall I say it? —a conservative family."

"The people here are different from other South Africans," Beatrix says. She uses "South African" to refer to the Afrikaners. Usually when whites speak of "South Africans," they are referring to whites only. "They have a much deeper sense of history and family background. The valley has kept more of its families. People have been here for five or even six generations.

"The first du Plessis came to South Africa in 1688. He fled for his religion. In those days everything was very wild in South Africa. There were lions right here in Wyndal and elephants. The governor of Cape Town gave him a farm, rations for a few months, an ax, and a plow. He was also given a quarter share in a *snaphaan*—a musket —a few pounds of lead, and some gunpowder. And then he had to fend for himself, just like the Voortrekkers.*

---

*The Voortrekkers were Afrikaners who, discontent with the British administration of the Cape, marched in the late 1830s into the hinterland to be free of the British.

"People in the Cape know that they come from the oldest part of the country. Look at the names of the farms. They are still the same after nearly three hundred years! Children come back to the valley. They miss it. My sister in Pretoria misses it. She is always a bit homesick and talks about making the trek back home. I don't know how to explain it. There is just something about the valley. It is our home. I don't think you Americans can really understand this."

"You think South Africa belongs to the Black man," Om Max interrupted. He always came in from his workshop when I interviewed his wife. "But we came here before the Kaffirs were here. There were some Bushmen and Hottentots. The Hottentots died of smallpox, like your Red Indians, and the Bushmen, well, they're the Coloureds now, they and the Malays. We call them Cape Coloureds. In the old days the Bushmen used to steal our cattle—we used to have cattle and sheep in the valley—but now that they're Coloureds, they live with us peacefully."

"And they miss the valley too when they leave it," Beatrix added. "They know their place is here."

"Yes, we have been here for a long time," Om Max mused. "We've always been a bit isolated. In 1900 war didn't touch us much down here. The train hadn't come in yet. In those days there were a lot of bandits on the road. There were no banks here yet, so they used to send the money up from Cape Town in cash to pay the teachers. They would tear the bills in half and send up one half one day and the other half the next. The teachers would put them together and use them. That way, if a courier were robbed, the bandits would only get a worthless half bill.

"Those teachers all taught us in English. I wasn't born until after the Boer War, but even when I was in school, we weren't allowed to speak Afrikaans. We did learn High Dutch. If you got caught speaking Afrikaans, you'd get a real hiding. One teacher made a sign, and the first one to speak Afrikaans in class each week was made to wear the sign until someone else was caught speaking it. Then he would give the sign to him. Whoever got caught with the sign on Friday afternoon would get a hiding. They wanted to make us forget Afrikaans. I remember one Friday—I was very little still —I got caught with the sign and was given such a bad hiding that I couldn't sit down at dinner. I was scared my dad would ask me what was wrong. Every time I got a hiding in school and he found out, he would give me another one just to make sure I had learned my lesson. I just sat there really stiff and hoped he wouldn't ask me what was wrong, but of course he did. I told him. He asked me why. I told him that, too. And he said he was proud of me, and I burst into tears. I can still remember those tears.

"I can laugh at it now, but there are some people who can't. They were too badly burned. Our language has survived. When I was little, there were almost no books in Afrikaans. There was the Bible and that was about all. Now we have books on every subject— university books. That is something to be proud of. The English have always hated Afrikaans. They tried to make us forget it when they first came out here. Lord Somerset—he was one of the first British governors of the Cape—had the idea that if our ministers could speak only English, we would have to speak it too. He brought in a lot of Scottish ministers, and now there are a lot of people with Scottish names who can't speak English. We gave them no choice. They had to learn Afrikaans!

"But now these English, these *inkruipers*, are coming into the valley," Om Max continued, suddenly getting angry. "They buy our farms. They live where our fathers and grandfathers lived, but they don't learn our language."

Beatrix looked at her husband with irritation.

"Well, they have crept in, haven't they?" he said.

"*Inkruiper*," which comes from the verb "*inkruip*," "to creep in," "to crawl in," as a snake crawls into its hole, has derogatory connotations. It can also mean "toady" or "adulator."

"They pay so much for a farm that no one in the valley can buy one anymore. They come in with money they've made in Durban or smuggled out of Zambia or Rhodesia. They make capital improvements none of us can make. They go to *our* Deciduous Fruit Board for advice or to Stellenbosch University. They're buying us out." Om Max paused. "They're not bad farmers," he admitted. "In the old days, we had loose standing trees. We never pruned them. We never sprayed them. Peaches were the most popular crop. I remember my dad began pruning in a haphazard sort of way. It must have been in the early twenties. I was just beginning to learn about farming. We didn't have irrigation. We thought that it would soften the peaches. We were afraid of softening the fruit because transportation took so long."

"There was something beautiful about the old orchards," Beatrix said. Her eyes were the same slate-gray as her great-granduncle's, but they were worried and always slightly suspicious. "I'm sentimental about history. I'm proud of the fact that I live in a village with history. When Max's father died, the farm was divided into two, and then when Piet, Max's brother, died, his farm was sold to Jack Freeling. It was sad. It's not that I mind the English being here. What I find sad is that the young are not farming; that the farms are leaving the families. We are slowly being infiltrated."

"In the past," Om Max said, "the farmers worked together. We were part of one big community. But the English here manage for themselves. There is no longer a community. I remember a few years ago there was a terrible rainstorm and a lot of flooding. Water came rushing down from the mountains and burst one of the dams on our farm. We were not the only ones who suffered damage. Then there was a real sense of *kameraderie*. All the farmers in the village came together and formed a committee. I went to the committee and told them about my dam. Other farmers came with similar requests. The farmers who had no damage supplied us with labor at their own cost. I don't think that would happen today."

"I'm not sure," Beatrix said more for my sake, I suspect, than out of any real doubt. I was always identified with the English if only because English was my mother tongue. "I think *we* would still come together in case of a crisis but I'm not sure *they* would."

Many Afrikaners, like Beatrix Roussouw, are "sentimental about history." They are proud of their past; they embellish it; they venerate it. Even a man as ready to debunk history as Hennie would sometimes become sentimental about it. He told me once that he was worried that my interviews with him, a renegade, were giving me the wrong picture of the Afrikaner and his culture. (Hennie was as convinced as anyone in South Africa that there was a correct picture of *the* Afrikaner!) He went on to tell me in a schoolboyish manner the saga of Afrikanerdom and ended up, as much to his surprise, I believe, as to mine, extolling the Afrikaners' entry into commerce and industry in the decades following World War II.

History for the Afrikaner, that is to say, *his* history, is no ordinary history. It is, as T. Dunbar Moodie and others have written, a sacred history, a biblicized history, the history of a chosen people, a revelation. D. F. Malan, one of the most eloquent proponents of Afrikaner nationalism, expressed this well when he wrote:

> The last hundred years have witnessed a miracle behind which must lie a divine plan. Indeed, the history of the Afrikaner reveals a will

and a determination which makes one feel that Afrikanerdom is not the work of men but the creation of God.[2]

It is a providential history, a heroic history, a history constructed on a few resonant events: a *via dolorosa* of the Afrikaners. It is a story of suffering, misunderstanding, and persecution. It is as well the saga of hope and ultimate redemption.

The saga begins with what Moodie calls a "scant 'myth of origin' ": the settlement in 1652 of about ninety men under the leadership of Jan van Riebeeck on the Cabo de Boa Esperance, then occupied by a reputedly savage, yellow-skinned people, the Khoikhoi, or Hottentots. Van Riebeeck was under orders from the Dutch East India Company to build a "fort and garden"—a refreshment station for the Company's ships, whose crews were dying of scurvy on the long haul between the Netherlands and the East Indies.

For the people of Wyndal the saga begins with the arrival of about 200 French refugees, Huguenots fleeing the religious persecution after the revocation of the Edict of Nantes in 1685. A handful or so of them were settled in the valley "to cultivate the vine"; the farms still bear their original names. The Cape government interspersed Dutch farms among the Huguenot ones—they wanted to integrate the French as quickly as possible—and the French language was soon forgotten. Only farm and family names remained—Lourmarin d'Orleans, Piccardie, La Dauphine, Malan, La Grange, du Plessis, Roussouw—and something rather more difficult to grasp: a bloodline that is preserved in family genealogies. Really little more than lists of names, abstract, devoid of any biographical or historical depth, these genealogies give a cultural, spiritual, and racial identity to their members. What little is known of the ancestors comes less from family stories than from what has been learned in school histories.

"And then the French refugees, my own forbears, arrived in 1688," one South African historian told me. "They form a very powerful element, you know. Look in the telephone directory and you will see their names. Look at university registries and the registries of corporation executives, and you will see their names. The impact of the French element is enormous throughout the country. They started off by having a French school and a French congregation, but that didn't last very long. The Company, the Dutch East India Company, was adamant that there be only one language and that that language be the language of the Company. But you would be surprised: the French Huguenots kept very much to themselves for a long time. It is an interesting fact that a man like D. F. Malan —he was seventy-six when he became prime minister in 1948—had only one non-Huguenot ancestor among his thirty-two most immediate ancestors. And it still happens. My son has married a Malherbe and my daughter has married a Marais. Most of my ancestors are French. It was a deliberate policy among them to marry their own kind, that is, until the move eastward, the Great Trek."

For the Afrikaners, less perhaps for those from the Cape than for those from the other provinces of the Republic, the Orange Free State, the Transvaal, and Natal, the Great Trek (1836–1854) is the centerpiece of their historical consciousness: an extraordinary flight of small bands of farmers—in all they numbered 6,000—from British rule into the wild and treacherous regions of the interior. It was the Napoleonic Wars that first brought the British to South Africa in 1795. They occupied the Cape until 1803, when the Batavian Republic was created and Cape Town was handed over to it. In 1806, after the Batavian government joined with the French, the British reoccupied the Cape and took formal possession of it in 1814. With their arrival, the Afrikaner historian W. A. de Klerk observed, "all contours, human and physical, had hardened."[3]

From the very beginning of Dutch settlement, there had been an uneasy tension between the essentially corrupt administration of the Dutch East India Company and those residents of the Cape who were not directly in the employ of the Company. Rebels, renegades, adventurers, and those who simply could not withstand the temptation of an open, unknown land ventured out beyond the Company's pale. They became a sort of frontiersman—trekboers they were called—seminomadic pastoralists who, as they moved farther and farther from Cape Town, lost more and more of their European heritage. Sir John Barrow, a by-no-means unbiased observer, described the trekboers in his account of *Travels into the Interior of Southern Africa in the Years 1797 and 1798* in what became the influential portrait of them. I quote him at some length.

> Placed in a country where not only the necessities, but almost every luxury of life might by industry be procured, he has the enjoyment of none of them. Though he has cattle in abundance he makes very little use of milk or of butter. In the midst of soil and climate most favorable to the cultivation of the vine, he drinks no wine. He makes

use of few or no vegetables nor roots. Three times a-day his table is loaded with masses of mutton, swimming in the grease of the sheep's tail. His house is either open to the roof, or covered only with rough poles and turf, affording a favorable shelter for scorpions and spiders; and the earthy floors are covered with dust and dirt, and swarm with insects . . . His apartments, if he happens to have more than one, which is not always the case among the grazing farmers, are nearly destitute of furniture. A great chest that contains all moveables, and two smaller ones that are fitted to his wagon, are the most striking articles. The bottoms of his chairs consist of thongs cut from the bullock's hide. The windows are without glass; or if there should happen to be any remains of this article, it is so patched and daubed as nearly to exclude the light it was intended to admit. The boer not withstanding has his enjoyments: he is absolute master of a domain of several miles in extent; and he lords it over a few miserable slaves or Hottentots without control. His pipe scarcely ever quits his mouth, from the moment he rises till he retires to rest, except to give him time to swallow his *sopie*, or a glass of strong ardent spirit, to eat his meals and to take a nap after dinner. Unwilling to work, and unable to think; with a mind disengaged from every sort of care and reflection, indulging to excess in the gratification of every sensual appetite, the African peasant grows to an unwieldy size, and is carried off the stage by the first inflammatory disease that attacks him.[4]

Barrow goes on to describe the "listless inactivity" of the Boer woman—a stereotype that is given literary expression in Olive Shreiner's Tant' Sonnie.

The mistress of the family, with her coffee-pot constantly boiling before her on a small table, seems fixed to the chair like a piece of furniture. The good lady, born in the wilds of Africa, and educated among slaves and Hottentots, has little idea of what, in a state of society, constitutes female delicacy. She makes no scruples of having her legs and feet washed in warm water by a slave before strangers; an operation that is regularly performed every evening. If the motive of such an operation were cleanliness, the practice of it would deserve praise; but to see the tub with the same water passed round through all branches of the family, according to seniority, is apt to create ideas of a different nature.

We learn that the women go around without stockings and shoes, even in freezing weather, but that they make use of a small foot stove.

The young girls sit with their hands before them as listless as their mothers. Most of them, in the distant districts, can neither read nor write, so that they have no mental resources whatsoever. Luckily, perhaps for them, the paucity of ideas prevents time from hanging on their hands. The history of the day is that of their whole lives. They hear nor speak of nothing but that such-a-one is going to the city, or to church, or to be married, or that the Bosjesmans have stolen the cattle of such-a-one, or the locusts are eating their corn. The young people have no meetings at fixed periods, as in most country-places, for mirth and recreation. No fairs, no dancing, no music, nor amusement of any sort. The cold phlegmatic temper and inactive way of life may perhaps be owing to the prolific tendency of all the African peasantry. Six or seven children in a family are considered as very few; from a dozen to twenty are not uncommon; and most of them marry very young, so that the population of the colony is rapidly increasing.[5]

Barrow's ethnocentrism is perhaps as revealing as his description of the Boer. It was undoubtedly in part in reaction to attitudes such as his that the Boers trekked into the country, first to Natal, and then when the British took control there, across the Vaal and Orange Rivers into what were to become independent republics in the second half of the nineteenth century.

Hugo Malan

"You must understand the bitterness of those Voortrekkers," Hugo Malan said. I was surprised, since Hugo rarely had anything sympathetic to say about the Afrikaners despite his own background. He is a tall, handsome, distinctly North German–looking man in his early sixties with a high, straight forehead that is moderately wrinkled; large, well-sculpted cheekbones; an angular nose; and tight, tawny skin that reminded me of one of Dürer's portraits of his father. He has identified so strongly with the English that he speaks Afrikaans through his bushy moustache with a strong English accent. An exceptionally intelligent man, he is well respected in the valley's English community and is treated with a certain awe by the Afrikaners. His rationalism frequently leads him to a cold, rather harsh, certainly judgmental, essentially conservative view of human nature, but, paradoxically, in his social encounters, he is warm and sympathetic, and given to trivializing his conversation with women and those men whose intelligence he finds inferior to his own. With his equals, his rationalism is relentless.

"My father used to tell me how his grandmother was cheated out of what little indemnification she was to have received for her slaves. When the English liberated the slaves in 1834, they agreed to indemnify the owners. It wasn't much—about a third of what the owners could have got on the market in Cape Town. There was one hitch. You could only receive the indemnification at Whitehall. Now, most of the slave owners could not afford to go to London, and even if they could, they would not have known how to get around. So people like my great-grandmother—she was a widow by then—resorted to agents who were traveling around the Cape collecting powers of attorney and promising to deliver the funds. Of course, once they got their hands on the powers of attorney, they were never seen again. My great-grandmother—she must have been a powerful woman—swore that this would never happen to her three sons. She insisted that they all become lawyers, and they did. She was bitter. Yes, they were all bitter, but she never really blamed the English. Her sons all married English girls.

"It is bitterness and vindictiveness that have held back so many Afrikaners. It's like the Boer War. There are still Afrikaners, even in Wyndal, too young for even their fathers to have fought in the war, who cannot bring themselves to forgive the English for it. It is their cancer. They become stubborn; they cling to their culture, to their language. They refuse to admit that it is inadequate to the world they are living in. It was this bitterness, this frustration, that drove the Voortrekkers out of the Cape—and not the liberation of the slaves. That's English propaganda. There was a lot of talk about the law and the rights of men after the English arrived in the Cape, but the Afrikaners found themselves deprived of what they considered to be their just rights. It was the Black Circuit that started it all, that led finally to Slachter's Nek . . ."

The Circuit Court, instituted in 1812 by Sir John Cradock, the second British governor of the Cape, was known among the Afrikaners as the Black Circuit. It was the first court in South Africa empowered to hear complaints by Coloured servants against their masters and was deeply resented by the Boers. "It was not so much love for the native that underlay the apparent negrophilistic policy as hatred and contempt of the Boer," F. W. Reitz wrote on the eve of the

Anglo-Boer War in that inflammatory history of South Africa *A Century of Wrong.*[6]* For the English, under pressure from such missionaries as Dr. John Philip, the court represented an attempt to extend the law to all the inhabitants of the Cape colony. Slachter's Nek, certainly one of the most resonant symbols in the Afrikaners' version of South African history, is the site where five Boers who had rebelled against British rule were hanged in 1815. Four of the ropes broke and, despite pleas for mercy, the four half-hanged men were hoisted back up on the gallows and hanged a second time.

The English put a stop to the slave trade in 1807 and in May 1833, Parliament abolished slavery. All slaves in the British Empire were to be set free by December 1, 1834. On February 2, 1837, the Voortrekker leader Piet Retief posted his famous manifesto, which purported to explain the cause of the great emigration. Included in his list were "turbulent and dishonest conduct of vagrants," losses sustained by the emancipation of the slaves, plunder by "Caffres," and religious prejudice from the English. Compared by Afrikaner historians to the American Declaration of Independence, the manifesto ends with the following words:

> We are now quitting the fruitful land of our birth in which we have suffered enormous losses and continual vexation, and are entering a wild and dangerous territory; but we go with a firm reliance on an all-seeing, just, and merciful Being, whom it be our endeavour to fear and humbly obey.[7]

The land was indeed wild and dangerous. Over the years that followed the first emigration, hundreds, thousands, died of hunger, thirst, disease, and war with the Black populations that had settled in the area. Stolid Calvinists, isolated from the great Enlightenment of the eighteenth century, the Voortrekkers believed themselves to be the Chosen of God. "For thou art an holy people unto the Lord thy God, and the Lord hath chosen thee to be a peculiar people unto himself, above all the nations that are upon the earth."[8] They likened themselves, sometimes in a fiery mysticism, with the Israelites, the British with the Egyptians, their treatment by the British with

---

A Century of Wrong was in fact written by Jacob de Villiers Roos and Jan Smuts and issued by Reitz, the state secretary of the Transvaal government. It was, according to Moodie (1975, p. 2n), the first "inspirational" history of South Africa.

Pharaoh's yoke, their trek with the flight from Egypt, their leaders with Moses, and saw their survival as God's deliverance and their suffering as purification. "Behold the armies of the salvation of the Lord," an Afrikaner clergyman preached on the eve of the Transvaal War in 1880, "we were as Israel of old—before us lay the Red Sea, behind us was the Egyptian host and on either side of us were lofty mountains. We could but look up and cry to God and He heard our voice."[9] The English at the time saw the trek as resulting from the Afrikaners ignorance.[10] On August 5, 1837, the *Commercial Advertiser* wrote:

> In the Boundless Interior the Frontier Boer sees, or fancies he sees scope for the gratification and indulgence of all these propensities (for love of land, love of cattle, love of ease, love of independence, for the desire to have his own way in everything); and looking with pity on the busy hive of condensed humanity in cities, or even in villages; and regarding with disdain the grand, but to him the unintelligible results of combined industry, the beauty of which he cannot know because they are intellectually discerned, he tosses up his head like a wild horse, utters a neigh of exultation, and plunges into the wilderness.[11]

We do not know how the Xhosa, the Zulu, the Basotho, and other Black peoples saw the trek. We do know that they fought, and fought savagely, against the white men. We know, too, that they desired the European's arms, his beads, his sugar, his coffee, his tea, his blankets, and his brandy.

4

HOME

Hennie

Hennie, the third of three brothers and a sister, was born in 1924 in a small town in the northwestern Cape near the Namibian border. His great-grandfather on his father's side had trekked into the Orange Free State. He was a restless sort of man who, like so many of the Voortrekkers, never seemed satisfied with the land he was farming. "He kept moving on," Hennie explained. "Those Voortrekkers were nomads. They could never settle down. The grass was always greener on the other side. And it often was. Trekking ran in their blood, and I suppose it runs in mine too. I've never lived in any one place for very long. We're not like the people in Wyndal. They've been on the same farm for generations. They have a sense of family history. It's in their homes and on their land. I am the seventh generation born here but I don't know where my ancestors came from. I don't even know where my mother's father was born."

Hennie's grandfather left his father in the Free State and settled down with his two brothers in the northwestern Cape. They staked out a vast farm in an area that was so dry—it was a desert really —that they moved around it according to where the rains fell. "They would settle down with their sheep where it had rained until the springs ran dry and there was no more pasturage. Then they would move on. Some of those farms were over forty thousand morgen.* Ours wasn't that big. I don't know how big it was. I'm not sure anyone did. It wasn't big enough though. There was a long drought. It lasted seven years. It rained on the neighbors' farms but not on ours.

"My grandfather was a stubborn old bloke. He wouldn't sell, but his sons didn't much fancy sheep farming. They sold off the few sheep they had left. My grandfather had given them a few sheep when they were kids—that was the custom—and it was those sheep that they sold. I don't think that between them they got more than two hundred rand, but land was cheap in those days and they were able to buy fifteen morgen of completely undeveloped land right along the Orange River. My dad had a lot of faith in irrigation farming. They started clearing the land, stumping the great trees out. They had to level it, too. For the first two years they planted just enough to keep themselves going. It was difficult, and eventually my uncle got out of the venture and started a cartage business with an old ox wagon and some donkeys. They hadn't built the railway to the southwest yet, and there was a lot of work for him, but the business petered out. Then he moved to the South West to look for diamonds, but I don't think he ever saw one. He was starving to death when my dad finally bought him a little plot of land.

"We used to have two and a half, sometimes three, crops a year. We would underplant one crop with the next so that as we reaped one, the other was already growing. We wanted to make maximum use of the land. The soil was so rich we had to fertilize only once a year. We always had something to eat, even during the Depression. We weren't rich, but we were never really poor. My dad used to say that he would never again farm more than a stone's throw from a river.

"After my dad married and had children, he sold the farm and bought another one, a smaller one, nearer town. It was about six morgen, but his kids could go to school by donkey cart. By the time I went to school, he had sold the second farm and bought an even smaller one, right in town. I used to walk to school. The farm was only about three morgen, but it could be even more intensively cultivated. The railway was in by then, and we used to ship fruit

---

*A morgen is a Dutch unit of land area equal to 2.116 acres. It comes from the Middle Dutch *morghen*, "morning"—a morning's plowing.

and vegetables up to the South West. It's very dry up there, and vegetables were so expensive that people began to write to my dad and ask him to send them ten bobs' worth a week. It wasn't long before the shops got hold of his name and started ordering through him. When I took over the farm, I stopped the small orders. It was easier that way. And then later a friend of mine and I started our own shop up there. We captured the market in no time."

Hennie remembers little of his childhood, and what memories he has seem flat to me, fragmented, and devoid of those resonances that make memories come alive. I was not surprised. Many of the Afrikaner men with whom I talked seemed unable to re-create the first years of their life in a vibrant fashion. I attributed this, without sufficient evidence, I suppose, to the presence of an authoritarian father who was never to be questioned.

"In the Afrikaans tradition you do what dad tells you," Hennie explained. "You don't question him. You want to be like him. There is a tremendous identification between father and son. The son puts on a show of masculinity. We have a special word for it in Afrikaans: *kragdadigheid*, 'power,' 'strength.' 'Potency,' I think, is the best translation. The son must show his potency, his *kragdadigheid*, before his father. He must show it, but he can't question his father's *kragdadigheid*. There's the rub."

Hennie laughed. "This all began in the early days, when people were living in a frontier situation. Once you started shaving, once you started growing a beard, you were considered a man. Now you could go with your dad on some of his hunting expeditions. You were allowed to ride with a rifle. The rifle was more or less a sign of manhood. And we have in our history, I believe, an example that has inspired more youth than anything else. That is the story of Dirkie Uys. He was only about twelve years old when his dad was mortally wounded by the Zulus. He stood over his dad until help finally arrived. Now, you see, that is *the* example for youth. The great thing was to prove your manhood, your *manlikheid*. And really it's a stupid sort of thing and carried to stupid extremes. 'If you can hold your liquor, then you're a man' sort of thing. If you're really a man, you don't need to prove it.

"Now, in many ways, my brothers and I were brought up differently. My dad never forced us into anything. If my brother wanted to go to university, that was all right. He never told him he had to become a minister. In the old Afrikaner tradition, the first clever son always became a minister. The next one became a lawyer or a teacher, and the third took over the farm. My dad never insisted that we go on with our schooling. I'll never forget, one day my eldest brother complained to my father that his teachers didn't know what they were talking about. My dad told him he didn't have to go back to school if he felt that way. Of course, he was back at school early the next morning. That was the way my dad was. He wasn't very strict, I suppose, given all the mischief my brothers got into. I was only given a hiding once. I can remember it, but I can't remember why. I think that my mother was more of the disciplinarian in our home.

"Of course, I was sort of catapulted into manhood when my dad died. I was only thirteen. My eldest brother was already up in the Transvaal in the mines, and my second brother was at varsity. I had to go to school and manage the farm by myself. My mother—she had always been rather ill—took to her bed after my father died. I hardly remember her during those years anywhere but in bed or, on summer evenings, on the stoep, staring out over the fields onto the river. That lasted two or three years.

"She was, in her way, a gutsy lady. She was over ninety when she died. She could talk to you on nearly any subject. The week before she died she took part in the talent contest they had in her old-age home. She had five books of poetry on her deathbed—she was already looking for a new poem to recite at the next do they were going to have at the home.

"During those years I was the man around the house. I just suddenly realized that I had extra responsibilities. I had to accept this. What else can you do? Your dad has died, and you just have to carry on. I don't think I thought about it very much. So, you see, in some ways, my dad's death protected me from having to prove my manhood. I didn't have to play rugby to prove that I was a man. That's what rugby's all about, you know."

Hennie had no time for rugby. He insists that after his father's death he managed the farm by himself. His brothers were away; his mother was ill; his uncle was not much of a farmer. He rarely mentions any relatives when he talks about his life immediately after his father's death, though there were some: cousins on his father's side and his mother's two brothers, who lived nearby. Nor does he mention the Coloured farm workers. Hennie prefers to remember himself alone.

I asked him who took care of him when he was a child.

"My sister Katrin did. We never had a nanny as such. There was a Coloured girl who stayed with us. My parents adopted her, and she grew up with the rest of us.

"There were Coloured people who lived on the plot next to us, and I played with their kids. Naturally, my first friends were Coloured. Children don't notice the color of their friends' skin. You only become aware of it when you're told that you're big now and must not play with Coloured girls anymore. I was about ten, I suppose, when I became aware of the fact that people had different-color skin. It didn't much matter. My parents were friendly with the *volk* who lived around us. My mom used to visit them, and they would visit us too. There was nothing odd about that! And yet somehow . . . Well, I remember there was a European who had married a Coloured woman. They didn't live too far from us. They had a lot of goats, and the goats kept getting into our yard. I chased them back one day and I told the European that my dad said he should be more careful with his goats. I called him *outa*. You only call Coloureds *outa*. He corrected me, and I said, 'But you're married to a Coloured woman.' I had to depart in a hurry. That was my first awareness of color, and I suppose that is why I always remember it. It is from moments like this that you become aware of differences. You begin to think about it. You begin to notice that there are certain people who are different and live differently.

"It started with the first settlers. South Africa was never colonized to the extent that Jamaica was for instance. For many years there was a very small minority battling against tremendous odds to keep their identity and their way of life—in a world around them that was terribly different. There are a lot of laws that we have today that got started then in that struggle. If an African or a Coloured man raped a white woman, he would be hanged. If a white man raped a Coloured woman or an African, he probably wouldn't even have had to go to court.

"In my younger days I was like a little rhino. I just went charging through life, and what didn't suit me, I kind of brushed out of the way. And if I didn't like you, I'd tell you in no uncertain terms. And if you didn't grasp it, I'd hammer it into you. When my father and his brother moved to town, they were only the sixth European family up there. All the land belonged to the Coloureds, and they had to buy it from them. My dad and his brother always used to say that they had tamed that part of the world. They hammered those others into submission. I suppose I shouldn't laugh, but that was the way it was in those days.

"I've been wondering whether I should tell you this or not, but as we're on the subject, I might as well. Everything about my family wasn't always respectable and good. When my uncle came back to farming, he grew a lot of watermelons. You get to know your watermelons. You've got to keep an eye on them to see which are ready for picking. My uncle suddenly found that some of his melons were disappearing. So one night he sat up in the bushes to see who was helping himself to them. There was a tremendous storm that night, and in the lightning my uncle could see this bloke coming toward him and eventually he recognized him. He was one of those very cheeky Coloureds who used to boast that no white man had ever hammered him. My uncle watched and waited and caught him red-handed. The bloke tried to make a run for it, but before he could get over the fence, my uncle had him down and was punching away at him. Then he started pulling out his hair—his eyebrows even, every bit of hair on his body. And when he ran out of hair, he pulled out his pocketknife and began stabbing him, just little stabs, on his inside thighs. The bloke couldn't walk for weeks.

"Now, I'm not telling you this with pride. But as a child, it made a tremendous impression on me. You see, here's a guy who boasted that no white man had ever hammered him, and then one of your own relatives—one you respect—puts him in his place. You want to imitate him. You don't even think about it. You do it automatically until something happens to make you really think about what you're doing. It just can't come from within. It's got to come from outside—from God. You need the courage to change.

"We've got to teach our children to question why they're doing the things they do. But when I was in school we just sat there like a lot of little birds with our mouths open, and the worms were stuck down. That was that. We never asked questions.

"When my parents were children, they didn't have the opportunity of going to school. One day, my dad told us, an old Hollander arrived at the farm and opened a sort of school there. What qualifications the old Hollander had, I don't know. I don't think my grandfather ever bothered to ask him. He was the teacher. He could read and write and add and subtract. In those days, the teacher was often only a step or two ahead of the students. The Afrikaner holds anyone with learning in awe. He is learned! He must know. That sort of unquestioning attitude must have rubbed off on us children.

"I had three teachers who inspired me. One was our headmaster. He taught us English as well. He made Shakespeare come alive for me, and to this day, I still read Shakespeare for relaxation. The second was my German teacher, and the third taught us maths and biology. He was different from most of my teachers. He was more critical of things. I admired him so much that I did not query what he said. I did query some of the other teachers, but I hero-worshiped him. I just accepted whatever he taught.

"I didn't have much contact with the teachers after school. Some of the boys did, but I had to rush back to the farm. I had enough to do there. I missed out on some of the things the other students were experiencing, but as I look back at it now, I don't think I missed much.

"I remember a school trip we made to see an eclipse of the sun. It was in 1936, the same year that Edward VIII abdicated. King George V dying, King Edward VIII abdicating, and King George VI being crowned, those are the first major social events I remember. Actually 1936 was a memorable year for me. That was the year my dad died."

I asked Hennie if his teachers were sympathetic when his father died.

"I think they were sympathetic, but I didn't really look for sympathy. I was bright enough to hold my own in school, and I was too absorbed in what was going on on the farm to be worried about anything else.

"I enjoyed my youth tremendously. I wouldn't have had it any different. Naturally, I would have preferred to have my dad around, you know."

Hennie does not have the love of his homeland that many of the Afrikaners with whom I talked, especially those in the valley, have. The ties that bind a man to the land are not easily understood. They extend over time and are subject to the vicissitudes of history. They are given various cultural glosses that permit an array of rhetorical, political, and economic ploys and that cover in one fashion or another his ambivalent relationship to the soil. It gives, but it takes as well. In some areas, as in southern Italy, the land is associated with struggle, with hardship, with poverty, with vipers, scorpions, and desiccation. It is the symbol, understood in its most causative sense, of the *misèria*. And yet in the dreams of many peasants who were fortunate enough to escape the *misèria* there is a nostalgia, not for it but for the land, a desire to return, with privilege, to conquer. In other areas, in Tuscany, for example, the land is associated with a richness and a beauty that mask the toil and the hardship that it imposes. In frontier areas, at least in those areas where the frontier is considered positively, the ties that a man has to the land are always threatened by possibility elsewhere, over the frontier. In South Africa, the frontier was fraught with danger, hardship, an alien and menacing population, and emptiness. And it was associated, too, for the Voortrekkers, with the *beloofde land*, the promised land, with salvation and escape from the evils imposed by the English.

At the time of the Great Trek, there were English who argued that as graziers the Afrikaners were not closely bound to the soil. "Most of the Emigrants are Cattle Farmers," the *Commercial Advertiser* wrote on August 27, 1836, "and a cattle farmer in this colony is bound to the soil by very slender ties."[1] Today, the Afrikaners claim that the English have no deep love for the soil of South Africa. They refer to them as *souties*, which is said to come from *sout peël*, "salt penis," because they have one foot in South Africa and the other in England. Land, like the Afrikaans language, the Dutch Reformed Church, and Afrikaans *kultuur*, has become a symbol of a fervent and, in my estimation, anachronistic nationalism that is grounded, perhaps like all nationalisms, in struggle: a struggle for survival. (There is in Afrikaans a word, *kultuurstryd*, which means "struggle for the maintenance of culture"!) Land figures in this struggle. The Afrikaner affirms stubbornly: This is mine—and, by extension, this is not yours. But although I often heard Afrikaners talk about the absence of strong ties to the land among the English, I have never heard them talk about the nature of the ties that the Blacks have to the land. Nor do the English talk about the Blacks' ties to the land, though they are angered by the Afrikaners' insistence that they themselves are *souties*. (The people of the valley will sometimes say that the Coloureds belong to the land. The Coloureds have worked the land for generations. They miss it, as Beatrix Roussouw says, if they immigrate to the city. But, they, the whites, will also say that the Coloureds take no pride in the land. "Look how they live," says Beatrix. "They have no gardens. They leave rubbish all about. They have no pride." Peggy Malan has made the same observation.

In the valley there is a positive attachment to the land. It is, as I have said, a fertile valley and a beautiful one. The land has been worked for hundreds of years and carries with it, for its inhabitants, all of the associations that accompany long years of cultivation. For South Africans who live elsewhere the valley embodies all of the charms of a simple, rural existence that is reminiscent of the European farmstead. They tend to have a romantic, an idyllic image of the valley, a literary one really, and many are drawn to it. Those who have moved "back" from the Transvaal or the Free State refer to their move as a "reverse trek," and contrasting the valley's gentleness to the harshness of the northern landscape, they romanticize their life in the valley and the meaning of the land. They do not understand, I believe, the significance of the land for the old families, and although the old families are certainly sorry to sell their farms, particularly to outsiders, *inkruipers*, their regret is tempered by monetary gain. Very few of them have been able to resist a healthy offer for their land for sentimental reasons.

The gentleness of the valley is exceptional. Elsewhere, as in the northwestern Cape, where Hennie was born, the landscape is often harsh, the land infertile and difficult to farm, and the climate uncertain. There are great variations in temperature—Hennie's hometown is reputedly one of the hottest in South Africa—and in rainfall. Many of the family histories that I collected are punctuated by memories of long droughts and the suffering and hunger that accompanied them. Harshness of climate and landscape, drought, and the struggle to keep a farm going, to survive really, are frequent themes in South African literature. Rural poverty among Afrikaners was a serious problem throughout the first decades of the twentieth century; the Carnegie Commission sent a team to investigate it in the thirties.[2] Hennie's family was fortunate, as he himself notes, in contrast to many small farmers.

The proclaimed attachment that the Afrikaner has to his land must be weighed not only against the trekking of the nineteenth century but also against the vast urban migration of the twentieth century. At the turn of the century the majority of Afrikaners were farmers. By 1936, 47.8 percent lived in urban areas, and by 1974, 88 percent did.[3] The English, primarily craftsmen and white-collar workers, were from the start an urban population. Even the 1820 settlers, the first organized agricultural immigrants to South Africa, who were to serve as a sort of human bulwark against the Xhosa, were not an agricultural population, and within three years of their

arrival less than a third of the original 4,000 remained on the land.[4]
As de Kiewiet notes, "The lack of intensive cultivation and the
exceedingly low rates of pay for agricultural labour discouraged the
crofters and labourers who went so numerously to Canada, Australia, and New Zealand in the middle of the century."[5]

Still, to dismiss the Afrikaner's professed attachment to the land
as a mere political gesture, a symbolic assertion of "this is mine and
not yours," or as a crude expression of identity is to lose sight of the
fact that this attachment, this love of the land, is often deeply and
sincerely felt. Decisions are based upon it or rationalized by it.
Cultural glosses often serve as cover stories, and not just for the
group but for the individual as well.

Irene Prinsloo

"I'm going home next week to see the flowers. My sister called this
morning to tell me that the rains have come. There should be a
bumper crop. There have been five years of drought, and always
after a drought, there is a wonderful crop of flowers. The soil rises,
and the flowers appear everywhere, fields of flowers, fields of color.
It is the most beautiful thing I have ever seen.

"The northwest is special. It breeds a special kind of people. Few
of them ever move away. It is so dry, so arid, so brown. They just
can't get used to the green. It suffocates them.

"It takes a hard, diamond sort of man to live up there, you know.
You can't be a soft man. Inside, they, the Afrikaners up there, are
a very soft people, but they're hard-living. There's a couple. I knew
them as a child. They have a big farm up there. They came down
to the Cape one winter a few years ago and got into a very serious
automobile accident. Oupa was in the hospital for a year and Ouma
for almost two years. There had been a drought, a tremendous
drought, and a few months before she was to be discharged, the rains
came. And the flowers came. And she knew I would be going up
to see them. I try to go up to see them whenever I can. She said,
'Irene, you must come back and tell me everything you saw. You
must describe every flower you see. You must make it come alive
for me.' I came back, and I went to see her, and I told her everything
I could. I spent the whole afternoon with her, in her hospital room.
I described the flowers, their colors, the feel of the soil. I told her

how Oupa insisted upon accompanying me even though he was on crutches. At the end of the afternoon we were both in tears. But when I left, I felt empty. I knew that I had failed. I hadn't made the fields come alive.

"And then two or three days later I got a call from Oupa. He said he was coming down to the Cape to see Ouma and wanted me to drive him to the hospital. He would drive as far as Wyndal, but he wouldn't drive into town. I drove him to the hospital and helped him out of the car. He opened up the boot, and there were two tomato boxes filled with sods of soil with different flowers. Some were already in bloom. Some would bloom in a week or so. Some were still seedlings. He had brought the soil of the earth for his wife. My words were not enough. The flowers alone would not have been enough. It was the soil of life that she had to see and feel."

Irene Prinsloo stopped. She was moved by her story, as I and our hosts, Carol and Duncan Reid, were. Irene is one of the most sensitive, most articulate Afrikaner women I have met. She moves easily between the English and the Afrikaner communities. She combines an intuitive grasp of a situation with a quick understanding of it. Her summations are frequently in story form. She is about Hennie's age, comes from a neighboring village in the northwestern Cape, where her father was a doctor, and moved to Wyndal about ten years before. She and her husband, an important lawyer in Cape Town, restored one of the most beautiful houses in the valley, hoping to make it into a sort of family seat. She did not know Hennie or his family—they were in her eyes poor whites—and she had made no effort to meet him. Although she is in many respects a liberal woman, an open-minded woman, a democrat among whites, she is a strict member of the Dutch Reformed Church and considers Hennie an apostate. (She is not as harsh in her judgment as some of the Afrikaners of the valley, who consider him a traitor.) Irene talks frequently about the northwestern Cape, which she romanticizes greatly, as she romanticizes her childhood, her marriage, and her home. She took me under her wing and spent hours telling me about her home and the people with whom she grew up. They are for her a pure, simple people: the authentic Afrikaners who have been corrupted neither by urban life nor by the power of politics. She frequently refers to Ouma and Oupa and the tomato box.

I told Irene once that her story reminded me of Bosman—a short-story writer whose beautifully written tales portray the rural

Afrikaner of the western Transvaal with a tenderness that verges on the maudlin. They provide a mythos that is greatly appreciated by both English- and Afrikaans-speaking South Africans. Irene smiled.

"The blood of Bosman flows in my veins," she said proudly. "Our plans are fixed. My sister and I are going up to the northwest at the end of next week. We are going alone. We want to go out and look at the flowers and cry. It's such a pity that so very few people from overseas ever see them. Even if they go up to the northwest, they don't know the language and can't speak to the people. Few of them speak any English. And if you don't know the language of a people, I always say, then you can't know their soul. The soul of the people up there has remained exactly the same."

Irene was excited, sentimentally so. She had invited me to tea just before she left the Reids'. "I can tell you many stories about the northwest," she had said. "But you must promise to stop me if they are of no help to you. I do rattle on, and I don't want to interfere with your work." I was particularly interested in finding out as much as I could about the northwest, to fill in Hennie's story. His was so dry. Irene talked and talked. She shifted back and forth from personal reminiscences to observations about life in the northwest as she had seen it or heard about it. Such shifts in narrative perspective were frequent among the people I interviewed. They reflected the ambivalent nature of our relationship. They knew I was interested in them as *white South Africans,* and this knowledge put a strain on our relationship—a strain that could be lessened through their description of others. Or, it could be lessened through the telling of stories, which I encouraged, since I was particularly interested in their rhetoric. (I also needed to lessen the strain, and I too would tell stories and make observations, about the United States and other countries in which I had lived.) Irene's shifts in narrative perspective reflected as well her ambivalence to the northwest and its people. Her father and mother were both outsiders. They were not farmers but professional people. They lived in a large stone house and had a "white girl" who took care of the children.

"Somehow Mommy and my dad managed to let us become part of the community irrespective of differences. We didn't realize it at the time, but they taught us to make up our own minds about people. They taught us that no two people are alike but that there is a way to choose. They guided us discreetly. We were never conscious of it. My sister and I ask ourselves to this day how they managed to do it. They were satisfied reading their Bibles every night, teaching us the Bible, playing music together. We had a little family orchestra. I played the piano or the banjo; my sister, the mandolin. Mommy would sing, and my dad would play the comb. Of course, they had books, and slowly they brought those books into our lives. We started with fairy tales and then we went on to *Little Women* and to Pollyanna. *How Did Pollyanna Grow Up?* They brought all this into our lives without ever giving us the feeling that our home was better than anyone else's.

"On New Year's Eve, I remember, we used to go out to a farm. The farmer would lie on the front stoep and try to shoot between the front wheels of the approaching cars. That would be our work-out. Then he would invite us all in for tea, and we would begin dancing. We danced all the night through, right into the New Year. Now, can you imagine Mommy doing this? But she did. There would be clouds of dust from the manure floors. They would have to water it down. Well, that farmer would dance so wildly that his shirt would be soaking. He would shout to his wife to bring him a dry shirt. I can still hear the way he rolled his *r*'s. And right there in front of everyone he would change shirts. We never once thought it was funny. We thought it was lovely the way he would carry us off our feet and lead us around the floor. And my parents were there, and they loved it. Everybody loved my parents."

Irene reflected, and as she did, I detected a sadness in her expression. "It would perhaps be fairer to say that everybody respected them," she went on, finally. "They were friends in time of need but . . . We have a lovely word in Afrikaans, *sielsvriend,* friend of the soul. They were not really *sielsvriende,* the farmer and his wife. My parents only had two close friends, the principal of the school and an English couple who lived nearby."

I asked Irene how she raised her children. "Just the same," she answered. "I think we succeeded. My youngest son lives in that part of the world. His soul craves friends with whom he can really talk, but he has become part and parcel of those people. He has gone even further than we were able to. He can sit and talk their language and laugh. They speak a language from the earth. It is rough. We could never really speak it.

"Mommy was a delicate woman—very sensitive. She taught us to see beauty in line and design. That's why the first time I took the children to see the Namibian desert, I told them to stand still and look at the shadows. 'You'll see convolutions,' I told them, 'and the color of the sand changing with the setting sun and the rising sun.' And this was exactly what Mommy had taught us. I remember when it was very dry, and we would take a walk. Mommy would say, 'That's a pretty stick. This is a pretty color. That's a pretty seed pod.' She taught us to make a lot out of very little.

"Do you know that she made sure that the indoor maid polished the silver every single day. It was a pink powder, and I can still see her polishing the silver. How it shone! She would set the table—we had such a beautiful table—and make the beds. We had a kitchen girl, a cook, who did the cooking, but the white girl would help Mommy with the baking and the sewing. Mommy would oversee it. She would do the cutting but the white girl did most of the stitching. The white girl would also make sure that my sister and I had our baths, that we were dressed nicely, and that our hair was brushed properly. Then she would take us to Mommy, who would put a bow in our hair and make sure we looked pretty.

"I must say this for my mother: She was a wonderful adminstrator of our home. It really ran on oiled wheels. There was never a fuss when a guest arrived unexpectedly. No running about. Everything just seemed to work.

"I get up early in the morning, just as Mommy did, and just as she did, I say, 'Praise the Lord for this wonderful day.' And then after I say my morning prayers, I make myself a cup of tea and have my quiet time. By the time the maid comes, I've decided on what I am going to cook, what I need from the market, and what special instructions I have to give her. Mommy never wasted any time. She would spend about twenty minutes in the kitchen, giving instructions. And that was how our house was run.

"When anyone in the household was ill, Mommy would come to my sister and me and tell us to make our own beds and to do other chores that we usually didn't have to do. There was never any argument. You never said, 'But, Mommy, I can't. I have music,' because she knew you had music. You just had to fit it in somehow.

"My father used to teach us that a child needs two things, and if he doesn't get them, he is going to be an unhappy child. One is routine, and the other is discipline. A child who has routine and discipline will not be a rebellious child. If he does not have routine and discipline, he will have all kinds of frustrations.

"My father was strict, but without being unkind. In the northwest the man is very much the man of the house. His word is authority. You don't argue. He has spoken, and that is it. If he tells you to be in at ten-thirty, you are in at ten-thirty.

"Some people think a child reacts badly to strictness. But that is wrong. A child is lost without strictness. He looks for guidance. Nowadays they put a lot down to lack of love or too much love or the wrong kind of love. Of course, love is important. There must be good feelings between parents and their children. But the child must also have a pattern. That way he knows he belongs. He must be given little tasks and made to do them regularly. I gave my children little jobs to do. On Saturdays we didn't have our garden boy, so that was the day my children had to rake the lawn, clean out the gutters, and take care of their own shoes. They didn't object. They were proud to do it. When they went away to school, they wrote me telling me how much they valued those tasks."

"Are mothers more lenient?" I asked.

"Yes. Mommy used to come in to us after my father had given us a hiding. She had a special ointment which she would rub on us. It made us feel better. We were always very frightened. My father wouldn't speak to us for a whole afternoon after a hiding. Nowadays you are taught to pick up a child immediately after chastising him so that he knows you still love him. They didn't have much psychology in those days, I'm afraid. But you can exaggerate psychology, too. And my father would never let us go to bed without first making up. He would wipe the book clean. Up there they believe that you should never go to bed bearing a grudge."

"Why are children given a hiding?"

"For lying. For breaking things. I have a good memory but I can't remember many hidings. My sister does though. My sister was a good speller. I was a terrible one. I came home with a bad report, and my father gave me a terrible hiding. I was very frightened, and I developed a terrible fear of learning. I only got over it when I dropped maths and started studying languages. Breaking things, lying, coming home late, playing truant, also coming home late after school or debating society, doing badly in exams—these are the reasons children were given hidings. And it is the same today."

"Did your father have a temper?"

"Yes, but he always managed to control himself. He taught us never to hide or chastise in wrath. You must never lose your dignity when you chastise a child. He also taught us never to tell a small

child to do what he is unable to do. Then you have lost him altogether. You must not tell him not to do what he can't help doing
either."

"How did your mother react to this?"

"She just accepted it. It is biblical, you see. We accept many
things because they are in the Bible. Sometimes children will not
accept things until they are told it is in the Bible. We have a lovely
word in Afrikaans, *skoei*. It refers to the mold for a shoe. You pull
leather over the shoe mold, and it gives the right shape to the shoe.
That is what we try to do with children: to mold them according
to the Bible."

Peter Cooke

"I have a very moral, a very Victorian mother," Peter Cooke said.
"You have to understand that Victorian attitudes lingered here in
South Africa much longer than in England or, I imagine, the States.
My grandfather on my mother's side was given a very Victorian
upbringing. It took him six weeks to consummate his marriage! My
grandmother had been given absolutely no instruction before the
wedding."

Peter is a romantic, a self-declared moralist, and a political drop-
out. He is one of the few whites in the valley who is not content
with giving stereotypic information about the other—the Afrikaner,
the Black, the Coloured—but makes an attempt to grasp the other
in his subjectivity. In their late thirties, Peter and his wife, Donna,
are considered to be "the younger generation" by the older English
farmers. They find Peter a bit spoiled, good-natured, but a foolish
farmer who lives by the grace of a handsome allowance from his
father.

Peter was born in a wealthy suburb of Durban. It was very
English, forcedly so, I imagine. Durban was always *the* English
colonial city, and its English-speaking inhabitants prided themselves, and still do pride themselves, on their genteel ways. Quick
fortunes were made in sugar, shipping, and, in the case of Peter's
family, canning. As fast as fortunes were made so were lowly family
origins forgotten. Class was imported with a vengeance and refor-
mulated with all of the *méconnaissance* of the upwardly mobile, who
recognize its outward signs but remain ignorant (so the privileged

maintain) of its inner workings. Position was marked by all of the trappings of wealth and few of those of family culture. Form, aped form really, masked but poorly an often cheap and tawdry material-ism and invidious social climbing. Empty snobbery was—and is— rampant. Great stock is laid in club membership, in school connec-tions, and in being an ODF, an Old Durban Family. The city is conservative, racist, and was early given to an unwritten apartheid that English critics of the South African government are eager to forget but their Afrikaner opponents are unwilling to forget.[6]

"My mother had a very difficult marriage and had to keep the most fantastic peace under the most extraordinary circumstances. My father was often irritable and easily angered, but he never actu-ally struck me. (My mother gave me a whack or two.) He could reduce me to nothing with just a few angry words. He could tear apart everything I stood for. In many ways it would have been better had he struck me. You are punished that way, and it is finished. You feel a certain remorse afterward for what you have done. But words linger. My father would just say anything that occurred to him and then forget what he had said. He did not realize that I remembered his words, that I saw myself and felt myself to be totally destroyed by his words. I wish I could repeat what he had said to me. I don't think he would believe that he had actually said such things to his son.

"But I have never been able to talk to my father. I wish I could have, but he is a very distant man. I have only recently come to realize that he hid himself behind a facade of strength. Underlying this facade was a profoundly unhappy man, a man who could never give way and relax.

"My father is a man without spiritual depth. Religion means nothing to him. It just doesn't begin to enter his way of life or his scheme of things or his way of thinking. My mother battled very hard to give us some sort of religious involvement. She was always very religious, but after her divorce she became even more involved in the church.

"I was sent to an Anglican school, but there you learn only the forms. My mother tried to inspire something more in me, but de-spite her efforts, I always found going to church a duty. I was always irritated by it and was usually irritable the rest of the day. And then a few years ago I suddenly thought to take the kids to Sunday school. I began to stay for the services. I enjoyed it. Then I was happy to get up on Sunday mornings and go to service and sit through it.

"It's been a bit awkward lately since Hennie has come. At first I attended his services, but I soon found that I couldn't in all conscience subject my kids to his teachings. He's a good chap, I am sure, but he is more of an inspiration for the Coloureds . . .

"Now we go to the Methodist church. The minister lacks charisma, but there is an excellent Sunday school. The kids stay only for the first part of the service, hymn singing mostly, and then they file off for Sunday school, while the adults listen to the sermon. It gives them more time, and they don't have to listen to preaching that doesn't relate to them.

"If we could relate factual episodes from our life to a religious power, we would all be believers. If these were as dramatic as seeing a wound heal miraculously in front of our eyes, we would have certain proof of a religious power. We would no longer sit on the fringes. It is a question of awareness, because there are so many things that happen to us that when we look back on them we see they could never have happened without some sort of incredible power behind us. Think of the British Tommy: the thin-legged, weedy little bank clerk who displays the most incredible courage under the pressure of war.

"My mother always managed somehow to maintain some sort of domestic atmosphere. Even on holidays. She set a fantastic example, a Christian example, which was in many ways to her detriment. It is a bit sad really. There is a lesson in it because she ended up as a bit of an artificial person. You never know what she really thinks. If you ask her to do something for you, she will never say that it is a bit of a nuisance. It is always 'with the greatest of pleasure,' even when you know it isn't. Sometimes I wish she would say, 'I'm sorry I can't manage it today, maybe tomorrow,' just so that you know that she is really human. She has got herself caught in a groove of just being pleasant about everything."

I have often noticed this "just being pleasant about everything" among women of Peter's mother's background. They appear, to me at least, to be caught in a cult of the pleasant. There is an exaggerated politeness about them, an oversolicitous concern for the wishes of the other, a stress on form, almost an embarrassment with content, a distaste for confronting, giving expression to at any rate, the *real*. They speak in euphemisms. If you thank them for something, they answer with "it is a pleasure" or more simply with "pleasure." A hostess will ask a guest "are you happy?" whether she wants to know if her guest is comfortable, has had enough tea, or wishes another biscuit. Such women seem to be protecting themselves from all that is unpleasant or potentially so. Peggy Malan, who is given to these euphemisms, once confided that she wished she could say exactly what she thought. "But it is just impossible. I don't even think I would know what to say."

"Your parents are divorced," I said to Peter. "How did your mother take that?" Peter's mother lives alone. His father has remarried a much younger woman.

"She left him. She was going to for a long time, but there was always something. My finishing school. My settling into the business. A cousin dying of cancer. She didn't want to upset the family. Finally she decided to leave. She actually moved out, and this put her in an embarrassing situation in financial terms. It is a pity because she is now suffering from that. But be that as it may."

Peter looked sad. "It's in her character: a reckless decisiveness after years of putting up with things. It was in her father, and so maybe it is coming to me as well. He was an accountant, and then one day—he was already in his fifties—he gave it all up for farming. He bought himself a farm, without apparently ever having talked much about it before he did it."

Peter remained in his father's business until it went public and control was taken by a large international conglomerate. He had been under his father's iron fist and had never been able to make an important decision, any decision, without having it countermanded by his father. He played only a technical role in the conversion and takeover, but he did hope for a significant managerial position when control was finally wrested from his father. Instead, he was given "a fancy title, a big salary, and no power." It was then that he left the commercial world and began farming.

"My grandfather was for me a father. I had no emotional relationship with my own father. He was so tough. There was no emotion in his life. Once I was having a conversation with a girl who was interested in spirit mediums and astrology. She told me about a fortuneteller. I went to her. She didn't know my name and didn't ask me anything. She simply asked for the signet ring I was wearing. I gave her the ring. She told me I had two daughters and a son, and she named the suburb where I lived. She said I truly wanted to be a farmer. She told me that Edward was interested in me. She did not know who Edward was. He was in the other world and had been a psychic. I too had the gift, she said, but it had to be developed. I did not know who Edward was. I asked my mother, and she told me that Edward was my grandfather's first name. We had always called him George, which turned out to be his middle name. He had died when I was fifteen."

"And the farm?" I asked.

"Oh, that was sold. There was no one to take it over. I was sorry. I missed my holidays. I had a native friend there who looked after me until I was old enough to play with him. When my parents and grandparents went out at night, he would sleep across my door. His mother was the cook. I think she had more Hottentot blood in her than Xhosa. His father was one of the senior guys. I used to go down to my friend's cattle hut—they call them Bantu huts now—and have a bowl of porridge with him. Then we would go out to play. Sometimes we would jog twelve miles in a day. He taught me to ride, and we used to ride to the station to collect my grandfather's post. It took a couple of hours. We used to take little hunting trips. At first we used catapults and then a two-two rifle. He handled the rifle of course. I think my grandfather turned a blind eye to the fact that he wasn't quite so actively involved in the farm. He also used to go to school, sometimes, but we always had the same holidays.

"He exposed me to nature. You know, one's eyes are closed until somebody opens them for you and shows you how to find things and where to look for them. It was a lovely experience. I went with him to ceremonies, and when he was initiated into manhood, I was allowed to visit him in the bush. I was very honored. I think it is important for a young man to have this experience. His initiation was an eye-opener for me. He was circumcised and had to spend three months in the bush. He talked to me a lot about the customs of his people. Boys of his age—I was fourteen, he must have been eighteen—are called *quadims*. I suppose we'd say 'young buck.' They had to wear white clay, which made them look ghostly. They would dress up in the most incredible finery on Saturday, stick a mouth organ in their mouths, jog to a party six miles away, and jog home again in the early hours of the morning playing the same sort of monotonous tune to keep them going. They would have bells and bits of sheepskin on their legs, beadwork, and great big turbans on their head.

"Part of the fun was the stick fight. They would hold a straight stick in the middle and wind their turban around their hand. It acted as a sort of shield. They would then climb into each other with a knobkerry and protect themselves with the stick. They'd try to hit their opponents as hard as they could. I suppose you could compare it to rugby really. There were rules, but sometimes they would come back with the most dreadful wounds. They have apparently a slightly thicker skull than we do, and so they can take more of a beating than we can.

"My friend taught me to fight with the knobkerry. We used saplings, the ends of which we would tap into a ball. It didn't hurt, but you could feel the blow well enough to learn to deflect it.

"There was tremendous discipline and self-control in my friend's initiation. He was made to spend the night with his girl friend in a special hollowed-out bush without being allowed to sleep with her at a time when everything is running very hot.

"He taught me to handle sheep. In those days they used to castrate sheep with their mouth. There was a film recently on television about those Afrikaners who after the Anglo-Boer War trekked to Argentina and have lived there ever since. They still castrate their sheep with their mouth. You actually bite the vas deferens with your teeth. They make an incision with their pocketknife and then literally put their mouth to the scrotum and do something. I don't know quite what it is, but it is revolting. The Afrikaners used to have their staff do it, but in South America they have no staff and have to do it themselves. The old farmers consider lamb testicles a great delicacy. Once I said to one of them, 'In the old days it was believed that if you ate a lion's heart you would be brave. What do you expect from a lamb's testicle?' He didn't think it was very funny."

I asked Peter if he noticed any changes in his friend after the initiation.

"Oh, hell, yes. He had taken in something and was now showing it through his personality. He had more dignity and a better bearing. He was proud of his position. He was glad to have gone through the experience, proud of the fact that he had emerged from it as a man and had not been cowardly about the very painful act of being circumcised."

Although Peter sounded as though he were repeating a lesson in a first-year anthropology course, there was something moving about his words. He seemed to be living his friend's experience. On another occasion he admitted that he had longed for a similar experience, and went on about how impressed he was with the social order that primitive societies have and how sad it is for those tribal peoples who move to the city and lose that pattern and order. "We lack it so terribly in our society," he observed. "We have no order. We drift about. We are lost.

"We've certainly buggered things up. There is a lot of hypocrisy among the natives in town. We maintain a double standard with them, and they maintain a double standard with us. They have their authentic world, which involves initiation, circumcision, their ceremonial life, and then they have the world in which they present themselves to us. We know bugger all about them.

"I've got a boy on the farm who wants to go through his initiation. He has asked me to get him a goat and a sheep. He will have to burn all his old blankets and the clothes he has worn. They are things of the past. It is very expensive. A sheep costs fifty rand. The expense doesn't frighten him. His family will contribute large sums so that he can go through the experience. I'm encouraging him. I think it is magnificent."

"Did your relationship with your friend change after his initiation?" I asked.

"My grandfather died after the holiday during which my friend had been initiated. The farm was sold, and I never returned. I've probably met him twice since then for very short spaces. He is working on the next farm. He speaks just a little Afrikaans, and I have forgotten my Xhosa, so we can't really communicate. He is married and has children, and so do I.

"I think there would be a lot of shyness between us were we to see each other more often. There comes a time when the Black man recognizes your position and respects it. This is particularly true in South Africa, whether we want to accept it or not. As children we could play together, wrestle together, throw balls at each other; but then suddenly there comes a time when all that stops."

Peter grew silent, and then after a few saddened moments he said, without, I think, realizing the irony, "I remember once, after my friend had become a man, jogging down to his hut in the evening. I said I'd race him to a tree, as we had often done in the past, and he refused. 'I am a man, and I must walk with dignity. I can jog but I can't run.' He could no longer carry a knobkerry around. He had to carry a staff."

5

UPBRINGING

Hennie

"I sometimes think that God gave many people their brains by mistake," Hennie said cynically. We were talking about preaching. "A spinal cord would have been enough. They just don't think. They don't question. They do what they've always done, automatically. You have to challenge them, but you must never challenge them before you've challenged yourself.

"I went to a cheese factory up in Rhodesia one day to get some milk and overheard two farmers talking about shooting a 'cheeky kaffir' in the foot. I listened casually without taking it in, and it was only when I was driving back to the mission station that I realized what I had heard: Some poor bloke had had his foot blown off! I had heard too many stories like it to pay much attention to it. Maybe it's because I'm lame that I finally appreciated that story. You have to be alert all the time, and you can't do that alone. You must have God's help, and He is always there ready to extend it . . . ."

I asked Hennie if he had ever been challenged by the sermons he had heard in the Dutch Reformed Church. I myself found the sermons I had heard cold and highly formal, abstract and rhetorical, overly dedicated to biblical exegesis.

"No," he answered flatly. "And even today the moral exhortations you hear on the radio are not really challenging. They answer your questions even before you can ask them. In Afrikaans we say, *'Die gewente maak die gewoonte.'* 'Habit becomes second nature.' And that's our educational principle. And the first habit we instill is the habit not to ask questions.

"The minister in my hometown couldn't have been a very exciting preacher because he never got called anywhere else. He stayed there for many years and had an absolutely devastating effect. During the last six weeks of my training for confirmation, we had to go to see him every evening for an hour and a half. On the Monday of the last week of training he began to talk about the *Rooms gevaar*, the Roman peril. I thought it was his duty to warn us against teachings in other churches that were not strictly according to the Bible. The first night I found what he had to say interesting, but by the third night I was bored. He kept pounding away at those poor devil-ridden Catholics. When he began it all over again on the fourth day—I remember, it was a Thursday—I asked him a question: 'For four nights now you've been telling us what lousy people the Roman Catholics are and how cockeyed their theology is. Why then are their lives so Christian?' There was a little convent not far from where we lived. Whenever one of us was sick, the nuns were sent for. Two of them would come out so that the family could get a good night's sleep. When my dad died, the first people to arrive at our house were two nuns. It was they who laid him out for the funeral—not my mom. Anyway, I told the minister this and asked him again why, with such a cockeyed theology, they were so Christian. 'If you want to argue,' he answered, 'then you will not be confirmed.' I left. We were to be confirmed on Friday, presented to the congregation on Saturday, and receive our first communion on Sunday.

"I was so angry. I wanted to refuse. I thought about joining up with the Catholics. I knew he would ask me about them, and I would have to answer in front of all those people. A friend of my late father's came to see me that night. 'Hennie,' he said, 'I think you are wrong.' He spoke to me like a father. He explained why he thought my attitude was wrong. He didn't just say, 'You are wrong.' I'll never forget that night. I have always remembered and admired him.

"I was confirmed on Friday, and the *dominee* [minister] didn't ask me about the Catholics. On Monday I went back to see him and said, 'Now that I'm confirmed, I want to start the argument over again.'

The old man threw a fit, and I stayed away from the church completely.

"I think there were already deeper issues there than this. What church can impose something on you without giving you the reasons why? If you look carefully at God's commandments, you can always find the reasons for them. It may take time, but with time you will find them."

I asked Hennie if there were many Catholics in the area where he grew up. There were only a few English-speaking Catholic families in Wyndal.

"There were only a few families, and they always had a lot of problems. The only thing I really knew about the Catholics, aside from their caring for the ill, was that once a year they would come to our place for date-palm fronds for Palm Sunday. We always thought they were a queer lot, but we did admire their priest because he didn't contract out their new church. He and his parishioners built it with their own hands.

"It was mostly a Coloured congregation." Hennie laughed. "If there had been a few more whites, I might have joined up with them."

Hennie's rebellion shows an independence of mind, which, given the conforming pressures of Afrikaner communal life, is indeed exceptional. The *kerk*, or church, is the spiritual, the social and cultural, in many respects the material, certainly the symbolic, center of the Afrikaner community. Membership in one of the three closely related Dutch Reformed Churches—the Nederduitse Gereformeerde Kerk (the largest), the Hervormde Kerk (theologically the most liberal and white supremacist), and the Gereformeerde Kerk (theologically the most conservative, objecting even to the singing of hymns in church)—is an essential prerequisite for membership in the Afrikaner community. "You can't really separate the Afrikaner from his religion," Hennie says. "It is almost like the Jews. You are a Jew by birth and by religion. You are an Afrikaner by birth and by religion." Ninety percent of all white Afrikaans speakers are members of the Dutch Reformed Church. (I use the term to cover all three Reformed Churches in South Africa.) Hennie is fully realistic when he says that he is considered "a renegade, an apostate, a damned man" because he left the church and joined the Anglicans. In the valley he is studiously avoided by many of the older, more conservative farmers.

The Dutch Reformed Churches in South Africa are strictly Calvinist. It has been pointed out by many historians that unlike their European and American counterparts, the South African Reformed Churches were not appreciably touched by Enlightenment thought and the more liberal theology that ensued.* Theirs is a primitive Calvinism embodied in the Heidelberg catechism and the decrees of the Synod of Dort. (All men are totally depraved. God has unconditionally elected a few to salvation. It is to these few that the atonement of Christ is limited. They receive, they cannot resist, the grace of God; they cannot fall even for a moment from His grace.) Great emphasis is placed on a sovereign, wholly other, wholly inscrutable God; on the inborn sinfulness of man as a result of the fall; on an inexorable predestination—the elect will be saved and those who have not been elected will be damned for eternity; on the glorification of God through work by building His kingdom on earth. The South African state as it has been envisioned by the Nationalists would in its perfection (were such perfection possible) be identified with that kingdom!

The Bible is not only the revealed word of God but, ultimately, the final source of all knowledge. It is read literally, fundamentally. Hennie, whose fundamentalism would be an embarrassment to any Anglican priest in England, claims to have been troubled by the fundamentalism of the Dutch Reformed *dominees* with whom he came in contact.

"As a member of the Dutch Reformed Church," Hennie says with some exaggeration, "I had to accept the fact that the world and everything in it was made in six days. I couldn't have an idea of gradual evolution, even though there was plenty of evidence around me for it. I simply couldn't accept the biblical version with my mind. And I had been taught to love God with my mind and heart. How

---

*Although there is considerable merit in this argument, it does somewhat oversimplify the position of the South African Reformed Churches, which were in contact with Europe throughout the eighteenth and nineteenth centuries. The *classis*, or presbytery, of Amsterdam exercised nominal control over the Cape church, and clergymen were trained in Holland and later in Edinburgh until the founding of the Stellenbosch Seminary in 1859. The seminary's founding was itself a reaction to the threatening, new-fangled notions, the *nuwigbede*, of Dutch theology. There was, moreover, within the South African church a tension between the more latitudinarian clergy of the Cape and the more orthodox clergy of the interior (Davenport).

could I? It was only when I spoke to an Anglican priest that I came to understand that it made no difference whether the world was made in six days or six million years. What was important was who made it and not how long it took. It was only then that I was able to get away from this literal reading of the Bible."

"The Word of God in the Old Testament," a Calvinist minister, John M'Carter, wrote of the Afrikaners in 1869, "has been to them not only a means of Grace, but in a sense what it was to the Israelites of Old, the means, in times of social dilapidation, of preserving and keeping them alive as a people. It has been their bond of union, their code of manners, their motive to educate their children when none other existed."[1] For the Afrikaners living on isolated farms in the hinterlands, the Bible, the Heidelberg catechism, and the Book of Psalms (hymns) were their only source of book knowledge, and there was—and still is—a certain pride in the possession of this untainted repertoire. In the valley today I have heard young university-educated men and women praise their elders for reading only the Bible. They find, I suspect, a certain innocence in this, and at least one young woman told me that since she had graduated from Stellenbosch University ten years earlier, she has not touched a book other than her Bible. To be sure, she reads newspapers and several women's magazines, but these do not appear to have the same value for her as a book. There was, and still is among the most traditional, a fevered anti-intellectualism, and even among many of the more enlightened farmers of the valley I detected a mistrust of nontechnical, nonscientific knowledge. (South African history, at least a certain version of it, was the exception.) Writers like André Brink and Breyten Breytenbach, who are considered apostates, are heftily condemned. J. M. Coetzee, whose writing is more subtle, certainly more difficult, is simply ignored.

The Afrikaners of the valley, like those of the hinterland, know their Bible and know it well. Their day, even among some of the more enlightened families in Wyndal, is punctuated by Bible reading, hymn singing, and prayer. A family organ is found in many of the traditional households; in many instances, family services are still conducted in the morning and evening. Several Afrikaners reported the dreaded honor of conducting their first services under the critical eye of their father or grandfather. Prayers are said upon awakening, before and after meals, and at bedtime. They are also said before starting on a trip or engaging in some important or potentially dangerous enterprise. They are said before rugby matches and tennis tournaments. Peter Cooke was amazed and somewhat disappointed to discover that his Afrikaner friends even conducted services on hunting and fishing trips. Children are frequently quizzed by their elders on their knowledge of the Bible. Not only do they go to Sunday school but they have Bible study groups in school as well. Education is determinedly Christian, and religious instruction is given to the Voortrekkers, the Afrikaners' equivalent of the boy scouts.

From the founding of the first Afrikaner schools after the Anglo-Boer War there has always been a strong religious emphasis in Afrikaner educational philosophy. The Dutch Reformed Church took an active part in establishing these early schools. Its ministers were (and still are) active on school boards, and the schools were founded on Christian National principles, an ill-defined ideology of fervent, romantic nationalism that is supposed to be grounded in Christian—read Calvinist—theology. It was yet another attempt to give the Afrikaner pride in *ons eie*, our own.[2] With the amalgamation of these early Boer schools with government ones after the Orange Free State and the Transvaal were granted self-government, the Christian National movement in education waned, but it grew strong again with the nationalistic fervor of the 1940s. The Dutch Reformed Church again agitated for Christian National Education. The National Institute for Christian Teaching and Education (Nasionale Instituut vir Christelik Onderwys en Opvoeding), which was founded in 1939 and was intimately tied to the Broederbond, published a highly influential policy report in 1948.[3] The report states that the school "should not be separate from, but should stand in the centre of, our national life, and must derive strength and inspiration from the soil of its culture and all its activities" (Art. 3). It advocates educational segregation of different national and ethnic groups, the importance of mother-tongue—single-medium—education, and the child's "subjection to the work of God in all things." Christianity is understood in essentially fundamentalist terms and determines the content of all instruction. "We believe that religious knowledge and subjects like the mother language (as medium and as subject), civics, geography, and history are subjects which, from their nature, if properly taught, inculcate a Christian and National view of life" (Art. 6. 1). The teaching of science "must start from the Christian attitude to life and to the World" (Art. 11. 2). The theory of evolution and other scientific knowledge that conflicts with the Bible are given scant attention in school, if not completely ignored. History must be taught "in the light of God's revelation and must be viewed as a fulfilment of God's decreed plan for the world and for the human race" (Art. 6. 6). The highest aim of education is, in short, "the moulding of people in God's image" (Art. 5). The report advocates "the principle of trusteeship of the non-European by the European, and particularly by the Afrikaners" (Art. 14). "We believe that the Coloured man can and only be truly happy when he has been Christianized and that he will be proof against his own heathen ideology and all sorts of foreign ideologies which promise him pseudo-happiness but leave him in the long run dissatisfied and unhappy" (Art. 14). "We believe that he [the Co-loured man] can be made race conscious if the principle of *apartheid* is strictly applied in teaching just as it is in his Church life" (Art. 14). "We believe that the education and task of white South Africa with respect to the native is [*sic*] to Christianize him and to help him on culturally, and this vocation and task has [*sic*] found its immediate application and task in the principles of trusteeship, no placing of the native on the level of the white, and in segregation" (Art. 15).

The report further states that native education should be under-taken as soon as possible by the natives themselves but under state control and guidance "with the proviso that the financing of native education be placed on such a basis that it is not provided at the cost of European education" (Art. 15).

Although the report was approved by the synods of the Dutch Reformed Churches in South Africa, it was never officially adopted by the National Party. Its principles have, nevertheless, been applied in varying degree in different school administrations, and it has been the inspiration of many Afrikaner educators, including Wyndal's headmaster. In reaction to this educational philosophy many English prefer to send their children to private schools, certainly to English medium schools, where they will not be exposed to such values. There has been a marked increase in attendance at Jewish schools in Cape Town, Johannesburg, and other cities with large Jewish populations. The reaction of non-Europeans is one of frus-trated anger and indignation.

The Bible provides the Afrikaner with a rich symbolic repertoire, a powerful, transcending idiom, through which he articulates him-self and his world. Even when he does not make direct reference to it, a biblical template seems to govern the form and content of much of what he has to say. Aside from the Afrikaners' biblicized understanding of their history, made so much of by Moodie[4] and other scholars, aside too from a marked propensity to envision reality in terms of a struggle between the forces of good and evil, between God and Satan, the Afrikaners understand in religious terms much of what, say, an educated American would understand in psychological terms.

A number of writers, among them Jan Loubser, have suggested that the absolute distinction that non-Arminian Calvinism* posits between the elect and the non-elect, between the order of grace and the order of nature, was understood in racial terms by the Afrikaners.[5] The Afrikaner saw himself as God's elect and the Blacks as damned.† The first South African–trained minister in the Gereformeerde Church, Venter, left that church rather than abandon his conviction that Africans bore the visible sign of damnation and that any attempt to convert them to Christianity was contrary to God's

---

*The Dutch theologian Jacobus Arminius (Jacob Harmensen, 1560–1609), founder of Arminianism, opposed the Calvinist doctrine of absolute predestination.

†This suggestion should be treated with caution. Although there is evidence to support it, particularly for rural Afrikaners in the nineteenth and twentieth centuries, there is less evidence for the seventeenth and eighteenth centuries. Racism based on skin color appears in the nineteenth century, after the arrival of the British. In the seventeenth and eighteenth centuries interracial marriage was treated in a tolerant and offhand manner and by the end of the eighteenth century may have accounted for as many as 6 percent of all marriages (see Fredrickson for discussion and bibliography). It is my impression that many historical studies have insisted on a rather too homogeneous and impervious view of the Afrikaners, an image that has suited both English and Afrikaner nationalist interests. It does not seem unrealistic to assume that the Afrikaners were influenced, positively or negatively, by the values of the English who arrived in the Cape at the beginning of the nineteenth century. There is certainly considerable evidence later in the century for their adopting Victorian morality and taste at least in the Cape and its immediate environs. It is also necessary to differentiate rather more carefully between those Afrikaners who lived in the vicinity of Cape Town and those, the trekboers, who lived farther inland. Given their isolation, and later the isolation of the Voortrekkers, their world view, and particularly their religious outlook, may well have "regressed" to a more primitive theological and biblical understanding, one in which the dualisms of Calvinism, of Christianity itself (of the elect and the non-elect, of the order of grace and of nature, of the forces of good and evil) were given great importance. Such reversions to basic unelaborated structural contrasts are not infrequent in isolated areas and among those who live in harsh and stressful environments.

will. As the anthropologists the Russells observe, Venter's exclusiveness probably remained popular among the ordinary *doppers*, as members of the Gereformeerde Church are sometimes called.[6] The Afrikaner's struggle to survive in a harsh environment, to preserve his identity in the face of racial and cultural extinction, to overcome the enemy, Black or for that matter English, was understood as a means of preserving God's kingdom on earth. The state itself, as envisioned by the Nationalists, is understood in Calvinistic terms as divinely ordained and created, as able to exist independently of the will of its citizens, over whom it has exclusive powers, and with rulers who are responsible to God and in whose name they act.[7] Although there has never been any *official* relationship between the Dutch Reformed Churches and the National Party, the church is "in a very real sense the National party at prayer."[8] Certainly, party politicians have made use of the biblical idiom and the religious sentiments of the Afrikaners in their political rhetoric and in their rationalization of policy, and the ministry in its turn has not been reluctant to provide the necessary orientation.

Unlike the other Christian churches of South Africa, principally the Anglican, the Methodist, and the Catholic, all of which strongly oppose apartheid, the Dutch Reformed Churches in South Africa have not only sanctioned apartheid but are themselves divided along racial lines.* (Calvinism in the Cape generally lacked missionary zeal and did not in the earliest days create a sizable non-white Christian community.[9]) The Nederduitse Gereformeerde Kerk (NGK), the largest, is divided into three sister churches, formally called daugher churches, each catering to a specific racial group and receiving some support from the white mother church. (The minister of Wyndal's Coloured church complains that the village's mother church has not increased its contribution to his church in years despite marked inflation and a dramatic increase in his flock.)

*In August 1982, after hours of "anguished debate and prayer," the World Alliance of Reformed Churches voted to suspend the membership of the Nederduitse Gereformeerde Kerk and the Nederduitse Hervormde Kerk because of the "heresy" of racial segregation (*International Herald Tribune*, August 27, 1982). The Alliance elected Alan Boesak, the head of the Coloured branch of the NGK, its president. The NGK is no longer a member of the World Council of Churches or the South African Council of Churches, nor does it have relations with the Dutch mother church.

To support their own position and the government's policy of apartheid, the Dutch Reformed Church has sought biblical justification. To cite one example:

> The principle of separate development so as to be able to serve one's own people is in complete agreement with the Bible teaching of unity in diversity, whereas integration and assimilation weaken this diversity and reduce it to a uniformity and monotony. The examples that are used for the Church of Christ clearly teach us diversity in unity as well as the fact that it must be maintained (I Cor. 12:12–27; Rom. 12:4–5; I Cor. 15:39–41). The Soma Christou does not permit the destruction of members of the community.
>
> "If the whole body were an eye, where were the hearing? If the whole were hearing, where were the smelling? But now had God set the members every one of them in the body, as it has pleased him. And if they were all one member, where were the body? But now are they many members, yet but one body" (I Cor. 12:27–30).
>
> We must therefore come to the conclusion that Scriptural pronouncements concerning the right or not to separate development are that respect for and the normal development of the autogenous in the community of nations, are indispensable to the Scriptural teachings of unity in diversity.[10]

This conclusion follows a convoluted argument in which it is shown that God willed diversity (even though diversity was the result of man's sin) and that it is the Devil's intention to weaken this diversity. Several Afrikaners in Wyndal said simply that as God confused the languages of the world and scattered His people after they had built the Tower of Babel, so must they, His believers, the Afrikaners, preserve these different languages. For them language stood for culture and race.

The Reformed Churches are organized along Presbyterian lines. The *dominee* is the most highly respected member of the community and is extremely influential. In Wyndal he sits on several of the most important committees and is a member of the school board. It is rumored that he and the schoolmaster, some say the police chief too, are members of the Broederbond. The *dominee* has been very careful to cultivate the English who have moved to the valley and has offered them the Church Hall for special occasions. He is aided by twelve deacons, who are responsible for the church collection, and by twelve elders, who are responsible for the spiritual welfare of designated sections of the parish. They conduct weekly prayer meetings, and the most conscientious of them make it a habit to visit every family in their sections at least once every two weeks. It would indeed be difficult for the parishioners to escape the vigilance of the church had they the mind to do so. The *dominee* or one of his elders is quick to visit anyone in difficulty, and he has at his disposal the help of a social worker. Aside from official prayer meetings, there are a number of unofficial Bible study groups that meet once or even twice a week. They are particularly popular among women, and I know of several women who attend at least one such group each day of the week except Sunday. The *dominee* encourages these groups and tries to attend at least one of their meetings each year. He complains that his parish is too large for a single minister but not quite large enough to justify an assistant minister.

Church services are held twice on Sundays, once in the morning and once in the evening. They are very formal. Men dress in dark suits; deacons and elders, in black ones with white ties. Women dress in "proper" dresses. Until recently they had to wear hats—and some of the more conservative still do—but even those who no longer wear them are careful to put up their hair for the occasion. (Hairdressers are busiest on Saturdays.) As I have said, I found the services to be cold and impersonal, and several of the younger parishioners have made the same observation. "You don't really get the opportunity to take part in the service," Irene Prinsloo's daughter-in-law, Margot, told me. "We sing hymns, and I quite enjoy that, but I don't really feel part of the community of worshipers. I find the sermons too abstract. I am not uplifted by them, and they usually don't concern my particular needs. I was at church this morning, and I don't think I could tell you what the *dominee* spoke about. It is not his fault. I have great respect for him. It is that way in all churches." (The *dominee* must in fact preach on doctrine twelve times a year.)

I myself was impressed by an insistent sense of community. Everyone seemed to be conscious of exactly who was present and who was absent, of how they were responding to the sermon, and of what they were wearing. But when the service was over, the parishioners immediately left for home. They did not wait to talk to the *dominee* or to greet one another. Sunday afternoons are somber. They are spent visiting family. Work is not permitted or any kind of recreation. English children complain that their Afrikaner friends are not allowed to play on Sundays. Afrikaner children make no comment.

Nagmaal, or communion, services are held four times a year and play a particularly important role in the South African interior, where they may be the only occasion on which a church member sees his minister.[11] (An attempt was made to schedule circuit court meetings to coincide with *nagmaal* services in the last century.[12]) The host may be withheld from those who have strayed from the church; adultery or premarital sex are the two principal reasons for being refused communion. ("They expelled me from the church because I was living with a man in sin," a visitor to the valley confided in me. "When I went to church, everyone looked at me. Such looks! I just couldn't get to my car too quickly after church. I kept going despite the looks. I didn't go to be seen but to say my prayers. Finally the *dominee* came to see me. He said he was not happy with the way I lived. I told him I was happy. He said that what I was doing was contrary to the ways of the church. 'You know,' I said, 'I'd give everything I had to somebody in need. I am generous. I believe in the good and in doing good.' But that didn't make any sense to him. My living with a man out of wedlock was a sin to him. That was all that counted. He asked me to leave the church. Now at home I go to the Catholic church. Father Maximillian is a wonderful man. He is very open with me—warm and understanding. I say my prayers and feel good. Nobody criticizes me. Father Maximillian has been an inspiration to me. I've been here in the valley two months now, and I haven't even seen the minister once, not even on the street.") Unlike the Anglican Church, in which the parishioners voluntarily step up to the altar to receive communion, the host is distributed to the parishioners in the Dutch Reformed Church. It is as though a judgment is being made and communicated. Of course, in those services I attended, all of the worshipers received the host.

In the back country, not so many years ago the *nagmaal* services were very special occasions, for families from isolated farms would travel sometimes for days to the nearest church. They were a time for gossip, for matchmaking, and for potlatching. As Irene Prinsloo describes them for the northwestern Cape they were certainly rather more joyous occasions than in Wyndal.

Irene Prinsloo

"The big *nagmaal* service was in the spring, in October. It would all start on Thursday. Farmers and their families from all over the district—a district of several hundred thousand square miles—

would come to town, on horses, in ox wagons, in cars if they could afford them, in anything that could be pulled. They would pitch their tents or make lovely reed huts, and they would spread the floors with manure. By six in the afternoon, fires would be blazing. It was so beautiful. We all knew one or two families, and they would bring us lovely sausages, homemade *boereworse.* My sister and I would look forward to it. On Saturday morning there would be an enormous bazaar, or so it seemed to us then. And in the afternoon there would be an auction for the benefit of the church. Even in 1933, during the terrible drought, there was a sheep that fetched over five hundred pounds and a cake that fetched over a hundred pounds! Those farmers used to bid on a sheep and once they got it, they would auction it off again. That year we made almost five thousand pounds—and from poor people who gave more than a tithe. I went to school with some of their children. They stayed in a hostel run by the church, and on Saturdays Mommy would invite them over in groups of twenty to play in the garden. They could pick all the fruit that they wanted, and then we would call them into the kitchen for tea with bread and our homemade honey and butter. Some of those children had to go to school in summer and winter alike without shoes, and the boys wore jackets that were lined with flour bags that had been put out in the sun to bleach. It was those families that gave so generously. And on Sundays we'd have three services. All the girls, no matter how poor, would have a new frock for church."

Peter Cooke

"You have to talk to a lot of people before you are able to evolve a definite idea of what constitutes the basic Afrikaner," Peter Cooke explained. Like many of the English I interviewed, Peter usually preferred to talk about the Afrikaners, the Zulu, the Xhosa, or the Coloureds rather than himself and his fellow English speakers, but unlike many of the other English, he has made a concerted effort to make friends with the Wyndal Afrikaners and speaks with a certain enthusiasm about them.

"The Afrikaners are a mixture of all sorts of things. On the one hand, they have a tremendous amount of so-called discipline, and on the other hand, they seem to have no discipline at all. Discipline was one of their big problems during the Boer War. They fought under a commando system. Since they were independents and not conscripted soldiers, they did basically what they wanted to and wasted a tremendous amount of fighting power that way. If they did not respect their commander, they saw no reason to obey him simply because he was a senior officer. They would simply refuse to follow commands if it so pleased them. 'No, I'm going to have tea now.' Or, 'It's time for some *biltong* [dried lean meat].' Or, 'I've got to get back to my place to take care of the sheep.' It would have been unheard of for a British Tommy to disobey his commanding officer.

"Oh, they have problems, and it comes out in all aspects of their life. They say one thing, and they do another. It is motivated by all sorts of things: inferiority, the feeling of being oppressed. There is so much that is wrapped up in them as a race. And then there is the church."

"Yes, that interests me," I said. "I have always wondered how a man and woman can sleep together after reading the Bible and praying together." Peter was one of the few farmers with whom I could talk about sex with some ease.

"I don't think they would find it offensive. They would regard it quite naturally as an act of consecrated marriage. I think they would have a roaring conscience if they were making love outside of marriage.

"A friend of Donna's stopped by a few weeks ago. She comes from an old farm in the valley, but she has been to training college and had just returned from a trip to the States. I don't remember how it came about, but I was showing her a copy of *Playgirl*, which a doctor friend of mine had brought up from Cape Town."

Playgirl, Playboy, Penthouse, and other similar magazines are banned in South Africa. There is quite a market for them in suburban Cape Town.

"She looked through the magazine and then asked me if I had any copies of *Playboy*. She had never seen it. For me it has reached a stage where all you do is look through parted legs, and it all becomes a bit distasteful. I'm used to it, but she was not. And despite her education and her travels, she still asked me whether or not I thought looking through such magazines was sinful. We debated it. We had a long pleasant chat about it. Hers was not a silly emotional reaction. She was being very honest with herself. She was really trying to make up her mind whether or not it was sinful."

Peter and Donna are accused by the older generation of English farmers of having tasteless parties. "They flirt with the idea of an orgy," one farmer put it. Margot and Tommy Prinsloo described their embarrassment at a birthday party for Peter to which they had been invited. "I had brought him a pen," Margot said, "and when we arrived I knew I had made a mistake. It was very noisy, and there was a lot of drinking and screaming and loud, boisterous joking. After dinner we went into the lounge to open the presents. Luckily mine was on the bottom of the pile, and they never opened it. I realized that all the other presents were imported from Amsterdam. All their friends—they were mostly from Cape Town—had got together and bought stacks of pornography. (They later put them in a filing cabinet.) There were all sorts of contraceptives that were blown up like balloons and were floating around. I just couldn't say a word. They must have known we were bored because they never invited us again."

"It was mostly showing off," Tommy added. "A lot of noisy drunk people showing off and missing the boat entirely."

Dominee Pieter Kotze

"The old Nationalists stand by certain moral standards," Dominee Pieter Kotze said. "Young people are more pragmatic today. They're ready to stab anyone in the back. They're more inclined to use violence and get away with it. The old people had fine scruples about these things. They were shocked by the Information Scandal,* our Watergate, a couple of years ago, and by the murder of Steve Biko.† Perhaps they do not express their doubts about the government openly, but they're bothered by it. Whatever one might think of their values, the old Nats are a moral people and consider corruption in the government a breach of faith. Some of them think the government is too pragmatic."

Pieter Kotze is a young minister in the Sendings, or Mission,

---

*After the Soweto riots in 1976, Balthazar Johannes Vorster, the prime minister, encouraged the Department of Information to engage in clandestine activities in and outside South Africa. Vorster did not inform his cabinet of these activities and financed them through a secret defense account. When the auditor-general made a critical report, a scandal broke out. Vorster resigned, and the present prime minister, Pieter Willem Botha, was elected.
†A popular young Black Consciousness leader. See Chapter 11.

Church, the Coloured branch of the Dutch Reformed Church, in a neighboring village. He often preaches in Wyndal when the local minister is unable to hold services. Pieter Kotze was a brilliant if rebellious student at Stellenbosch, and unlike the majority of graduates of the "Angel Factory," as the English call Stellenbosch's Theological Faculty, he refused to accept a calling to a white Dutch Reformed congregation. "Apartheid," he says, "is simply unsound theology. I don't want any part of it. But of course by accepting a position in the Mission Church, I am participating in it (even though our church is open to all)." Pieter Kotze's passion is the Old Testament. He knows Greek and Hebrew and is well versed in the German commentaries. Aside from the commentaries, his bookshelves are lined with Kierkegaard, Jaspers, Heidegger, and Barth. "I took a course in Nietzsche, Foucault, and Marcuse. I didn't make much out of Foucault. I have trouble with the French. Marcuse was difficult because, as his works are banned in South Africa, we could only read them in the library with special permission." Pieter Kotze says he has been most influenced by the Dutch philosopher C. A. van Peursen, who takes a moral position in theology. "He sees facts as the fossil remains of values." Pieter Kotze dreams of studying in Basel—he has never been overseas—and teaching at the university. He justifies preaching in a village church on existentialist grounds. It is his "absurdity"—an absurdity that confirms a peculiar faith under attack by a cynical intellect, a penchant to question everything, and a fascination with "godless" theologies. He says somewhat enigmatically that South Africa has a terrible sense of history without knowing it. He also says that every South African walks around with a pocket revolution.

"Would you say that the younger clergy in the Dutch Reformed Church are pragmatic?" I asked.

"There are many sides to your question. Everyone, I would say, has become more pragmatic, the radicals and the right-wingers who advocate violence. I was shocked once. There was a chap in my class who said that the riots in Soweto were a good thing because they gave birth to African nationalism and would lead to the flow of blood. He was very reactionary. Many right-wing extremists take this position. It's as though they are looking forward to bloodshed.

"I myself had a lot of trouble fitting into Stellenbosch. It is a Dutch Reformed school and, therefore, very conservative and very Calvinist. The professors there want to set high academic standards but they do not want to trespass the sacred preserves of conservatism. Calvinism is largely opposed to pietism, although there is a conservative group that is open to it. Fundamentalism is for the Dutch Reformed Church more acceptable than liberal theology. Whenever I argued a more liberal position in class, my professors would smirk. They might have agreed with what I was saying, but they had to put a face on. They didn't want a liberal reputation. They were intimidated by their students. They would accept their fundamentalist, pietistic criticism but not my liberal criticism. There is in fact a huge gap between what the syllabus states is desired and what is actually taught. You can get a degree knowing very little theology.

"I do not really like talking about the time I spent at Stellenbosch. I found it very unpleasant. I lost my temper. I wanted to shout and scream. But I learned to be nasty in a cool sort of way. I'm not going to cry about it. I don't blame those who hissed at me. I learned never to be afraid of my own position—never to succumb to social pressure. I was determined not to sell myself as many of my professors did. I felt quite alone; in other classes, outside theology, there were a few independent students, and then I must admit, there were several of us in theology who went about expressing our position with missionary zeal. There were about sixty of us in a class. At first there were only two of us who defended a liberal position, but by the end of the semester three or four others joined our camp and about a dozen were not unsympathetic to it. Today there would probably be a few more.

"Most of the students put me off. I remember one who was a very rigid Nat. He should have been a communist because he believed one should do whatever one is told. There was another who was a party organizer for the Nats. He was older and quite brilliant. He had liberal theological views. In fact, he was a total relativist in theology, but in politics he was right-wing. Personally, I believe that the relativists carry things too far. They never seem to be convinced of anything. One has to take a position. One of our greatest problems, certainly I feel it, is an inertia that is decorated with sentiment and keeps us in our place."

South African universities, like South African schools, are divided according to race and language. There are separate universities for whites, Coloureds, Indians, and Blacks. With the exception of the

University of Port Elizabeth, the ten white residential universities are either English- or Afrikaans-speaking. Under very exceptional circumstances, which the government is presently trying to limit further, non-white students may attend white universities. Of the students in 1983 at the three largest English-speaking universities, approximately 12 percent at Witwatersrand in Johannesburg were non-white (mostly Indian and Black), 14 percent at Cape Town (mostly Coloured), and 19 percent at the University of Natal in Durban (mostly Indian). Less than 1 percent of the students in the same year at any of the five Afrikaans universities were non-white. Of the total university student body in South Africa in 1983, approximately 69 percent, were white.[13]

There are striking differences in social and intellectual tone between the English- and Afrikaans-speaking white universities. The Afrikaner universities are conservative, authoritarian, ideologically oriented, and subject to a pervasive and usually uncritical Christian Nationalism. They are staffed almost entirely by Afrikaners.[14] Students dress conservatively, tend to be religious (especially at Potchefstroom, the "Dopper University"), support the Nationalist government, and are fiercely proud of their cultural tradition. They master what is assigned in an unquestioning rote manner and seem to find little adventure in their studies. Their approach is pragmatic; their goals are well articulated and, even among many students of theology, materialistic. They suffer few of the identity crises that characterize American university students, though according to many Wyndal residents they drink a great deal. They tend to accept the status quo in South Africa. English students who attend Afrikaans-speaking universities form isolated cliques. They feel estranged and excluded, and they are often troubled by the uncritically conservative attitude of Afrikaner students. "I cannot really talk to my roommate," an English medical student at Stellenbosch told me. "She is an Afrikaner. She does exactly what she is told. She never questions her prof. She memorizes everything even when she does not understand it . . . I tried talking to her about politics, but I had to give up. She just repeated what her father had told her. She doesn't have a mind of her own . . . She has a boyfriend, and all she wants to talk about is marriage. She goes home every weekend—to church."

The English universities are less conservative (though conservative by American standards), less religious, less nationalistic, and less ideologically oriented (although among liberals there is some "play" with Marxism) than the Afrikaner universities. The faculty is recruited from both within and outside South Africa. Students dress more extravagantly, play more with ideas, question their professors and their country's politics (student demonstrations and protests are frequent), and are sexually more permissive than Afrikaner students. Students in the sciences and engineering tend to be more conservative than those in the arts, and there are a number of conservative student organizations.* Liberal Afrikaans-speaking students try to attend English-speaking universities. Some of the students, "especially the Jews," Hugo Malan once observed, have personal crises, but these seem to be less disruptive than the ones American students go through. Psychotherapy does not play the same role in South Africa that it does in the United States. In general, I found that most English and Afrikaner students accept their parents' career advice rather more readily than American students do. Like the Afrikaner students, the English students' goals in life tend to be governed by a strong materialism. Their problems have to do with weighing their moral and political commitments against material and social self-interest. They have less to do with "what am I going to do in life" than with "where am I going to lead my life." Most of them entertain the possibility of leaving South Africa, and some do.

I generalize here—to give a sense of contrast. There are of course exceptions to both the English and Afrikaner universities. Most Afrikaners in Wyndal who send their children to university send them to Stellenbosch. "It's nearby," one mother explained. "My children can come home on weekends. It's our oldest university and the best. It's more in the Cape tradition." Most of the English send their children to the University of Cape Town although Jack Freeling, one of the first English farmers to settle in the valley, let his eldest daughter go to Rhodes University in Grahamstown, which has the reputation, at least in Wyndal, of being a party school. He was criticized by other English residents of the valley for giving her such a free hand. "He'll be lucky," one neighbor said maliciously, "if she makes it through with only a diploma." One very conservative English family sent their children to Stellenbosch rather than

*Since my research, there has been, I have been told, a conservative turn among English-speaking white university students.

to Cape Town, where they would be exposed to "communists, sexual promiscuity, and a generally disruptive atmosphere." The University of Cape Town, which is located on a foothill of Table Mountain, is sometimes called the Kremlin on the Hill by conservative South Africans. It is not especially liberal by American standards.

Jack Freeling

"There was an embarrassing experience at my son's school a few years ago. A recruiting officer from the army came to address the school. He was met with great rudeness and was booed. It was pretty uncomfortable."

Jack's son, Tony, had just started boarding school in Cape Town. He and his sister Ida, who also went to boarding school, were home for the weekend and had just left us for a friend's. Tony had been telling us what a relief it was to go to a school where you didn't have to study the Great Trek every year for half the year. Ida had told us earlier that the girls in her school avoided talking politics and race because, as everyone had different ideas, such talk caused friction. Jack and his wife, Constance, always treated my interviews as family occasions and invited their children to participate if they were home and available. The Freelings were unique in this respect. (Tony was fourteen at the time, and Ida was sixteen.) Most parents tended to dismiss their children's ideas, at least in front of me. Jack told me that his children enjoyed talking to me because I asked interesting questions and was interested in their opinions. "They both want to visit the States now," Jack said. "It's important that they show an interest in other parts of the world. Who knows where they will end up?"

Jack went on: "The big question is: Do you do your military service after you leave school or do you do it after varsity. I think it is important to do your university first, because if you go straight from school, you're open to the brainwashing techniques of the armed forces. You must build up a little cynicism. Once you've got that, you can stand any mental onslaught."

Two years of active military service followed by an active reserve requirement in the commandoes is compulsory for all white males in South Africa, and despite recent legislation, conscientious objectors (137 in 1981, 312 in 1982) continue to be imprisoned. The South African Defence Forces (SADF) are, however, multiracial and do not discriminate in terms of pay and status. In 1982, 92 percent of the permanent forces of the SADF were white, 6 percent Coloured, 1 percent Asian, and 1 percent Black.[15] English and Afrikaner farmers in Wyndal view military service positively as building up a young man's character. They did not seem to be overly distressed by South Africa's Angolan war. Both groups were convinced that the "communist threat" had to be contained.

"Most of the senior boys at Wyndal are planning to go directly into the army," I observed. "They say it will give them time to decide on their future. It's a debt, they say, they have to their country."

"That's the headmaster. He's an old Broederbonder and very active in the commandoes. He runs the school along military lines. Most of the boys are active in the school's 'pre-commandoes.' "

The commandoes (basically active reservists who have completed national service) are a local militia that, in the event of a national emergency, are supposed to keep order. Since completing their active service, many of them have been called up for additional active service on the Angolan border. There are about 300 commandoes in the unit to which Wyndal belongs. Many of the Afrikaners in the valley remain active members of the unit after they have completed their reserve requirements. For the most part the English do not. The commandoes have detailed maps of the valley with files on each farm: who lives there, what firearms they possess, and what fire-fighting capacity they have. Commandoes keep their rifles at home, much as Swiss soldiers do. Weapons with repeating mechanisms and mortars are kept at local headquarters. "Ever since the riots in Soweto, everybody's armed to the teeth here," Jack told me once. There is an active woman's pistol club in the valley, and rifle practice is a favorite activity among high school students.

"How do you feel about Tony's military service?" I asked Jack.

"Well, it's still a few years off. I'd hate for him to do it. But I don't think there's much danger of his getting shot. You're a damned sight more likely to get run down by a bus in Cape Town. Things might escalate of course."

"But what about the front in the South West?"

"I don't think very much is going on there. The casualty figures are really very minimal."

It was reported in June 1981 that since 1961, 841 members of the South African Defence Forces had died in clashes with guerrillas, in training, or during military operations.[16]*

"The boys mix with roughs and toughs. It shapes their character to a large extent, and from that point of view, it's good for them."

"Does Tony ever talk about military service?"

"No, not to me at least. I think he feels it's something he owes his country. They're taught it's a sort of payment for their education."

"Do you feel that way?"

"Well, I suppose I must."

Whenever we talked about the Nationalist government, Jack vacillated between an attitude of pained resignation and one of moral and political indignation. A member of the opposition, he fumed over his—its—impotence.

"Why did you send Tony to Cape Town?"

"It's a tradition. I went to his school. We're very English that way: school ties and Old Boy networks. That sort of thing. Of course his is not one of the fancy 'private' schools . . .

"We could never have sent him here. It's fine if you're just an Afrikaans-speaking farmer's child, but that's all. There's no intellectual stimulation whatsoever. It's supposed to be a dual medium school, but even English is taught in Afrikaans. And then it's all on Christian National Education—you know, love your country; love your God; love your Christian duty, your spiritual duty to your race. How could any reasonable parent send a child to a school like that? We sent Ida and Tony to Mountainview for primary school like all the English here. It was quite an adequate school and truly dual medium. In fact, they were quite good at the basics. You learn to read and write, and your multiplication tables are hammered into you. It's fine until thirteen. After that you must go. Otherwise you're molded into a narrow street."

"Do they teach subjects like mythology?"

"Oh, dear, no. How could they? It would interfere with the Bible.

---

*In 1982–1983, 77 members of the SADF died in action in South-West Africa and Angola. 1,268 SWAPO insurgents were killed; 71 civilians were killed in cross-fire or by land mines; 70 civilians were victims of political murder; and 171 civilians were abducted by SWAPO (South African Institute of Race Relations, 1983, p. 610). For further information on SWAPO, see footnote on p. 172.

In primary school, in the Afrikaans reading books for English children, there are little folktales—what little Janie did when he found a bed of ants, that sort of thing. But none of the great mythologies of ancient Rome."

"And what is Tony's present school like?"

"It's very progressive—high academic standards and excellent teaching. Standards have risen about fourfold since I graduated in '49. The matric [final examination] is somewhere between the English O and A levels. Some of the fancier English schools still prepare for London A levels, but that's being phased out."

"So you think standards have improved. Several people have told me the level of South African education has decreased," I said.

"I don't think that is true. Many people complain about languages. Instead of learning a *legitimate* European language they say their children have to waste time studying a made-up one. Yes, I would prefer that Tony and Ida—she's talented in languages—have more time to study French or German, but we do live here. And more than half the population, that is, the white population, speaks Afrikaans. If we lived in Zululand, I would want the children to learn Zulu. Languages aside, I think standards in science and maths are higher than in my day."

"And Ida's school?"

"I think the same is true. My eldest daughter—you've not met her —is at Rhodes and studies modern languages. I'm sure she's not as fluent as European children at her level, but she has a good grounding in grammar and vocabulary and will pick up her fluency when she goes to Europe. She plans to get a job as an *au pair* in France as soon as she graduates."

"I don't understand the status of your children's schools."

"They are government boarding schools. We have quite a tradition of them here. We've got the old private schools as well. They're based on the English system and dedicated to an ethic of fagging and prefects and a stiff upper lip. All of them are in financial trouble, as I believe your schools in the States are. When one of them opened the door to Coloureds and Blacks, there was a reaction from the Old Boys. They approached the Board of Governors and forced them to limit the number of non-whites to ten percent of the student body.

"Tony's school is an English school, but it is more liberal. You get a better education, and it's half as expensive. We pay about one hundred sixty rand a semester for tuition and board. It's the same at Ida's school. Of course, there are no non-whites in either of their schools, and that's a pity. But, quite frankly, given the fluctuations in the fruit market, I couldn't swing sending them to private schools and my eldest to varsity."

"Are there any Afrikaners in the schools?"

"Yes, it's the policy at Tony's school to bring in Afrikaans-speaking boys from the country as part of a leavening process. They have the most furious arguments—political ones. Apparently they shout and shriek at one another. 'You can't treat the Blacks that way.' That sort of thing. It's on a friendly sort of basis. Tony says the Afrikaners go on the defensive and start quoting their fathers.

"The father is very strong in the Afrikaner family. Right or wrong, his opinion is laid down as law. It's backed up by the church, and the church by the government. The Afrikaners have a strong-knit family. A child is subservient to the father right through almost to his father's death. If you step out of line, you get hammered physically. The women are very committed too, a lot stronger than most people think. They seem to be more vicious in their opinions. There's no broadness at all—almost in a witchlike way.

"The Afrikaners have a sort of simplistic outlook on life. There is no critical content. They're a simpleminded people, as greedy as hell when it comes to money. Somebody expressed it well the other night at the Wentworths'. He said the Afrikaners were lower-class Germans mostly, with lower-class German genes, and they've kept that genetic streak right through. You know all their talk about the Boer War—you've talked to Dr. Steyn?—symbolizes a genetic mental pattern. I'm sure it does.

"They learn in a completely different way. There's a syllabus laid down by the Ministry of National Education. They learn the damned books by heart. It's a very narrow form of education. They learn the facts, they swap them, they regurgitate them on exams, and of course they get fantastic results. But there is no broad education and no critical content whatsoever. It's a form of parrot learning, and it's the same at Stellenbosch for the first year or two. 'You will read from page so-and-so to page so-and-so and you will be tested on it on Monday.' I think perhaps at the higher echelons it improves. It must, because, for God's sake, we can't go on like that."

"Do you know anything about the non-white schools?"

"Little enough. We have no contact with them. They're in a

shabby state. The government spends little on them. The students
protest, boycott, get beaten up and expelled, and, of course, nothing
is accomplished. You were here during the riots last year. How
many people were killed in Cape Town?*

"There's a small shack of a school down here for Blacks. I don't
suppose you've ever noticed it. It's on the road to Mountainview.
It's mainly for contract workers. It's so sad. Forty or fifty kids of
all ages stuffed into a little room with a wood stove that smokes until
they're all in tears. How the hell a Black child ever gets anywhere
I don't know. He'd have to be an absolute genius. And they have
to pay for that—and the transportation to it."

Estimated per capita expenditure during 1981–1982 on pupils of various racial backgrounds was as follows: 1,221 rand for whites, 798 rand
for Indians, 419 rand for Coloureds, and 165 rand for Blacks. Teacher-pupil ratios were 1:18 for whites, 1:24 for Indians, 1:27 for Coloureds, and 1:43 for Blacks. Per capita expenditure is considerably
lower and teacher-pupil ratios considerably higher in the homelands.[17] Education is not compulsory for Blacks, and drop-out rates
are very high in part, it has been argued, because of malnutrition.[18]
In white areas, between 50 and 60 percent of the adult Black population is literate, having passed Standard 2 (fourth grade); 98 percent
of the white population is literate. Since the Bantu Education Act
of 1953, private and missionary schools have come under increasingly
strong government control.[19] New regulations for African schools,
gazetted in 1980, provided for the expulsion of students who boycotted classes and launched protests.[20]

*In 1980 Black and Coloured students boycotted schools in protest of educational
discrimination. In the Cape there was a meat workers' strike and a strike at Fattis
and Monis, a western Cape food processor. In June, during the commemoration
of the Soweto riots, riots broke out in the Cape. The government admitted that
thirty-four people died in the riots. Unofficial figures were much higher.

6

POLITICAL CONSCIOUSNESS

Afrikaner nationalism increased dramatically during the first half of the twentieth century. Louis Botha, the first prime minister (1910–1919) of the Union of South Africa, and his successor, Jan Christian Smuts (1919–1924), favored the merging of the English and the Afrikaners into a unified white nation that would maintain close contact with Great Britain. Theirs was a politics of white racism and egalitarian liberalism. (The Union left 1,250,000 whites with complete political control over 4,250,000 Blacks, 500,000 Coloureds, and 165,000 Indians.) Botha and Smuts's pro-British position was resented by the more virulently nationalistic Afrikaners, who were afraid of losing their national identity. These nationalists opposed South Africa's entry into World War I on the side of the British— their "enemy." In 1914, James Barry Munnik Hertzog, one of their champions ("only one person has a right to be 'boss' in South Africa, namely the Afrikaner"[1]), formed the Afrikaner National Party, which opposed South Africa's participation in the war. (Hertzog had been a member of Botha's first cabinet but had had to be dropped because of his nationalism.)

In 1922 the Smuts government came under increasing attack because of its handling of striking white mine workers who were protesting an attempt by the Chamber of Mines to relax the color bar and cut their wages. Smuts called in the Defence Forces, and in a five-day battle, more than 200 whites were killed. In the end, the color bar was more firmly entrenched than ever, and in 1924, with the support of the British Labour Party, the National Party came to power, and Hertzog became prime minister.

Hertzog advocated a two-stream policy, in which South Africa's two principal white groups would maintain separate identities. ("Community life in South Africa flows in two streams—the English-speaking stream and the Dutch-speaking stream, each stream with its own language, its own way of life, its own great men, heroic deeds, and noble characters."[2]) He gave South Africa its first flag, made Afrikaans an official language, and helped articulate the notion of "dominion independence" within the British Commonwealth. However, as a result of political intrigue and a disastrous economic policy, Hertzog's National Party was forced in 1933 into coalition with Smuts's South African Party. The two parties became the United Party in 1934.

The thirties were a difficult time for the Afrikaners. Aside from the effects of the Depression (exaggerated by Hertzog's refusal at first to follow Britain's example and abandon the gold standard), there were serious droughts. Poverty was widespread. Several South African observers have compared the economic situation of the Afrikaners in the thirties to that of the Coloureds today, forgetting of course that unlike today's Coloureds, the Afrikaners were never subject to the restrictive laws of apartheid.[3] Farmers streamed into the cities for whatever jobs they could get. Most of them were unskilled and were competing with workers of other races for the same jobs. (Black migration to the cities increased during the same period.) "From being easy-going, slow-moving, friendly, tolerant men of the land," the journalist-historian René de Villiers observes somewhat simplistically, "they tended to take on the characteristics and philosophy of the urban worker without the comforts and easy living of country life. They began to take their new approach to life in the Nationalist party, which itself came to reflect some of the harsher, relentless, isolationist, and authoritarian philosophy of the 'new' Afrikaner for whom life in the cities was often grim and earnest."[4]

Antagonism toward the Blacks and hostility toward the English —who by and large were in an economically more advantageous position—were rampant. To solve the problem of "poor whites," Hertzog gave state support to industrial and agricultural development, and by expanding the bureaucracy and state-run railway personnel, he virtually subsidized the existence of thousands of Afrikaners who would otherwise have found themselves unemployed or forced into menial labor "unworthy of a white man." He increased racial segregation, disenfranchised the only partially enfranchised Cape Bantu, and expanded native reserves.

Hertzog's coalition with Smuts was considered in some Afrikaner quarters downright treasonous. Daniel François Malan, *dominee*-turned-politician, ardent, mystical, fanatical nationalist and racist, and from 1948 to 1954 prime minister, refused to join the coalition, preferring a purified (*gesuiwerde*) national party. (Images of purity and pollution characterize Afrikaner political oratory.) Malan and his followers, staunchly supported by the avowedly nonpolitical but politically highly influential Broederbond, opposed ethnic fusion, *samesmelting* (among English, Afrikaners, and Jews), and advocated a reunion, a *hereniging*, of "those who belong together"—namely, Afrikaners whose loyalties would not fluctuate between England and South Africa. Malan and his Nationalists promoted a republicanism in which the English would be given a choice between becoming true South Africans (subject, to be sure, to Afrikaner national interests) or returning to their homeland.

Hennie

"My dad had tremendous admiration for General Smuts, and so did I," Hennie said. "But our admiration wasn't shared by everyone. There were a lot of Afrikaners who thought Smuts had sold out to the English. 'He's abandoned us to the enemy,' they would say. 'And now he wants us to fight for the enemy.' I had a teacher who spoke that way. I had fights in school. I was just a kid, and I didn't really understand what it was all about. I knew my dad liked Smuts, and I was determined to defend him.

"In 1938 we had the Ossewatrek, the great ox-wagon parade. In many respects it was a political thing: a way to bring about Afrikaner unity. Old General Hertzog and Smuts had joined forces, but Malan wouldn't have any part of their desire to share power with the English. It was Afrikaner all the way, and that was what this parade was about.

"Nine wagons set out to celebrate the Great Trek. Seven of them were scheduled to arrive in Pretoria on the Day of the Covenant,

December 16, 1938, where there was going to be a tremendous celebration. They were going to lay the cornerstone of the Voortrekker Monument. The other two wagons were to meet on the same day where the Battle of Blood River had taken place, where Sarel Cilliers had made his covenant. I had to recite it in school."

Hennie recited in Afrikaans the covenant that the great Voortrekker Sarel Cilliers made with God before the Battle of Blood River, in which the Voortrekkers successfully defeated some 10,000 Zulus. They suffered only a few casualties but 3,000 Zulus were killed.

" 'Brothers and fellow countrymen, we stand here before the Holy God of Heaven and Earth to make a vow that, if He will be with us and protect us and give the foe into our hands, we shall ever celebrate the day and date as a Day of Thanksgiving like the Sabbath in His honor. We shall enjoin our children that they must take part with us in this, for a remembrance even for our posterity. For the honor of God shall herein be glorified, and to Him shall be given the fame and honor of the victory.' " Hennie could not resist smiling with satisfaction upon completing his recitation. It was a schoolboy's smile.

"These wagons reenacted the whole trek. Everywhere people dressed up in traditional costumes. There were a lot of speeches, and they even renamed streets after the heroes of the trek. One of the wagons came through my hometown. I remember it well. I'd never seen such crowds. The mayor gave a speech, and the old *dominee* thanked the Lord for the preservation of the Afrikaners and blessed the wagon and even the oxen that pulled it. I wasn't very much part of the whole thing because I never had the right clothes.

"I was only about fifteen. I could feel a rift between the Nationalists and the supporters of Smuts and Hertzog. I don't know how it happened, but I became a sort of rallying point for the English and the Jews, who didn't feel part of the whole thing. When the wagon finally left town, a lot of people followed it for miles on foot or on horseback; some went all the way to Pretoria. We got into a tremendous fight, and I came home with a bloody nose."

The Ossewatrek to celebrate the centenary of the Battle of Blood River was organized by Henning Klopper, who had founded the Broederbond in 1918 and then in 1930 the Afrikaans Language and Cultural Union of South African Railways and Harbors (Afrikaanse Taal en Kultuurvereniging, or ATKV), one of the most powerful cultural associations in South Africa, representing over 18,000 Afrikaner railway workers. The message of the trek was a fervent claim of unity, of *volkseenheid*, which would override all the splits and potential splits of party politics and regionalism, and those inspired by British imperial interest. "Let us build a monument for Afrikaner hearts," Klopper said on August 8, 1938, as the first wagons set off from the foot of van Riebeeck's statue in Cape Town. "May this simple trek bind together in love those Afrikaner hearts which do not yet beat together."[5]

Feverish enthusiasm for the trek spread throughout South Africa. Men grew beards and wore traditional black corduroy jackets and checked scarves—the clothes Hennie did not have. Women wore aprons and *kappies*. Committees were set up to organize processions to greet the wagons. One woman I talked to remembers having been chosen to carry "a glorious floral wreath" to the wagon approaching from Cape Town as "the most significant event" in her life. "I was made to ride a beautiful white horse. I was scared—I have always been scared of horses—but I knew God would help me overcome my fear, and He did." Several other farmers remember with moist eyes the folk songs and dancing, and the little plays about the trek that were performed in the evening in the towns where the wagons halted. Children were baptized when the wagons arrived. Young men fought to get to the wagons to smear their handkerchiefs with axle grease.[6]

No wagon came through the valley, but most of the farmers managed to get to at least one celebration in a neighboring town. Many of them accompanied the wagons across the southern Cape and some all the way to Pretoria. One farmer, considered by English and Afrikaners alike the most bigoted man in the valley, ran in the marathon and carried a torch of freedom and civilization to Pretoria. The runners were greeted by 3,000 Voortrekkers, each with a torch of his own. The torches were thrown into a huge bonfire at the monument site, signaling for other fires to be lit on the hilltops surrounding Pretoria. Elsa Joubert, the author of the recently published *The Long Journey of Poppie Nongena*, the first book in Afrikaans to treat the experience of an African woman living on an urban Black location, was sixteen at the time and a Voortrekker. She described the scene this way:

> The hill is on fire; on fire with Afrikaner fire; on fire with the enthusiasm of Young South Africa! You are nothing—your people is all. One

light in dusk is puny and small. But three thousand flames. Three thousand! And more! There's hope for your future. South Africa![7]

There was in the Ossewatrek an almost mystical conviction that it would culminate in the declaration of a South African republic free from the stifling and demeaning control of imperial Britain.

Hennie

"There was a kind of letdown after the Ossewatrek," Hennie said. "I suppose that's why there was some fighting among us kids. You can excite people with nationalist ideals. You can raise their spirit to a feverish pitch. But you can't sustain such a pitch. It's a bit like those revivalists you have in the States. They pitch their tents. They thump their Bibles. They fill everyone with the 'spirit of the Lord' and they leave. They abandon their children. A mother just can't give birth to a baby and leave it to survive on its own. You have always to be with God . . .

"There was a lot of talk about Afrikaner nationalism in school. I had a big fight with one of my teachers because he thought the Germans were going to win the war. I said, 'Oh, rubbish,' and he and the whole class turned against me. They called me a traitor to my people. There was a lot of admiration for the Germans and even for Hitler. I don't think those poor blokes really knew what Hitler stood for. They knew only one thing: He was against England. That was good enough for them. They were damned if they were going to fight against England's enemy.

"There's been a lot of talk about how the war split South Africa, but the war was also a turning point for South Africa. Until then we were dependent upon imports from England and Germany. These were cut off, and we had to make do on our own. And we did it. I had a friend. He was in the testing department for the railways. We used to import steam traps from England. They cost something like three pounds ten. They would drain water from the heating system on the trains so that only steam would pass through the heaters. Well, my friend designed a trap that cost only forty-two cents. It was so simple. He drilled thirty-seven holes in a copper disk. When steam passed through the hoses between the trains, to which the disk was attached, the copper heated up and expanded, closing the holes. When water began to accumulate, the copper cooled down, opening up the holes through which it could flow out. It's a little thing really, but it was that kind of thing that gave us confidence. That was the beginning of South African industrialization."

"And how did the war affect you personally?"

"Well, suddenly I began to take part in politics. I remember that the first effect the war had on us at the farm was that we couldn't buy trucking. We used to import all our farm implements: spades, forks, garden hoes. Now we had to find substitutes or make them locally. How often we longed to see the good old stamp 'Made in Germany,' which we knew was a mark of quality. Oh, we had a lot of teething problems then, and of course lots of people saw this as a moment for establishing our own industry. In many ways I myself longed for peace so that we could go back to our old standards and our old way of life. Then we could buy just what we liked.

"I was at varsity then studying engineering. I had to do practical work every year as part of the course. My cousin was with the army engineers in Pretoria, so I went up there to work in the army workshop. I had to cut up pieces of metal into squares and oblong shapes and drill little holes and tap the pieces of metal down to a certain size. I had no idea what I was making. I asked my cousin to find out, and he found out and told me, although strictly speaking he shouldn't have. I was making the prototype of an aerial camera!"

I was struck by the naïve excitement in Hennie's voice.

"Armored cars were being made in railway shops, where they had welding equipment. They were assembled in other factories. And these were being built for the South African army!

"And it was just at that time that a Coloured bloke came to a Jewish friend of mine who had a farm along the river. '*Baas,*' he said, 'you know these stones here is really good stuff. I used to work in a mine where we had to dig them up.' 'You look after the sheep,' my Jewish friend said. 'Leave the stones alone. They won't run away, and the sheep will.' A couple of days later the Coloured man brought another sample to his boss and told him they were good stones. So eventually my friend sent them away for analysis and found out that they were tungsten, which was in great demand. Suddenly a man and a couple of slaves could pick a ton in a week and make four hundred pounds. Some of the neighbors came to me and asked me to design a magazine to keep dynamite in for blasting. I became part of the war effort that way, although I was just farming.

I noticed how things that had never mattered could become important! Here we were living on top of all these stones that never mattered, and then suddenly they did. People were making a living out of them, and soldiers' lives were being saved by them. Putting a tungsten tip on a bullet can help smash armored plate. Suddenly South Africa became a supplier of a much needed element. Handpicking and blasting in a small way were no longer sufficient. Bigger deposits had to be found, and they were. They had to be developed, and they were. Those little stones were being exported to America! And really and truly these are the things that began to expand my perception of the world. At the same time, it was affecting South Africa. I don't think we realized at the time how much. All these young men who had grown up in their little corner were going out into the world and seeing a different way of life."

"Were there many Afrikaners who fought in the war?"

"Yes, yes. My eldest brother was against the whole thing. He was pro-Nationalist. I had a cousin who didn't care one way or another. He just wanted to lead his own little life. And then there was my cousin, the engineer. He was very much involved in the whole thing, but he was not allowed to go to war. He was too valuable to lose. And, oh, I forgot my second brother. I'll never forget how he looked in uniform."

"How did all these differences of opinion and service affect your family? Were there arguments?"

"No. You see, my eldest brother, the pro-Nationalist, was not around much. He was working in the mines. My cousin was in Pretoria, and the other one just didn't talk much about the whole thing. My second brother (he had been working in the mines too) wasn't around either. He came down to see us in his uniform, and that's how I remember him. He never did go up north to Europe. You had to volunteer for that, and I don't think he did."

"And you?"

"I wanted to join up. I was at varsity. I tried to join the air force, but unfortunately Erroll Flynn joined the army before I did the air force so there was nothing left for me to do. He won the war."

"So did you do any military service?"

"No. I had to get permission from my mother before I could join up, and she said that I was needed back on the farm, that she couldn't manage without me."

"Was that true?"

"It was a small piece of land, but, once again, circumstances determined what I was going to do. I wonder how often we are victims of circumstances."

Hennie went on to tell me how successful the vegetable farm was during the war. I did not feel I could ask him how he felt about not being allowed to fight. Nor could I ask him more about his brothers. He was always very reluctant to talk about them.

"People say that the war was a rallying point for Afrikaner nationalism, and I suppose it was. There were patriotic organizations like the Ossewabrandwag—it grew out of the Ossewatrek and was important down here in the valley—but there were a lot of Afrikaners who fought in the war too. And my family was not unusual: some fighting, some refusing to fight, some wanting to fight and not being able to, and some just not paying any attention to the war at all. There were a lot of those. There always are."

Pro-German attitudes were widespread among Afrikaners during the years immediately preceding World War II and in the first years of the war. Smuts's determination to declare war against Germany shattered his party's alliance with Hertzog's—Hertzog had advocated neutrality—and eventually brought about Hertzog's resignation and put Malan's purified Nationalist Party on firmer ground. Pro-German, pro-Nazi sympathy was encouraged by the Ossewabrandwag (Ox-wagon Sentinel), a "cultural" organization founded in 1938 by Colonel J. C. C. Laas and soon commanded by a staunch admirer of Hitler, Dr. J. F. J. van Rensburg; it aimed at perpetuating the "ox-wagon" spirit. Rabidly nationalistic, militaristic, sympathetic to National Socialism and fascism, dedicated to a unified Afrikanerdom and a South Africa purified of English and Jewish influence, and not averse to sabotage and terrorism, the Ossewabrandwag rapidly spread among the Afrikaners. By 1940, it had a membership of over 200,000.[8] The Afrikaners with whom I talked about it (they included several local leaders) claimed that the organization was not particularly anti-Semitic, simply pro-German and anti-English, but there was in fact a strong current of anti-Semitism in its political and philosophical outlook. At first Malan flirted with it, but he soon came to realize that it posed a threat to his own National Party and he disclaimed any connection with it. As it became evident that Germany would lose the war, as Malan distanced himself and his party from the Ossewabrandwag, and as the

Ox-wagon Sentinel's acts of sabotage and terrorism became extravagant—van Rensburg was a member of its extremist branch, the Stormjaer—more and more Afrikaners switched their allegiance to the National Party.

Dr. Jakobus Steyn

"War broke out when I was in standard eight or nine," Dr. Jakobus Steyn said. "We were of course anti-British. We were not really Nazis—or pro-German. I don't think that was our attitude. I personally was anti-British. Now we had another enemy fighting our enemy so we had a sort of common enemy. That is why most of the Afrikaners sympathized with the Germans. It was just that we thought England was going to get back what she deserved. We were called Nazis. It was a terrible time for the Afrikaners and South Africa as a whole. It was father against son many times because you had many poor Afrikaners who had to go to war to earn enough money to live on. We, of course, had no time for those people, those *verraaiers*, joiners (literally traitors) we called them, because of our history.

"After the cinema we used to have to stand at attention while they played the British anthem and showed a picture of the King and Queen. Now, *that* was asking too much of us. We would walk out before the anthem started or, if there were a few of us, we wouldn't stand up. We had many fights. Grown-ups would slap us.

"We had more or less the same problem in Cape Town during the war when I was a student at Stellenbosch. When the cannon was fired at noon to give the correct time, we were supposed to stand at attention for three minutes and pray that the British would win the war. Anyone who moved was attacked by soldiers and sailors in town. Now, many times we, students from Stellenbosch, would come into town to cause a bit of trouble. It was, as I say, forced down on us."

"But what about the relationship with the Nazis? Was there much anti-Semitism?" I asked.

"I never knew it. There were Jewish children in our schools, but I never noticed any anti-Semitism. There were English-speaking kids too, and they were very outspoken. We had a couple of fights. I would say that the English-speaking people would very much like to associate the Afrikaner with the Nazi, but that is actually not right. I say, it was just that we felt, like anybody, a common sympathy. If you were beaten by a bloke and then suddenly you find there's somebody else who beats that bloke, well, without words, you become friends with his enemy."

Dr. Steyn remembers the Ossewatrek. He and his grandmother would sit next to an old radio and listen to the progress of the wagons to Pretoria. "The Afrikaners as a whole were swept up by it psychologically, and in that way it contributed to our victory in 1948."

"And the Ossewabrandwag?" I asked.

"Oh, that was a cultural organization to bring the Afrikaners together during the war while we were fighting alongside our enemy against the Nazis. There was a feeling among the Afrikaners that we all had to get together because in our own ways we were boycotting the war. This cultural organization grew and grew, and people felt that it would provide the necessary organization for us all. Then a bloke came forward, van Rensburg, and he changed the Ossewabrandwag into a militant organization. He wanted to sabotage post offices and other government buildings. Well, we didn't go along with that. Nor did Dr. Malan. So we left the organization."

"Were you at university at the time?"

"No, I was still in school. There were junior and senior sections of the Ossewabrandwag at that stage. As a kid I decided—and my dad also told me—not to follow the militant direction. We wouldn't have liked a rebellion to start. There was quite a lot of feeling against the militants. So we all switched our loyalty to Dr. Malan and his Nationalists, and began to work for the party. Our victory in 1948, like the Boer War, is an event we will never forget. We had given up our republic, and now we were on the path to becoming a republic once again, out from under the English flag and British rule. We were proud that day. I had been in England doing my housemanship [internship] but I was happy to be back for the election."

The Ossewabrandwag played an important role in Wyndal during the war. Two of the largest and most established farmers in the valley and the town clerk were leaders of the organization. They met clandestinely in an old farmhouse, its windows boarded up so that no one could see or hear what was being discussed. Although the three leaders—in their late seventies or early eighties now—are reluctant to talk about the activities of the Ossewabrandwag, they are proud of having been part of those activities. They insist that they were not anti-Semitic. "How could we be?" one of them asked me. "We have suffered the way the Israelites suffered." He went on to say that they collected money for German prisoners of war and for the orphans of Germans killed in the war. Two of the three leaders adopted German children, and one of them, "the most bigoted man in the valley," has kept close ties to Germany since the war. It is he who said to me once, "You Americans are always putting pressure on us South Africans to change. You do not understand our problems. You do not understand that when our ancestors came here, the kaffirs didn't wear clothes. Now they do. It is only three hundred years, and *that* is not a very long time for such a big change." It is he who wrote a letter protesting the presence of "kaffirs" at a celebration in a nearby town a few years back. "Soon you'll have them dancing kaffir dances in front of our children." And it is he who tacitly admitted that the Ossewabrandwag never really disbanded but went underground, leaving each member with an important mission to accomplish in the event of a British or Black takeover. I had heard talk of this underground organization from several English farmers, though since they could find no concrete proof of its existence, they dismissed it as another example of the fantastical scheming and intriguing of the Afrikaner. The fact that one English farmer was able to buy and restore the old Ossewabrandwag headquarters, despite protests from its original owner— it had been sold once since the war—was proof enough of their impotence.

For English South Africans World War II was of immense symbolic importance. It figured significantly in every life history I collected. It reaffirmed their ties to England and confirmed them as capable and courageous fighting men. Such memories are particularly significant for people who feel that they have lost control of their political and economic destinies and who, as the years go by, are forced to acknowledge, however reluctantly, that England can no longer offer them a home. "I have learned to distinguish between pride in one's country and love for one's country," Hugo Malan once said. "We assume that they go together and usually they do. You Americans are both proud of your country and feel a love for it. The last time we South Africans felt both pride and love for our country was during the war. I can now say that I love my country, as much as any Afrikaner, but I can no longer take pride in it."

Hugo's distinction spread rapidly among Wyndal's English. It seemed to clarify their feelings.

In 1948, much to the surprise of everyone, Smuts's United Party was narrowly defeated by a coalition of Malan's HNP and Nicholaas Christiaan Havenga's more moderate Afrikaner Party.* The coalition had a majority of five seats in Parliament. Malan became prime minister, and Havenga deputy prime minister and minister of finance. Malan and Havenga had placed less emphasis on republicanism in their campaign than on mother-tongue education, apartheid, and the communist peril[9]—issues around which Afrikaans unity could always be evoked. The Afrikaners were elated by their victory. Malan said, "Today South Africa belongs to us once more . . . May God grant that it will always remain our own."[10] The Nationalists proceeded to consolidate their power base in quite ruthless ways. Six seats were given in 1949 to strongly Nationalist South West Africa, officially not even part of the Union: Malan's and Havenga's parties were merged into the National Party in 1951; election districts were reorganized twice in the decade following the 1948 victory; Coloureds were removed from the common voting roll in the Cape in 1956; native representation in Parliament was abolished in 1963.

The English were shocked by the results of the 1948 election and its immediate sequel. They had always taken political control for granted and did not realize that they had been losing political ground for some time.[11] Jack Freeling recalls English feeling then: "Well, my God, the whole English-speaking community was plunged into the most dreadful gloom. You know, this was the end of the world. It was absolutely dreadful. It was a shock. Nobody expected it. Gradually, of course, as things got a little easier, as they kind of relaxed, people started accepting it. And then a chap like Vorster, for instance, played golf. So he must be a good chap! But this small acceptance has been lost in the last four or five years."

Duncan Reid says, "None of us believed it. We were sure the elections were rigged. In fact the United Party had more votes than the Nationalists, but rural districts, Afrikaner districts, had great parliamentary weight. We never had time to consolidate."

Hugo Malan says, "How, we asked ourselves, could a man of Smuts's stature, a real statesman like Churchill or De Gaulle, lose?"

---

*Havenga, sometimes called Hertzog's Man Friday, founded the Afrikaner Party in 1941, to continue Hertzog's two-stream policy.

Carol Reid explains it: "He was getting old. He had lost touch with his country. He was more interested in international matters, in the United Nations. He had surrounded himself with men who would never question his wisdom."

"Oh, they were shocked all right," a student at the University of Cape Town says. They were jostled a bit, but then they began to see what was happening elsewhere in Africa, in Kenya, Tanganyika, the Congo. They knew they had a government on which they could rely. They could afford to be liberal, to indulge themselves in their anguish. What did they lose really? They're living in big white houses with lots of servants, driving their Mercedes."[12]

"We were too cocksure," Catherine Fox says. "We were dreadfully complacent. Complacency has always been our failing."

Catherine Fox

Catherine Fox is a woman of strong moral conviction. She settled in the valley a few years before to be with her family. She is by far the most "cultured" person there. Well into her eighties, she drives to Cape Town to concerts and the theater. She goes to music festivals in Europe and, despite arthritis, maintains a lively correspondence with friends in England and the United States. She went to school in England and had little contact with Afrikaners before she moved to the valley. Unlike many of the other English, she has begun to learn Afrikaans. ("It was as though I found myself in some little foreign land whose language I did not understand. I've met some Afrikaners who are very nice, but I feel as though I am standing on the outside. We'll be talking, and suddenly they say something in Afrikaans. They'll go into hoots and peals of laughter. I don't know what it is about, and stand there like an imbecile. I have to understand. So I've been learning a bit of their language.")

Catherine disapproves of the South African government. Her husband was active in liberal Jewish circles in Johannesburg. He was a strong supporter of Helen Suzman and the Progressive Party,* and Catherine herself helped out in their campaigns. "I am

*Helen Suzman, a well-known South African liberal, was the only parliamentary representative of the Progressive Party during the 1960s. After Smuts's defeat in 1948, the United Party became the opposition party, until its disintegration in the

not a political beast," she says. "My love is music. But I could help my husband entertain and could canvass." When Catherine's husband retired, they moved to Malawi. After his death, Catherine decided with great reluctance to come back to South Africa. "I had taken a very great dislike to the republic. I see a very, very dim future here. I can remember my father always saying that he didn't want us to remain in this country because it was not a white man's country. He said that before World War I. He foresaw what is happening now.

"We didn't of course. We were very lighthearted. We didn't realize what was going on around us when we were younger. We simply accepted it. People had a very good life, an easy life, a comfortable life. Black people are very remarkable in a way. They made magnificent domestic servants. Somehow or other you didn't think that they were unhappy.

"I haven't really thought about this period in a long time. We must have grown up in a very selfish atmosphere—not thinking deeply, I'm afraid, not thinking at all. In the early stage of my marriage, I was very occupied with survival. (My father didn't approve of my marriage and didn't give us a bean.) It was very exciting to be on our own, but we had a lot of anxiety, too, because we were determined to have children. You've got to think about how you're going to bring them up. My husband was only just beginning his career, and we had a house. He was determined to have a house—he wasn't going to *do* without one. So we really had to think a great deal about ourselves. I don't think I gave the problems of the Blacks any thought for the first five or ten years of my married life.

"When we started to be on our feet and established, I began to think about things. And then afterward, when we were really in a very comfortable position and my husband had done extremely well and had a partnership in this great firm, which had a wonderful reputation and was highly respected—it was all very lovely and I knew I had done the right thing in marrying him—I began to look around the world. I became a Zionist. I became very conscious of what was going on with the Blacks. I joined the Black Sash."

The Women's Defence of the Constitution League, known popularly as the Black Sash because its members wore black sashes in

_____

1970s. The more liberal Progressive Federal Party (PFP) grew rapidly at this time and became the official opposition.

their silent demonstrations, was one of several organizations that developed after the Nationalists came to power to protest unjust laws and acts by the government. It was founded to challenge the packing of the Appeal Court and the Senate and the taking of Coloureds off the common electoral roll. Today it is one of several white liberal organizations, primarily staffed by middle-class English women, which give guidance to non-whites and protest, as best they can, discriminatory acts and laws.

"The Black Sash was rather like the suffragettes: a group of madly dedicated, brave women who used to live with little suitcases packed and quite prepared to go to prison. I was very keen, but I don't think I'd have been brave enough to go to prison. I worked very hard for them—and for Zionism. I felt that after what had occurred with Hitler I was lucky not to have been sent to a gas chamber and that I must do my little bit.

"We protested the government's expulsion of the Black people's representatives from Parliament. We used to form long lines of vigilantes. We would go wherever we knew a minister or anyone else in power was arriving—airports, stations, docks—and stand there in our black sashes. They would be greeted by lines of downcast and miserable women making a public protest. It sounds a bit theatrical, but it made the people in power very uncomfortable. We brought the world's attention to it. We read about the Black Sash in overseas newspapers. But we couldn't stop the government. It was very depressing. And now the demonstrations have stopped. We are not permitted to 'assemble.' "

"Who was in the movement?" I asked.

"Mostly English, people of Scotch and Irish descent, a few Afrikaners, very few, and not too many Jews. I think the Jews were a bit afraid. Some of the husbands wouldn't let their wives join. They were frightened. It was just after the war.

"We protested the pass laws, too. They were dreadful. If our garden man left our garden to water some plants on the other side of the hedge and if he didn't have his pass in his working shirt (not wanting to get it dirty and spoiled because without it he was a lost soul), he could have been carted off by any policeman who happened to walk by. We wouldn't know where he was. We wouldn't know what had happened. We'd ring up the police stations, and if we happened to strike somebody a bit simpatico, we might learn his whereabouts. This used to happen all the time in the suburbs. It was driving us mad. Every evening you used to see lines of these people handcuffed to one another being dragged to the nearest police station. We succeeded in getting that done away with. Of course, the passes still exist, but there is usually less harassment.*

"When I began thinking, I was distressed to have to write a piece of paper. This was before they issued passbooks. I had an African man servant whom we absolutely adored. He had worked for us for over twenty-five years. We had built very beautiful servants' quarters for him and our other help. We all loved him. And this man was really noble. He was old enough to be my father, and yet he had to come to me if he wanted to go out. I would have to scribble, 'Please pass Amos until six o'clock—or eight o'clock—tonight.' Suddenly I became sort of revolted and ashamed about this. I talked to my husband about it. It made me eager to leave the Republic."

On May 31, 1961, fifty-nine years after the signing of the Treaty of Vereeniging, which ended the Anglo-Boer War, and fifty-one years after the establishment of the Union, South Africa became a republic. The dream of the Afrikaner Nationalists was realized. (A referendum on the issue of becoming a republic, limited, of course, to white voters, had been held the year before, on October 5, 1960: 850,458 votes were in favor of the republic; 775,878 were against it. The republic was created by a majority of 74,580 voters!) Celebrations were held at Vereeniging. A statue was erected. It depicts a man who was felled by a sword—Boer defeat—and the same man who brandishes the sword before the world. The inscription reads GEWOND MAAR NIE OORWONNE ("Wounded but not conquered").

*In 1982 a total of 206,022 people, roughly 23 per hour, were arrested for pass-law offenses. This was a 28 percent increase over the 160,000 arrests in 1981 (South African Institute of Race Relations, 1983, pp. 262–263).

7

MARRIAGE

Hennie

"I went on farming after the war. I had joined up with my cousin, and we weren't doing too badly. So I decided not to go back to varsity to finish up my engineering degree. I liked farming. I'd been doing it since I was twelve. I liked being independent.

"Well, one day I had to go up to Jo'burg for some farm equipment. We were beginning to import parts again, and I wanted to see whether or not I could get hold of some parts for a tractor we hadn't been able to use since before the war.

"My cousin asked me to stop in to see his daughters, who were in high school in Kimberley. He wanted me to give them some pocket money and to pay some of their fees. When I got to the school, I found that the older one was spending the weekend with Rose—her piano teacher. As I had to pay her too, for the lessons, I went out to see her. So that's how I met Rose.

"And the strange thing is that the moment I clapped my eyes on her, I was interested in her. I'd met many girls in my life, but Rose was the first one who really interested me. When I got back home, I said to my cousin's wife, 'I think you'd better invite this teacher down here for the school holiday.' And she did, and the very night Rose arrived, I asked her to marry me. So I always maintain that love at first sight is one of the biggest time-savers.

"When my cousin's wife discovered what was happening, she started spreading all sorts of rumors about Rose. She did everything she could to split us up, but I refused to listen to her.

"You see, Rose was English, and my brothers and cousins were never able to accept my dad's admonition to forget the war. They hated the English. It was just that simple. Rose's mother was an Afrikaner, but that didn't make any difference to them. Her home language was English, and that was what was important, that and the fact that she was Anglican. Even my mother got caught up in it and tried to stop me.

"We got married anyway. I wasn't going to let them stop me. We got married, and we left. My brother came down from the mines to take over the farm. He said he wasn't going to let me dishonor my father's name by bringing an English woman into the house that my father had built with his own hands."

Hennie stopped. He did not like talking about his marriage. I found this true of most Afrikaner men and, for that matter, most English-speaking ones too. Marriage talk among South African whites is very much woman's talk. For the Afrikaners, at least, this reluctance to talk about marriage is part of a general reluctance among men to talk about the more intimate side of their lives. It is unmanly. In part, I suppose, it can be attributed to their Calvinistic heritage. In their conversations with me, it was also a way of keeping distance. But Hennie's reluctance to talk about his marriage had less to do with manly *pudeur* or a desire to keep me at bay (he had ample means of doing this) than with the pain he felt. He left home angry at his brothers, his cousins, his mother, his entire family. He never made up with his brother who took over the farm, and he was only reconciled with his second brother a few years before. He did see his mother after his first child was born, but they were estranged again when he became an Anglican.

Although Hennie did, nevertheless, bring up his marriage several times in our meetings—it marked an important departure in his life —he could never bring himself to describe in detail exactly what had happened. (I did not push him. I hoped someday to find out about it from Rose.) I suspect that his cousin's wife accused Rose of looseness. Rose was a piano teacher and an *entertainer*. She had organized shows at the English school in Kimberley. One particularly malicious member of Hennie's congregation ("Of course I haven't been to the church since *he* asked us to embrace each other") said she found Rose a bit sallow and added that there was "a touch of the tar brush" in every Afrikaner. Like other members of the white congregation, she did not consider Rose properly English.

Rose is a sad, retiring, otherworldly woman in her late fifties. She was once clearly a beautiful woman, and she carries herself with the grace of a woman who knows herself to have been beautiful. She is in fact rather sallow, and spends much of her time in bed suffering from arthritis. Her deep-brown eyes show her suffering. They are nervous, distracted, sometimes bright and understanding and at other times hollow and uncomprehending. When they are hollow and uncomprehending, Rose seems to carry out her tasks automatically, without emotion or interest. When they are bright and understanding, she is alive, interested, and charming. Despite her arthritis and the other ailments she seems to suffer from, she carries out all the duties (and there are many) of a clergyman's wife with discipline and responsibility. She is a deeply religious woman—Hennie says that it was she who taught him what it means to be religious—and devotes much of her life to prayer. Like Hennie, she is charismatic and acts in accordance with the words of the Lord that she hears during her prayers. Her world is a sort of personal purgatory filled with symbolic significations that are lost to those about her. She views her suffering, the troubles she and Hennie have had, her sadness, as a test of her spiritual commitment and, like a martyr, she takes a certain solace in her suffering, her troubles, her sadness. They are signs that she is favored.

"There were incredible differences between us," Rose once told me. "I expected it because I had been in love with an Afrikaans cousin. I learned Afrikaans, Afrikaans cooking, Afrikaans songs, Afrikaans dancing. And then one day I realized that I could never be an Afrikaner. The differences are too great. It is impossible to straddle both worlds.

"Human beings hate difference. There is an apartheid of the heart. I have learned this through self-observation. And this apartheid of the heart can only be overcome through the power of the Lord. I am a very fastidious person and a very clean person. There is nothing I like better than to bathe. I sometimes have to go into Coloured houses. I have to walk through dirt. I have to see people who are black with filth. It upsets me. I hate filth. Still I do it. I embrace these people. I love them. But it is not a human love. Such love would be impossible. It is a love that comes from another power, a transcendent love, the love that comes through Christ."

Hennie is devoted to Rose with a devotion that comes with years of shared hardship. Their life was never easy. Rose's suffering, her nervousness, her distraction, her fragility, were always a burden to Hennie. At first he responded with irritation and anger and then with guilt-ridden patience. Today, like Rose, he looks at his life, their life, as a sort of spiritual test, but he does not endow it with the same sort of personalized symbolism that she does. He is too down to earth. He is at times inordinately proud of Rose, of her musical talent, of the poems she has written, of her ability to withstand the pressures she has been under, of her commitment to Christ. He is often worried about her as well. He fears for her health and seems concerned about what she will say or do in those situations that are not altogether routine. When I asked to interview her, he seemed reluctant to let me talk to her. In one of those gestures that are at once so frustrating and so revealing, she agreed and then refused. It seems that, praying to the Lord the night before we were to meet, Rose was "instructed" not to talk to me. "It was not because He thought it would be difficult for me," she explained a few weeks later, "but because He knew how much I liked to talk." Hennie seemed relieved, although our relations were embarrassed for several weeks after that. I was relieved too.

Rose's mother's family were Afrikaners, poor farmers who trekked for decades, hoping, always hoping, to find a promised land. Finally they settled in Kimberley. They watched fortunes being made and lost after the discovery of diamonds in 1867 along the Orange River. There were no diamonds on their few acres. They watched, too—with some satisfaction, one suspects—the disappointment of English adventurers who came to Kimberley and found not fortune but the grueling work of deep mining. (With the discovery of diamonds in the "blue earth" of some of Kimberley's volcanic pipes, diamond mining was transformed from a gamble into a big business, for such diamonds could only be retrieved through deep mining.) Rose's great-grandfather on her father's side was one such disillusioned fortune seeker. His sons took jobs where they could, and with the exception of Rose's grandfather, who remained in Kimberley, they left for the Transvaal when gold was discovered there in 1886. Rose's father was a bookkeeper for De Beers, which had by that time the monopoly on diamond production. He was a quiet man who was satisfied with balancing his books and a few beers after work.

Rose's mother was ambitious. It was she who pushed Rose, her only child, into piano playing. She had known poverty. She had married, as best she could, to climb out from under it. She was disappointed, I imagine, with her husband's lack of ambition. She spotted Rose's talent—and there was talent—at an early age and made sacrifices, tremendous sacrifices, to buy a piano and to give her daughter lessons. The piano would be her salvation. She watched Rose practice each day and pushed her further and further until the poor girl collapsed on the eve of an important competition for a scholarship to London. Then Rose's mother lost interest in her daughter. Rose became a piano teacher in Kimberley and not the great concert pianist of whom her mother had dreamed. When Rose announced her engagement to Hennie, so Hennie tells it, her mother didn't even bother to ask her fiancé's name. It was Rose's father who made a feeble attempt to dissuade her from marrying an Afrikaner.

"Rose didn't teach after we got married. We moved around a lot and didn't have the money for a piano. Then when we weren't doing too well financially, she decided to help out by teaching again. She got permission to use the school piano, and when she was sure she could still play well enough to teach, we hired one, and she gave lessons at home. She was always a perfectionist. When she was in school, she belonged to a little theater group. Once she submitted a play—she wrote and produced it—and won first prize in a national competition. Her English teacher came in second. She won a couple of more prizes, but when the national theater in Rhodesia asked to see her plays, she read them over, decided they weren't any good, and tore them up.

"She also wrote a lot of poems. I'll have to show you some of them. They would just come pouring out of her. I was much influenced by a lot of what she wrote. She was always more religious than I, and it was actually witnessing her that made me want to be a Christian. It was she who made me realize for the first time that there was a difference between being a Christian and a member of a church. I was a member of the church but I wasn't a Christian. No one can argue with me about that. That's how I saw myself, and after all, I think it's how you see yourself that's important. I saw that she was getting more out of life than I was. She had God in her life, and I didn't. And that made all the difference. It was then that I really wanted Him.

"Rose was always very close to God, but it wasn't until David,

our youngest son, became a Christian that she came to understand
the experiences she had been having all along. She never told anyone about these experiences. I didn't even know about them. She
didn't know that she was receiving the baptism of the spirit. She was
upset by these, and I acted strangely. She lost all her confidence. She
couldn't do the shopping. To cross the street was a major operation.
One night I actually had to ask a friend of ours, a Roman Catholic
priest, a man of great spiritual wisdom, to talk to Rose. I could do
nothing.

"He spent most of the night with her, at her bedside, and talked
to her. 'You talk about love,' he told her, 'well, then, you must take
it up. It's your cross, and you must bear it.' Then she went on a
retreat at one of our mission stations. She talked a lot to one priest
there—he's a bishop now—about her real desire to know God. That
night she prayed to know God and that night she met Christ for the
first time. They walked hand in hand, you know, even on the street.
Nobody else could see Him, but she knew He was there. And for
three days and for three nights He remained with her. And ever
since then she has never had another breakdown, and she never
will." Hennie uttered the last phrase with great conviction.

"Teaching had always been a tremendous strain for her. She
would get so emotionally involved in the whole thing that after a
while she wouldn't be able to take it. She always wanted everything
done the right way. I must say she was very talented as a teacher.
Other teachers used to say that she was the only one they knew who
could take a piece of wood and teach it to play the piano. She really
took to kids who were thought to have no musical ability whatsoever. If they had two hands, she could teach them to play.

"After that retreat, she began to organize musicals at an African
school to keep kids off the street and to give them something to do.
She got a friend to teach them dancing and another to set up a
percussion group. Eventually those kids got so good that she decided to have them give a public performance. A lot of African
artists began phoning up from all over Rhodesia to ask if they could
take part in the show. And that is when we first came up against
apartheid in Rhodesia. There were no apartheid laws for public
theater in Rhodesia, but the only hall that was big enough for Rose's
show was a farmers' hall. In its constitution it was stipulated that
Africans could only enter the hall to vote. Rose wanted to have a
multiracial audience. The parents of the African children who were

performing obviously wanted to see their kids. For six months Rose was climbing the wall, going from farmer to farmer to talk them into allowing the show. Finally they did. We invited a lot of top brass. That was to ensure a big audience. And they came, and the show was a great success. We actually made a profit, and Rose convinced the government and the State Lottery to contribute funds for a youth center for the Africans. That's the way she has always been. When she gets an idea into her head, there is no stopping her."

Irene Prinsloo

"On Saturday my husband and I went to a wedding. We came out of the church—it was a lovely service—and went to a very posh hotel. After the speeches, there was music and dancing. Kobus and I got such headaches that we had to take something for them. There was so much noise. There was a tremendous drum, beat after beat, louder and louder, and there was the blaring of the horns. I couldn't even hear what Kobus was saying, and he was sitting right next to me. There was no room for thought. I don't say a wedding must be all heartache and tears or even laughter, but there must be time to think about the fact that you are getting married. It seems to me young people today want to block everything out of consciousness. They don't want to think about the more serious side of life, the more biblical side of life. I don't know what they're trying to block out, but I do know that they are blocking out everything that is good and solid.

"Where I grew up, marriage was a big thing. You knew what you were doing. You were told what you were doing by your parents. It was the parents' privilege and duty to tell you about the virtues of marriage. I remember when Kobus came up to my parents to ask permission to marry me, my mother told me that she had always prayed that I would find the right man and that the Lord would guide me in my choice. She told me that I was very young to marry, too young, but that since Kobus was a very Christian man—a man who understood the meaning of Christian marriage—she and my father would give their consent.

"My father talked to me about the seriousness of marriage. He told me—and I have never forgotten his words—'Irene, if you find marriage to be a bed of roses, you lie in it. If you find it to be a bed of thorns, you lie in it, too. You don't get divorced.' There was a more stoical attitude to life up there. My father would say that it was a life of complete opposites. There would be no flowers for five years, and then suddenly there would be too many flowers for anybody to conceive of. It was the same with food. It was like slaughtering an animal. There would be a superabundance of meat, and then no meat. It was a different rhythm.

"I can't remember any unhappily married couples up there. There were no marriage problems. There were no problem children. People didn't look for problems. The problems were drought, sickness, and money. There wasn't even such a thing as happiness or unhappiness in marriage. It was a settled thing: Once you decided to marry a man, that was the man you would live with for the rest of your life. That was never questioned. Divorce was unheard of. Today we have one of the highest rates of divorce in the world.

"I do remember one woman, Tannie Frieda, who came to stay with us. Her husband drank too much. She wanted a divorce. When my parents heard about it, they insisted that she come to stay with us. The *dominee* came each day to talk to her. My father talked to her, and my mother did. Her friends came, and ours too. Everyone came to persuade her not to get a divorce. That was the way it was in those days. People rallied around someone who was in trouble. We were children and didn't know what was happening. I remember asking my mother why Tannie Frieda was staying with us when she had a house of her own. I remember asking why the *dominee* was always talking to her. Mommy explained that she was in a bit of trouble and that the *dominee* knew what was best for her. That was all she would tell us. Children were more protected in those days. (Now they watch *Dallas.*) Tannie Frieda did go back to her husband and remained with him until he died. It was never a question of her happiness. It was a question of fulfilling a promise she had made."

The Dominee

"We do not have many marriage problems in the valley," the *dominee* of the local Dutch Reformed church said. He has lived in Wyndal for nearly twenty years and is the most respected man in the valley. He has a calming presence and immediately inspires confidence in even those who approach him with mistrust and hostility. He has made a determined effort to improve relations with the English and offered them the church hall on several occasions. He has allowed them to use his church for those funerals that were too big for Hennie's church or the Methodist hall. He is, however, on poor terms with Hennie, and he has remained very distant from the liberal white *dominee* in Wyndal's Mission church. He has not encouraged the church board, so it is said, to increase the allowance they give the Mission church each year. It has remained the same in Wyndal, as in many South African parishes, for at least a decade, despite marked inflation in South Africa and the apparent financial need of the Mission church.

"The Dutch Reformed Church takes marriage very seriously. Our major problem is alcohol abuse. The husband drinks too much. Sometimes husbands and wives are not compatible. I've had several cases since I've been here. People do make mistakes. I try to find a solution, especially if the couple has children. A broken family is a *terrible* thing for children. If divorce is inevitable, then I try to arrange it in such a way that the husband and wife remain friends. This is not to say that the church thinks lightly of divorce. It does not.

"Sometimes an unmarried couple will come to see me because the girl is pregnant. I've had several cases in the last few years. They want to know whether or not they should marry. I always ask them if they intended to marry before the pregnancy. If they say yes, then I ask them if they love each other and feel they could be faithful to each other. I explain that they must not get married to solve the problem. I cannot put myself in a position of someone who has to give up a child, but I think it is better to give up the child than to be forced into a marriage that ends in a divorce. The church is, of course, against abortion. We have a social worker who comes here each week. It is she who would arrange for the adoption.

"Although the church is against all premarital sex, we have to face reality. We have to be tolerant. Living together without being married is another thing altogether. The church puts great value on the closeness of the family. The family is the cornerstone of the community. We stress the importance of maintaining good relations among family members. We believe in infant baptism, because it gives the parents a sense of responsibility toward their young. It enhances their own relationship to each other. Fortunately, here in the *platteland*, in the country, people living out of wedlock are very rare."

* * *

The older generation of Afrikaner farmers in the valley are all married to Afrikaner women. Nearly all of their children married Afrikaners. (It is in this generation that there have been several divorces.) It is still too soon to determine whether or not their grandchildren will marry within the Afrikaner community. Even for the older generation, however, the valley is not an entirely endogamous unit. Many of the farmers married women from neighboring villages or elsewhere in South Africa.

Beatrix Roussouw says that it is better for children to marry within their own culture. There are enough strains in any marriage, she explains, without adding those that come from living with someone from another background. ("Background"—"agtergrond"—is frequently used among white South Africans to refer in a rather neutral way to cultural, regional, and class origins. Racial identity is of course assumed. Language, religion, and family are important components of one's background.)* Beatrix speaks from experience. Her son, Andre, married Tamara, an English-speaking woman who, in Beatrix's eyes, has led him astray. He has left the church and become a Baptist. (I should note that many of the farmers who married English women have left or have flirted with leaving the Dutch Reformed Church for one of the more enthusiastic churches that are spreading among the middling middle classes in white South Africa.) Beatrix feels that the English are sexually freer. She asks me how American men feel about marrying girls who are not virgins. "I think it causes divorces," she says. "It is all a question of religion. The more religious you are, the more you are against premarital sex." She admits that divorce is no longer the disgrace it was when she was a young woman, but she would be very unhappy if her children were to divorce.

Beatrix approves of birth control provided that it does not harm the woman, but she is against abortion, which is illegal in South Africa. She did admit that if a white woman were raped and became pregnant by a Black man, she should be allowed to have an abortion. (She told me about a woman who was given permission to have an

---

*"Background" relates to the notion of ethnos—roughly ethnicity—that pervades Afrikaans anthropological thinking (Sharp, 1981). "Culture," "ethnos," and perhaps to a lesser extent "background" can all substitute for "race" in white South African social rhetoric.

abortion and then could not find a doctor willing to perform it.) She is against abortion in those cases where a white woman had been raped by a white man and sees no reason for an abortion if a Black woman were raped by a white man. She had difficulty acknowledging such a situation. She is very much in favor of birth control for Blacks, who, she says, reproduce like rabbits, and like other whites in the valley, she has tremendous praise for the government nurse who literally chases after those Coloured women who fail to show up for their trimonthly birth control shot. (There is a local, multiracial clinic in town that is concerned with family planning, immunization, venereal disease, tuberculosis, and child welfare. It caters mostly to Coloureds. Birth control pills or shots, as well as condoms, are given free of charge. Sterilization can be arranged for those who request it and for those afflicted with certain heart and kidney conditions, as well as for those who suffer from mental retardation, provided a psychiatrist, a minister, and a physician all agree.) Both Om Max and Beatrix Roussouw are against interracial marriage. They fear that if such marriages were legalized in South Africa, there would be no controlling their number. Many of the older Afrikaner men with whom I spoke could only conceive of encounters between men and women of different races in mechanical, sexual terms. As male-oriented as they were, they did recognize the complexity of relations between white men and women. Om Max asked me whether there were a lot of interracial marriages in the United States. He doubted me when I said that there were relatively few. "What would stop them?" he asked. "If Black men and white women are allowed to go dancing together, well, then, they . . . There'd be a lot of marriages."

Tamara Roussouw

"I think women are very lonely here. Their husbands are out working all day. They have maids who do the housework. And what have they to do? Marketing. But you can only do so much marketing. I think that is why birthday parties are so important. It gives mothers a chance to get together while their children play. Some mothers bake fancy cakes and make other food, which the children only throw away. I just make a simple tart. I don't give expensive presents. I'd never spend more than a rand, but there are mothers here who spend five rand or even more for a present. And I don't believe in giving children little trinkets to take home. I don't think children should be spoiled."

Tamara had just invited my daughter to a birthday party for her son and was briefing my wife on birthday customs. Tamara is a handsome woman in her late thirties, with fine leathery skin and a deep, throaty voice that suggests a sophistication she does not in fact possess. She seems never to have really blossomed. She is anxious to differentiate herself from the Afrikaners with whom she lives but has never been accepted by the English farming families. When they talk about the first English to have moved into the valley, they never mention Tamara. Nor do the Afrikaners. In English eyes Tamara not only married beneath her but made the tragic mistake of marrying an un-Anglicized Afrikaner. Although they show some concern for her—"she had a very unfortunate childhood"—their concern is tempered by the "fact" that she should have known better.

"I came from Eshowe in Zululand. We were mostly English there. (Both my parents are descended from the 1820 settlers.) I didn't really know any Afrikaners until I met Andre. We fell very much in love. I was a nursing sister, and Andre came to the hospital with one of his boys, whose foot had been crushed under a tractor. That's where we met. I was immediately swept off my feet. He was shy, very shy, and I was afraid I would lose him. But I didn't. It was hard. I wanted very much to marry him, but we couldn't even meet in public. It would be so scandalous for him to marry an English woman! After his mother found out about me, she would say, 'Now it's not proper for you to be seeing Tamara every night. You should only see her on Saturdays.' Imagine, he was twenty-five! She did everything in her power to curtail our relationship.

"Andre kept saying that he was going to tell his mother and father that he wanted to marry me, but every time he went home, he got cold feet and said nothing. Finally I couldn't stand it any longer. I booked a passage to Australia, where I had managed to get a nursing job. I told Andre that I was going for a year, that he would have to live without me, and that he could see how he felt at the end of the year. In fact, I planned never to come back. I wanted to make a clean break of it: to forget Andre, to forget South Africa, to begin a new life.

"When I got to Australia, all I could do was to think of Andre and South Africa. I missed him so. I couldn't stand the Aussies. I couldn't stand the way they talked. It was so rough, so uncouth. They were always cursing and swearing. I knew I'd made a mistake. I wrote to Andre, and a few months later he sent for me. He had finally told his parents. They agreed reluctantly. His mother was particularly upset. She told Andre that he was making the mistake of his life.

"My father didn't care what I did. He never did. My mother asked me why I wanted to lead the life of an Afrikaner. 'You'll be stuck in a little village,' she said. 'Whatever the other women wear, you'll have to wear. Their manners will have to be your manners. You'll be closed in, confined, unhappy. You'll lose all your freedom. Don't do it.' But I did it." There was a muted determination in Tamara's voice.

"I was so in love with Andre that I surrendered to him completely. I told him that our children could be Afrikaners. I agreed to send them to Afrikaans schools and to the Dutch Reformed church. (We were married in the Reformed church.) I agreed to everything he asked. I didn't realize that it was not he who was asking but his mother. Now, of course, I don't think it was such a good idea."

Tamara described the rules by which Afrikaners name their children. The first son is named after his paternal grandfather; the second, after his maternal grandfather; the first daughter after her maternal grandmother; the second daughter, after her paternal grandmother. Other children are named according to parental whim. Often Afrikaners will create new names by combining family names. This was Tamara's tactic. She was not getting along with her mother-in-law when her first daughter was born. She wanted to name her Camilla, but Beatrix and her son would not hear of this. She was to be named after her maternal grandmother (even though she was English). Tamara agreed but only if she could name the baby Dorothana, a combination of her mother's first two names, Dorothy Anne. Camilla would be the baby's middle name. Beatrix and Andre had to agree. Of course, no one could bear to call the child Dorothana. She is in fact called Camilla, as Tamara had planned all along.

Tamara laughed triumphantly as she described her ruse. "Camilla was my second child. The first one died at birth. I wanted to go to an English doctor in Cape Town, but I was made to feel like a spoiled little English girl. Was I too good for an Afrikaans doctor?

I didn't have much confidence in him. I had worked in the local hospital. In fact he kept me in induced labor for forty-eight hours before he performed a Cesarean. The baby—it was a little boy—was perfectly healthy but he died. Any reasonable obstetrician would have performed the Cesarean in twelve hours. He never gave me anything to ease my pain during the whole forty-eight hours of labor. I don't know how to describe it. It was as though it was my lot to suffer. He never talked to me about what happened. He knew I was a nursing sister and wanted to keep me in ignorance.

"Andre didn't talk about it either. He had the baby buried before he was named. This was very offensive to me. For an Anglican— and I was still an Anglican then—a baby that is buried without a name is forever doomed to purgatory. I still think about him, always without a name. I have never been able to give him a name even in my imagination. It is as though part of me just disappeared."

Tamara could not go on. Finally I asked her why Andre had had the little boy buried without naming him. Had Andre named the boy after his paternal grandfather, she explained, the family name would have been lost forever. He could not give a second son the name of one who had died. " 'But couldn't you have named him anything?' I kept asking Andre, and he kept saying that had the baby been named, it would have had to be named after his father. I couldn't understand. I don't remember very much from that time except that I was very lonely. There was no one I could talk to.

"I was pregnant again within six months. My wounds had barely healed. Camilla was born by Cesarean, and Beatie, my second daughter, too. The doctors told me that I was not to have any more children. (After the death of my first child, I was allowed to go to Cape Town to an English doctor. Andre still wanted a son who would take over the farm one day, and so I found myself pregnant again. When Maxie was born, the doctor tied my tubes. I had asked him to do so without telling Andre. I hadn't wanted to name Maxie Maximillian. I wanted to give him a lighter name, an English name, but Beatrix fumed and fussed and Om Max stomped around looking very hurt. What choice had I?

"I have always been able to speak to the girls in English, and from time to time even Beatrix speaks to them in English. Andre will not allow me to speak to Maxie in English. I do sometimes when he is not around, but when Maxie talks English, it is always with an accent and an Afrikaans inflection. 'I want you to me up pick.' It saddens me. My own son is not able to speak to his grand-mother. And the girls, they are always taking advantage of him in English."

Tamara in fact runs an Afrikaner household. She dresses as other Afrikaner women in the valley do, and she has adopted their man-ners and mannerisms. She has even begun to speak English with an Afrikaans accent, and I have caught Afrikaans turns of phrase in her speech. A few years ago, shortly after Maxie was born, she became a Baptist, and now Andre too has received a second baptism in a cold mountain stream above the valley. He has been expelled from the Dutch Reformed Church. ("When someone is baptized a second time," the local *dominee* explained, "he is rejecting an important doctrine of the Reformed Church: He is rejecting the covenant his parents made with God when they had him baptized.") Andre and Tamara now pray together daily for instruction from the Lord on all manner of things. Andre had hoped to modernize the farm, to put in irrigation, and to replant his fields in palmettos, but he could not raise sufficient capital to make the improvements. He works hard, harder than most farmers in Wyndal, and sometimes talks about selling the farm. Such talk is fantastical: Shortly after Maxie was born, Om Max and Beatrix had the farm placed in trust for their grandson in such a way that neither Andre nor his wife could sell it. They were afraid that Tamara would convince Andre to sell the farm and, in their eyes, his and Maxie's cultural heritage.

Marriages are always more than the union of a man and a woman —even in the most modern societies, with their atrophied families and hypertrophied individuals. They end a waiting. They bring together in a ritual instant—an instant that denies the daily routines that will inevitably follow—members of two (in a certain sense four and even eight) families, each coming, as it were, from somewhere else. They are moments of tension, moments of structural and sym-bolic reorientation for all the participants. Marriages are flush with emotion and feeling, the emotions and feelings that ought to be— love and affection, tenderness and warmth—and those that ought not to be but are. They echo a past. They anticipate a future. They "come," in William Carlos Williams's words, "to have a shuddering implication." Old dreams are forgotten, even before new ones can be formulated. Secret expectations, always at the edge of magic, come to a halt before that empty instant, that void, that marks both an end and a beginning. Dreams, hopes, and expectations begin again. A new waiting starts—a new realism.

Caroline Du Plessis

Caroline Du Plessis does not live in Wyndal, but she grew up there. She still thinks of it as her home. She romanticizes it. She describes brilliant weddings with red carpets leading from the church and magnificent banquets with traditional dancing. She thinks a lot about the past. She suffers from cancer, as have all the women in her mother's family for several generations now. She is descended from Sarel Cilliers, the extravagant prophet who made the covenant with God on the eve of battle with the ferocious Zulu chief Dingaan. She says that the cancers that have ravished her family are God-given tests of her faith and the faith of her sisters and cousins, her mother, her grandmother, and aunts, all of whom, she is proud to admit, died, some in excruciating pain that could no longer be dulled with morphine, without ever questioning their faith. They remained true to Cilliers's covenant.

"I have sat at the bed of the dying. I've seen people die. And I have observed that there is a vast difference between the children of God and those who do not believe. The children of God look as though they are greeting the heavenly Father. Those who have lived a wild, godless life show a terrible struggle. They can't seem to cross over."

Now in her late fifties, Caroline is a bitter woman. It is not the cancer that has made her bitter. If anything, it gives meaning to her life. It is a sign of God's recognition, of her worthiness to bear a cross, of the significance of her family. No, Caroline is bitter because her worldly dreams have never come true. She never had a red carpet (purely apocryphal in any event) rolled out before her as she and her husband, Dietrich, left the church. She never had a grand banquet, although she had a nice party with lots of mutton and ham, watermelon and fig preserve, milk tarts and a big white wedding cake, and, of course, dancing. Caroline is bitter because she and Dietrich are poor. He was to have inherited a farm, an important farm—though not as vast a farm, not as productive a farm, as Caroline would have had it—but then his father died and his mother remarried and somehow managed to leave the farm to his half brother. "We fought for it in court. We spent what little money we had on lawyers, and we have nothing, absolutely nothing, to show for it."

"My daughter, Christina," Caroline explained at our second meeting, "married an agricultural engineer. They have an eight-month-old son. After they married they moved to the northern Transvaal. They're divorced now. He divorced her before the baby was born. She is now a nursing sister in Port Elizabeth. Christina loved him, but when she told him she was pregnant, he told her that it was the most unfortunate day in his life, that he never wanted a baby, and that he had not loved her for the last three years. Christina divorced him because she felt she was committing adultery. He still lives up in the Transvaal. All the engineers up there are divorced. Life is rough up there. It is no place for a family.

"Christina loved a Hollander. He was a lawyer. He was very bright, but he was a Roman Catholic. When Christina told me about him, I was very upset. I told her that her forefathers were Huguenots and had fled France because of the Roman Catholics. Now she wanted to betray that tradition by marrying a Catholic. We finally persuaded her, and she gave up the Hollander and married the engineer. We feel sorry now that we interfered. She might have been happy with the Catholic. But we could never see our way to letting her marry a Catholic. We prayed, my husband and I, that she give him up. She met the engineer soon after she broke off her engagement. He was a friend of the Hollander and asked her if she still loved him. She said she still did, and he told her he would make her love *him*. When they announced their engagement, we were thrilled. His father was a minister in the Dutch Reformed Church. They were more in our tradition.

"When Christina called to tell us she was divorcing her husband, we were shocked to our roots. We could not understand what had happened. She came to stay with us. Her baby was born here. I will never forget the morning the baby was baptized. She stood up all alone in the church. Everyone in the congregation cried. She was given envelopes with ten, twenty, and even fifty rand for the baby.

"She worked in a hospital here until the day the baby was born. It was born by Cesarean. It was very tragic. The child choked on the amniotic fluid and could not breathe. They had to give it one-hundred-percent oxygen. Normally under those circumstances, the child would have been an imbecile. But we prayed. We went to

Dominee Malan—he has the power of healing—and he prayed for the baby. He said, 'We didn't ask for an imbecile but for a baby born in Your image.' It is remarkable how the baby thrived on the oxygen."

A year later I met Caroline again. She told me the baby was doing fine. He walked at ten months and was talking now all the time. She had gone back to Dominee Malan, a charismatic minister in the Dutch Reformed Church who occasionally leads prayer groups in Wyndal, and had asked him to pray that Christina remarry her ex-husband. He did, and since then, according to Caroline, the engineer has been coming down from the Transvaal to see Christina and the baby whenever he can. Caroline thinks they'll remarry.

The English farmers also have their marriage stories, but as they are only recent arrivals, few take place in Wyndal. Although they speak more openly (to me at least) about family, by which they also mean class and money, they are reluctant to enter into details about themselves and others. They prefer a quick, summary phrase or two. They often talk about someone marrying into money or into a good family. They understand the success or failure of a marriage less in terms of background or tradition, terms that, like *kultuur* and *ethnos*, the Afrikaners tend to reify, than in terms of character. (Rarely do they talk of things like unconscious motivation or blind desire. Their understanding of "character" is reminiscent of a Victorian popular novel.) It is not that background is unimportant but rather that it is so obviously important that only a fool, like Tamara Roussouw, would marry out of it. Of course, marriages upward (on whatever basis) are praised and envied by those below and "understood" by those above.

Marriages across ethnic boundaries, to Afrikaners, Germans, or Jews, are at best acceptable, providing the spouse comes from a good Anglicized family, preferably with money, and is willing to forfeit his or her background. In such marriages, English—English South African—culture is dominant and sets the appropriate standards of demeanor and decorum. It is my impression that marriages between English men and non-English women are more acceptable than those between English women and non-English men. Given the dominant position of the man in the white South African family, it is felt that there is a danger the husband will revert to type in such marriages and draw his English wife into an alien and unacceptable way. Such marriages are always carefully watched. At times even Hugo Malan's relationship with Peggy is interpreted in terms of his Afrikaner background even though he is almost obsessively English in his manner and thinking. Several English mothers were concerned that, having moved from distinctly English communities like Durban or Salisbury to a predominantly Afrikaner community, their children might well fall in love with an Afrikaner. I was sometimes led to believe that this fear of intimacy was in part responsible for the English families' sending their children off to school in Cape Town.

Although divorce, always a source of gossip, is frowned upon by the English farmers, they do not attach much stigma to it. "It is better to get divorced than to have an unhappy family," Carol Reid says. They are all in favor of birth control, and a few of the more liberal believe that abortion should be legalized, although the majority feel that it should only be permitted under certain circumstances, when, for example, the life of the mother is endangered or when there is a high risk that the baby will be deformed or mentally deficient. Premarital sex is acknowledged as a reality, but most parents prefer not to consider their own children's behavior. There are several families who have refused to send their children to Rhodes University in Grahamstown because it is notoriously "free."

Boys should be given an "international education," that is, one in which they will be able to find a good job abroad if they have to leave South Africa. There is less stress on girls' education, though ideally they should also be prepared to find work abroad. Both sons and daughters are expected to take their father's career advice very seriously and, at least in the valley, they usually follow it. Jack Freeling's son had thought of studying law but readily agreed to study accounting when his father pointed out that if he studied the Roman-Dutch law of South Africa, he would never be able to find a job in the law anywhere else in the world. Peter Cooke says that he does not much care what his daughers do. They will probably be married if they have to leave South Africa, and girls can always find a job as a secretary or a receptionist. Boys are expected to complete their military service before marrying, and they are even expected to complete it if they plan to leave South Africa permanently. "They have a debt to their country," the parents say, and young men echo, "I have a debt to my country." Women are expected to work until they are married or until they have their first child, and then to give up their careers. In their free time, they can serve on charity boards or get involved in various arts and crafts. Several women in the valley are potters, and others make lamp shades, macrame hangings for flowerpots, crocheted wall hangings, and country-bohemian dresses and blouses. They are subordinate to their husbands, and although there is some talk about feminism, no one takes it particularly seriously.

Carol Reid

Carol Reid says she was relieved when her daugher Janet gave up an Afrikaner whom she had been seeing for over a year, but she is worried about Janet's future. She would like to see Janet married. She is now twenty-five and, Carol says, should be starting a family.

"I didn't put any pressure on her to stop seeing Piet. She must lead her own life. But I think she would be happier with an English man. She had a wonderful boyfriend when she was at varsity. Duncan and I hoped she would marry him. But it didn't work out. She is an independent girl. She wanted to spend a year in England. In fact she spent almost two years there. She earned her passage and left with a few hundred rand. I was so worried about her. But that is what girls do nowadays. She managed to get odd jobs here and there and had a wonderful time. When she returned to South Africa, she said she no longer loved Michael, though he was still deeply in love with her.

"She shares a flat in Cape Town with two other girls and works at a wildlife commission there. She studied biology and was always a bit of a tomboy. She's very different from her sister, Helen, who was always a homebody. Helen is happily married and lives in Durban with her two sons. Her husband works for an office supply company. She's just written to tell me that he may be transferred to Johannesburg. I hope not. I don't think Jo'burg is the place to raise children. It is really the rat race. They say it is like New York City, but I don't suppose it really is. It isn't big enough.

"Little Duncan—we always called him Little Duncan so as not to confuse him with his father—works for Anglo-American. He married just before you came out here, and he and his wife live in Rondebosch in a flat near the university. They're saving to buy a house, but with the price of houses going up every day now, they have found themselves having to wait longer than they expected. Duncan's wife, Anne, works for IBM. She says she'll go on working even after they have children. Of course, she can do a lot of her work at home. She is apparently very clever and designs programs. She's still young and doesn't realize what a responsibility children are."

Carol continues in a grandmotherly fashion. What she fails to tell me, others in the valley have: Janet has led a wild life, Helen is a sweet but not overly intelligent homebody, and Duncan's wife is half-Jewish. Gossip is intense among Wyndal's English farmers. What they keep to themselves is often revealed by their neighbors. Returning to the valley after a ten-month absence, I found that people had forgotten what they had already told me and gossiped freely.

RHODESIA

Hennie

"When we got married, Rose and I bought a new car and went up to Rhodesia. We went for a month, on holiday, but also to look around. A farmer up there gave me a job, so we stayed. I wanted to make a complete break. A cousin of mine had been telling me what a wonderful country Rhodesia was. That's what put the idea in my head. He was planning to move up there too, but he never got there.

"Rose and I liked the country. It was a young person's ideal—stacks of opportunity. It was a wide-open country. The sky was the limit. It was all up to you. There was a kind of frontier spirit about the place. I suppose it was like your Wild West. It wasn't an easy life. In the beginning everyone struggled together and helped one another. There would be a bloke who had a string of farms. He would sell one off to someone who had five or ten years to pay for it. He was getting a good rate of interest and was helping out someone else who needed the money. But then suddenly things changed. The price of tobacco jumped incredibly. Everyone started making money, and a new group of farmers moved in. They weren't interested in developing the country. They were just interested in making a quick buck. No one helped anyone else anymore. It was at this stage that the crookery began.

"Basically I don't find much difference between the Rhodesian and the South African. The lives of both are based on having a lot of servants in order to have time to do the things that really matter. Of course, what really matters is having time to do nothing. They don't want things to change because that means they'll have to give up their way of life. It's this way of life, not Western civilization or Christianity or anything like that, they're defending. It's just privilege.

"In the old days things were different. Agreements were made on a handshake. There was an old man named Mac who discovered gold but didn't have the money to develop his mine. He was standing at a bar one evening talking to two strangers. He offered them each a third of his mine if they would give him x amount of money. They took out their checkbooks and wrote down the amount he wanted and shook hands on it. He went off and opened up his mine and for the next fifty years the mine was run on that verbal agreement made in a pub over a pint of beer or a whiskey. That was the old spirit.

"Then there was a bloke who came to Rhodesia with five pounds in his pocket. Some little bank clerk made a mistake in his account, and one of his checks bounced when it shouldn't have. He sued the bank for defaming his character, and they settled for five thousand pounds. With that he bought a farm and had a very good first season and bought a second farm and then a third. He wanted to be a millionaire and even divorced his wife because she couldn't enter into his spirit. He never paid any salaries. He just gave bonuses at the end of the year—fantastic bonuses if the year were good. It was always a gamble. He never let up on his men. There was one young bloke who came to work for him and whose wife was expecting her first child. He asked for a day's leave to take her to the hospital. 'My lorry is scheduled for tomorrow,' the old bloke said. 'She can go in on the lorry. Your job's on the farm and not running around town.' So the poor woman had to wait a day before giving birth and had to go into town on a lorry. And when she was due to come home from the hospital, she had to wait again for the scheduled lorry.

"I was actually offered a job on one of his tobacco farms, but thank God I didn't take it. It was fifty miles to the nearest doctor. With children you can't take that kind of risk. The bloke eventually made his million, but the number of others who were trampled around along the way isn't to be believed.

*   *   *

Hennie tells many such stories. They are a white Rhodesian's folk-lore. They are stories of extravagant possibility, ruthless success, and wild failure. They are not tales of moral edification or spiritual growth. They pose no questions. They cast no doubt. They proclaim a cliché of rugged individualism and a boundless materialism. Success and failure are measured in Rhodesian dollars. They are the stories of a wild frontier, but a frontier without noble heroes, without the cowboy of virtuous heart and solemn purpose who sets himself like Saint George against the powers of evil in a Manichaean universe.[1]

There was never the lawlessness of the American West in Rhodesia—the British South Africa Company quickly set up a rela-tively efficient administrative structure[2]—and the tales are of a fron-tier whose possibilities are of the diamond fields of Kimberley or the gold mines of the Transvaal. They are perhaps more realistic than the tales of the Great American West, which, for whatever reason, was always cast in grandiose mythic terms. They do at times, as does Hennie, refer to a sort of golden age of disinterested reciprocities, in which a handshake was worth more than a contract, but it was still an age of checkbooks and suits at law.

The golden age of Rhodesia contrasts with the self-interested world in which millionaires are made and little men falter. They, the little men, are the necessary sacrifice of the big men, the millionaires. "But the number of others who were trampled around along the way isn't to be believed." Richard Turner, Mary Turner, and even the newcomer, the still sensitive Tony Marston, are the sacrifice to men like Charlie Slatter in Doris Lessing's first novel, *The Grass Is Singing*.

> Slatter had been a grocer's assistant in London. He was fond of telling his children that if it had not been for his energy and enterprise they would be running round the slums in rags. He was still a proper cockney, even after twenty years in Africa. He came with one idea: to make money. He made it. He made plenty. He was a crude, brutal, ruthless, yet kind-hearted man, in his own way, and according to his own impulse, who could not help making money. He farmed as if he were turning the handle of a machine which would produce pound notes at the other end. He was hard with his wife, making her bear unnecessary hardships at the beginning; he was hard with his chil-dren, until he made money, when they got everything they wanted; and above all he was hard with his farm labourers. They, the geese

that laid the golden eggs, were still in that state where they did not know there were other ways of living besides producing gold for other people. They know better now, or are beginning to. But Slatter believed in farming with the sjambok. It hung over his door, like a motto on a wall: "You shall not mind killing if it is necessary."[3]

What distinguishes the novelist's tale from the tales of Rhodesians, and even Hennie's, is the presence of the laborer, the Black man. The Black man, the *sine qua non* of success, is as irrelevant as the tools the European uses.

The tales that Hennie tells are told too, with greater passion perhaps, by those Rhodesians, the "when we's," who have moved south to a "safer haven." (Hennie and Rose never really considered themselves Rhodesians.) "When we were in Rhodesia" has become a sort of paradise. Rhodesia itself is idealized and romanticized. The "when we's" talk of its beauty: the balancing rocks split by white-barked figs, the baobabs, the kaffir-orange trees, the elephant troops, the lion prides, and the occasional leopard, the jungly low-veld. When they speak of the smell of the fields of sunburnt wheat and tobacco, tears often come to their eyes. (Olfactory memories appear strongest for them, as they often do for the *pieds noirs* who were forced out of North Africa.) They tell the same tales of success and failure that they used to tell when they were in Rhodesia, but now they are more intensely personal, as though they are filling the dead space of memory with illusory intimacy and life. They are stories of an age that is no more. They are filled with nostalgia, rancor, and bitterness. The "when we's" say they were let down by the British —by the outside world with its economic sanctions. In Durban they have an Independence Dance on November 11 to commemorate the day in 1965 that Ian Smith declared Rhodesian independence.* Their stories are followed inevitably by a new genre of tales: tales of how the Black man has messed everything up now that he has come to power. They warn the white South Africans of the peril of giving in to the Black man—and are resented as such. The Black man is at least recognized in these new tales.

The tales the "when we's" tell are, of course, part of the folklore of South Africa. Rhodesia was for many white South Africans the

*In 1983 the Independence Dance was held in the meeting hall of the Moths, the Majestic Order of Tin Hats, a British veterans' organization. A portrait of Queen Elizabeth II, against whom the Smith government rebelled, loomed over the gathering (New York *Times,* November 30, 1983).

"positive" frontier they never knew in South Africa, and today they often forget the danger, the risks, and the hardships of early farming there.[4] By contrast, the South African hinterland was less a land of rich possibility with close ties to the Cape than an emptiness in which to take flight, to escape, as the Voortrekkers did, the evils of the British, to isolate oneself even from outposts like Cape Town of a distant and untrustworthy civilization. A "negative" frontier, it was always fraught with danger. It was the place of the laager, the circle of ox wagons that formed each night to protect the trekkers from hostile natives, savage animals, and all of the personifications of evil that must surely have haunted their minds. The Dutch East India Company never took southern Africa seriously nor, for that matter, did the British, until diamonds and gold were discovered. Then there was a rush into the emptiness; but a rush is different from the settling of a frontier. It is quick, singleminded, exploitative, a thrust that is ultimately indifferent to the landscape. One need think only of the ugly dross mountains of the Rand. Diamonds are to be found, gold is to be mined, they are to be exported, and gain is to be made. No one on a rush thinks of settling down, though many, if not most, do. Theirs are not the dreams of the frontier farmer, who sees his future there before his eyes. Their dreams are back home. (The rush for diamonds, for gold, for whatever rather than the settling of the frontier, has given the opponents of imperialism much of their most potent imagery.)

Something of this spirit of the rush affected the way in which at least some of the whites saw Rhodesia—the newcomers Hennie talked about who moved in after the skyrocketing of the price of tobacco, but earlier adventurers too, who sought gold but were willing to try their hand at anything else that promised them wealth. On any frontier that offers large prospects there are of course the grand schemers, cunning, callous, and unscrupulous, who as often as not hide under the guise of gentlemanly manners and a self-righteous moralism, and the lesser swindlers and cheats, petty scoundrels who prey on men like Hennie—who see in the handshake possibilities not to be found in the written contract or the registered deed. But even for these schemers and scoundrels, as for most Rhodesians, I imagine, Rhodesia offered the possibility not only of becoming a millionaire back home but of building little kingdoms in which one day they could lead "the good life." It was for these kingdoms that they fought for twenty-odd years, and it is back to these kingdoms, the farms, the homes, the businesses, that those who left, the "when we's," look with nostalgia and bitterness. Their tales of Rhodesia idealize the kingdoms. Their tales of Zimbabwe justify their move, for they have always to convince themselves that they had to move and that they did move at the right time.

For the South African the tales of Zimbabwe are proof of his need to hold firm against the Black man. Zimbabwe has become a stage on which one possible scenario of South Africa's future is played out. Its news is reported daily in newspapers. It is talked about continually. One of Duncan Reid's Rhodesian friends sent him a tape in which he described melodramatically his fears and hopes during the first few months after Robert Mugabe's election. Duncan played it almost nightly to friends, many of whom recorded it for themselves and their friends. Zimbabwe is a place both of hope, for there are utopian fantasies that it will all work out in the end, and of dread, for there is the more prevalent "knowledge" that it will never work out. No one, in Wyndal at least, talks about South Africa's interference in the internal affairs of Zimbabwe. What was once a frontier has become a border. The old magistrate in one of the Empire's outposts in J. M. Coetzee's parable *Waiting for the Barbarians* observes:

> But last year stories began to reach us from the capital of unrest among the barbarians. Traders travelling safe routes had been attacked and plundered. Stock thefts had increased in scale and audacity. A party of census officials had disappeared and been buried in shallow graves. Shots had been fired at a provincial governor during a tour of inspection. There had been clashes with border patrols. The barbarian tribes were arming, the rumour went; the Empire should take precautionary measures, for there would certainly be war.[5]

From a land of possibility Rhodesia, now Zimbabwe, became like Angola, Mozambique, and even Botswana, a land of danger to be guarded against. It is the preservation of a frontier, rather than the establishment of a border, that the fighting in the South West is all about.

Hennie

"Yes, in many ways it was difficult." I had asked Hennie if his life had been very difficult in Rhodesia. "Once I actually got myself a job in Canada. Rose didn't want to go though. She said she couldn't bear the cold . . .

"I did find the farmers in Rhodesia more in touch with what was happening on the experimental stations than farmers in South Africa were. They were prepared to put new ideas into practice. South African farmers are very conservative, especially the fruit farmers here in the valley. It wasn't until the English started moving in that they stopped farming the way their great grandfathers did . . .

"Things don't always work out the way you expect them to. I think partially it was God who wanted me to do something completely different. I was on the wrong track, and that's why whatever I tried didn't work out. If it had, I never would have become a priest.

"I wasn't getting much of a salary on the first farm I worked on but I was to get quite a bonus at the end of the season. The man I worked for had had polio and was confined to a wheelchair. It turned out—I didn't know it at the time—that he had had sixteen managers in the previous two years! Some of them didn't last a week. He had about seven thousand acres, a big dairy, and there were pigs and of course maize. About twelve hundred acres were under cultivation.

"He must have had a hundred fifty workers. I remember arranging for three hundred fifty kids to get vaccinations. Most of them were Mashona, but there were a few Matabele to work the cattle. They're cattle people. They're born with a sense of how to handle cattle. The Mashona are farmers. They can't handle cattle. They're a clever people. They've had to learn to live by their wits because the Matabele were always chasing them. We also had some Malawis. I like working with them. Whenever I start up a farm, I like to get a gang of Malawis. They're terribly loyal. Once they've accepted you, they'll never look for another job. They'll die with you. They're more subdued than the Matabele. Once a Matabele has had a few drinks, he becomes aggressive . . .

"Well, the first year we had a most devastating season. The rains came late and six weeks later it was all over. Hardly anybody had any crops that year. I was getting a little bit on the pigs and a little bit on the flock, but the big profit was to be on the maize, and that didn't come. So there's your big chance you see, and then suddenly there's nothing.

"So I chucked that job and went to work on a big ranch. They could pay me a little more. They had about twelve thousand acres and wanted me to open it up. We arranged everything but the commission I was going to get on the cattle sales. We did fairly well the first year, but I found that they had had such big losses the previous year that they didn't make any profits and I didn't get a commission. Fair enough, I said to myself and stayed on for a second year. During those two years we spent an awful lot of money. I put up two hundred fifty miles of fencing. That's an awful lot of fencing. We had to put in water lines, too, so that every paddock would get water. It takes a lot of capital developing a place like that. You don't show much profit at first. Once we began showing a profit, I wanted to put in a big vegetable garden. We had eight and a half miles of river frontage. This was my background, and I was excited by the possibility. By the third year, everything was ready, and we stood to make a handsome profit. We had a lot of siltage, and when the cattle was ready to go to market, the owners came to inspect. I told them I wasn't going to let the cattle off the ranch until I knew how much I was going to get out of it. 'Now,' they told me, 'we'll have to wait and see.' So I chucked the whole thing. I suppose I should have stayed on for another year or so. Maybe, maybe not.

"But I found myself a third job, with a bloke who had an auctioning business and a lot of other little businesses. He didn't really have the money to develop them. He had all sorts of little mines, and my job was first to visit his auctioning businesses and then to get the little mines, mostly gold, on their feet. Once I got them started, he'd put in a manager. He was manufacturing bricks. When I started working for him, they were costing him about seven pounds per thousand, and he was selling them for six pounds. I went in and reorganized the whole operation. By the time I was finished, we were producing bricks for one pound five or ten per thousand and selling them for six. I was supposed to get a bonus for each half million bricks we sold. It wasn't much, but by the time two million were sold, my bonus would increase substantially. Well, there were about two million bricks standing in the field when a tractor toppled over and crushed my leg. Whilst I was off duty, the owner got a Coloured bloke in. He had run the brick factory before me, and now that I had reorganized it all, it was easy for him to keep making a profit. The day I came back to work, the old bloke told me that he didn't need me anymore. It was cheaper to keep the Coloured bloke on."

Hennie describes his first years of work in Rhodesia in a monotone. His description carries no emotion. "It was really a tough place," I say. "No one seems to have had a sense of responsibility," I try again. Hennie ignores my comments and goes on as monotonously as ever with his narration.

"Then I went to work on a farm owned by the BSA company. It's the old British South Africa Company. I think it is owned by Anglo-American now. It was the company Rhodes formed to develop the region, and until 1923 it *was* the government. Big companies like that don't pay very much, but they don't diddle you out of anything. They're not going to pay you enough so you'll be able to go out on your own. They're not interested in making a rich man out of you. But they always pay you enough to make you think twice about doing anything else. They're just a business. You have to make budgets, estimates, and yearly reports. Sometimes I think that companies like BSA and Anglo-American run these farms for the prestige of it. They don't make any money off them. They can move off some of their profit. Their real business is mining—the copper mines in Northern Rhodesia, I mean, Zambia. They've a vast empire. It was BSA that built the railway line into Rhodesia, and when Rhodesia became independent, the government had to buy it from them.

"Anyway, the BSA farm I was working on had about four thousand citrus trees, a citrus nursery, a lot of maize, tobacco, and some cattle. The cattle was mainly for feeding the laborers. When I started, there were four white managers, but then they reorganized and left only two of us. At first I was only in charge of tobacco, but then, after the reorganization, I took over the maize and cattle. We were planting two hundred fifty acres of maize, and we had another two hundred fifty acres in rotation. We didn't really have enough implements or labor to farm that many acres properly. I changed over and farmed only eighty acres and reaped as much maize as they had been reaping on the two hundred fifty acres. And I was able to save two thirds on fertilizer.

"Whilst I was working for them, I was getting more and more disenchanted with the farming life. I was getting to the stage where you begin to take stock of your life. I was over thirty-five. You know, half your life is gone. You ask yourself, Where am I? Here I have been living out the best years of my life, and what have I done? I've grown some maize, and there's always an overproduction of maize. It's an embarrassment to the government. I've grown some tobacco, which nobody was really interested in. I would grow orange tobacco, and they would want lemon. I would grow lemon, and they would want mahogany. You grow a heavy kind, and they want a light kind. You grow a light kind, and then they want a heavy kind. You're always growing the wrong kind. Even the few head of cattle we were marketing, everyone assured me, were as tough as leather. What was I doing? Was I going to spend the rest of my life in a rut?

"I began thinking about all this the day my leg was crushed.* Something dramatic had to happen to get me to think. Up until then I was just living, just existing. Suddenly I realized that I could have died. What would have happened to me? The idea of lying in a coffin all dressed up with nowhere to go just didn't appeal to me. It was then that I started going back to what my dad believed. He believed in the Bible. He believed in God. I asked a Dutch Reformed minister up there to help me find God. I asked an Anglican priest, too. From what I know now, I don't think either of them could have known Him. Otherwise it wouldn't have taken four years to introduce me to Him. If someone wants to know Him, I introduce Him chop-chop.

"A priest came up there. He was involved in the healing ministry. Rose went to a service he had performed, and she came back and told me about him. She wanted me to hear him. I went one night, and Rose went the next. Somehow what that bloke was talking about made sense to me. I began to look at myself from a completely different angle. I wasn't exactly liking what I was seeing. I knew something was going to happen. By the end of the week it did. I was ready for a change. And within a week of my conversion, I handed in my resignation to the BSA Company.

"Everything had been coming to a head. It was the whole atmosphere up there." Hennie was speaking with excitement. "Everyone was taking advantage of everyone else. A lot of farmers up there would take on a bloke and pay him twenty or thirty pounds a month and promise him a twenty-five-percent bonus at the end of the year. But how many of those blokes ever saw a bonus? There was always one excuse or another. There was one man, for instance, who, if he found you at home at eleven having tea, would knock a hundred pounds off your bonus. By the end of the year, he had lopped off

*Hennie has moved back in time. His leg was crushed before he started to work for BSA. It was while he was working for BSA that he became an Anglican.

so much that you had nothing left. There was nothing you could do about it. He was under no legal obligation to give you a bonus. Blokes were changing jobs every season. Or they were stagnating. I couldn't go on with it. Of course, it was no better in South Africa. There, they only paid a lousy wage and never even bothered to promise you a bonus.

"I went to see the Dutch Reformed minister. I told him that I wouldn't be coming to church anymore. I told him that I had decided to join the Anglican Church. He gave me a little book to read. I read it, and the next day I took the book back and told him, 'I'm not only going to become an Anglican, I'm going to become an Anglican priest.' "

There was defiance in Hennie's tone. On another occasion I asked him what his family thought of his becoming an Anglican priest. "I'm a complete and utter outcast, a real renegade. I'm an untouchable because I left the Dutch Reformed Church to join the Anglican Church. I was joining the enemy."

"Was it difficult for you?"

"A week before I converted I told the priest that he would never catch me doing all these bowings and scrapings and lighting candles. And then God spoke to me, and I went to him, the same priest, and told him I wanted to become a priest. God can change anything, even me.

"Fortunately I was far from my family. They couldn't affect me immediately. When my brother found out, he told me that if I became a priest, I could never set foot in his house again. He even promised to put pressure on the company he worked for to give me a job in Salisbury if I didn't become a priest. (I could never have worked anywhere where everyone knew I had got my job because of my brother. I couldn't have handled that.) The fact that Rose was an Anglican helped, too. Most of our friends were in fact Anglican. And when I think back about it, I have to admit that the Dutch Reformed minister was with me on this whole thing. We were good friends. When I told him I was going to become an Anglican, he said, 'Hennie, I've been waiting for this for two years.' When I told him that I had decided to become an Anglican priest, he said, 'Hennie, I've been waiting for you to tell me this for two years.'

"Now, you see he'd seen something happening in me that I myself hadn't seen. He'd seen the change. And when I went to see the priest, he said the same thing. 'Hennie, I've been waiting for you to tell me this for two years.' Other people were seeing things. I said to him, 'All you people must have been talking behind my back these last two years.'

"I'll never forget that day—the day I told the priest that *I* too wanted to be a priest. It was a Wednesday. He wrote to the bishop in Salisbury. The bishop was out on a trek in the district and didn't get back to him until the following Tuesday. He phoned the priest and asked to see me. We went to Salisbury the next morning and spoke to the bishop. I had to see various other people who asked me a lot of stupid questions. By afternoon I was told that I had been accepted as a candidate for Theological College. I'm probably the only man who was accepted for college before being confirmed in the church."

Hennie tells several versions of his conversion to Anglicanism. They each reflect an aspect of the experience, but the experience itself is never described. Each version does relate back to his accident and to his discovery of his own mortality. They are each marked by a tone of defiance—a defiance that reminds me of his refusal to condemn the Roman Catholics at his confirmation. They are tales of a change of identity: the death of an Afrikaner, Hennie might say, and the birth of a Christian.

"When I became a real Christian and a priest, I suddenly discovered that I had an identity other than that of an Afrikaner. I was a Christian. My citizenship was elsewhere. I can't get terribly excited about being an Afrikaner. That we have an Afrikaner government does not alter my situation. I've still got to buy my own beer." Hennie's tales of his conversion are all overshadowed by a charismatic experience he had about a decade later. When he speaks of being "a real Christian," he collapses time: for, as he has told me several times, his becoming *a real Christian* did not take place when he became a priest but when he first "met Christ." The decade that follows his conversion to Anglicanism is not "inspired." He describes it mechanically. He speaks of God's immanence, His presence, in an intellectual way. He does not speak of His companionship or of the intimacy of their relationship. At times he condenses his conversion and his "meeting of Christ" into a single, mythic instant, which marks his transformation.

"I couldn't go directly to Theological College because there was no room at the college. They were very fully booked. So they sent me to a mission station in the east, where they were having a lot of trouble with their farm. I spent eighteen months there. I was in charge of the farming section. My predecessor had been more interested in politics than in farming. He had actually led the farming side away from the church. But the church was the whole reason for the mission station's existence. In the early years, when they converted these African people, they had to take them out of their tribal situation and put them on a mission station so that they could live like Christians. They didn't want them to lapse into their old heathen ways. The government gave the stations huge tracts of land to settle these people on, and the church became the dominant thing in their lives. Everything revolved around it. In order to establish his own authority, my predecessor had to break the people away from the church.

"When the bishop asked me to go to the station, he asked me to try to get the farming side back to the church again. I wasn't interested in the political side of things. I merely tried to do my job and do it as a Christian. As a result, I encountered a lot of resistance from the people. The farm was deeply in debt. I figured that even if I were able to turn it around, it would take twenty-five years without a bad season before the debt was paid off. Eventually I recommended we sell the land back to the government and let it become private trust land. After a lot of resistance, they finally agreed.

"Then came the real problem. The land was cut up into small holdings, and the people at the station had to be resettled on these holdings. Originally they didn't fancy this, but eventually they got used to the idea. I helped them go over their land and plan where to build their houses, their *kraals*, and where to plant their crops. In the evenings I used to give lectures on farming in the community hall. I spoke their language pretty well by then.

"When I came back from Theological College on holiday, most of those people who had been against me were standing there to greet me. This one had brought a chicken, and that one had brought a few eggs. Another brought a pumpkin, and still others came with a few sweet potatoes. There was a whole string of them waiting to welcome me back. Their leader said he was sorry he had given me so much trouble. 'If you hadn't come,' he said, 'we would never have got what we wanted.' "

"Did you have any friends among them?" I asked.

"Yes. I'm godfather to quite a number of them."

"Did your attitude change toward the Blacks after you became a Christian?"

"No, I don't think so. I just loved them all. Well, maybe it did. I wasn't treating them as servants anymore but as friends. There was one bloke in particular whom I liked. He was a busboy, really more of a foreman, a Malawi. He was an elderly man and was trying in many ways to be a father to me without realizing that I was his boss. He wanted me to understand the others. We became very close. You know there are some people who always seem to know what you're thinking even before you speak. He was one of those. I think these Africans have an inborn ability to assess you and to know exactly how you are going to operate in certain circumstances. He would often come and talk about work. He made suggestions, and very often I would follow them. I think that he was afraid that I would louse things up. The more advice I accepted, the more willing he was to give of himself. I've never really analyzed the whole thing. I think that when you acknowledge someone as a person, you can get a lot more out of him. It becomes a personal relationship rather than an impersonal job situation."

Hennie went to Theological College in South Africa. Rose and their two sons stayed behind in Rhodesia. Rose gave piano lessons and supported herself and her sons and was even able to send pocket money down to Hennie. "She worked hard and never complained. She was happy with my decision. I think she had wanted me to become a priest all along." With the exception of a short trip or two to see his mother, Hennie had not been back to South Africa in almost a decade. Like so many other Rhodesians, he and Rose and the children spent their vacations by the sea in Mozambique. (A Rhodesian's vacation in Mozambique was rather like an Englishman's vacation in Spain or Portugal. Mozambique was a place to taste the not quite exotic. It was a place to let go: to put up with the noise, the dirt, the confusion, the racial disorder, the language no one could understand, and the food, especially the seafood, that tasted so good and then always gave you stomach trouble. It offered hardships as the perverse pleasures they in fact were.) Hennie was most impressed with the rapid industrialization he saw on his return to South Africa. He studied with great energy, so several of his fellow collegians told me, and was able to complete a three-year program of study in two and to start a Sunday school as well.

"Three of us started a Sunday school in an African township. The thing took off and within three months we were teaching between twelve hundred and fifteen hundred children every Sunday morning. It wasn't a Sunday school anymore. It had become a youth center. After services these youngsters used to come up to us and ask us to pray for those who were sick in their families and to help the needy. The need was so great that we had to put a limit on our help. If a person earned five cents or more a day, he couldn't be helped. We simply didn't have the funds.

"The township was in Grahamstown, and Grahamstown is one of the most backward places in the world. When the government wanted to build a railway line through the town, the people stopped it because it was going to put the ox wagons out of commission. When someone wanted to open a second brick factory, they stopped it as well, because of the pollution. The result is that there is only one pottery and one brick factory. That's the sum total of industry in Grahamstown. There's no work. When the university's in session, there is some work for domestic servants, but when the university's closed down, there is no work at all. Blacks there literally starve to death. They scavenge on dead bodies, looking for bits of food. And this is where the government's created its Bantustans!

"I met a man there. His family came from the Ciskei, but he was born in Cape Town. He was seven when he visited his homeland for the first time. He married a woman from the Kimberley area. Well, this poor bloke lost his job in Cape Town and was sent back 'home' to Grahamstown. Of course, he couldn't find a job, and as his wife wasn't a Xhosa, she wasn't allowed to come with him. She was sent back to Kimberley."

"How did you feel about the situation?" I asked.

"I had had no experience of it. There were only Coloureds in the northwest, and they were part of the farm. Conditions were better in Rhodesia. I wasn't too worried because in actual fact I wasn't part of it. I was a guest there to study. I was going back to Rhodesia. I used to collect all kinds of clothes and dish them out. I did whatever I could, but the situation was far too big for a couple of dozen theological students. I suppose I should have been more concerned, but really, there wasn't much I could do."

Hennie returned to Rhodesia just after the dissolution of the Federation of Rhodesia and Nyasaland in 1963. He was given a country parish. He does not talk about his ordination, the excitement he may have felt when he conducted his first mass, his priestly

activities, or, for that matter, his family. His son David showed me
a snapshot Rose had taken of Hennie at his ordination. He is very
much "the little guy." (Another shot shows Rose beaming with
pride.) From what little he tells me about this period, and from what
his sons have told me, I have the impression that Hennie had become
a church bureaucrat. He managed his parish very much the way he
had managed the farms on which he had worked. It was a difficult
period in his life. Rose was ill. His sons were growing up. (They
were away at school much of the time.) He was given immense
parishes with overwhelming evangelical responsibility. Although he
never spoke of it, I suspect that he was never fully accepted by his
white congregations. He was the apostate Afrikaner, for them as he
is for the Wyndal farmers.

At one point we talked about his sons. Both were raised as Anglicans. English was spoken at home. Zachary, the oldest son, was
always a pacifist. Only once, in Hennie's memory, did he get into
a fight: He defended several African students who were being bul-
lied near his church-school dormitory. His headmaster observed the
fight and wrote to Hennie about Zachary's moral integrity. Both
Zachary and his brother, David, had always had African friends.
"They could not share in the hatred of the Black man that was
building up in Rhodesia. The hatred kept building up, especially
among those who didn't have a relationship with God. It's only too
easy to build up a really intense hatred. It hadn't really existed before
the terrorism began. Then the Africans were simply there. No one
bothered to love them or hate them. They were inert: to be worked
and cursed.

"I found a lot of this hatred in my first parish. There had been
some terrorism in the area when the Federation had been broken up.
Some terrorists threw a petrol bomb into a school dormitory, and
a lot of children were very badly burned. An old couple, in their
seventies, was found in a pool of blood one morning by their servant, who had come to prepare them coffee. She had the presence
of mind to call their son, who managed to get them to a hospital in
time. They both survived. The old man had fourteen chopper
wounds in his head. Two square inches of his skull were missing at
the temple. Lots of farmers found their cattle with hamstrings cut
or udders cut off. It wasn't a very sophisticated kind of terrorism in
those days, but it was enough to rouse fear and hatred in the farmers.

"The first thing I was told when I got to the parish was not to mess around in politics. Evidently my predecessor had been very political. 'Fair enough,' I said. 'There is more than enough to do.' Then on November 11, 1965, when UDI [Rhodesia's Unilateral Declaration of Independence]* was declared, these same parishioners asked me to bless the new Rhodesian flag. 'Sorry,' I said, 'I can't do it. It would be a political act. You told me not to take part in politics, so I can't go along and bless the flag. I'm not living under the protection of a flag. I was born under the Union Jack, and I've lived under the South African flag; when I came up here, I was under the Union Jack again, then under the flag of the Federation, and now a Rhodesian flag. All this time it's been God who has protected me and not the flag.' They hated my guts for that. I wasn't being true to Rhodesia and what it stood for—European civilization. I think I was more concerned about preserving a particular way of life.

"I'll never forget the day I took these parishioners into an African township. There had been a big party rally for the Rhodesian Front (that was Smith's party), and the next morning, three cars arrived at my door filled with buns and meat and other leftovers. They wanted me to give the leftovers to the poor. I said, 'Come with me,' and I led them beyond the church into the African township. It was the deepest they'd ever been into the township. 'How can you tell me that you know these people when you've never even seen where they live?' I asked. I took them into some of the houses. 'Look how close together they live,' I said. 'You allow them to be poor, but you don't allow more than one person in a grave. These people here are living closer together than they would be if they were in a grave. You tell me you understand them because you speak their language. But you don't know how they live. You can't tell me you know them. You can't make decisions for them.'"

Hennie stopped. He was carried away by anger and disgust—the anger and disgust he must have experienced at the time. I asked him how his parishioners reacted.

*As a price for their acquiescence to the dissolution in 1963 of the Federation of Rhodesia and Nyasaland (Northern Rhodesia, Southern Rhodesia, and Nyasaland; today Zambia, Zimbabwe, and Malawi, respectively), Winston Field, the Southern Rhodesian prime minister, and his successor, Ian Smith, asked for independence as soon as either Zambia or Malawi gained theirs. The British government refused on the grounds that the white-dominated Rhodesian government was not truly representative. Angered, the Smith government declared unilateral independence on November 11, 1965.

"Oh, it was a tremendous eye-opener. We grow up without knowing the other. That is one of our major problems. It has got much worse in the last thirty years or so, with apartheid. Previously we had lived closer together. We had no choice. We knew how *they* lived. Now, you have to make an effort to get to know the other man. Most people don't want to make the effort, but we must. We must learn to see things from the other man's point of view. We must feel his agony. We must get involved at quite a different level. Ultimately this getting to know the other man is the only thing that will save us."

"Terrorism also separates people," I observed.

"Yes, that is true. You can't get to know a man if you are afraid of him. I remember one occasion well. I had been transferred to the east, near the Mozambique border. There had been some terrorist activity in the area. Late one afternoon I went out along the escarpment with my rifle to shoot something for the pot. I came upon an African village. I was terribly thirsty and farther away from home than I realized. You know, I was afraid to enter that village. I can't explain it really. I was just afraid. I stood there in the shadow of a tree and looked. Finally I pulled myself together and entered the village. The people couldn't have been nicer. They thought I was lost and invited me, a complete stranger, to stay the night. They offered me food. They said they'd help me find my place the next morning. That's the real African—the African I knew—but for a moment I had forgotten him because I was scared.

"You know, years ago Rose would go through those reserves on her own—a woman alone in a car—and she wouldn't hesitate to stop and pack in as many Africans as she could into the car. It didn't matter who. Man or woman. Friend or stranger. She was never scared. She never even thought they would do her any harm. And Rose wasn't the only one doing this. Everyone did. But then she stopped, and they stopped too. And here in the valley she never gives anyone a ride unless she knows him. Whenever there is a clash, especially along racial lines, a bitterness and a mistrust develop inside you like a cancer. It is something that has to be dealt with, and it is only through Christ that we can be freed of it. It has always been one of my biggest jobs, trying to stop resentment and bitterness and unforgiving attitudes from creeping in—to stop hating all Blacks because some Blacks have committed atrocities."

"Did you ever have any personal experience with the terrorists?"

"No, not really. (David did, of course, when he was in the army.) The terrorism took place in the outlying areas. In the beginning they would attack a farm, and then the Rhodesian army would move in and wipe them out in a couple of days. The terrorists weren't well trained then, but in '73 and '74, when they started moving in from Mozambique, they were better trained. It was no longer a question of knives and choppers and handmade petrol bombs.

"One day some terrorists put a couple of stones across the road. This one bloke came along—he used to work on the roads—and got out of his car to remove the stones. He was attacked and stabbed, but he managed to get back into his car and to drive a few yards before he slumped over his wheel dead. The terrorists threw four gallons of petrol on the car. They were standing some distance away and shooting live matches at the car. For some miraculous reason the car never took a light. His wife and children were in the car and managed to escape. The next day, when I came along, the place was swarming with troops. I don't think they ever got the terrorists. They could slip back across the border, and they had relatives in the area who would protect them. They were forced to protect them.

"The Rhodesian troops used to come into the villages and question the villagers. They weren't always too worried as to how they got their information out of these people. The villagers were torn between answering to the troops or to the terrorists. They were caught in the crossfire. They had a tough time. The terrorists would round up women and children and bayonet them or shoot them to death. It was a senseless slaughter.

"I see the same thing happening in the South West now. So we knock off two hundred terrorists in a month. That's really a very small number. In the meantime they're murdering their own people, ambushing them and setting land mines. All the people want is peace. Mugabe won because he promised the people peace, and SWAPO will win because they promise peace.* The people don't want SWAPO. They want peace."

*SWAPO, the South West Africa People's Organization, headed by Sam Nujoma, has opposed both politically and militarily South Africa's attempt to install a white-dominated government in Namibia. The Ovambo people, who make up half the population of Namibia, are its principal supporters. When in 1973 the UN General Assembly declared SWAPO to be the "sole authentic representative of the people of Namibia," South Africa took the declaration to be a sign that the UN was determined to impose a SWAPO government on the South-West. Since then, little real progress has been made toward a solution to the Namibian problem.

"And the whites?"

"Well, the funny thing is that they never panicked. When that old couple I told you about was found, the townspeople didn't worry because it had happened on a farm, and the farmers didn't worry because the farm was isolated. They had their rifles anyway."

"How do you account for it?"

"For one thing, the farmer's servants were always very loyal. When a farm was attacked, it was always attacked from the outside. And then the younger ones were used to it. A youngster born in the mid-fifties would have known it all his life. It was part of life. They knew no other way."

Zachary van der Merwe

"I was born on a farm in colonial Rhodesia," Zachary van der Merwe began when I asked him to tell me about his life, and immediately went on to ask me whether his father, Hennie, had already given me their family history. I told him that Hennie had spoken about it but that I had no clear idea of it. "He's quite tricky actually," Zachary said. "He prefers to gloss over a lot of it. It's an incredible story. You should insist that he tell it to you, but he'll probably heave himself right out of it.

"In a sense that's been my experience of him as a father. He's been a kind of cardboard cutout figure. I've never really got to know him as well as I've got to know my mother. I find that a strange sort of experience. My father and I don't really communicate. We have certain set conversation areas that we sort of walk around and that's it. He's always been somewhat of a loner. I think he's always felt a difference about himself, a sensitivity, which he doesn't naturally yield to or want to expose."

Zachary is also a bit of a loner, although he surrounds himself somewhat defensively with women. Unlike Hennie—at least as he understands him—he indulges his sensitivity. He is a set designer for a small experimental theater in Johannesburg whose productions are frequently closed down by the government, and he also freelances as he can. When his work brings him to the Cape, he visits his parents but rarely spends the night in Wyndal. I have seen him rush into Cape Town after one of Rose's immense Sunday dinners —she always has at least a dozen parishioners to Sunday dinner— in order to babysit for a friend. Zachary is, as he says, close to his mother and feels a very strong responsibility for her. With his father he is tense and evasive. Hennie listens to what he says carefully—uncomprehendingly, I am tempted to write—but rarely addresses him. Hennie is both proud of his son and disappointed in him. He is proud of Zachary's work so long as it is not pornographic—Zachary has been taken with "porno-political" gestures, exposures really—and he is convinced of his son's moral fiber. "Even when he was a kid, he would stick up for what he believed even if it meant getting a good hiding." Hennie is disappointed, however, in his son's idea of religion. Zachary has studied Hinduism and other Oriental mysticisms. He has been an adept of an Indian guru and once thought seriously of joining a Zen monastery in England. He has been involved in several spiritualist groups—groups that Hennie in his more fundamentalist moments likens to Satan worshipers—and has most recently been attending the services of a neognostic society whose members come from the wealthiest strata of Johannesburg's spiritually enlightened. Hennie says that Zachary is a seeker and has gone astray but will eventually meet Christ. He and Rose often pray for him.

Hennie clearly prefers his younger son's total commitment to Christ. (David is a preacher for the Assemblies of God and lives in Port Elizabeth. He rarely gets to see his parents.) Rose is spiritually closer to Zachary. She shares his introversion and tends, like him, to take refuge in an otherworldliness when she confronts South Africa's large social problems. She is also attracted to David's innocent Christianity—the way people who dwell on their spiritual life are often moved by those whose spiritual commitment is outgoing and gregarious.

There is a fine camaraderie between Zachary and David. Zachary is in his late twenties. He is thin and not very healthy-looking. His face tends to the gray, and he has Hennie's weak slate-blue eyes. He was once a runner. David is stocky and muscular. He is in his middle twenties. He is a surfer and is usually beautifully tanned. He has Rose's dark-brown eyes. When the two brothers are alone, they joke easily about themselves and reminisce about their childhood in Rhodesia. Both say that Africa begins north of the Limpopo River, and both are tempted to return to Zimbabwe. They never engage in intellectual or religious talk. It is a kind of taboo, so different do they know themselves to be. When they are together with their mother, then they compete strongly for Rose's affection and attention. They become childish and seem to be replaying past dramas. Rose simply observes them—and not without regret. Hennie will actively defend David, who is perhaps more immediately likable than Zachary but no intellectual match for him. Zachary is apt to scandalize his brother in these situations. He finds David's fundamentalism foolish. He is troubled by his militarism. (David fought the guerrillas in Rhodesia. Zachary was excused from military service because of a kidney ailment.) On one of the rare occasions when the two brothers were in Wyndal together, Zachary appeared on a friend's motorcycle with a loud, sexually provocative woman, an artist, whose hair was dyed bright orange and who was wearing a zebra-striped satin blouse, wine-colored harem pants, little black cowboy boots, chartreuse socks with yellow fleurs-de-lis, and an olive-drab combat belt. Hennie did not seem to notice her discordant costume. Rose ignored it, and treated her warmly. (The woman was in fact quite warm and rather more innocent than she appeared to be.) David's wife, a bland, whispery woman of consummate English lower-middle-class values, said nothing to Zachary's friend. Zachary himself did not have much to say to her. He had met her the night before at a friend's party. David was most attentive to her and so clearly embarrassed by her looks that he took to proselytizing her. Over coffee the two of them were at loggerheads, for David argued, citing biblical verse after biblical verse, that women were created to be subservient to men. Zachary listened bemused, but I detected a certain hurt in him as his brother got into deeper and deeper water.

"His sensitivity," Zachary went on hesitantly, "well, there is a story that my dad was madly in love with a girl. She turned him down, and that was the last time he experienced love, so to speak. He met my mother shortly afterward, and in three weeks they were married. They arrived in Rhodesia with nothing, just a buggy and luck. All their possessions were in the back of the car, and they had just enough money for petrol to go around looking for my mother's cousin, their only existing relative in Rhodesia. He worked in a garage. That is all they knew. Just before closing time, that first day, they found someone who knew where he was, and they had their big meeting. There had evidently been some confusion because my dad thought there was a job waiting for him. There wasn't. They stayed with this cousin for a few months, until my dad did find a job on a farm. They were sleeping in the back of a store, and then when he got the job, they moved into a converted garage. That's where I was conceived. There was a flood about them, and they were cut off from everything for five months.

"My dad wasn't much of a success. He had a very bad temper, and he was always being fired because of his temper. He was beating Africans and fighting. He was a barman for a while. He is very much a frontier kind of man, very rough, but there is his incredible sensitivity and perceptiveness about people.

"And then his leg was crushed. I was with him when it happened. I think that's a trauma he hasn't really got over. When the tractor toppled over on him, all he said was the Afrikaans equivalent of 'ouch.' The tractor boy wrapped his leg in a blanket—he was bleeding badly—and we managed to get him into the car. I was seven at the time. He drove himself to the hospital, which was three miles away. I was crouching on the floor beside him, pushing up and down on the accelerator pedal as he told me to. He had to lie there for five hours before they could do much to him. He was in shock. They couldn't even give him painkillers because of the shock. I just kept crying, telling him not to die. 'Please don't die.' I don't remember the months after that.

"Because of his crushed leg, he couldn't continue as a farm manager. He looked for a job and finally found one on a mission station. It was here, because of his association with a priest, that he decided to join the priesthood. For three years we hardly saw him. My mother supported us while he was studying. She taught piano and worked so hard that at one point she came down with malnutrition. She just wasn't eating. It was horrific because sometimes we didn't know where the next meal was coming from. At Christmas time we wouldn't be able to afford any festivities or even a special meal. And then on Christmas morning we would find a huge box or boxes of things. It just happened to us all the time. Things—fruit cakes and groceries—came to us, and we never knew where they came from. People would send them to us anonymously.

"Yes, I think it is worthwhile getting the story of my father's early life and my parents' early life because it is like out of a novel."

"But what about your own early life?" I asked. "What were your earliest memories?"

"My earliest memories were of not having any white friends, only Black ones. I spoke their language fluently. We used to play with stones or make cars out of a couple of boards and some old bicycle wheels. Most of the time we just explored the bush. I had all sorts of farm experiences, like going to have a crap in the bush and then wiping my bottom with a leaf covered with wasps. Or, disappearing from the house to have a beer in the compound on Sundays. Outdoor experiences: running across snakes, being chased by snakes, climbing trees, coming across a leopard. One night I was alone in the house. I was about five. The back of the house was sunk down, and there was a shelf of earth at window level. I saw a leopard looking in the window. It was a really terrifying experience. And then I remember my father having to get up every five hours or every two and a half hours to make sure the curing temperature was right in the tobacco barns. A sense of African space, life, texture. Servants all the time. Huge houses. Dressing up in explorer's gear and going out into the bush." Zachary often spoke in short phrases, piling image on image to create an effect.

"When I was twelve, we moved into town for the first time. One day we went out to a strange farm—I'd never been there before; my mother was visiting friends. I went for a walk and met an African on the road. I felt like a friendly wrestling match and asked him if he wanted to fight. He looked at me very ugly. 'Well, do you want to fight?' I asked. He was bigger than me and shook his head. Before I knew it, he slapped me very hard on my face. I wasn't suggesting that at all. Then he slapped me on the other cheek. I just started running. He picked up these huge rocks, and they went whistling past my head. If one of them had hit me, I'd have been killed. I was cheeky."

"Did your parents ever say anything about your playing with African children?"

"No."

"When did you begin to see them as being different?"

"When I was seven and started going to school. There were two white kids just about two miles down the road. I used to play with them. I found it strange at first because there was a whole different, well, I suppose, sophistication about them. One sort of became aware of differences that way. I didn't enjoy playing with them. I identified with the Black kids.

"We had one boy—he must have been about fifteen—who used to look after us before we started school. He used to take David and me for walks. Once, I remember, he took us to the country club. We walked down to the golf course. There was a little shed there, and we sat down on a bench in front of it. He took out his penis and started playing with it. He asked us to fiddle around with it a bit. It was a very curious experience—a kind of pungent experience. Once he took us for a walk, and we came back an hour and a half late for lunch. We had seen my father looking for us and ducked into the grass and carried on with our walk. When we got back, my parents were in a panic. I got a hiding for not bringing David home. And this guy got a walloping from my dad. He broke his jaw, and we didn't see him for a few days.

"When I was thirteen, we moved to another part of the country. My dad had just come back from college. We had all sorts of vagrants staying at the house. I remember one of them well. My dad was away for the weekend, and he tried to rape my mother. My brother and I were witness to that. We all ran to the car and managed to get to a friend's house and slept over there. Immediately after that I was shunted off to boarding school so as not to have to witness this kind of thing again. And that was a crazy experience, one of the most terrifying in my life, because suddenly I was in the midst of white Rhodesia. I had never felt any kind of bond with the white Rhodesian. I always felt myself to be an observer, and whatever their antics were, human or otherwise, they kind of fascinated me. They were like a strange insect that I was observing. And here, suddenly, I was in their midst. They all came from very different backgrounds. There were a few Black guys, too. I ended up having two very good Black friends. One's father is a minister in the government, and the other's, a headmaster. I also had three white friends. The only level of interaction between these white and Black friends of mine was banter, especially about sports. There was a definite pecking order, and I found myself between the two groups. There was a lot of discrimination but it wasn't institutionalized. Everybody shared dormitories, and study hall was integrated."

"What kind of a school was it?"

"Anglican."

"How did you like school?"

"I went to five junior schools and five senior schools, two of which were in England. By the time I was nineteen and went off to university, I'd say we had moved twenty times. Every time I started to know my way around and to make friends, I was uprooted. I think that is why I experienced such solitude as a youth, why I was always an observer."

"And what was it like when you first came down to university in South Africa? Was it your first trip?"

"Yes. The first thing I noticed was how different Blacks in South Africa were from those in Rhodesia. The South African Blacks weren't concerned with greeting you or establishing any kind of natural and exuberant rapport with you. This is not the case in Rhodesia, where most whites speak an African language. Here I was immediately aware of a very real split. I felt threatened, frightened by it, and dismayed, too. I thought, Oh, well, there's a big black cloud hanging over this country. That's what it is. I'm only here for a specific purpose. It's not my worry.

"I was very aware of the Rhodesian's attitude toward South Africa. The Rhodesians think themselves the cream of the crop. They know how to farm. South Africans don't. Rhodesians can get fifteen, twenty, thirty bags per acre, while South Africans can only get five. This was very much my dad's way of thinking. We all had our stereotypes, especially of the Afrikaner. All of this flashed through my mind, and I realized that there was a whole lot more about people than just being people. I was trying to find my own identity. I saw everything with irony, as absurd or as a potential satire. I felt a certain dislocation insofar as I didn't feel at home here. It was definitely a foreign land."

"Did your parents talk much about South Africa?"

"No, they didn't. They considered themselves Rhodesians. They moved up when they were a very young couple. I never thought of myself as anything but Rhodesian. Whenever I came home from university, crossing the border was an amazing experience because I was immediately released from the fear I always sense in South Africa. And there were the open expanses. The air was easier to breathe.

"For me to get the feel of a country, a train journey is very important. It's the quality of the sidings, the signs, the nature of the metal, the physical things you pass—they become congealed demonstrations of a much larger thing. They become emblems, symbols, of the whole thing. In a sense even the metal takes on the quality of the emotional atmosphere around it. I went back and forth to Rhodesia by train about five times. It's a long journey—three days and three nights—very slow. There's not much to do, just drink beer and get drunk if you can afford to get drunk. Everybody gets drunk. I used to stick to myself and peer out the window, but I also really enjoyed going into the bar. It was like a zoo. It was an endless entertainment, watching all those people drunk and taking themselves so seriously."

"And at the university were you also an observer?"

"In the beginning, yes. I made a few friends my first year, but it was only toward the end of the year that I began to feel close to any of them. They're married now and living in the suburbs—in the slums of Constantia.* I was the only guy in a class of fifteen girls. So, I was given cups of tea all over the place, but in return for all the favors, I had to do all the heavy work in art class. My best friends were older. Some of them were lecturers."

"Were you happy at the university?"

"It was the first glimmer of consciousness that I experienced. I began to see things, place them, understand them. It was a very painful period emotionally because I was confused about who I was and what I should be doing, who I should be talking to, and how I should be behaving."

"Did your parents have any special aspirations for you?"

"No, not really. I always had the ability to be alone and to become involved with books. I was always artistically inclined. My mother encouraged this. My dad was neutral. When I decided to go to university, he did support me. He had to struggle to get me a government grant. He had to make quite a big scene."

"How did they feel when you decided to be a set designer?"

"I sort of fell into it—and they fell into it too."

*Constantia is one of Cape Town's wealthiest suburbs.

9

OVERSEAS

Hennie

"In England I discovered a sense of history, which we do not entirely have here. I was working in a church built by Christopher Wren! He had only been a name for me. One day I had to conduct a wedding in a church dating back fifteen hundred years. The granite steps leading up to the sanctuary had been worn down more than an inch by the knees of those who had been in prayer. How many knees had pressed on those steps to whittle them down an inch? It was incredible. Kneeling there praying I suddenly thought of all the prayers those walls had soaked up over the years. What if they were to reveal all their secrets: people going to war, people losing their loved ones . . . The joy and every kind of emotion those walls had heard! That is something we haven't got here in South Africa.

"But I was disappointed, too. All those monuments seemed to me to be typical of England at the time I was there. They were monuments to the dead. The English were going around with a kink in their neck, looking back at their past and forgetting that England has a future. They were a big nation once, and they can be again. But they forget about this because they keep looking back to their glorious past.

"In some ways their attitude is completely contrary to ours. My high school class was the second to pass through. We didn't have a past to look back to. We had to establish our own tradition. We had to look to the future to find our tradition. Of course, there are many South Africans who try to invent their tradition. But for me, through my experience in that school, I learned to doubt those who are always looking backward. Why worry about the past? There is nothing I can do about it. I cannot recall it. What can I really learn from it? Only that which will help me prepare for the future. I live today and plan for tomorrow.

"It was that traditionalism that I found disappointing in England. Otherwise I loved every minute I was there. Rose and I could easily have stayed there had the children settled down. Zachary was at a very difficult age. He was fifteen or sixteen. He had grown up all his life on farms in Rhodesia and had had a very free and easy life. Suddenly he was landed in the concrete jungle—in the slums of London. He couldn't get used to it. It was easier for David. He was younger and always more outgoing. Zachary would talk to his schoolmates about the lions and elephants he had seen. At first they were interested, but then they would get jealous. Who does this guy think he is? Most of them had never left London. They would beat him up. We couldn't let it go on."

Within five years of his ordination, Hennie had proved such a successful evangelist that he was invited to England to become an urban missionary in one of London's worst slums. He and his family moved into a small, dilapidated rectory in the heart of the neighborhood. "It was so cold that in the year we were there we were never able to warm the place up. In August Rose would be sleeping with a hot-water bottle." The boys were sent to a local school. Neither of them adjusted to London. Zachary often came home badly bruised. Given Hennie's casual attitude about the boys' education, their failure to adjust must in fact have been quite serious. Rose liked London immensely, made several good friends with whom she still corresponds, and went to as many concerts as she could afford. She gave no lessons but was asked just before she left to join the faculty of a small but well-known private music college. Hennie does not talk much about his life in London. He worked hard and probably would have stayed had the boys adjusted. Occasionally he jokes about the conditions in which they lived. "They had to find somebody who had lived in a real jungle to live in *that* jungle."

* * *

History, tradition, age . . . I have heard similar reactions to the age of England, Europe, the Old World, from many Afrikaners. For the most part they do not take as violent a *parti pris* for the future as Hennie does, but they express wonder at the age of Europe—a wonder that even in the most unpoetic often becomes poetic. They find there in the Old World what they are seeking in their own world: a tradition that roots them in their land. They envy the taken-for-grantedness of the European past, a past that simply is, a past that offers, however constricting it may be, security, so that the future, though less than certain, is never altogether uncertain. Above all, I believe, the Afrikaners envy the relaxation that comes with having a past that does not have to be created and re-created continually—a past that has neither to be retold nor reenacted to be authentic.

And yet, many Afrikaners (and English South Africans for that matter) with whom I spoke, even the most conservative, felt constricted by the weight of Europe's past. "It's all already there," is the way one man put it. The Afrikaners miss an openness, an excitement, a freedom, to do in Europe what, in those magical moments when they lose realistic sight of their own future, they associate with South Africa. (Symptomatically, the images they use to express this openness, this excitement, this freedom, are spatial. Despite the "encroachment" of Black Africa, space affords a more positive, a more vital image of possibility for them than does time.) Those Afrikaners who have visited the United States (and in Wyndal, at least, they are becoming more numerous) identify with the openness, the excitement, the freedom to do, and the doing they see there. They are distressed, however, by what they see in America as an arrogant disdain for things past, a looseness, a violence, a disorder, an absence of control.

In the Afrikaners' symbolic geography, Europe (that is, Western Europe) and the United States, the Old World and the New, represent extremes between which the Afrikaners situate, or would like to situate, *their* South Africa. They say in their most stubborn mood that they will not make the mistakes of the Old or the New World. They, God's chosen, are here to establish and maintain a new social order in which racial purity is guaranteed, as are harmonious relations between different racial and ethnic groups. They will resist the temptations of the Old and New Worlds. They will fight incursions from the East, the Soviet Union and China, and from the *natuurvolk* of Black Africa who in their innocence have succumbed to the communist devil. Their identity seems at times to be constituted by their defense against outside influence of whatever sort. They draw a tight boundary around themselves—a laager.

The Old World is the place of origin in the Afrikaners' historical consciousness. It is the place from which their ancestors came, a place that is little more than a name—abstract like the name of the valley farmer's first ancestor who came to the Cape of Good Hope and the year in which he arrived. They know little about these places, just as they know little about their ancestors. The names, the places and personages, mark the spatial and temporal beginning of the Afrikaners' individual and collective histories. The Afrikaners' first trip to Europe is in a certain respect a pilgrimage to their place of origin. It is frequently combined with a trip to Israel, to the Holy Land, the *Heilige Land*, their spiritual origin. It is analogous to their trips to the museums and monuments that dot the South African landscape. Despite the fact that Holland is known to be unsympathetic to their cause, to be degenerate and corrupt, filled with drug addicts, prostitutes, and brazen long-haired hippies, it is usually visited, as is England, the land of their enemies. The one is despised: The Afrikaner feels a cultural betrayal. The other, ironically, is liked: The Afrikaner feels at home and is forced to differentiate between the English from England and those of South Africa. He does. Even the swiftest pilgrimage, the cheapest tour, designed to solidify a view, fragments the view. People are differentiated. Other social arrangements are witnessed. Other cultural outlooks are noted. Other possibilities are recognized. These are, for the most part, relegated to *die vreemde*, to those others who lived abroad, where conditions are different. Yet such trips have their effect.

The United States, and to a lesser extent Canada, Australia, and New Zealand, are not places of origin, temples of the past, but places of possibility. The United States is associated with an open future, a future that is neither numbed by waiting nor cast over with gloomy images of apocalypse. The Afrikaner, as I have observed, seems stunned by the violence of America's possibility. He is also swept up by it. He envies America's "burdenless" future. No holding action is necessary. No resistance is required. Come what will. America can afford to be irresponsible. "You killed off your Red Indians," he says. "And your Blacks are a minority. Ours are the majority. We're the minority." He looks for problems. He sees them. He knows about the slums of New York, Washington, and Los Angeles. "How can you condemn us for Soweto when you have the South Bronx?" he asks. He sees anger and frustration in the eyes of American Blacks. He sees violence in the Puerto Rican. He listens intently to stories of mugging, rape, and riot. He is shocked by miscegenation, distressed by racial hatred ("We do not hate the Black man; we know his place"), and offended by those who condemn him without hearing him out. Above all, he is wounded by those, in America and in Europe, who know nothing of his country and who are surprised to learn that there are *white* Africans.

Piet Viljoen

"In 1972 my wife and I were in Vienna. I remarked at how beautiful the streetlights were. Someone in our tour asked me if we had streetlights in South Africa. It shows you how little people know of South Africa."

Piet Viljoen is a boyish-looking man, a sort of innocent, in his early forties. He is a builder. His father and mother moved to Wyndal at the beginning of the Depression. They had lost their farm in the Karoo and were literally starving when they arrived. Piet's father became a *bywonner*, a hired hand, one step removed from the Coloured workers, on one of the largest farms in the valley. He saved every penny he could, and with his savings he rented a small plot of land only to discover that it had no water. The owner would not return his money. Piet's father saved again and rented a second plot, with water rights at night only. He grew splendid vegetables and in fifteen years he had saved enough to buy a small farm. When his father died, Piet sold the farm. He did not have his father's green thumb. With the proceeds from the sale, he built himself a sturdy Cape Dutch house, which marks his determination to remain in the valley despite the fact that neither he nor his father before him was ever accepted by the old Afrikaners. In the foundation of his house he buried his family history. "The Afrikaners are not like Jews," Piet says. "They do not help one another."

"A lucky thing happened to me. We went overseas. I won a free ticket to Greece in a raffle for an old people's home in Bellville. My wife and I were visiting her cousin, and a chap came by and sold us each a ticket. Mine was the winner. We decided that it was not worth going all that way without seeing more of Europe. I spent two thousand rand more to see the rest of Europe. It was worth it. We started in Greece and then went to England, Belgium, Holland, Germany, Italy, and France. Then we returned to England.

"I found everything very crowded in Europe. Everyone seemed to be acting for himself. There was a rat race. I did find it much neater than in South Africa. There, the workers know what they are doing. Here, the Coloureds do not have enough experience. Perhaps it is our fault. Europeans are better organized, especially when it comes to garbage disposal. I looked at things that were of concern to me. I have been concerned about garbage disposal in the valley. It is one of our biggest problems . . .

"I like to travel, to learn. If I go to Europe again, I will do things differently. I will try to visit people. I would like to know how they live. You can't learn that on a tour."

"What impressed you the most about Europe?"

"Well, that in less than four hundred years we in South Africa have come a long way. We are not that far behind Europe. We saw a lot of old buildings. We came to a door that was over four hundred years old. It was a privilege to touch it. So many hands must have touched it. And yet, when I came back to South Africa, I realized how proud we should be of our own accomplishments. Look at how much we have done in the age of that door.

"There is no place like home. I was so glad to be home—back in the old, familiar routine. To be sure, there are many beautiful places in Europe. I liked Lucerne and especially Boppard. I wrote 'Boppard' down in my journal and next to it I wrote, 'The most beautiful place in the world.' It is a village on the Rhine, next to the Lorelei. But when you have been away from your home for a couple of weeks, and you return, you feel happy."

Dr. Jakobus Steyn

"Now, I liked the English in England," Dr. Steyn said, referring to the year he had spent in London in the early fifties as a postgraduate student in medicine. "There were no screams against apartheid in those days. You could see that the man in the street had a policy completely different from that of the government. What I appreciated most about the English in England was the fact that whether a man was a Tory or not, if you attacked his King, he'd go for you. The Labourites and the Tories didn't like each other very much, but when you'd meet them in Paris or Germany, then they were English through and through. They'd stand up for England no matter what. They're not like *our* English.

"I was invited to a party one night given by some English South Africans. There were a couple of Blacks there. I didn't mind because it wasn't my country. One of them, an anthropologist from Nigeria, asked me a few questions. When I mentioned the Bushmen, he said I was discriminating against them because I called them Bushmen. Why shouldn't I call a Bushman a Bushman? Isn't that what you anthropologists call them? He should have known better. Well, we got into quite an argument over that. And then I asked one of the South Africans at the party if, when he was overseas, he wasn't also always being put on the defensive—always being put into a position of inferiority. He had to admit that.

"I knew our statistics pretty well in those days. I had to defend myself. I knew how many Blacks were at school in South Africa and how many were at school in other countries in Africa. I knew how much we spent on medicine for them and how much other African countries spent. Things like that. Then one of those Blacks said I couldn't be telling the truth, but I was. I asked the same South African to confirm what I was saying. He was a *liberal.* He said he didn't know anything about it. He thought that maybe I was right, but he didn't really know. *That* I cannot appreciate. A real Englishman would have defended his country right or wrong if he were in a foreign land. But not one of those liberal English-speaking South Africans."

Dr. Steyn was completely disdainful. "Of course, such types are becoming more and more exceptional. I think most English-speaking South Africans realize that *this* is their country and not England. But you still get some of them who are neither here nor there. If things get bad here, they'd like to pack up and return 'home.' I just read in the paper this morning that an English-speaking woman said she doesn't have a South African passport because she can't travel with it. She has an English one and can go all over the world with it."

Many countries refuse to grant South African citizens visas. These include the countries of Black Africa, North Africa, and the Middle East.

" 'It's worth more,' she says, 'than a South African passport.' Now, I think that is wrong. Why should she go to a country which doesn't accept her as she is, as a South African? I have no time for people like that." Again there was contempt in Dr. Steyn's voice.

"When I sailed to England the first time, there was a woman on board who couldn't wait to get 'home.' I met her again about six months later in Europe. She could hardly speak Afrikaans *but* she spoke to me in Afrikaans. She kept saying how wonderful South Africa was and how she couldn't wait to return. England wasn't what she thought it would be. Of course, things aren't so good in England now. My wife and I were there a few months ago. Now England has the same problems we have. But no one is telling England what to do about them.

"That is one of our biggest problems: you people from overseas interfering with us. We would like to speed up evolution a bit. We are trying to do that. But we can't rush things too much. If you rush things, you'll have chaos. That is what you overseas people don't realize. You come over here with your ideas; you tell us we are wrong; you tell us what to do. We've got no standing. Believe me, if you had the recipe to solve our problems, we would take it. We've been told we're racists and that we are doing the most terrible things. But who tells us? The English, with only a million and a half Blacks, who have had more race riots in the last six months than we have had in years!"

The South African news media gave a strong racial slant to the riots in England in the spring and summer of 1981. I was tempted to correct Dr. Steyn—to point out that the winter before, over forty Coloureds were killed in riots in Cape Town alone and many, many more were mutilated. But I restrained myself.

"Now I don't want to be told what to do by people who can't even keep their own households in order. I wouldn't like an Australian to tell me what to do. Look what the Australians did to their aborigines. They murdered millions. There are only a couple hundred thousand left, and they have no civil rights at all, nothing in comparison with the whites. But they have loud mouths. They tell us we are racists. The same is true of New Zealand. Look how they have been protesting against our Springboks."

There were serious, at times violent, protests in New Zealand in the summer of 1981 against the South African rugby team and the government of Robert Muldoon, which had granted them visas.

Although New Zealanders of diverse and highly respectable backgrounds protested, the South African press suggested the riots were caused by *skollie* elements—just as they blame the riots in South Africa on the *skollies,* or hoodlums. The Springboks later played in the United States, and again there were serious protests. Many countries and their athletic clubs have refused to play rugby, cricket, and soccer with South African teams until the teams are fully integrated. As a gesture, the Springboks put one Coloured player, Errol Tobias, on the team.* All of the Coloureds and Blacks with whom I talked thought Tobias was a sellout.

"But what did these New Zealanders do with the Maoris? They killed them off by the hundreds of thousands. The white man is in the majority there. That's a nice and easy spot to be in. And America did the same. Where are all those Red Indians? We are told that our homelands are pitiful, but you have your reservations. Today, if you want to see a Red Indian, you have to take your car and travel quite far to see one. I know. I was there. Well, the result is that we become antagonistic as soon as overseas people tell us what is wrong with us.

"You see, we made a mistake three hundred years ago, when we came to South Africa. We just didn't kill off the Black people. My ancestors were religious people. We tried as hard as possible to teach the Bushman and the Hottentot about Christianity. We gave them work. We taught them. If you compare us with other countries, you'll see we are the only country that didn't kill off its primitive people. We are the only country in which the white man is in the minority.

"One of the nice things about memory is that it is quite easy to forget. Australia forgets her past. New Zealand would like to forget her past. It's only South Africa's future that has got to be remembered. Our past—well, I would like to dish it up and show the world what we did in comparison to what you did in America, and the Australians did in Australia, and the New Zealanders did in New Zealand. We still have our Blacks. Where are your Red Indians? Where are the aborigines? Where are the Maoris? We don't get a chance to voice our past."

Dr. Steyn could barely contain himself. "And you," he finally sputtered out, "you condemn us for what you yourself have done."

* * *

*A second Coloured player, Avril Williams, has been added to the team.

Europe is more than the place of origin—the goal of pilgrimage.
The United States is more than the place of possibility. Both are
places of judgment and, like Australia and New Zealand, places that
refuse to be judged. The Afrikaner, and to a lesser extent the English-speaking South African, are very conscious of their image
abroad. Newspapers in either English or Afrikaans print little news
from overseas, and what news they do print is usually related somehow to South Africa. A statement by a minor official in Germany
about South Africa may well make headlines, while a major political
controversy between the Social Democrats and the Christian Democrats that risks toppling the German government may not be reported at all. Or great attention will be given to an event that
somehow mirrors events in South Africa, like the riots in England
(understood in racial terms). (For more "objective" accounts of
overseas news the South African depends upon *Time* magazine and,
to a lesser extent, *Newsweek.*) History is also taught largely with
respect to South Africa. The South African sees his country as
having far more importance than in fact it does. Hennie, Piet Viljoen, Dr. Steyn (in a conversation that I do not report), and several
other Afrikaners with whom I spoke complained about the ignorance about South Africa they found overseas. They felt, as I have
noted, wounded.

Many white South Africans describe being put on the defensive
when they are abroad. They are constantly having to justify themselves and their country. The Afrikaner, who tends, in my observation, to identify rather more strongly, certainly with less irony, with
his country than does the American or European of similar social
background, finds himself a sort of emissary for his people. Dr.
Steyn is not the only Afrikaner who arms himself with statistics
when he travels overseas. One frequently hears tales (again they
become a living folklore) of the insults, the slights, the discrimination, the Afrikaner has had to suffer.

Irene Prinsloo

"We can't seem to get our point across to people overseas. I don't
think they really want to understand.

"My father was a very debonair sort of man. He had a sort of Old
World courtesy. He never put the wrong foot forward. When he

was eighty, he traveled around the world on his own. On shipboard, he met some people from America. One of them took a liking to my father and asked him to come to dinner if he ever came to Washington. He did. He was picked up by the man's car and was warmly welcomed to the house. The man introduced his wife and a few friends. 'Irene,' my father said, 'the minute I sat down they started to tackle me. I took it and I took it and I took it. And then I saw that the man was not reasonable. He was not giving me a chance.' My father folded his napkin, put it down on the table, slowly pushed his chair back, and said, 'Excuse me. Will you please call me a taxi.'

"I can tell you this much—there must have been a strong provocation for my father to do that. They never listened to him at all. You can imagine my father being thrilled to get this invitation because now he could put his case before people who had their wits about them. He thought it would be a wonderful opportunity. And he hadn't a chance.

"And when we were overseas the last time, people asked us about South Africa. Every time we would try to explain, they would say, 'But you've got no Black representation in the government,' and they would listen to nothing else we said. That was as far as we could get."

The English-speaking South Africans sidestep the questions they are asked abroad. They blame the government, the Nats, the Afrikaners. They talk about their political impotence. They cast themselves as victims. They pretend to a liberalism that I, at least, am not always convinced is as strongly held as it appears. (I am not questioning their sincerity. There are those whose profession of liberalism is indeed sincere. There are those in whom it is hypocritical. And there are those, probably the majority, who announce it in what Jean-Paul Sartre would have called *bad faith*. They are ambivalent. They are torn between the security, illusory to be sure, of the *status quo* and the insecurity of a change that they know to be inevitable.) They act abroad (slightly more defensively perhaps because they are more provoked) as they do in South Africa. When they are asked, as they frequently are, why they remain in South Africa, they talk about South Africa as their home, about their love of the country, its beauty, its potential, and even about the need to stick it out for the good of the country. Or sometimes they speculate about leaving—and of course some do—or at least providing their children with the opportunity of leaving. Or, in their most realistic moods, they admit that their business and professional interests are in South Africa, their careers, their reputations, their contacts. They admit the privilege they will have to forgo if they do leave, and they complain about the restrictions on the outflow of capital that tie them down. "Were I just starting my career," I have heard men in their early thirties say, "I would seriously consider leaving."

The English-speaking South Africans consider themselves to be part of an international English-speaking community. They are South Africans by residence, by citizenship, and by an ill-defined congeries of sentiments that perhaps can be best summed up as "attachment." They do not, in my observation, identify as strongly, as quintessentially, with their country as do the Afrikaners. Although they are infuriated when the Afrikaner casts doubt on their feelings for South Africa, they do recognize—they often contemplate—the possibility of living elsewhere. They do not consider emigration a betrayal, although those who do emigrate, like my friend Carl, do at times consider their move an abandonment. They suffer, too, the inverse feelings of being betrayed and abandoned by their country. When the English-speaking South African travels overseas, he does not consider himself an emissary of his people whose mission it is to enlighten the world about South Africa and about how he and his people have been misunderstood. Overseas is not a place of judgment. If he feels his country has been unjustly criticized, he will defend it. He does not immediately gather himself into a psychic laager. He does not feel inferior, although at times he may identify with his critics and suffer a kind of crisis of conscience. He attempts to be *objective*, and this "objectivity" permits him some rhetorical distance from himself and his country—a distance that I have found less often among Afrikaners. Their commitment to Afrikanerdom is too violent. Consider Dr. Steyn's belief that a man should defend his country right or wrong when he is in a foreign land.

The English South African is more at ease abroad. Parents who can afford it arrange to send their children to Europe when they are at university or immediately afterward. (A trip to the United States is left for the children to arrange for themselves when they are launched on their careers.) Europe is the locus of culture. The Useless Man in the Junction Avenue Theatre Company's political farce *The Fantastical History of a Useless Man* says,

After matric I went overseas. Everybody told me, that's where the real culture is, overseas. I mean do we ever see anything great here? Like the Beatles or the Stones? No. Nothing! And they don't let you rest. Everywhere you look. The magazines, the books, the movies. Even at school. My teacher says we've got nothing. No literature, no drama, no culture, no home . . .

We've been taught all our lives that our home and our culture lie somewhere else. There's been a conspiracy, a tacit agreement that we must never look around us. "All things bright and beautiful." And our culture lies somewhere else. I couldn't understand one thing. If this was the case, the truth, what the hell were all these people doing here? Pining for their lost lives somewhere else . . .

If the truth and the life and the art is 6000 miles away, what are we doing here? I asked all these people who taught me what they were doing here and they refused to answer. And finally I determined to go and find out for myself. I went on a search to find my culture and my art and my life and I found that it was all a blind. The people here —my teachers and peers and mentors—didn't want art and culture and life. They wanted a device to cloak themselves from the reality around them. They fed and clothed their bodies here, but averted their eyes. They kept their minds in Europe. They went on mind-fucks in museums, browsed around bookshops and luxuriated in theatres and averted their eyes. They made us believe that there was nothing of value here; they imported a culture and civilization like a deepfreeze and averted their eyes. And what I want to know of all you visitors to Pettycoat Lane, why don't you look at Diagonal Street?[1]

Diagonal Street is in Johannesburg's "Black" street. The Useless Man's monologue is interrupted by a "bourgeois ritual" in which his parents and other guests give him "going overseas gifts"—passport, traveler's checks, binoculars, opera glasses, long underpants, ski cap and glasses, ski jacket, scarf and gloves, *Europe on 10 Dollars a Day*, spring balance, side-pouch, sleeping bag and haversack, contraceptives, and an Instamatic camera with flash—each placed on a copy of Kenneth Clark's *Civilisation*. When he returns from Europe, his father arranges eight copies of *Civilisation* on a bookshelf.

I am not convinced that European culture is simply a device to "cloak" the whites from the reality around them. Certainly many English in Wyndal and in Cape Town traveled as often as they could to Europe. They went to museums, they went to the theater, they went skiing and hiking—they did not browse in book shops very often—and they talked and shopped. They seek, and at times experience, a cultural rejuvenation, but they do not use Europe to divert their attention from the world around them. They have ample ways of avoiding Diagonal Street. One should not forget that the Coloured section of Cape Town, District Six, at the very center of the city, was razed in the sixties and its inhabitants resettled in monotonous little houses in Mitchell's Plain, about twenty miles from the center of town.

Several of Wyndal's wealthiest English families spend part of each year in Europe. They go to England for the theater and to see friends; they attend musical festivals in Scotland and Austria; they ski in Zermatt, Davos, or the Engadine. Most of the other farmers have been to Europe or at least England in the last five or six years. (They tend to have gone less often since moving to the valley because of the weakness of the rand and because of the expenses involved in modernizing their farms.) Their trips tend to be more touristic, or else they are restricted to visiting friends, usually in England. They talk frequently about their trips, especially at dinner parties. They repeat themselves.

Catherine Fox

"They are really very bored here," Catherine Fox says. "I must confess, I am bored too. When I moved here, I thought I would find people who shared my interests, who loved music and the theater the way I do. I haven't. I have a little music group, but we don't meet very often, and I try to keep up with my French. It is very difficult. People here just don't have that much to say. They don't read. I mention Proust or Thomas Mann, and I am not even sure they have heard of them.

"My father had a great love for European culture and music. He came from a little village near a lake on the Lithuanian-Polish border. The great fear there was that the boys would be swept into the Polish army. When men were taken into the Polish army, not only Jews, they were often never seen again. They all tried to escape. At the age of eighteen my father got away. Somehow he managed to get to England. I don't remember how. He got odd jobs there, like becoming a rent collector. He lived on absolutely nothing and just put penny to penny until he could pay for the lowest form of sea travel to South Africa. He came with absolutely nothing, not a bean. He was Jewish and he came to a country where there was anti-Semitism but no persecution. He found that everyone here had a chance. If you had the brain and the desire, you could make good. He did. People could make fabulous fortunes in those days. He went to the Transvaal.

"It was a very adventurous period. It was a dangerous, wild country. From a health point, I don't know how any of them survived. The country was just one mass of blackwater fever and malaria. It was terribly hot. But they had a wonderful life. A lot of these young people got together, and amongst them of course were all these young Jews, bursting with music. They formed an operatic society and had concerts and dances and a very happy life. They went into trade. You see, the mines needed engineers, but people like my father had no training; they could only go into trade. When gold was discovered on the reef, they all pelted down to the reef, which wasn't even Johannesburg then. When my father got there, there were just tents. It was very interesting to listen to him, when he sat in enormous comfort in a beautiful house, recollecting how he had got all this from nothing. It was really quite like a fairy tale. He had warehouses and traded extensively with England. I really must take my hat off to him. It was wonderful how he worked his way up. Of course, this was typical of the crowd of young Jews who got away to freedom and were enjoying the fact that they could now live without fear and could educate themselves and their children. And, by Jove, they educated their children. Nothing was too much. If they showed any talent, they were immediately given lessons. We, of course, went to England.

"My father always felt European at heart. He sent me to one of those horrible little snob schools that used to take very few pupils. We were highly specialized and very spoiled. There was a splendid headmistress, who took an interest in each little girl. We weren't just a name and a number. The girls were mostly English county. I and three little Sassoon girls were the only Jews. The school concentrated on teaching us how to behave. It never prepared us to work. At that time no girl ever thought of earning a living. I sometimes think I was born too soon. We specialized in art, music, literature, and languages. We weren't taught maths, only elementary arithmetic to do household accounts. We were taught fine needlework, dancing, and riding both astride and sidesaddle. I still remember the lovely horses. We had regular teachers in music, art, and dancing. If the teacher saw that any of us had a little bit more than the average feeling for a subject, she reported it immediately to the headmistress, who would then have a special teacher come down from London. I was particularly good in music, so they sent down a music teacher.

"My mother was a very delicate person who was a poor traveler. She was so ill on board ship to England that the doctor told my father that she might not make it. This gave Papa such a fright that he took a holy vow unto himself that he would never again subject her to anything like that. So he settled us in England, and he trotted back and forth the whole time until my mother died. Then he remained with us. I was nine. He was in his forties. He devoted himself to us. He was very strict with us, but he was also interesting. He kept a strictly kosher house. And you have to live in one to know what *that* means. It's really awful. You have to keep everything apart. You dare not use a knife to cut meat that has touched anything to do with milk. If you do, you'll go straight to hell. He didn't have Jewish servants but gentile ones. They were so terrified of doing anything wrong that they were stricter than he was.

"When I was fourteen, my father moved us back to South Africa. We thought we were returning for a holiday, but my father got very caught up with big business developments. There was so much opportunity here, and he was in a position to increase his fortune by playing the stock exchange. So we stayed on. I went to school and then to the conservatory. And when I had done everything I could there, I asked my father to let me go to London. I had been accepted by the Royal Academy. The head of the Johannesburg conservatory had arranged it all. I was to go into digs with another girl. Then my father put his spoke in. He said I wasn't going. That was a real shocker for me. Imagine what it meant to an eighteen-year-old girl who had worked as hard as possible to go to the Royal Academy and on to Europe. But he wanted me to go to one of those terrible snobbish schools in Switzerland. He put it off. I remained in South Africa and met my husband . . .

"I've always been attracted to things English. When South Africa became a republic, I was personally deeply upset with the thought of South Africa divorcing itself completely from England. The National Party just got stronger and stronger and stronger. And here we are in this beautiful valley, living in a beautiful little fool's paradise. People go on with every comfort you can think of, with their servants and their beautiful homes, and yet awful things are happening around us. We all say, 'Isn't it ghastly.' But what do we do? We do nothing. When I was younger, I was part of the Black Sash. I felt that we should make some kind of public protest. But you can't get enough people to do it. After we moved out to Malawi, we used to return to see our friends. Each time we returned, we discovered, to our horror, that more and more of them had become Nats. My husband asked one of them, a lawyer, why he had joined the Nats. He said, 'Expediency.' I think, Vincent, you'll find as you move through life that economics is the greatest power in the world.

"It was painful for my husband. He loved South Africa. He had fought for his country, and he had very nearly died for it. He was a true South African. He fought in German South West Africa. He was in the cavalry. When the campaign was over, he came back to Johannesburg and wanted to join Alistair Miller's Airmen, but they told him that at twenty-four he was too old. So my husband put his few pennies together and got over to London on his own steam and joined the Royal Flying Corps to fight for South Africa. They were the ancestors to the RAF. It was a miracle that he survived, that any of them survived. They were given a lifetime of four hours over France. They were flying little things that looked like paper kites. They had no radar, no parachutes, the crudest of instruments, hardly a decent map. My husband survived because his plane crashed in England. The other pilots in his group were all killed over France. He had only one-half hour more of solo time before he was to be sent on his first mission to France. He didn't want to fly that morning. He felt he was going to crash, but you could never say you didn't want to fly. He went up. He stalled his plane the way you stall a car. He wasn't high enough to pick up flying speed again, and he was too high to make a controlled landing. He was picked up with a shockingly broken leg and rushed to a hospital. He lay in hospital for thirteen months and was then sent back to South Africa on a long leave. He was waiting to return to the Flying Corps when the armistice was declared."

Catherine is an eloquent speaker. She has an extraordinary memory and can literally repeat the program of a concert she attended in Buenos Aires in 1932. She often entertains the English farmers with her travel stories, though she sometimes irritates them with her *cultural* presumption. She herself is aware of this, and she watches herself carefully. Some of her stories have poignant metaphorical connotations, which, without being fully acknowledged, are disturbing to her listeners. I remember her describing a trip to South America in the thirties. She was on a cargo ship that was carrying Japanese immigrants to Brazil.

"These immigrants were taken from the poorest people imaginable. They were literally starving. They were moved as families. The oldest and the youngest had to come. They would never see Japan again. Never, never, never. It was an enormous enterprise. One man explained it all to me. He was the head Jap.* He traveled with them. He was an enormous man. I had thought all Japs were tiny, but this one could easily have touched the ceiling. He was very cultured and spoke perfect English. There were over a thousand Japs on board. He would deliver them and leave them. We watched them disembark. It took a whole day. It was a very interesting thing, very sad in a way. When the ship eventually steamed off, leaving them all standing on the dock, each of the children waved two little flags they had been given. One was Japanese and the other was Brazilian. This big Jap, the man who was managing it all, was standing next to me. Tears were pouring down his face. 'This is the part,' he said, 'I can't bear. We just leave them standing there wondering what on earth will happen to them.' "

There is one set of travel tales that Catherine does not tell the valley farmers. These have to do with her trip to Israel. Catherine is proud of being Jewish. She has, in fact, a rather romantic picture of being Jewish. She knows, however, that it is awkward to talk about being Jewish among the valley farmers. It is not that they are anti-Semitic—some are, some are not—but to discuss the matter is to acknowledge a difference that is best left unacknowledged.

"We flew from Athens to Tel Aviv and spent twelve days in Israel. I was interested in seeing all the work the Zionists had done. I had worked for their cause for years. I think that from the time I could think straight, I was a Zionist. I was very keen to see what we'd done. It was quite extraordinary. Israel benefited from the great happening in Europe. There were top people everywhere—even on the kibbutzim. I was taken all over by WIZO—that's the Women's International Zionist Organization. (My husband had a

*"Jap" is used rather more frequently by white South Africans than by Americans. Although it has a derogatory connotation, I do not think Catherine Fox was being derogatory when she used it. "Jap" for her was a "relic" of the war.

cousin who was one of the very big noises in the organization.) They have everything possible for children—even the premature ones. They concentrate on them. They have the most wonderful wards for these children. They have fantastic doctors—all the top brains of Germany and other parts of Europe that had to flee Hitler. Everything is absolutely the latest . . . It was very exciting."

"Did you ever think of settling in Israel?"

"I thought about it a lot after my husband died. I thought I would like to go but that it was too late. I wouldn't be useful enough there. There is really no reason to go if you can't pull your weight. They don't want people just sitting around—redundant people. I think there are quite a lot of rich people who have gone from South Africa. They have adopted Israel. But that does not appeal to me very much. If I'd been younger, I would have gone and worked there. I feel there is a tremendous purpose there."

"Which you don't feel in South Africa?" I asked.

"No, not at all. You feel the energy, the purpose there, the future. It's vibrant. You can feel the throb of the country. You can feel that everybody's working with tremendous purpose. If you want to plant a seed in the garden, you probably have to remove six huge stones to make room for it. You have a sense of achievement when you've cleared the tiny spot and planted your seed. You know the seed is going to do something. I don't feel that here. I don't know why. When I was busy raising children and leading a full life, I felt absolutely at home here, comfortable and happy, but I never felt South African. I never felt I belonged here."

The other English-speaking inhabitants of the valley do not talk about England with as much longing as Catherine Fox does. Few of them have spent as much time there as she has. England is, however, of central importance to their lives. It represents a richness, an authenticity, a meaning, a texture, they do not find at home. Listening to them talk about England, I sometimes had the impression of people talking about a play they had seen and with which they had intensely identified. They knew the scene. They knew the plot. They knew the actors. And yet there was a distance—the distance of representation—between them and their England. They simply were not English.

England is for them the source of their cultural life and the values they hold most deeply. It provides them with a model of social understanding. To listen to Peggy Malan and her "mates" gossip is at times like listening to someone read from the *Tatler*. There is something distinctly literary, Victorian, in Peggy's understanding of social relations. Carol Reid, one of the few English-speaking women in the valley who has not visited England, recognizes her completely literary knowledge of that country. "Whenever I think of England, I think of the stories my mother read me when I was a little girl. I think of the great novels we read in school, of Jane Austen, the Brontë sisters, Dickens, and Galsworthy. I have always wanted to visit England, but I am afraid I would be terribly disappointed. My England is not the England of today." Carol accepts the England of her stories and novels as having once been. She allows no room for literary convention.

Carol's nostalgia, if it is possible to refer to her feelings as nostalgia, is by no means unique. England is for the English of the valley the England of stories and tales. It is an England of memory revived through the telling of these tales and stories. It is through memory that England—and the connection with England—come alive. It is through "living an English life" that the connection also comes alive. Narrative performance and the performances of everyday life serve the same purpose. They are both in their own way magical performances and removed as such from the reality of whatever it is that South Africa is. Despite the allegiance that the English-speaking South Africans have to South Africa, their locus of meaning and values, of significance, is elsewhere. It is in part this displacement that leads the Afrikaners to call them *salties*.

I do not mean to suggest that other immigrant populations—settlers abroad, expatriates of several generations, or exiles—do not experience this displacement of values and meanings. I am certain they do. But I am equally certain that to the extent that they live in a society with, in their terms, an "open future," the external locus of values and meaning is gradually replaced by an "internal" one. For today's white South African the experience of the future is "closed." Just as the Afrikaners "who have no place to go" dig themselves into a laager, so the English maintain their *connection* with England. Israel and the larger Jewish community abroad serve, I believe, a similar function for the South African Jews.

For many English South Africans England represents not only a locus of significance but also a refuge: a place to go if they are forced to leave South Africa. In recent years, however, with the economic and social difficulties in which England finds itself, the inflation, the unemployment, the social unrest, the strikes, the apathy—all of which are stressed in the South African news media—it no longer offers the secure refuge it did in the past. When I asked Jack Freeling where he would go if he had to leave South Africa, he answered, "I'd go to England from my point of view. I'd probably go to Australia from the children's point of view. I think there is probably a bright future there. But we'd go to England first, certainly. I find the Australians brash and vulgar. Of course, the children would get used to it. They'd grow up there. Also, I have a feeling for this country. To run away is not part of one's setup really. I shall certainly stick it out, but the children might leave. My nephew is finishing university this year, and he is going to England. He's up to where he has had it. His father went through hell to get him a job in an international firm. I have talked about the possibility of leaving with my own children—they're really too young to consider it—but I had to stop because they got so upset and so insecure. We'll just see what will happen. They must find their own way and see where their future lies."

Jack Freeling is one of the angriest farmers in the valley. He talks at times of becoming a librarian or an archivist in England. His wife, who has even closer ties to England than he does, notes that their children consider themselves South Africans in a way in which they themselves never did. Even though they go to English medium schools, they no longer prepare for English examinations but for the South African matriculation. "We knew *our* kings and queens, *our* battles and treaties; I knew the names of all the counties of England before I ever saw a single one. The children today learn none of this. They learn South African history. I suppose it is as it should be." The Freelings' eldest son, who was listening to his mother, said, "But, Mom, how many times must you study the same thing? Each year we study the Great Trek."

For many of Wyndal's English, England is also the land of lost possibilities. It is the place where one could have gone before it was too late. It is the place where one should have stayed if one spent any time there. Hugo Malan, who studied at Cambridge, often talks of the offers he received from British engineering firms upon his graduation. When his friends from Johannesburg or Durban visit him, they talk late into the night about lost possibilities of opportunities never taken. I was at first reminded of the lines of the Portuguese poet Fernando Pessoa

> If at some point in time
> I had turned left instead of right;
> If at some moment
> I had said yes instead of no, or no instead of yes;
> If, in conversation,
> I had used the words which only now I drowsily devise—
> If all that had been so,
> I'd be different now, and perhaps the universe itself
> Would be subtly induced to be different too.*[2]

But as I listened more carefully and came to know Hugo and his friends better, I realized that I was not listening to stories of regret —though, to be sure, there was often regret in them—but to stories of self-affirmation. Great stock is laid in international offers. Talking about them not only gives one prestige and a competitive advantage *vis-à-vis* one's contemporaries, but it also gives assurance that being wanted elsewhere, overseas, in England, is not an impossible dream. Time in narration and the time of narrating are collapsed for a magical instant even among men as coldly rational, as pragmatic, as Hugo and his friends.

Hugo's stories—and many others I heard—end with the decision to return to South Africa. They affirm one's ties to South Africa and justify the life one has chosen. Hugo romanticizes his Cambridge days, but he also recalls the cold winters, the "bed and breakfast" with dank sheets he lived in in Manchester during a summer's apprenticeship, and the unfriendliness of his colleagues there, that is, until they discovered at the end of the summer that he was a tennis player. Then they had something in common and could be

---

*Se em certa altura
Tivesse voltado para a esquerda em vez de para a direita;
Se em certo momento
Tivesse dito sim em vez de não, ou não em vez de sim;
Se em certa conversa
Tivesse tido as frases que só agora, no meio-sono, elaboro—
Se tudo isso tivesse sido assim,
Seria outro hoje, e talvez o universo inteiro
Seria insensìvelmente levado a ser outro tembém.

friendly. Hugo missed the openness of South Africa. He expresses no wonder at the absence of productivity in England.

England is also a place of disappointment. Almost all of Wyndal's English who have visited England describe a certain disappointment on their first trip there. They did not find it as genteel as they expected, as honest and upright, as well spoken, as welcoming, as beautiful even. They were shocked by the poverty. They felt constricted by the social forms. Like Hugo, they missed the openness of the veld, the vast stretches of unpopulated land, the savage mountains, and the warmth of South Africa. They missed the possibility, the adventure, of South Africa. England seemed too fixed. They felt at times snubbed; they realized, and this was most disturbing, that they did not really belong, that despite themselves they were not English but South African. England could not live up to the England of their imagination, the England of bedtime stories, novels, and tales told by their parents and grandparents. They felt cheated by these idealized stories, but, I think, they knew the need for them, for they themselves tell them now.

Peter Cooke

"I was sent overseas as an apprentice. It is a tradition in my family. My dad did it, and I was expected to do it. It was my first trip abroad. I was unhappy for the first four months. People in England were aloof, and the family with whom I was living did not take much of a liking to me. I had been raised with the idea that all things English were the best, that the English were hardworking people, that English values were the most moral, that the English language was the most wonderful, that the English were kindly.

"When I got to England, I was terribly shocked. I had lived in a very sheltered environment. I had not really experienced the world. England was a vast opening up. I suddenly discovered how people could be cruel to one another. I was shaken by this. I was made to do menial things: to run errands, to stamp papers, to proofread. I suppose that is a good thing. It was the way in which it was done. But there was no sense of growth. There was no sense of direction. It was a little like a balloon. You can press the balloon, and it moves in a certain direction. Or you can let it be just as it is. That is the way it was in England. It is the older men who do all the work. The young ones leave early. They don't really work very hard. They begin work at nine or nine-thirty in the morning, and they take many tea breaks. In Germany it is different. The Germans begin work at seven in the morning. They were supposed to be our enemies!

"I began to play rugby and squash, and finally I began to make a few friends. I probably should have stayed longer. My godfather —he is English—wanted me to stay longer, but I didn't like it there and came home on my own terms. I never really took seriously the idea of staying in Europe. I found it all too conservative. I was keen on getting ahead in the world of business.

"I realized that I was not in fact English. South Africans are always pretending to be English. Have you been to any of the clubs in Cape Town? They have special railings for the old men to get out of the baths. They have huge palm trees in the halls and a big bust of Queen Victoria. They serve onions and tripe at lunch on Wednesdays. My English friends from England laugh at them. They find them more English than the English.

"Of course, my parents and their generation remember England from another time. I was terribly confused when I returned to South Africa. The English-speaking community was in tremendous political despondency. South Africa had become a republic while I was away. We, the English, were being more and more excluded from everything, and the Afrikaners were rushing into business everywhere. Why bother with politics? we asked ourselves. I concerned myself with my business activities."

10

CONVERSION

Hennie

"The first time I experienced the in-filling of the Spirit I was in Rhodesia. I was told that two women in the parish had this experience of being filled with the Spirit and praying in tongues. I didn't much worry about it because there were only two of them. I did notice that they were different from the other members of the congregation. They seemed more dedicated. They were really moved by the Lord. I couldn't give them enough to do. Then, when I was transferred to another parish, one of my best friends there told me that she had been filled with the Spirit. What could I say? I saw that she was very devoted.

"It was about this time that David was becoming difficult. He was sixteen and was very much involved with the hippies. I could see that if he went the wrong way, he'd do it in a big way. That's the sort of person David is. One weekend a friend of mine invited David to a youth camp near Bulawayo. When David came back, he told me that he had committed his life to Christ, that he had been filled with the Spirit. The camp was run by the Assemblies of God. When I saw the transformation in David, I went back to my Bible and discovered that being filled with the Spirit is scripturally correct. I became interested myself. I asked a minister in the Assemblies of God in Salisbury to pray for me and to lay hands on me. I was sure that God had touched me, but nothing spectacular happened.

"I was then transferred to the Cape. I asked the archbishop to lay hands on me. Again nothing seemed to happen. A week or so later I was conducting a retreat, and it was then that I realized that something dramatic had in fact happened in my life. When I prayed for people who were sick, they recovered! Or they were filled with the Spirit. From that moment on, *that* was my ministry. I rejoiced. I started to minister in my own parish with tremendous success.

"It was about this time that the archbishop asked me to take over a particularly difficult Coloured parish. The archbishop had sacked the previous priest for a financial scam, and no priest in the diocese would take it over. The congregation was too rebellious. I eventually agreed. I started a Bible study group—to get the parishioners to know Jesus. Three months later, I asked them if they wanted to be filled with the Holy Spirit. If they did, I said, I would pray for them. About eighty people came up to the altar. I started laying hands on them. Each and every one of them swooned under the power of the Spirit. They were lying there before the altar like dead people. We had to drag them away to make room for the next lot. Something had happened. People were so scared that they ran from the church. Those who came to know Jesus knew He was alive. When I first came to the parish, there was scarcely any church attendance. Two months after the people had been filled with the Spirit, you had to come early to get a seat. The church seated six hundred!

"It was the first time I had seen anything like it. Never in such quantity. You could feel the power of the Spirit so mightily. It was frightening. I felt absolutely drained. That evening I asked two of the Coloured ministers to lay hands with me. I didn't want people to think it was me. With three you knew who was responsible. One of the blokes didn't have time to lay hands on the people. He was so busy catching those who were falling!

"The other bloke asked me the next day how I knew it was going to happen. I answered that I believed God's word. Jesus had said, 'If you who are evil know how to give good gifts to your children, know then how much more your heavenly father will give to those who ask.' I was, I suppose you could say, inspired. I was filled with the conviction that I could rely on God to do this.

"Praying in tongues is like praying in any other language. You can start and stop when you like. Initially, I find that most people start babbling and can't stop. I remember a woman who was sitting next to me in a service in Port Elizabeth. She was filled with the Spirit. She praised God, on her way home even. At home she said, 'Lord, there is so much I want to tell you but I don't know the words. You have to give me a language to express it.' At that moment she burst into tongues and went on for an hour. It was as if a dam had broken in her. She wanted to tell God that she loved Him. You can't say it in simple words. You have to let the dam empty. Afterwards you can control it.

"Once you have experienced the in-filling of the Spirit, your whole outlook changes. Someone can ask you to do something, and you do it out of loyalty or because of some outward pressure. That is the way most of us act most of the time. But when you are doing it out of love, there is an inner urge. There is no hardship no matter how hard it is. You enjoy doing it. This can only happen when God does something to you. He writes His laws on your heart, and those laws become the inner urge. You can't be thinking about keeping the law. You just want to please Him so in the process you're keeping the law.

"It is God who pours His love into your heart when you've been filled with the Holy Spirit. Paul describes it, especially in Romans. It is not the love for God but the love for mankind that God pours into your heart. But it is not a vague sort of general love that doesn't mean anything. It is a particular love for a particular individual. You know He loves you even though His love for you isn't the same as His love for another individual. His love for you is not the same as His love for me because you are a different person. So God loves differently, simply because we are different. But I know that He loves you, and because He does and because I love Him and He loves me, I also want to love you irrespective of the kind of person you are. I may not like the kind of person you are, but I still want to love you.

"Yes, it is something outside coming in, but you sort of feel it from inside. You want to do it. You want to love. It is something God put there. You've got to have courage to change. You can't force the change on anyone. Too many of us expect a gondolier church, where the priest does everything, to just sit back and let the other guy do the rowing. But you can't change people that way. Change will only come when you have no option. The commitment must already be there."

* * *

Hennie's reference to those who expect a gondolier church is to those who are complacent. Hennie is an activist. His activism is at the heart of his commitment to Christ, and it is expressed in his intensely evangelical ministry. He is distressed, if not downright angered, by those, especially those whites in his congregation, who shield themselves through their faith from the disturbing realities around them—from their own consciences. One's faith in God should not, he argues, lead to a complacent acceptance of the world around one. It should inspire one to change the world—to make it into a true Christian community. Such change cannot come about by "fussing" with the institutions of society as political activists would have it. It must come about through one's commitment to Christ. "It is only when you have met Christ," Hennie says, "that you have the power to love your fellowmen as they are, in their difference. Such love, Christian love, the love of one's fellowman through Christ, must be at the base of society." Institutional change will follow of itself.

"The Renewal," Hennie insists, "is not the same as a revival. The Renewal must take place in an established community. You need the support of others. There must be someone to supervise the whole thing. I wouldn't dream of preaching in Jo'burg and then leaving the people who had received the Spirit. I'd feel immoral. I've listened to Billy Graham. I think he is sincere. But he is acting as a midwife and bringing people into Christ and then leaving them. You can't take a newborn baby and leave it with a pile of apples and let it take care of itself. I remember one bloke who said he had been saved four times by Billy Graham!

"What you are seeing in Wyndal is a real Renewal. It is part of a much larger movement. It is not limited by denominations. People all over the world are being called by the Spirit. It is very strong in the Cape, but it is also strong in the Natal and growing in the Transvaal and the Free State. Of course, it is not new to this area. It was in 1910, I believe, that a minister in the Dutch Reformed Church and his congregation began to pray in tongues. They were eventually forced out of the church, and they formed the beginnings of a Pentecostal Church in South Africa. Unfortunately, they laid too much stress on speaking in tongues and on being rebaptized. It's obvious they never made the impact they should have. If they had just preached the power of the Holy Spirit, I think they would have won over the whole territory. But they confined themselves to those who actually spoke in tongues.

"And this is happening again today. Some people in the Renewal are putting too much stress on the symbols rather than on the reality of Christ and His teachings. They demand a second baptism, and neither the Anglican Church nor the Dutch Reformed Church nor any mainline church can accept that. It's causing a real crisis in the Reformed Church here. I will have to speak to the *dominee*. If he's not careful, he'll lose half his congregation. Andre Roussouw has just joined up with the Baptists. His wife already had last year. And there are many others. They are turning to the Renewal because there is more freedom than in their own church. They have to seek the experience of the Spirit outside the church! People who felt powerless in their own churches suddenly find power in the Renewal. They see a type of early church which has the power to convince and convert. It is a very strong experience.

"The Dutch Reformed Church frowns on this. They set up a special committee to investigate it, and I believe the committee has made a provisional report in which they admit there is some truth in it. A number of ministers who have been moved by the Spirit have formed a sort of spiritual community, *koinonia* they call it. I've spoken to them, and many have received the Spirit."

Hennie is always careful not to question the faith of those who do not display the signs of being filled with the Holy Spirit: trances, praying in tongues, visionary experiences, and other "encounters" with Christ. He refuses to call those who have had the baptism of the Spirit Christians in such a way as to imply that those who have not had the experience are not *real* Christians. Many members of the Renewal in South Africa do refer to themselves as Christians in precisely this way. In what must surely be regarded as a Calvinistic twist, they regard themselves as God's elect. Hennie has learned, he says, through his meetings with Christ, through prayer, to be patient. God's will will be done in its own time. It is not for man to question. This patience was, I should perhaps add, an important factor in his relationship to me; for Hennie, always the evangelist, hoped, I believe, that through his talks with me I would come to experience the in-filling of the Spirit. He never once made an active attempt to convert me. I was never convinced that he much liked me.

Charismatic Christianity is, from what I could observe, spreading

among South African whites.* The Renewal is particularly important in the Anglican Church, in the Catholic Church, and in such
Pentecostal Churches as the Baptists and the Assemblies of God.
The Dutch Reformed Churches, which, given their stance on apartheid, are not on the best of terms with the other Christian churches
in South Africa, have generally looked askance at recent enthusiastic
worship. There have been several interdenominational Renewal
conferences in the last few years. The Cape Renewal Conference in
1981 had over 6,000 registered participants of all colors and creeds.
Hennie has been active in organizing less formal interdenominational fellowships and Bible study groups. He is, at times, almost
heretically anti-establishmentarian. When he is carried away, I have
heard him argue that the church hierarchy and even the buildings
themselves—"they impose a formality"—interfere with true Christian fellowship in Christ. He would like to see a return to simple
household churches, where Christians can worship without encum-
brance.

The Renewal in the Anglican Church is particularly strong in the
Cape and is increasing elsewhere in South Africa. The former archbishop of the Anglican Province of Southern Africa, who was based
in Cape Town, was charismatic and encouraged his fellow clergymen in that direction. With considerable exaggeration, Hennie says
that when he returned to South Africa fifteen years before, only
three of the hundred and eighty priests in the Cape diocese were in
the Renewal, whereas today almost half of them are. More realisti-
cally, about thirty of the priests have had charismatic experiences.
Since the entire staff of St. Paul's College, the Anglican seminary
in Grahamstown, was charismatic in 1981, priests in the Renewal
were hoping for a marked increase in the movement in the next few
years.

Members of the Renewal, like Hennie, tell stories of extraordinary conversions, miraculous healings, and "groups overcome
mightily by the Spirit of the Lord." They attest to the power of the

---

*Among Jews, particularly of what I call the middling middle class, the Lubavitch
movement—a legalistic fundamentalist movement that advocates an isolating com-
munitarianism—is spreading. Members of this movement, like many members of
the Christian Renewal, remove themselves from active political engagement and
concern. There are, to be sure, many politically active Jews—most liberal, but
some, like the members of the Students' Jewish and Zionist Association, very
conservative.

Lord and the strength of the Renewal. Saint Paul is frequently the model for individual conversions, Christ for miraculous healings, and for the enthusiasm of groups. Trances, praying in tongues, visions, and extraordinary auditory phenomena are understood as the in-flowing of the Spirit of the Lord and implicitly at least as a sign of divine election. The in-flowing of the Holy Spirit is sometimes referred to as the baptism of the Spirit. It is associated with rebirth. Several charismatic priests with whom I talked defined the charismatic experience as rebirth by the power of the Holy Spirit or as renewal through the power of the Holy Spirit. They did not much like definitions. They smacked of an intellectualism to which they were generally opposed. What is important, they argue, is the experience itself. Emphasis is on the life of prayer. One awaits the word of Christ. Hennie prepares his sermons now by praying as fervently as possible until Christ tells him, quite literally from what I could make out, what he ought to preach. One well-known priest who is active in the movement refused to see me until he had prayed to Christ and received His consent. When I arrived at the interview, he talked nonstop for two and a half hours, jumping from subject to subject, closing his eyes and remaining silent for long stretches of time, preaching at times, confessing at others, and arguing at still others. His mood shifted from elation to despair, from optimism to pessimism, from intellectual engagement to emotional release. I felt as though I were witnessing a performance, which reminded me of shamanistic performances I had seen among the Navaho or among exorcists and mystics in Morocco. His performance was extreme, but I observed something of this "letting go," this succumbing to emotion, this loosening up of the conventions that bind normal discourse, in several of my more charismatic acquaintances. Hennie, I should add, never *let go* in my presence, although once in talking about Satanism he seemed to have lost his critical perspective for a few moments.

"The Renewal is God's response to the evil that is spreading throughout the world, but, fortunately, the growth of the charismatic movement is much faster than the growth of the Satanic churches. But evil *is* spreading. I think that God has allowed a Marxist regime in Rhodesia to cleanse His church there."

I was taken aback by Hennie's equating of Satan, evil, and Mugabe's government.

"I remember a man came to speak to us about the church of Satan. They had given him a wafer to chew and to spit out, and instead of wine, the blood of a black cat. He was made to promise to do everything he could to dishonor the name of Christ. They had sexual orgies. Sometimes people became ice-cold. They were demon-possessed. He said they used to pray for the moral breakup of clerical marriages.

"I myself came across a case of a man in prison whose sister was messed up with one of these Satanic churches. She had gone out with a man from the church, and then she found a chicken bone in a pint of black paint she had bought. She showed it to her brother, who threw it in a dam. He was immediately bitten on his thumb by a snake, and then every night demons would enter him in the form of cats. To discourage them, he gave up eating meat. That did no good. I prayed with him and got him to make a commitment to Christ.

"There are times when you perform an exorcism that you can actually see the demons leave. They look like monsters in old pictures. Satan and the demons are the defeated enemy. They have no real power. They just pretend to have it. You have to be filled with the Spirit and have the power and authority of Christ. You name the demon and command him to leave.

"I've been told that there are about fifty thousand members of the church of Satan in South Africa. They do not advertise. You are brought in by a friend. The head of the Assemblies of God here says there are about thirty-five million worshipers of Satan in Brazil alone.

"Now you may have heard about the Illuminati," Hennie went on after a somewhat overly dramatic pause. I was disconcerted. I felt as though I had suddenly tapped into a current of irrationality that could not be stopped. "Personally, I don't know much about them. They are a group of leaders, intelligentsia, whatever you'd like to call them, operating behind the scenes in every country in the world. They want to take over the world. Nobody can tell you who they are or where their head office is. That's what makes them so frightening.

"I myself have never taken them very seriously," Hennie said reflectively. He seemed to come back to himself. "Obviously God is ultimately in control. I believe in the victory of good over the forces of evil. You will find in the Bible that God sometimes makes use of what looks evil to us for His own ends. He then discards it.

So I'm not terribly worried about these Illuminati. I can't really believe that they have the power to manipulate every government and to control the world. It's pretty fantastic.

"People today are willing to believe just about anything they read in the newspapers, see on television, or hear on tapes. There are a lot of tapes in the religious field coming into South Africa from America. They can be very damaging to people who come newly into the experience of the Spirit unless they are firmly grounded in a church where there are some guides."

I asked Hennie if any Afrikaners had turned to his church.

"No, not here. It's easier for them to become Baptists or members of the Assemblies of God. There they have models. There is a Dominee Hugo who was baptized a second time and forced to leave the church. Have you met him? He comes out here every so often to lead a Bible study group at Andre Roussouw's. (I used to go myself but then I started my own Bible study group.) And there is Rudy Malherbe. He's the expert on the Illuminati. I don't think he's been out here yet. He was a *predikant* [minister] who had a vision one day and received the Spirit. His message was too much for the church." Hennie laughed.

"But don't you think it would be harder for them to become Anglicans because of community pressure?"

"You mean joining the enemy?"

"Well, yes."

"No. I don't think there would be that much pressure. Community pressure is no longer so great here. The Afrikaans element is becoming diluted. I don't think they can pressure anyone anymore. There are so many English here now. The character of the place has changed completely."

I asked Hennie whether he thought this a good thing. He answered that he did not necessarily think being an Afrikaner was a negative thing. I explained that I had meant that through the Renewal Afrikaners and English were coming together. So it seemed to me, at least in the valley.

"If they discover that they are South Africans," Hennie answered skeptically, "then it will be a great step forward. You can't live cheek by jowl and not come together."

I laughed. Whites and Coloureds had been living "cheek by jowl" for generations without coming together. Hennie did not understand my laugh.

"In the first nine months that I was here," Hennie went on, "over a thousand people were filled with the Spirit. The church of Satan cannot boast of that kind of success. The Devil is panicking because he knows his time is short. He's got to make the most of it. You see the transition: The hippies have given way in America to the Jesus Freaks."

The stories that Hennie and other charismatics tell have a strong prophetic quality about them. (Hennie's talk about the Satanic church and the powers of evil is rather unusual for a South African Anglican charismatic, but it is not unusual for members of the more Pentecostal churches.) Bible study groups among Wyndal's Pentecostals stress divination and prophecy. They look especially to the Book of Revelations and the prophetic texts of the Old Testament. They propose gloomy futures from which the true Christians—the Christians of the Renewal—will be saved. Debate concerns whether or not the "Christians" will be saved before, during, or after the time of troubles. Plans for the future frequently involve establishing little communities of the faithful that will help one another resist the temptations of the devil and live together as good Christians.

The Anglican charismatics place less stress on the Last Judgment and the Apocalypse than do the Pentecostals, Hennie says. Nevertheless apocalyptic thinking does occur. I was told, for example, that during the Renewal Conference in Johannesburg in 1977, an Anglican dreamed that there was a terrible stench in the lounge. He asked God why. God showed him seven coffins labeled "Black," "White," "Coloured," and so on. God said, "If you go on using labels, you see now what my judgment will be. Neither run ahead nor run behind but stay together." Word of the dream spread through the conference. Works like Nadine Gordimer's *July's People*, J. M. Coetzee's *Waiting for the Barbarians*, and other recent South African novels and short stories concerned with the future are, in my friend Carl's words, rehearsals for the future.

The Anglican Church is perhaps the most politically active church in South Africa. It is certainly the most vocal in its criticism of the South African government and its policy of apartheid. It is concerned more with bringing about change in the here and now than in some other place and time. The former archbishop of Cape Town, Bill Burnett, wrote in the August 1980 issue of *Good Hope*, the church's monthly newsletter:

We are not in Christ prisoners of our history. Jesus is Lord and not our past. We are free to accept change and to be changed. We do not have to wait for everyone always to have acted rightly before we talk or negotiate with them and before we find one another in Christ . . . If we really believe we can be a Christian fellowship only when our future is absolutely secure or when justice prevails, we shall remain of all men most miserable because we shall never find what we hope for and we will have totally missed the point of the Gospel of Grace. We will be thinking as the world thinks. We will continue to act with the mind of the flesh.

There is considerable conflict today between the charismatics and the non-charismatics in South Africa's Anglican Church. Many of Wyndal's English refuse to attend Hennie's church not only because he has invited in the Coloureds but because he is a charismatic. Some of the former parishioners go to more conservative churches in neighboring communities. One priest, who is Anglo-Catholic in orientation, tried at first to sidestep the Renewal issue by explaining that he considered himself charismatic even though he had never had a "charismatic experience."

"A Christian can only be charismatic because one can only really be a true Christian within the power of the Holy Spirit. One cannot function otherwise. One needs a spirit far greater than oneself. I know that in my own life I alone could never have done the things I've done. I haven't the necessary background or education. I believe that there is a greater power at work, and for that reason I believe that I am a charismatic.

"I am only against the charismatic movement when it becomes sectarian. What I can't handle about them is their assumption that they alone have God on their side. They make other Christians into third-rate citizens in the church. Only God can judge what level Christian you are. As an Anglican priest I feel that I've got to try to minister to a diversity of people who fall within my parochial boundary. I would not like to exclude anyone.

"I don't want to condemn the charismatics. I think they have taught us the importance of small groups worshiping together. I think it is only in small groups that the church can survive. And perhaps God has worked through them to show us that the Anglican Church in South Africa is too British—too cold, too formal, without emotion. But one must be careful about one's emotions. This is the dangerous side to the charismatic movement. One can become very emotionally orientated, coming back each week for an injection of emotion."

Many members of the South African Anglican community are offended by the importance given emotion by the charismatics. Peggy Malan says that she stopped going to church when she was told that she ought to give open expression to her emotions in church. "For me," she says, "religion is a very personal and a very private matter. I don't want to share my innermost feelings with just anyone who happens to be next to me. I certainly don't want to show my emotions. Perhaps I am wrong. Perhaps it is good to show one's feelings. I simply can't. I wasn't brought up that way." She adds with unusual anger that now that she has learned that the Anglican Church contributes to the World Council of Churches, which supports the guerrillas on the border, she will never set foot in the church again. (While I was living in the valley, word spread that the Anglican Church was supporting freedom fighters in Angola, Namibia, and elsewhere in southern Africa. I was never able to discover any evidence for this assertion among the people with whom I talked.)

Carol Reid, who is equally angered by the Anglican Church's supposed contribution to the guerrillas, says that she is distressed to see the beauty of the liturgy supplanted by handclapping and the singing of crude hymns. "If they must swing their bodies, why don't they go to a discotheque?" one of Carol's friends asks. Jack Freeling, who attends church in Cape Town when he can, says that he wishes the charismatics would all join the Baptists, and Hugo Malan, who hasn't been to church since he was married, says he is worried about the irrationalism that is creeping into the church. He does not believe the church should interfere in politics. "One of the great advances in civilization," he says "was the separation of church and state. The Afrikaners never learned this lesson. They are always confusing the two, and now the Anglicans are doing the same." Still another English farmer, who, rumor has it, votes for the Nats, quotes Paul: "Let every person be subject to the governing authorities. For there is no authority except from God, and those that exist have been instituted by God. Therefore he who resists the authorities resists what God has appointed, and those who resist will incur judgment."[1] Although he is one of Wyndal's richest farmers, he says that he will not "give one bloody penny to a bunch of old blokes who foam at the mouth when they pray and incite revolution."

One of the most passionate Anglican priests I talked to says that the English cannot deal with emotion. He insists that the problems in South Africa are not of a moral nature but of an emotional one. Those who think they are of a moral nature are misguided. The English cannot express emotion; the Afrikaners express emotion— look at their "hot" parliamentary debates—but can't control it; the Blacks and, to a lesser extent, the Coloureds "have the purest emotion that gives correct expression to the Spirit. It is a joy to work with them. There is something so fresh about their emotional expression. To solve South Africa's problems we must all learn to give expression to our emotions—not an uncontrolled expression but a controlled one. Such a controlled expression can only come through the Spirit."

Mysticism, emotion, politics, exclusivism, and hierarchy are all confused with one another in the conflict between charismatic and non-charismatic Anglicans. During the 1981 election of a new archbishop for the Province of Southern Africa, the charismatic faction was apparently opposed to the election of the Black bishop Desmond Tutu because he was not sympathetic to the Renewal. Blacks, I was told, have not been particularly active in the charismatic movement. Hennie says that in his experience, in Rhodesia, they preferred the most colorful possible ritual of the High Church. (The charismatics are very Low Church.) Bishop Tutu's supporters opposed the charismatics because they were not politically active enough. A compromise candidate, neither Black nor charismatic, was eventually chosen. Bishop Tutu, who was to win the Nobel Peace Prize in 1984, was elected General Secretary of the South African Council of Churches.

One Black Anglican priest with whom I talked said that he was very disappointed in the election. Given the plight of the Black people, Bishop Tutu should have been elected and would have been elected, he argues, had the charismatics been willing to forgo their political position and their "personal salvation." He said he is increasingly troubled by the accusation of more militant Blacks that the Anglican Church is a white man's church—an instrument of imperialism. Since the election of the new archbishop, he has considered leaving the church. Given the Dutch Reformed Church's support of apartheid, many politically conscious Blacks have come to see the Christian churches, and not just the Dutch Reformed Churches, as "clothing naked oppression in Christian vestments."[2] It is indeed ironic that Hennie's talk of "the love for mankind that

God pours into your heart" is taken from Paul: "More than that, we rejoice in our sufferings, knowing that suffering produces endurance, and endurance produces character, and character produces hope, and hope does not disappoint us, because God's love has been poured into our hearts through the Holy Spirit which has been given us."[3]

II

VIOLENCE

Hennie

"It was God strengthening the people for what they would suffer," Hennie said, referring to the mass conversions he had brought about in his Coloured parish in Cape Town. "They became towers of strength during the Cape riots. The riots began on Monday or Tuesday in September. It was about three months after the conversions, which, by the way, took place at about the time of the Soweto riots. On Wednesday I had to organize a relief party to get my assistant priest out of the area. No Europeans were allowed in. But we had discovered a back road in. Every day my assistant—he was white—and I went in to see what we could do to help. It was terrible: The roads were blocked with stones, drums, concrete blocks, and burning tires. The riot squad was there. They were shooting and using tear smoke. Every once in a while we would have to sneak away from where the tear smoke was.

"During the riots we had to cancel church services because it was too dangerous for people to come out onto the streets. If they refused to throw stones, they themselves would be stoned. The police would just start shooting whenever they saw a crowd. They were so heavy-handed. The *skollies*, white and Black, were having a marvelous time throwing stones, shooting, looting. I have no idea how many people were killed—far more than the papers reported. And, of course, they never count the wounded.

"My assistant priest was an Israelite, without any guile in him. He saw a group of people and went over to preach to them. One member of my congregation saw him and realized that he was going to be stoned. She grabbed him and took him to her flat. He was virtually a prisoner. (You see, even during the height of the riots, we could go anywhere provided we were recognized. We hadn't been in the parish long enough to be known by everyone.) She phoned me. At that stage I couldn't get in. The police had the whole area blocked off. I got a Coloured lad with a car to go in. I hid on the floor in the back, and we managed to get through."

"Were you terrified?" I asked Hennie. He had been describing the riots and his participation in them so matter-of-factly.

"It was quite exciting." He laughed. "Well, we finally managed to get the bloke out. The two of us crouched down in the back with some old sacks thrown on top of us.

"The riots lasted a week. We got people to start little prayer groups in their homes. It was the only thing we could do to restore some sense of sanity. They used to invite their nearest neighbors. They prayed to God that peace might descend upon them. When the riots were over, we used the prayer groups to start house churches, and these house churches became the backbone of the parish. I used to train house-church leaders, and they would train others. We started out with seven—there had been more prayer groups during the riots—and we had about fifty by the time I was transferred to another parish."

There were between 80,000 and 100,000 inhabitants in the township in which Hennie's parish was located. It was one of the poorest in Cape Town.

"What was the reaction of the people to the riots?" I asked.

"I think they grew spiritually. The church was the only thing that remained constant in a world that was going mad. The two Coloured blokes who helped me lay on hands and I formed a team. One of them became very anti-white during the riots. The other ministered to him. He asked him how he could hate all whites. Did he hate me? Did he hate my assistant? It was then that he realized his own tremendous racial prejudice—a racial prejudice that he had to overcome.

"After the riots were over, I called all the youth together. They weren't always church people. We had a couple of meetings in the church to discuss the whole thing. I asked them why they had burned down a particular shop. 'Oh, well, we wanted to get the European shop on the other side of the street, but we couldn't get to it because the police stopped us. So we burned this one down.' It didn't seem to matter who owned it, a Coloured chap or not. Or, 'Oh, the police climbed on top of it to shoot at us, so we decided to burn it down the next day.' They didn't have any logic. Most of the time they simply said that the chap had it coming to him.

"Of the two hundred youngsters I interviewed, only one of them could tell me why he was rioting. The others simply said they began to throw stones because everyone else was. And the one who could answer my question was one who had always refused to accept any authority. He knew the answers, but I'm not sure how committed he was to them. I found those who had committed themselves to God were less likely to throw stones because they had another set to identify with. Christianity transcends all barriers. You no longer feel a closeness to that kind of nationalism—Coloured nationalism, any nationalism.

"Of course, this is what many of the Coloureds have against Christianity and the Renewal. By expecting them to forgive, we stop them from doing anything. Once you've had this experience of Renewal, you suddenly see the white man as your brother. You don't feel the same toward him as you did when you lived with him as a Coloured. You find your identity in Christ and not in the color of your skin. You can't press the nationalism part anymore. And this the Nationalists find threatening. I think it is God's way of bringing people together. There are two ways you can get rid of your enemy: One way is to kill him and the other is make a friend of him. The choice is yours. The choice is ours. I've been talking to a lot of Coloured youngsters about these school boycotts."

In 1980 Coloured students in the Cape area, and in other parts of South Africa, began a school boycott to protest the inferior quality of their education.

"They ask me why there is still discrimination if Christ has broken down all dividing barriers. I tell them it is man who has erected these barriers anew. If it is the government that has created the barriers, then it is our job to pray for the government that they may see the light of Christ. Whether you cooperate with the state or you oppose it, even with a revolution, you are supporting a state. The church cannot participate in this. We must establish God's kingdom of justice. The church cannot ignore the social implications of this. A man has a right to earn a living wage. He has the right to live with his family. In the Bible there is some discrimination—against those who do not believe in God. If we all believe in God, then differences do not count. I must tell those who do not believe in God about Him. The church and the world have to become one for there to be the kingdom of God on earth."

I asked Hennie, "But don't you believe that some political action is required in the here and now? It is fine to forgive one's neighbors, but you must remember that the majority of South Africans do not earn a living wage and have no political representation. Their families are divided, and they suffer terrible discrimination. Are you not preaching a passivism that is exactly what the government and its supporters want?"

Hennie smiled, and after a long pause he said, "Well, somehow or other God will do the thing. He gives us each responsibilities, and we must follow Him. He is not going to relieve me of mine. And loving my neighbor is my job. Now, when I still want to pick my neighbor, then I am not really doing my job . . ."

Hennie sidestepped my question as he had done so often in the past. His position, a radical refutation of the state as an interference with God's commandment to love one's neighbor, seemed to me to be praiseworthy enough but so obviously unrealistic—an indulgence that was in no way appropriate to the conditions in which the majority of South Africans lived. Social existence in South Africa is overwhelming. It seemed to me, an outsider, that Hennie, like Rose, could escape it only by losing himself in an otherworldly utopianism.

Albert Jordaan

"It was less dissatisfaction than the perception of difference that triggered off the school boycott and the riots last summer," Albert Jordaan said. He was referring to the school boycott and riots in Cape Town in June 1980. Albert was a lay priest in Hennie's Coloured parish in Cape Town. It was he who had helped Hennie on the morning of the mass conversion, and it was he who ministered to Hennie's other assistant priest who had become violently anti-white during the 1976 riots. "The students realized how great the discrepancy was between their education and the education the whites were receiving. They compared their facilities with those of the white students. They knew the government spent more than twice as much on a white student as on a Coloured one. They knew how inferior their schoolbooks were . . .

"It started at the University of the Western Cape among the students there. They organized discussion groups, they drew up a petition; and they started a protest march that entered the white area. It was this that caused the security police to intervene. The students wanted a peaceful march, I believe, just to vent their feelings, but the security police came and began to beat up children."

"In other words, it was the security police who stimulated the violence," I said.

"Yes. They stimulated the violence."

"Does this happen often?"

"Yes. They usually don't understand the whole situation. It is possible to have group discipline without violence, but the police get too excited."

"Do you think they get too excited or do you think they want violence?" It has been argued with considerable justification that the police do in fact encourage violence in order to quell it, demonstrating their strength to the rioters. Manifestations of violence affirm for the whites the need to keep order even if it involves bloodshed.

"I don't believe they really want violence. No, I can't believe that. They just don't know how to handle the situation. They think they can suppress it by scaring people with force. But force just causes rebellious feelings and terrorism. They deny the people the opportunity to vent their feelings."

"Were you involved in the Cape Town riots in 1976?"

"Yes. It was the riots in Soweto that triggered them off. They also had to do with education. We acted in sympathy. We were all in the same boat. It was difficult as far as the church was concerned. Whose side were we to take? The side of 'law and order' or the side of justice. It was really a false question—a question of misunderstanding—since the question really concerned not law and order versus the absence of law and order but just law and just order versus unjust law and unjust order which we were told were just. We knew better, but we saw the violence and bloodshed.

"I had never been in a riot before. I had seen protests. The people's frustrations mount and mount because there is no place where they can vent their feelings, no place where they can express themselves to a higher authority. They have no one to go to. All channels are shut off. They can only protest and riot. Now they are creating this Coloured Representative Council, but it will have no power. It is not from the people to the government but from the government to the people. It is like a son who wants to go to his father to explain himself. It is terribly frustrating. I have such terrible frustrations in myself. I have no one to go to."

I was not sure whether Albert was using the *I* impersonally to make his point or talking more personally. He went on to criticize the President's Council, which had been proposed by the government as a sort of substitute for Coloured and Asian representation in Parliament.* He did not question the government's refusal to include a Black Council. (The government argued that no Black Council was necessary because all Blacks in South Africa were citizens of their own homelands, which were or would soon be independent.) Like many Coloureds, Albert was not particularly sympathetic to the Blacks, whom he did not understand and whose interests he saw as conflicting with those of his own people. He feared that in the event of a Black takeover his own people would become scapegoats, for they had had more privilege than the Blacks and were not as powerful as the whites. Albert himself, who attended a theological college in Umtata, the capital of the Transkei, the Xhosa homeland, had felt discriminated against by the Xhosa people and other Blacks there.

"If it wasn't for the Anglican Church, the riots would have blown all out of proportion. It helped prepare the people." They became more committed to Christ. They internalized more of his teachings. They understood. They didn't get so cross. The church stemmed the tide. Yes, it did not solve the problems but it stemmed the tide."

"But if it only stemmed the tide . . .?"

"As a Christian I believe that God is leading His people. He is bringing them, in His own time, into step."

Albert seemed nervous. He jumped from sentence to sentence. Each was a theological cliché. Ultimately he argued that it is only through the Spirit that people will come to know one another. "At the moment the church is one of the only places where people of

---

*It is now instituted and despite protests from many liberal Coloureds and Asians, and from Blacks, it has been accepted by the Coloured Labour Party.

different races can come together. It is the only place where they can talk together."

"What was the aftermath of the riots in 1976?" I asked.

"A lot of pupils were shot, and many were killed. The people still bear these scars. Those who were shot or who lost their children will never forget. Unless the government does something concrete about the situation—and they haven't yet, and it is five years now—we are only seeing the beginning of violence."

"Are the Europeans hated?"

"No. The people do not hate the European. They hate his ideology. They hate what the European stands for." Albert was evasive.

"Did those families who lost their children or did those who were hurt come to the church for solace?"

"Actually, they didn't come to the church, because the church preached love. They had to work it through themselves. Many of the people who were most committed stayed away from the church for quite a while. But they came back eventually. They felt that resorting to violence was wrong. The frustration was so great that they could not help themselves. It took time for them to make peace with God.

"And then there were those who talked about the church as being the white man's church. In the office where I was working at the time they talked about the church softening the Black man. It keeps them going in the face of suffering and poverty, but it weakens them so they don't protest.

"My answer to this is that were all men, Coloured, Black, and white, really committed to Christ, they would be able to live together in peace in the body of Christ."

"But what do you say if someone comes up to you and asks you why you are participating in a church that is softening up your own people?"

"The realist will see what the guy means. I believe that I am answerable to God and to God alone. I am not answerable to him. I belong to the church not because it is softening me up but because I believe it is what God wants me to do. It is the only way I can have a relationship with Him. I belong to the church because I belong to God. If God wants me to go into a situation, I will. If He wants me to protest the government, I will. If God wants me to speak out against my brothers, I will. I'm not one-sided, you see. I'm actually, as they say, an ambassador of Christ."

* * *

Since World War II, protest movements by non-whites have followed one another with ever-increasing rapidity. (Gandhi's campaign of passive resistance between 1907 and 1913 to protest
discrimination against the Indian community was the first dramatic
non-white protest movement in South Africa.) Sixty thousand African miners went on strike in the Rand in 1946. In 1949, 142 were
killed and over 1,000 wounded in anti-Indian riots in Durban. Zulu
men looted Indian shops, which they thought had been exploiting
them. At first the police did nothing to quell the rioting; then they
shot at the crowds indiscriminately. There were passive resistance
campaigns in 1952, bus boycotts in Johannesburg in 1956, and protests by African women against the pass system in 1958. The Pan-
Africanist Congress (PAC), later joined by the African National
Congress (ANC), the two strongest Black political organizations in
South Africa, both exiled today, organized anti-pass campaigns in
1960, which led to the Sharpeville massacre.

Sharpeville marked a turning point in Black-white relations. On
March 21, 1960, the police in Vanderbijlpark, in the Transvaal, fired
on protestors who had gathered without their passes in front of the
police station to await arrest and who refused to disperse even when
aircraft dived at them and tear gas was sprayed at them. The police
killed two men before they could disperse the crowd. A few hours
later police reinforcements shifted to the Sharpeville location outside Vereeniging, where thousands had gathered to protest the pass
laws. Apparently, in a moment of panic, police fired on the crowd,
which, according to many eye-witness accounts, was not hostile
(though the police and those sympathetic to them maintained it
was). The police killed sixty-seven Blacks—the majority were hit in
the back as they fled—and wounded one hundred and eighty-six
others. Riots spread to Cape Town. Police killed two demonstrators.
By March 30, the South African government had declared a state of
emergency. Gun shops sold out their stocks to panicky whites.
Inquiries about emigration flooded the Canadian and Australian
embassies. There was massive selling on the Johannesburg Stock
Exchange. It was believed that outside investment in South Africa
would come to a halt. The police arrested and detained thousands.
The strike was finally broken in the second week of April. Authorities began to enforce the pass laws again. (Blacks had burned thousands of passes.) The government banned both the PAC and the

ANC under the newly enacted Unlawful Organization Act. Although many Blacks had caught a glimpse of the potential of civil disobedience, they were highly demoralized by the end of April.[1]

Now underground, the ANC and the PAC both turned to violence. In 1961–1962 Nelson Mandela and Walter Sisulu organized a sabotage unit, Umkhonto we Sizwe (Spear of the Nation), which carried out a number of successful bombings. Police arrested Mandela, Sisulu, and other Umkhonto leaders in July 1963, and the courts sentenced them to life imprisonment. Mandela and Sisulu are still in prison. Sporadic violence and sabotage continued through the early sixties. The government responded with mass arrests and bannings. In June 1963 the minister of justice, B. J. Vorster, later to become prime minister, told Parliament that the police had arrested 3,246 suspected members of the Pan-Africanist Congress and its terrorist wing, Poqo, and that the courts had already sentenced 1,162.[2] The Nationalist government banned multiracial political parties in 1968 and tried to deflect some of the political discontent through its homeland policy. Steve Biko started his militant nonwhite South African Students' Organization (SASO) with its politics of Black Consciousness, which some critics felt was playing into the hands of the Nationalists' apartheid through its rejection of white liberals.

On June 16, 1976, 20,000 students, many of whom were inspired by Black Consciousness and SASO, as well as by the African National Congress, protested discriminatory educational policies in South Africa. The immediate issue was the use of Afrikaans in their schools. Riots broke out in Soweto, the southern slums of Johannesburg, where Blacks are required to live in demeaning poverty. Within a few days, 467 people were killed according to conservative estimates and hundreds more according to liberal ones. Violence and unrest spread throughout the country. For the next six months or so there were school boycotts and strikes, marches and demonstrations, the burning of government buildings, beer halls, and liquor shops, and continual clashes with the police, who went so far as to attack mourners at funerals. Over sixteen months some 700 deaths were publicly recorded, with most of the victims being shot by the police.[3] It is probable that many more went unrecorded. There are no reliable figures for the number of wounded and mutilated, and of course there is no way to measure the disruption, pain, and frustration of the riots and their aftermath. "The figures for those killed or wounded in the Soweto uprising, plus others for those imprisoned or flogged," the Rockefeller Foundation–sponsored Study Commission on U. S. Policy Toward South Africa reported, "only begin to convey the depth of the passions aroused on both sides by the clash between students and police. There are also hundreds of eyewitness accounts of youthful Black fury and of indiscriminate police shooting and brutality. The combination of anger and fear stirred in youths is suggested by the fact that two years afterward, according to the head of the security police, 4,000 of those who had fled were in guerrilla training camps outside the country."[4]

Since Soweto, as the 1976 riots and their sequel are called, violence has increased dramatically in South Africa. There is considerable labor unrest, and whenever there are strikes, the police usually end up using tear gas and frequently fire on unarmed crowds. Newspapers report almost daily incidents of police brutality and torture, forced suicides, indiscriminate arrests, unjustified detentions, and often absurd bannings. Incidents of political violence and sabotage rose from 59 in 1980 to 114 in 1981, 230 in 1982, and 395 in 1983.* Over 150 people have been killed, nearly all as a result of police action since riots broke out after the Coloured and Asian elections in August of 1984.†With this police brutality comes more violence in the locations. One Soweto resident described the atmosphere of fear this way: "People live under perpetual fear in the townships. In the first place a policeman infuses so much fear that the very sight of a police car attracts the attention of all people. The reference book is the chief source of fear. Fear is further increased by the presence of hordes of hoodlums in the location . . . Butcheries are perpetuated in the townships in a degree unprecedented in the world, of course, excluding wars."[5]

I observed such fear and suspicion during my own visit to Soweto‡ and other townships and heard tales of violence from their inhabitants. I also heard them from whites, for whom the savagery of the *skollies* and the *tsotsis*, or Black hoodlums, justifies the existence of apartheid, the locations, and strong-arm police control.

*South African Institute of Race Relations, 1984, p. 568.
†The New York Times, November 8, 1984.
‡Men, women, and children simply disappeared when they saw me, a white man. When, from behind their windows and doors, they caught sight of my ten-year-old daughter, Wicky, undoubtedly one of the only white American children to have visited Soweto, many became curious and were quite open with us.

They occur frequently in contemporary South African literature (for example, Fugard's T*sotsi* and Sepamla's *A Ride on the Whirlwind*), inspiring fear in the white readership rather than understanding of the demeaning conditions in which the youth of the locations grow up.

In the winter of 1980 a SASOL (South African Coal, Oil, and Gas Corp.) plant, which produces oil from coal, was blown up in the Transvaal. Workers went on strike in Uitenhage, and terrorists bombed shops in Durban. In Cape Town, Coloureds and Blacks boycotted schools, meat-packers, and buses, which had increased fares to the townships. Newspapers reported on the investigation of the medical reports on Steve Biko's death in September 1977 while in police custody. It was generally assumed that the medical examiners had covered up his murder. At one point Om Max, who was clearly bored by the affair, asked me, "Who is this Biko? I never heard of him until the papers began to make a fuss. If they hadn't, he would be forgotten, but the papers are always making trouble." I could not help feeling that as the Blacks were making Biko into a martyr, the more liberal whites, wittingly or unwittingly, were trivializing his death into one more instance of police brutality and of a corruption in Nationalist politics that extended even to the medical establishment.

On June 16, 1980, over 70 percent of the Coloured and Black workers in Cape Town stayed away from work to commemorate Soweto. Riots broke out. Over forty people were killed, and many more wounded. One medical student who was on duty at a local hospital told me that they did not have nearly the facilities to take care of all the injured who were brought in. Many died, he said, many more than the papers reported. He described listening to the radio announce that all was quiet as he heard gunshots from his open window.

Coloured and Black observers said that had the police not overreacted, the "stay-away" would have been peaceful, but that sensationalistic news reports, sandbagging, helicopter buzzings, and sudden artillery practice at a military camp where artillery practice was rare, primed the police and everyone else for violence.* I myself

---

*I myself witnessed similar provocation in the winter of 1981 when peaceful demonstrators, who were protesting the razing of a squatters' settlement on the outskirts of Cape Town, marched a few hundred yards from the Anglican Cathedral of Cape Town to Parliament, singing "We Shall Overcome." Within minutes, riot police-

was surprised at how peaceful life was in the white neighborhoods of Cape Town while a few miles away men, women, and children were being killed.

There was, of course, much talk of the riots among whites. English liberals blamed the police for overreaction. On June 18, 1980, the police Directorate of Public Relations announced that police had orders to shoot to kill, and on June 19, the minister of law and order, Louis le Grange, had the "unfortunate choice of words" withdrawn. Frederik van Zyl Slabbert, the leader of the Progressive Federal Party, said on June 18, "The police find themselves in an almost impossible position. They have to maintain law and order and prevent anarchy and looting in a community that finds itself in a political vacuum."[6] On June 19, the charismatic archbishop of Cape Town, Bill Burnett, observed, "As a Christian, I must condemn any misuse of power. While it is true that present disorders in Cape Town are at least in part a response to the misuse of power in our society over a long period, the burning and looting of shops and attacks on vehicles which happen to pass by simply cannot be condoned."[7] More conservative Afrikaners and English blamed the *skollie* elements for instigating violence. On June 18, Le Grange stated, "All I say is that we no longer have to do here with school, meat, or bus boycotters. We are concerned now with criminal, violent, *skollie* elements and we will act relentlessly against them."[8] I talked to many Afrikaners, who complained about foreigners, communists, and ANC guerrillas encouraging violence. A police colonel with whom I talked on a flight from Johannesburg to Cape Town said that there would be no problems in South Africa if foreigners would mind their own business. He blamed one man in particular: a KGB officer who, he said, was stationed in Lusaka, in Zambia. The police accused "certain unnamed, especially overseas press and TV men" of inciting youths in the riot areas to throw stones.[9]

Most people in Wyndal said little about the rioting, and when

---

men in camouflage uniforms appeared with attack dogs. The demonstrators were forced back into the cathedral. Violence was in the air, and one woman was fortunately pulled away from a dog as it was about to pounce. Had she been attacked, I have no doubt that violence would have broken out, and I was told that on the following day, when another demonstration was planned, police ambulances were parked in the vicinity of the cathedral. Were they in anticipation of violence? Were they a warning that there would be violence? The second demonstration was called off.

they did talk about it, they tended to repeat what they had read in the newspapers or heard on television. The conservative Afrikaners seemed to accept what people in authority, like Louis le Grange, said uncritically. One outraged woman put it this way: "History has proven their lowly condition. The Voortrekkers bought land from Dingaan, and then when they went to their land, he massacred them. You just can't go on their word. They never mean what they say. They are untrustworthy. In the riots, they are told that the land is theirs, that the white man took it away from them. This is not true. The white man bought it from them. They don't have the mentality to understand. Too few of them are educated. The government is trying to uplift their morality. But look what the children are doing. They are burning down the schools that the government built for them, for their upliftment. It's the *skollie* element. That's what I think. But that does not reach the seed of the matter. They are rioting for the show. They don't know what they are doing. There are other ways of expressing your grievances. They could go to the government and explain themselves. The government does a lot for them. Look at Mitchell's Plain. They have beautiful houses. They have all the necessary facilities: playgrounds for the children, tennis courts, schools, shopping centers, transportation. They just want to air their grievances. The riots are an exhaust valve."

Om Max also blamed the *skollies*. He was not so angry, and he did not confuse Blacks and Coloureds. Mitchell's Plain is the monotonous township to which the Coloureds from District Six in Cape Town were forcibly moved. Dr. Steyn said that if people from overseas would give the government a chance, there would be no trouble in South Africa. "There would be riots, for sure. They are occurring all over the world. Where races clash, you are bound to have problems. When a lower class aspires to be white—tries to become civilized in a year—you're going to have violence. If I were a Black man, I suppose I would want everything the white man has." He added that a lot of problems were caused by white (by which he meant English) South Africans. Duncan Reid also blamed the *skollies*. One of his neighbors, Glen Ross, talked about overpopulation. Hugo Malan was at times tempted by the overseas conspiracy theory. His wife, Peggy, talked about the appalling conditions in which the Blacks were forced to live. She added that she could not blame the Coloureds. Their schools were inferior. They were forced out of their homes in District Six and made to live miles out of town, and now their bus fares had been increased. "It's like rubbing salt into a wound," she said. "I can't understand how the government can go on making such tragic mistakes."

"What tempers the idea of Black violence," a *dominee*'s wife told my wife, "is the guilt I think that one feels. One almost feels that it would be just retribution." All of the farmers paid special attention to reports of violence in their area of the Cape and watched their workers carefully.

Jack Freeling

"In those days the heat wasn't really on," Jack Freeling said. I had asked him if there was unrest in South Africa in 1968. "People hadn't thought deeply about the future. They thought of it as controllable. We knew there was a looming threat, but it wasn't as evident or as probable as it is now. It was with Soweto that we began to realize how little control we had. There had been minor riots before, but Soweto was climactic. We realized we were on the brink. And, of course, we had riots down here in the Cape. Even in the valley there was a bit of nonsense. There was a little group of workers outside the Coloured pub who got aggressive and started turning over a car. A great big farmer plunged out of the European bar and shot one of the chaps dead. Of course, that was the end of that. There was never an inquest. Nothing was done. The chap still lives here and is accepted by the community. The whole thing has been forgotten. But there was no real rioting. It was bad in Stellenbosch and in Cape Town.

"People here all went into their houses, especially after the chap was killed. You didn't see a white person on the streets. I had to take my son through to Stellenbosch to see a doctor, and I got stoned. It wasn't all that serious. I remember, I had a pistol next to me, and the chap stood there cursing me, ready to throw a stone. I said to myself, 'Now, do I pick up this revolver and shoot the man dead because he wants to throw a stone at me.' You can't take a man's life because of one rock bouncing off the side of your car. One has to have perspective on these things. One gets a fright, but what the hell."

"Did you or any of your friends think of packing up at the time?" I asked Jack.

"No. Not then for that. We knew perfectly well it would be contained eventually. It's not the individual flash points that worry us so much. It's the dread black cloud hanging over us in the future."

The "individual flash points" have come to punctuate recent South African history. For whites who, like Jack Freeling, see themselves "on the brink" or under a "dread black cloud" and their future as a "looming threat," the "flash points" are portents. They embody the object of waiting, and by offering a glimpse of one possible future, they give a certain, ultimately intolerable, solace. Freeling usually ends his grim pictures of the future with "Well, it will all work out in the end." In her little treatise on violence, Hannah Arendt observes that "violence harbors within itself an additional element of arbitrariness; nowhere does Fortuna, good or ill luck, play a more fateful role in human affairs than on the battlefield."[10] Does this "all-pervading unpredictability, which we encounter the moment we approach the realm of violence," offer an escape from the overwhelming certainty of the future? Or do these "flash points" give only the solace of death and extinction? Finding himself politically impotent, Jack Freeling, like Peter Cooke and many of the other English farmers in the valley, has dropped out. He has limited his world to family, farm, and friends, but he is aware of what goes on outside his "beautiful little fool's paradise," as Catherine Fox calls the valley. He reads the newspapers and listens to the news on television. He indulges himself in despair from time to time.

For those who are more active in orientation than Jack Freeling, mainly Afrikaners and some English who feel themselves part of the political process, the "flash points" are also portents. They are warnings of what will happen if one gives way to the demands of the Blacks—or for that matter to anyone who pushes for change. Om Max and others of his generation condemn the riots. They show no interest in, certainly no sympathy for, the rioters. They do not blame all the Coloureds and Blacks. *They* know no better. They blame certain "elements": the *skollies*, the politically indoctrinated, the "scum of the homelands," as one ex-Rhodesian refers to the communists. These bugaboos prevent, rhetorically at least, more menacing questions. Younger, more liberal Afrikaners, like Irene Prinsloo's children and their spouses, are also warned by the "flash points," but they respond in a more "realistic," more "pragmatic" fashion. They talk about the need for *realistic change*; they talk about

improving the conditions of non-whites; they talk about their market potential. Tommy Prinsloo says that if any real change will
come about in South Africa, it will come about through business.*
Businessmen will discover—are discovering—that with improved
lives and increased salaries the Blacks and the Coloureds buy. "They
are our biggest market, right in front of our eyes, and we have
ignored them." But Tommy and others of his generation and political persuasion state that violence must be controlled. A firm hand
must be taken to prevent chaos and disorder, which will impede the
"natural evolution" of a free market open to all. Chaos and disorder
are resonant symbols of the demonic in South African political
theology.

It takes either too little imagination or too great an imagination
to understand what the "flash points" mean to the Coloureds, the
Asians, and the Blacks. The very word "flash point" is itself a
symptom of the callous self-reference of the whites. (Jack Freeling,
I should point out, is more understanding of the non-whites than
most white South Africans I interviewed.) For them, I imagine, the
riots—the disorder and chaos that are, after all, usually contained in
their locations—both indicate and commemorate misery and hardship, frustration and anger, impotence and rage, acts of courage and
failed courage, hope and despair (a despair that cannot be dismissed
as an indulgence), loss and death.

Of course, I cannot elaborate on these responses. I had very little
contact with non-whites, but I suspect that what contact I did have
with them was freer because I was an outsider. My relations were
not so governed by convention. I could pass over, just a bit, without
destroying the supports by which the Coloureds and Blacks, and the
Asians, too, held up their identity in the face of the white man. I
had, in any event, nothing to lose.

During the riots in June 1980 I talked to one Coloured law student at the University of Cape Town. (Non-white students may
study at white universities if their own universities do not offer
their chosen course of study.) He was in despair. His family was
in danger. Several friends had been injured. His examinations
were approaching. He had had a test the day before. He had not

---

*Tommy is echoing the position of Harry Oppenheimer, the chairman of South
Africa's biggest corporation, Anglo-American. Oppenheimer argues that the
growth of modern free-enterprise economy will undermine apartheid (Study Commission, p. 140).

taken it. (He was, I should add, automatically excused because of the riots.) He thought of quitting school. I encouraged him to continue. A friend, a white student, joined us unexpectedly and asked him how he had done on the test. He said he hadn't taken it. His tone was so cold that his friend left us puzzled and speechless. "He thinks he's my friend," the Coloured student said, "but how, tell me, how can I be friends with him? He doesn't understand. How could I study, how could I think about a test, when my family is afraid to leave the house and my friends are arrested? He tries to understand. But what does he know? He reads the newspapers. He looks at the pictures. But he worries about whether or not he'll pass his test. I'd like to also." I mentioned my conversation to several professors at the university. They said, with little sympathy, that whenever there was trouble, Coloured students wallowed in self-pity.

Other Coloured and Black students with whom I talked about the riots were more ideologically oriented. Some thought the violence was encouraged by the police. "They want to show us their strength." Others thought the violence had started with the *skollies*, but they asked why there were *skollies* in the townships. They talked about the divide and conquer tactics of the government. They insisted on calling themselves Blacks and not Coloureds or Xhosas or Zulus. They talked about terrorism: the sudden and unexplained searches, the interrogations, tortures, detentions, and arrests. They talked about crime, assault, murder, and rape in the townships. They talked too about the unpredictable in their lives, the arbitrariness of the responses they would elicit from whites, any whites and not just those in authority, and they seemed to equate this arbitrariness, this unpredictability, with violence. Violence functioned as a metaphor for the unpredictable.

The "flash points" are, as I suggested, portents. They embody the object of waiting. They are also rehearsals for the future—in the fantasies of those who, like Jack Freeling, have dropped out, in the flesh for the more active, the politically committed, the police, and of course those who demonstrate, riot, and sabotage. The acts of violence are not merely symptoms of the present; they are orientations toward the future. They are at once affirmations of one possible and not altogether unrealistic version of the future and an attempt to master, indeed to destroy, that future. Events, Hannah Arendt writes, "are occurrences that interrupt routine processes and routine procedures." She adds:

> Predictions of the future are never anything but projections of present automatic processes and procedures, that is, of occurrences that are likely to come to pass if men do not act and if nothing unexpected happens; every action, for better or worse, and every accident necessarily destroys the whole pattern in whose frame the prediction moves and where it finds its evidence.[11]

Violence, we noted earlier, is the realm of a kind of pervasive unpredictability. One illusory way to master it is to rehearse it, to routinize it, to mechanize it, to render its processes and procedures automatic, to eliminate, so to speak, every accident. As peripheral as this illusory mastery of violence through violence may seem, it is, I believe, an essential dimension of all violence. Illusory as it is, the mastery of violence through violence, through rehearsal, can never succeed. Violence can only follow on violence. *Action* and *accident* can never be eliminated. The future is never predictable. The object of waiting can never be fully known. There is fascination in this. Violence, the realm of all-pervading unpredictability, offers escape from the inevitable. It is missed, alas, by those who have experienced it.

Zachary van der Merwe

"I was sleeping in a photographer's studio just above a nightclub near the docks. It was a club that operated until three-thirty in the morning. It's closed now. It was rather eerie: all very deserted at night, just empty offices, except for this club that was filled with drunken sailors and Coloured prostitutes. It was real rough. I was witness to three occasions of police brutality: sort of taking Coloureds and beating them up. One time, I can't swear to it but I'm fairly sure that I saw them put a woman inside the van and do something to her. I didn't even want to look. I just heard the sounds. I was shocked. I had never seen anything like it.

"And on the docks—I worked there for a couple of years while I was studying—I used to watch the crane operators pick up Africans on those big steel loading nets and drop them into the water for the fun of it. One guy lost his arm. They were real brutes, those dock workers. You should be talking to them . . .

"And then there were the riots in '75. School kids marching into the city center . . . Hundreds of police in riot trucks, in camouflage, with guns, shooting tear gas on the streets . . . All those guys with guns, and Blacks just fleeing, and windows getting broken, and cars getting burned, and people getting shot . . . Headlines all over the place, all the time . . . And the sense of living in a dream, feeling quite excited about the whole thing because at last it was coming out in the open—the whole thing was being made clear . . .

"I had a sense of incredible, anonymous brutality. None of the police had numbers. There were instances of unmarked cars going about the townships, white people shooting at random, anybody, and just speeding off . . . People killed that way.

"I felt incredible anger at the police. I saw them as villains, pigs. I was really emotionally involved, but as far as doing anything, I didn't see that there was anything I could do. It was all on such a vast scale. There was so much happening that all I could do was feel tremendous pain and a sense of hopelessness and despair, and helplessness as well. But what does one do? What can one do—apart from getting a gun and going out and shooting all the policemen one sees?

"I'm always tempted to feel a great deal of anger toward the power of the government. And now I realize that I can't allow myself to feel that because then I'd be one of the mob.

"I was visited by the Special Branch once. It was actually by default because I was working at a friend's house. They had come to inquire about a party that had happened a few days earlier. They wanted to know why Blacks were coming into his house. I said I didn't know anything about it because I hadn't been there. I was sketching at the time—sets for a play that never happened. They saw one of my drawings and asked me why I was drawing in black and white. I almost said I couldn't afford color. They took my name and address and left in a huff, promising to see me again. I never saw them again.

"This whole political thing is a big farce because those dummies on top who wield real power are always selling themselves short. No doubt, they are affecting people's lives. They think in the short term, and short-term policies in this land, or in fact in any land, are doomed to failure in the long run. I don't feel anyone has to lift a finger to make an overt statement. In a sense an overt statement is distasteful because it's really playing their tune. They enjoy people showing their colors. I think it's more subversive not to respond to them on their level."

* * *

It is worth noting that Zachary includes in the middle of his pointillist description of the riots "headlines all over the place, all the time."
Violence rarely, if ever, exists in pure form. It always has a narrative
dimension: the stories we tell about it—the reports, descriptions,
and confessions—or keep secretly, inaccessibly even, in the recesses
of our mind. There is, we imagine, mastery in the telling of it. We
distance ourselves from it. We exorcise it. We impose a grammar
on it. We give it structure and shape. We incorporate it in familiar
genres. We present it or, better, re-present it in images that resonate
with other images—the images of past stories and tales—and
through the evocation of these other stories and tales we embellish
or trivialize ours. We play with our stories in ways we cannot with
the *violence* itself. We cast ourselves as heroes or anti-heroes, men
and women of delicacy and sensitivity or crudeness and insen-
sitivity. We participate in our stories, identify with the protagonists
we create, or disengage ourselves from them. We use the stories and
tales to seduce, inspire, and captivate, to banish, benumb, and repel,
our listeners, and they, in turn, through their listening, through the
responses they give, surrender to us, resist us, or lead us in still other
directions. For the listener and the storyteller the stories and tales
of violence are a kind of rehearsal for stories and tales of the future,
which may have to be lived as well as told. They give cover to the
terrifying silence of the pure act.

Newspapers assiduously report the violence. The border war,
riots, and strikes make headlines. They are often accompanied, in
the English-language press, by garishly colored photographs. (The
photographs are more subdued in the Afrikaans newspapers.) The
English press is cheap and sensational. Every edition has its headlines and its photographs. When there are no wars, riots, or strikes,
then individual acts of violence, rape, and murder, government
scandal—the death, say, of Steve Biko—and of course rugby make
the headlines. Violence and scandal in Zimbabwe are, for example,
constantly exploited. When there are no noteworthy photographs
of riot and bloodshed, then frequently there is a picture of a bikini-
clad chippy with a caption about how mild the weather has been.
The equation of violence, sex, scandal, corruption, and sports (surrounded by advertisements) is striking. Violence, certainly its meaning, is trivialized. The headlines and the photographs that
accompany it are essential to its depiction—its appreciation—in
South Africa.

Zachary also talks about the photographers who triggered off shootings by asking some children to throw stones at the police for a photograph. He claims to have heard about it from a reliable friend. The same story is told about all the riots. It reflects the attitude that South Africans take toward journalists and photographers—toward truth, in a sense. It reflects something more, too. Violence is no longer just followed by tales and stories—replays and rehearsals. It is now instantaneously replayed and rehearsed. It is recorded, photographed, and televised. It is wrenched from its context of occurrence. It is distanced, embellished or trivialized, almost as it occurs. It is depersonalized and derealized. Indeed, the depersonalization and the derealization of the experience of violence, so often described by those who have been in battle, are themselves given a reality for those who are not *actual* participants but only observers.[12] A new dimension has been added to violence through our technology: a new illusion of mastery has been created. The gap between the act and its telling has been collapsed but not completely. There is still the terrifying instant of silence. The stories of the journalists and photographers who stimulate the violence—stories by no means unique to South Africa—are, I believe, desperate attempts to eliminate the gap entirely, to fill the instant of silence. For there to be total mastery, that act and its telling, the occurrence and its representation, must be one. It is an old quest: the quest of magicians and poets.

12

WORKERS

Hennie

"I can't just arrive at the pearly gates and say, 'Lord, I've led a moral life,' and expect to enter the heavenly kingdom. He will say, 'Where are those who were on earth with you?' I can't answer by saying, 'Sorry, Lord, they didn't want to lead my kind of life. I left them behind.' The Father sent Christ into a hostile world so we've got to go into a hostile world. 'As thou didst send me into the world, so I have sent them into the world'—that is what Christ says in his last high priestly prayer in John 17."

Hennie was repeating part of a sermon he had given the previous Sunday on discipleship. He had irritated the few remaining whites in his parish who regularly attend his services. He had argued that those who "try to live little moral lives in their little world" are opting out of the world. They're not committed to the Lord but to their own good life. They live in "little holy huddles" and think that such huddles are the church. God loves the world, and the world includes drug addicts and prostitutes and alcoholics. He doesn't love *moral lives*; he loves the world, His world, His creation.

"I insist on discipleship. I just don't want church members. Christ says that if you want to be my disciple, you must take up my cross and follow me. That is what I would like from my parishioners: discipleship."

Hennie was angry. He was losing more and more of his European congregation. He claimed rather arrogantly that although he had lost half of them, church revenues had increased threefold in the last several years. His white parishioners contest this. He says that many of the Coloureds give more than a tithe. At a church council meeting, one Coloured parishioner apparently said, "Tithing is for the Jews. We have much more than they have so we want to give more than a tenth." Hennie insists that the Europeans have stopped attending church because he has invited Coloureds to attend the traditionally "white" parish church. He does not realize that many of them have dropped out of his church because they find his theology too fundamentalist, his sermons inelegant, his style too earthy, and his stress on the in-flowing of the Holy Spirit disquieting. They are embarrassed by his prayers for rain, for the sick, and for the government ("that they may realize the sins they are perpetuating") that he includes in all his services. They are offended by his failure to minister to them, which is often blatant, and by the attention he pays to their workers, especially their drunken workers. His sermons, his prayer groups, his Bible study sessions, are all directed to the Coloureds. With them he is tolerant and exquisitely patient. With the whites he is not. He has disturbed the delicate balance of his "non-apartheid" church. His criticism of the whites is too apparent. He expects from them *discipleship*. They ask angrily, "To whom, to Christ or to himself?"

"In the peninsula we have between two and three hundred cases of assault, mostly stabbings, each week, and we average about eight murders a weekend. It's mostly Coloureds, mostly the result of drink. It's the biggest problem in my congregation. I can't blame the Coloureds because it is the white farmers who first introduced them to wine. They gave them a bottle in the morning, one at noon, and one in the evening. On Friday nights they gave them two, and if they worked on Saturdays, they got three more bottles. Now, thank God, the farmers are giving up the *dop* system,* but they've already made alcoholics of the Coloureds. Children are born in an alcoholic state. If there's a party and the kid is teething, the mother will quiet

---

*The *dop* system refers to the wine allowance farmers gave to their workers "to keep up their morale" as one farmer put it. "To keep them working—happy," another said. The old Wyndal farmers gave their men as much as three quart-bottles a day.

him down with some wine. Well, by the time the child is twelve or thirteen, he's a confirmed alcoholic.

"The only way to cure an alcoholic is through prayer. I have never stopped a man from drinking any other way. Well, I have, in Rhodesia, but in those days I didn't know you could pray with a person. I used to take blokes into my home and spend months and months struggling and battling with them. Occasionally I would succeed in getting a bloke to see it another way and to give up drinking. Now I know an easier way. One prayer is all that is needed, if the bloke really wants to give up the bottle."

"Does it last?" I asked.

"Well, I have got quite a number of leading lay people who have taken the course seriously for three years," Hennie answered evasively. He would never admit his failures to me.

Hennie is well known for his cures of some of the most die-hard alcoholics. Shortly after his arrival, he started a Bible study group on Friday evenings, locally called the Bushman's Christmas, because of the Coloureds' drinking. No other minister had ever dared to organize such a group on a Friday evening. Within three months he had over 200 participants. Many had undergone dramatic conversions and had apparently given up drinking.

"One Friday night our study group was interrupted by a drunk. Some men wanted to kick him out, but I said no. We can't let him go. We must pray for him. We brought him up to the altar rail and started praying for him. Within five minutes he sobered up, and by the end of the evening he had made a commitment to Jesus Christ. The following week he was filled with the Spirit"—Hennie laughed at his pun—"and has never again had a drink.

"And then there was one bloke—I never laughed so hard when he gave his testimony—who used to play hide and seek with his mother on Friday evenings. He would follow her around asking for money for drink. She used to hide out at friends', but he always managed to find her. One evening she was praying very hard for help, and the Lord spoke to her: 'You have never been to Hennie's Bible study group?' 'No, Lord,' she answered. 'Well, why don't you go on a Friday evening,' the Lord said, 'and let your son look for you there.' And this is what she did. That Friday there was a knock on the door. 'Is my mother there?' I said I didn't know who his mother was and added, 'Whilst you're here why not come in and meet Jesus.' You know the rest of the story."

There is in Hennie's evangelical mission, perhaps in all evange-
lism, a paradoxical striving for the very domination he denounces.
Hennie believes that he has the power to convert and to heal. He
cannot separate the two. Unlike many faith healers, he insists that
his failure to cure is not the result of his patient's lack of faith but
of his own. He is—and I do not mean this necessarily in a negative
sense—a spiritual bully. His preaching is often aggressive, certainly
insistent, frequently iconoclastic. He takes, at times, a prideful pleasure in toppling the pillars of sanctified wisdom: the *status quo*. He
scorns the complacent; he decries liberalism; he mocks paternalism;
and he undermines all assumptions of superiority. And yet, if not
precisely the master, he strives to master. He is, his English parishioners will say, an Afrikaner after all.

"One bloke was the church warden here for seventeen years. He
never once spoke about conversion. He never won one soul for
Christ. When I spoke to him about it, he said he didn't consider
conversion his job. But, according to the Bible, my job is to prepare
everyone for the work of the ministry. I am not the minister. I have
certain gifts given to me by Christ to prepare the laity for the work
of the ministry. The ministry is *their* job.

"When I came here, the Europeans were not prepared for this.
They still aren't. They've never thought deeply about their religion.
They know which parts of the liturgy to say, when to pray, and
when to stand, but, for the most part, they are unwilling to give
themselves to Christ's teachings. They are satisfied with form
. . . As long as they think they are not grossly underpaying their
laborers, as long as they don't beat them, they think they are doing
what they ought to for them. They are satisfied. They will get no
closer. It's like communion. You've noticed how all the Europeans
sit up near the altar. That's so they can be the first to receive
communion—before a Coloured bloke has sipped from the chalice.

"So much of our church is hypocritical. This has nothing to do
with the government and its apartheid. It's how people feel. This
church was built for the farm owners. When I came here, there were
only two or three Coloured families who came to mass. They were
schoolteachers, the so-called better Coloureds, and they always sat
in the back of the church. The farm owners built the other churches
in the parish near their laborers' quarters. They expected them to
attend the church nearest them so long as it wasn't theirs. There
were Coloured folk, I discovered, living for the last fifty years

within a few hundred meters of this church who had never been in it. They used to trek six or seven kilometers to one of the other churches in the parish. Or they didn't go to church at all. How can you expect a man and his wife and their children to walk six or seven kilometers in the winter rain to attend a service when the church next to them is half empty? Well, *I* invited them in, and they came in. And do you know that a group of whites got together and sent a delegation to the archbishop to ask that I conduct two services every Sunday! They said the church wasn't big enough."

Hennie laughed. The parish church seats seventy. Hennie or his assistant priest conducts one service there every Sunday. They each conduct two services in the other churches in the parish. Without exception, the Europeans attend the parish church. There are seldom more than twenty of them. There are rarely more than forty Coloureds. They prefer the other churches because the services are more lively, and there is more singing. (The singing *is* impressive, especially compared to the dutiful cacophonies of the white parishioners singing to the ill-tuned organ of the parish church.) They also prefer them because they are their own churches and because they find them more respectable. "We put on our best clothes," one Coloured lady said. "They may not be as fine as those the whites wear, but they are our best. The whites—I hope you do not mind my saying this—save their best clothes for parties. I always wear a hat to church. I know I don't have to, but I don't feel right without one." (She was making an oblique reference to European women, who seldom wear hats to church.)

Hennie himself loosens up considerably when he is preaching to the Coloureds. He is at ease in Afrikaans. He sways as he sings, and he walks up and down the center aisle as he preaches. He smiles frequently and seems to enjoy preaching, at a simple level, to his Coloured parishioners. He embraces them, jokes with them, and creates a sense of conspiratorial camaraderie with them. He will talk lightly and then suddenly, melodramatically, turn serious and fill them with awe as he talks about demons and devils. He does not threaten them, for his preaching is always down to earth, very human, and full of his odd humor. His Coloured parishioners genuinely like him. They certainly enjoy his services.

"I think they regard me much more as a friend than any other priest we have had here. I've told them to call me Hennie—and not Father as they would normally. We have a special relationship.

Partially this is because I speak Afrikaans. I'm the first priest with whom they can actually communicate. My predecessors didn't speak Afrikaans. I've also shown them a completely new way of life and given a tremendous depth to their religion, which they never had. The fact that I'm white is quite immaterial to most of them.

"When I first cáme here, the Coloureds would often sit through a whole church meeting without saying a word because they were used to a white man doing all the thinking for them and telling them what was going to happen. They were token members of the church council, and they accepted that. They were too scared to say anything that differed with what their 'masters' said or thought. Now they're beginning to participate a bit more in the meetings. A little while ago I was sick and couldn't attend a meeting. The council actually elected one of the Coloureds chairman in my absence!

"In the past, the Coloureds depended too much on their priest. The priest was the master, and they were his servants. Now we teach them not to rely on any one person but to rely on God. They don't come to me as much as they go to Him. Once they have had experience of the Holy Spirit, they talk to God and listen to Him. It is no longer a one-way communication. It is two-way. You feel the need—the desire, I should say—to communicate. This has loosened people's dependence on me tremendously."

Hennie went on to discuss the insidious effects of the master-servant relationship. It governs all interracial encounters. The English, he said, are particularly prone to treat their workers paternalistically. The Afrikaners are harder on them but more respectful of them as men and women. It is only through the power of Christ that the Coloured ceases to see himself as Coloured, as *boy*, and the white man as *baas*, or *master*.

"But even the Afrikaner treats his workers with an 'I know best' attitude. You'll find that on the average the Afrikaner looks after his workers much better than the English do. He gets to know them as people, but, at the same time, he is always boss. He does what he thinks is right. He tells them exactly what to do. He promises that if they do *x*, he'll do *y* for them. You'll find they have a TV set in the shed for them."

"But that's not really taking the part of the other," I said.

"No, it's not entering into the other man's agony. It's more like a doctor who just tends you professionally. You are just a body to be dealt with, and he deals with you, and that's that.

"Of course, you get some Afrikaners who really care. My uncle had a servant who had worked for him for a donkey's age and was very old and sick. I've forgotten what his sickness was, but he used to smell terribly. I couldn't stand the smell and would run away whenever my aunt asked me to visit him. He lived in a little shack on the property. Every day my aunt went to wash and dress him. She brought him something to eat three times a day. They were very poor, but what they had, they shared with the old man. She put up with this for years. He wasn't discarded because he couldn't work anymore."

Hennie's tale of his family's treatment of the old farmhand is a familiar one. Even before my arrival in South Africa, I heard many like it from South Africans living abroad. I also read them in Bosman's stories and Brink's novels. The Afrikaner is cast as an uncouth, rather simple farmer, who pushes his workers as hard as he can, often making unrealistic demands on them, pays them little, frequently loses his temper, and at times beats them. Yet, when they are sick or old and infirm, he, like Hennie's uncle and aunt, will share everything he has with them and nurse them through the most vile illnesses. In his short story "The Coffin," Uys Krige writes of one rascally old farmer who gives the coffin he has carefully saved for himself to an old servant and then dies and has to be buried in a makeshift one. (Given the scarcity of wood in the Karoo and in the veld of the Free State and the Transvaal, many farmers trekked with their coffins. I know one old man in Wyndal who keeps his coffin in the attic.) Emphasis is given in all these stories to the peculiar, often romanticized, symbiotic attachment between the Afrikaner and his Coloured (or occasionally Black) worker.

The stories are told, with slightly different slants, by Afrikaners, English, and Coloureds. Irene Prinsloo gives at times the impression that the old Afrikaner farmers, as yet uncorrupted by the ways of the city, and their workers formed one big happy family. (The image of the *family* dominated the Afrikaners' description of the traditional farmstead, the *boereplaas*.) She talks about the care the farmer's wife took of her workers. "They were like children," she says. She talks too about the Coloured midwife, the *vroedvrou*, who taught the farmer's wife herbal medicine as well as the secrets of womanhood. Like other Afrikaners, she laughs at the contradictions in the relationship between the farmer and his laborers. She tells me about one cranky old man who worked hand in hand with his workers. "They were his closest friends," she says. "He knew them the way you can only know someone you have worked with for years. They shared the feel of the soil. But once you entered the *tuindeur*, the garden gate, he was lord and master. He didn't know his workers there. It was his kingdom. His son used to play with one of the Coloured boys, a bright little boy, who, the farmer made sure, went to school every day. One morning, it was raining, and the farmer's son asked his friend into the house to play, just as they had always played outdoors. They played so quietly that the farmer's wife never knew they were there. When the farmer came home and discovered the Coloured boy in his house, he lost his temper. 'Where do you think you are?' he screamed. 'In the Congo?' He gave the little boy a terrible hiding."

Shifts in attitude are dramatic. René de Villiers refers to the relationship between the Afrikaner and the Coloureds and Blacks as schizophrenic.[1] I have also noted a profound difference between the Afrikaner's working relationship with his laborers and what he has to say about them in other contexts. Then he sets off on some racist tack or another, without seeming to regard his own experience, and ends up referring to the Coloureds and Blacks at best as children and at worst as animals. Such shifts are often treated with humor by those who talk about them. They are part of a characterology that enters into the white South African's folklore.

I remember having dinner with a group of younger Afrikaners in the Valley. They asked me a number of general questions about life in America and eventually brought the conversation around to race relations. One farmer, a graduate of Stellenbosch University, argued that racial mixture produced "bad blood" and inferior intelligence and that the most successful societies in the world were homogeneous ones. He went on to say that in nonhomogeneous societies there was always a threat of a communist takeover because of the "inferior biology" of the people and the social unrest that resulted from a mixture of races. A second farmer argued that racial mixture produced social unrest but that it did not necessarily produce inferior intelligence. He pointed out that Coloureds were more intelligent than Blacks. The first laughed and said that was because they had white blood in them. The third farmer argued it had nothing to do with white blood. There were plenty of Coloureds who didn't have any white blood and who were more intelligent than the Blacks. It was a question of culture. They were in longer and more intimate contact with the whites, and this contact was bound to affect their evolution. No one took issue with his Lamarckian position. The first farmer returned to the subject of homogeneous societies, and this embarrassed his wife, who thought that I would take it personally as an attack on my own country. I tried to explain that in the United States everyone criticized the country, its people, its government, and that that criticism was considered to be an important part of the democratic process, but no one seemed particularly interested in what I was saying. The third farmer's wife changed the subject and told us how her father, one of the most *verkrampte* men in the valley, had insisted, just two days before, that one of his boys—a Black fellow who had worked for him for more than forty years—lead a cow he had bought thirty-five kilometers back to the farm. Twice her father drove out in his *bakkie* to make sure his boy wasn't dawdling en route. She thought her father's behavior was cute. "These old-timers know the Bantu. They're cattle people. My dad knew his boy would respect him. Of course, we're a different generation. We wouldn't dare do such a thing."

Her husband echoed his wife. "Of course, we don't know the Bantus here. We only know the Coloureds, but my father-in-law is from the Transvaal. He always had a Bantu houseboy and a couple of other boys in the field. He's supposed to be very conservative, but his houseboy comes in after dinner and watches the telly with him."

"He always sits on the floor," his wife interrupted. "He knows his place. He's not like these cheeky young Bantus who think they can have everything a white man has just for the asking."

Glen Ross

Glen Ross is a heavyset, miserly man in his mid-sixties, an Afrikaner of Scottish origin. "Being brought up on a farm, farming was in my blood." Before moving to Wyndal, Ross had been a bank clerk and then a government bookkeeper. "I sacrificed my pension, but I bought when prices were low." He is a loner. "I prefer to have a couple of spots and lie down than live the high life." Most Europeans do not know him, but the Coloureds do because he is reputed to be the most unscrupulous employer in the valley. In 1980 he was paying some of his workers less than 7 rand for a fifty-five-hour week. He has a violent temper and frequently has his two sons beat his laborers. He has made no improvements in their housing since his arrival. He belongs neither to the Farmers' Association ("It's a waste of time, and time's money") nor to the Dutch Reformed Church ("I had to give them so much money that I quit"). He takes interest in politics. "My politics are simple: There are twenty shillings to the pound." He does not vote. "There's no democracy in this country. Everything's decided in the caucus." He treats his wife like a maid. "I give the old girl a Maria six hours a week. Why should I give her more? She's got nothing to do with her time."

"The English blame us for misusing our kaffirs. But who's worse off? Would you prefer to have your brother working on the docks or someone else? You say you've been here for six weeks. You're looking at the situation from the balcony. Our Blacks and Coloureds are living in clover in comparison with the way they used to live during slavery. We don't hate them. We have to speak their language. Otherwise they don't understand. City people say we talk coarse to them, but I say it's all they'll understand. You can't insinuate. You can't suggest. You've got to tell them straight. Then they'll respect you. My boys will protect me. We understand each other. A few years ago there was an incident on the farm. Someone tried to rob me. The boys caught him. They said, 'Bass, let's slit his throat.'

"Humanism has given out too many handouts. I think this desire to live on handouts runs in the blood of the Coloureds and Blacks. We've spoiled them with welfare. Whites couldn't buy a house for the price the government's selling them to Coloureds. Now that freedom is served on a platter, people are taking advantage of it all over the world. Look at England, with its Jamaicans and Indians. They're throwing England out of gear. She made a mistake. She broke up the Commonwealth too soon. She dropped the kaffirs like hot potatoes. Kaffir politics are simple: *Be against whatever the white man is for.* The outside world will always stick up for the white man in the end. We forget this sometimes. Look at Soweto. Would there have been a greater outcry if we had killed ten thousand kaffirs instead of a few hundred?

"Now they're making education compulsory for Coloureds. We'll have more unemployment. Will an educated man want to work on a farm? He'll want to work in an office. I suppose I'd want the same. The government has made a big mistake. They have two standards for the matric: one for whites and one for Coloureds. The Coloureds' is much lower, but they're told that it's the same as the whites'. They expect the same jobs and the same salaries. Who can blame them? Of course, if they applied the white standard to the Coloured matric, seventy-five percent of the Coloureds would drop out."

Glen Ross said this with some satisfaction. The government maintains that although the matriculation examinations for whites and Coloureds are different, they are at the same level. Many Coloureds accept this position and say that those who have passed the matric should receive the same benefits as a matriculated white. Others recognize that the standards are not the same but insist, nevertheless, that a matric is a matric. Both groups argue that whites who talk about differences in examination levels do so in order to justify giving Coloureds inferior jobs and lower salaries. No one, I should add, seriously bothers to argue the equivalence of white and Black matriculation examinations.

Of course, the whole argument is based on false premises. Regardless of examination standards, there can be little doubt that the education of Coloureds and Indians, certainly of Blacks, is far inferior to that of whites in South Africa. School facilities and teacher preparation for non-whites are far inferior to those for whites. Even the most superficial comparison of prescribed books for the different racial groups reveals enormous differences in academic standards.

"If I take the forty-odd souls who live on this farm, I doubt if more than one would be able to pass the matric I had to take. (Of course, standards are lower now for everyone.) I don't have a single boy I'd entrust with my tractor. I contract a Xhosa. They make good drivers. A lot of farmers are in debt because of their workers. They buy a tractor for ten or fifteen thousand rand and then they give it to one of their boys, who has probably been drinking. In no time it is all dented up, if they're lucky. If they're not, it's been turned over and is in the shop.

"The farmers complain that they're not making enough on their farms. Well, that's because they don't know how to manage them. They have too many laborers, and they don't use them adequately. I farm about twenty morgen, and I use eight boys all year. During the picking season I hire on the women. I pay them a little less of course. I have about fifteen people working for me at the height of the season. But I never keep on a single soul when there is no work, and I pay them according to their worth. I have one boy who is too old to do anything but light pruning. I keep him on but I pay him a bit less than the others. He's happy enough to be getting a salary. I came out here without much capital. I had to replant, and still I was able to pay off the farm in eight years. Interest is dead money. I gross about sixty-five thousand rand a year and clear between twenty-five and thirty thousand. Nowadays the farmers are paying too much for their land. It's going for over ten thousand rand a morgen, and they complain because they can't lead the high life. What do they expect?

"In the olden days there were squires in England and barons in Germany. The masses had absolutely no say. There were all sorts of punishments. People were placed on racks and wheels and pulled apart. The world was cruel then. Today we are ruled by the mob. Our problem is different. It's overpopulation. The kaffirs breed like rabbits. I'm battling to get my women *volk* to have birth control injections. I've had the district nurse out here every week. The women want the shots, but the men tell them not to. They're afraid their women will run around if they get the shots. I don't know why they care. They do anyway.

"I don't see a solution. Actually there is one. The world needs a Hitler in every country. But who would want that? Hitler made only one mistake. He tried to take Russia. He got power hungry. The world is too sophisticated today to put up with the likes of him. We've even done away with the cane in prison."

The Coloureds, the Afrikaners, and even some English say they prefer an Afrikaner to an English boss.

"We're harder on them, but at least they know where they stand with us," the Afrikaners say. They tell a joke about a Coloured beggar who asks an Afrikaner for a handout. Without listening to his story, the Afrikaner curses him out and then tells him to go to the kitchen for a plate of food. The same beggar approaches an English man. The English man listens to his story sympathetically and tells him how sorry he is for him and how he wishes he could help if only he could manage it. He closes the door without giving him as much as a crust of bread.

The Afrikaner stereotypes the English farmer as a hypocrite his workers can't trust. The English farmer, he says, sympathizes with his laborers' life. He pays them more than the Afrikaner does; he does not work them as hard; he gives them better housing. *But,* the stereotype goes, he does not treat them as human beings. He keeps his distance. If a worker is sick, he will make sure he gets to the hospital, but he will not nurse the worker himself. If a worker is too old to work, he will give him the correct pension, but he will not share his food with him. He does not work comfortably hand in hand with his workers. He must preserve his image as a gentleman farmer.

A few of the English farmers in the valley accept this image. Others see it as a projection of the Afrikaners' own feelings about the English. Still others, the majority, are simply irritated by it. They agree that the Coloureds prefer to work for the Afrikaners because they understand each other better. They speak the same language and have lived on Afrikaner farms for generations. With a certain haughtiness they claim that Afrikaners and Coloureds are very much alike. They argue, however, that when they arrived in the valley less than a decade before, the Afrikaners were paying their laborers 5 rand a week, were working them on cheap wine, and housing them in leaky huts with dirt floors and no sanitation. "It's fine to talk about understanding, but what counts in the end is not understanding but decent housing, a living wage, and healthy children," one of the more progressive English farmers put it, angrily. "When I bought this place, more than half the children were suffering from chronic malnutrition. They were sickly, and two died in the first three months I was here. There must have been twenty-five children on the farm, and nearly all of them had upper respiratory infections. Now I make sure they get Pronutra [a protein cereal] each morning. The improvement in their health has been dramatic."

Peter Cooke

"It always comes down to the same question: What is the basic salary for these people?" Peter Cooke said. We were talking about drinking among the workers. Many farmers argue that there is no point in increasing the laborers' wages because they will only spend it on drink. "What is the effect of giving a lot of money to an unsophisticated people? This tears me up. Should I pay them more even though they don't know how to spend their money? Here's a lovely example: Last week one of my chaps asked for an increase. He has no education but he's a hard worker—thick as hell. Give him a spade, and he's fantastic. He's an average pruner—a very excitable guy. Anyway, he asked for more money. I said, 'Let's talk about it!' He explained that he couldn't afford to buy his child a birthday present. I said, 'Henry, that's terrible.' We chatted a bit about kids' birthdays, and then I asked him if he had bought any wine the previous weekend. They buy wine in two-and-a-half-gallon containers for two rand fifty. He said he had. 'And the weekend before?' I asked. He said he had. And then I asked him if he would rather buy wine for himself or a birthday present for his kid. Silence. I explained to him that when you need something special, you have to save for it. 'If I want to go on a holiday, Henry,' I said, 'I have to save for it. I have to do without other things. If I want to buy a motor car, I've got to put away for it. It means sacrificing other things.' You see, he would never think of giving up his wine for his kid's birthday present. That just doesn't register as being important. I made my point, but it was totally lost.

"After five years on this farm, I've found that my tremendous disillusionment with the Coloureds comes from my attempt to relate my own standards to them. It just doesn't work. I've got to keep pinching myself and saying to myself, Look, boy, they're not brought up the way you were. They don't think as you do. Don't get upset. Relate to them according to their own background. This has helped me a lot."

Earlier in our conversation Peter had asked me about some testing he had read about that proves Blacks have an intelligence inferior to that of whites. Such tests are frequently reported in the press. There was a particular flurry in June 1980, when the minister of posts and telecommunications, Hennie Smit, said that "the Blacks' thought processes are still slower than ours."[2] I explained to Peter that from a scientific point of view such tests were unconvincing. "I'm pleased to hear that," he said simply.

Racial and genetic arguments are frequently brought up by the farmers to justify the differences they perceive between themselves and their workers. By accounting for the differences in essentialist terms, in terms of race and genetics, they free themselves from any responsibility for the differences. They can preserve the *status quo*. They don't have to bother about *real* change. Among many of the more "enlightened" farmers, who attribute the differences they perceive to differences in culture, culture is, in my experience, also understood *essentially* as a given. For many Afrikaners, apartheid is justified on the grounds that it preserves in their *purest,* most *authentic* forms the cultures of South Africa. Some romanticize the natives' cultures as they do their own *kultuur.*

"I started a farm shop. I could buy what my workers needed in bulk and undersell the cafés in town. I thought they would appreciate it. I expected them to make a spot-check to see whether or not I was charging them more than the cafés. Some farmers do, you know. Well, they didn't make much use of the shop. They told me they didn't want it. I asked them why. There was dead silence. I couldn't get them to explain. I began to do some research. I went to the cafés and the Cooperative and priced the items I was selling them. I showed them that I was selling at by far the lowest price. I told them I was happy to give up the shop. It was fantastic. I would save myself time and bookkeeping. 'Have you chaps thought about this?' I asked. 'It will cost you more in town. You'll have to walk all the way. I can only lend you the tractor when there's a licensed driver, and he's going back home in a few weeks. And I will not let you carry any booze on it. I'll make spot-checks. It will be more inconvenient. What the hell are you guys achieving?' Again there was dead silence. Finally, one chap muttered something about seeing other things he wants when he goes shopping in town. I said, 'Well, go into town on Saturday morning and choose the other things you want. You'll have more money for them.' I just ended up with a blank.

"I'm not relating to them. I can't understand their point of view. I think, well, maybe they're growing up. They're flexing their muscles. Let them go through it, I say to myself. Let them go down to town on a Friday evening when it's raining and go through it all because they've got their full pay packet and can spend it the way they want.

"The *dominee* at the Mission church says that this all comes from mounting feelings of frustration in the Coloured community. He says that he himself is losing touch with them rapidly. They want to be independent of whites. They work for me. They get their money. They want to be as free as possible from my influence.

"I pay my workers as well as anyone in the valley. I treat them well. I give them good housing by comparison with the other farmers. I've given them a telly. At first they misused it. They'd leave it on all night. Once, one of them bashed it in. I made them pay the repairs. Now I deduct thirty cents a week from their salaries for repairs and electricity. I don't care about the cost of the electricity. I give it back to them in their bonuses. Paying for electricity gives them a sense of respect for the telly.

"Yes, I treat them well. I like them. When I was in commerce, I did the same. But then I always had workers knocking on my door asking for a job. Here I've had no one knock at my door and say, 'I want to work for you because you're a good bloke.' "

Peter looked hurt. When he had been in "commerce," he had made a practice of hiring workers whom no one else wanted because they had criminal records or bad reputations. He did this behind his father's back, and from what he told me, he was immensely success-ful in his hiring. When he left the business, most of the clerks and bookkeepers were Coloured, and several held positions superior to those of whites in his office.

I told Peter that I could find no necessary correlation between the salaries and the quality of housing and facilities a farmer offered and his reputation as an employer among the workers. Two farmers who, in my opinion, exploited their workers the most, beat them, and gave them only leaky hovels for homes had the best reputation as bosses. (Glen Ross was not among them.)

"It's like the old story of the whipping dog," Peter said. "You try to take the dog away from its whipped environment and give it a nice home, and it runs back. I don't know what it is inside us that attracts us to such situations. Maybe, it's the security that you know precisely how far you can go."

Among English-speaking farmers in the valley, Peter is the most involved in community affairs. Not only is he active in the Farmers' Association, but he plays an important role in the Verhoudings— Relations—Committee, which is aimed at improving relations be-tween whites and Coloureds. Ideally, Peter would like to make his community into a perfect one, removed from the problems of the rest of the country.

"There are Verhoudings Committees all over the western Cape, wherever Coloureds and whites are living close at hand, but we haven't been that successful here because of the Coloured popula-tion. We have a complicated constitution. You can't vote as such. You have to reach a consensus without a show of hands. For every white there has to be a Coloured of like position—or as near as we can come to it. The Coloured equivalent of a farmer would be a farm manager. There are a few of them in Wyndal, but they don't come. They're too shy.

"Basically what happens at our meetings is whites confronting whites over Coloured issues. The Coloureds don't say anything much. They just sit there in silence. We're supposed to meet once a month, but we are having a lot of trouble getting a quorum. A lot of Afrikaners belong to so many committees that they have little time for the Verhoudings Committee. It takes a bit of a backseat.

"Committees are the Afrikaners' passion. Tommy Prinsloo counted them up. There are over thirty committees in Wyndal. The school board, several church committees, the Farmers' Association, the Women's Agricultural Association, the Chamber of Commerce, the Cooperative Association—there are three committees—the commandoes, the junior and senior Rapportryers,* and so on. Of course, the Verhoudings Committee is not as close to the Afrikaner's heart as the commandoes. So we have to battle to get a quorum. We usually have a representative from the Department of Coloured Affairs present.

"We've managed to make some changes, particularly in the plans for the Coloured Community. We've cleared away an area for sports facilities. We'd like to get them a meeting hall—and then, of course, there's the school. There's always a tremendous fight about that. The municipality says it should only build a school for the Coloureds in the municipality and not for those in the district. They're the majority. I asked them if they had planned the white school just for the municipality. If they had, it would have been a tenth the size. As it is, it's far too big for the community, and they've just spent three quarters of a million for a new gymnasium! Everybody was angry with me, but the point was made. We haven't accomplished anything yet. We are only an advisory committee. There are three Coloured schools. Conditions are appalling. They're totally over-crowded. My farm children are in school. They go down in three shifts. It's most unsatisfactory. How they learn anything, I don't know.

"I try, but frankly between the mentality of the old Afrikaners and the government, I am always banging my head against one wall

*A conservative Afrikaner men's club, likened to the Lions or the Rotary, sometimes called the junior Broederbond.

or another. I've thought seriously about resigning, and then I ask myself who will replace me."

Peggy and Hugo Malan

"When we first moved here," Peggy Malan said, "Hugo had a very frank talk with the *volk*. He told them that the farm was very rundown and that he expected to improve it with their help. He explained how they would benefit from the improvements. He promised to pay them more, improve their homes, and send them to special training courses run by the government."

Hugo went on to tell them that as *he* expected to work hard, he expected them to work hard too. He wanted discipline and would not put up with sloth or insubordination. He would pay each man according to his worth. There would be no drunkenness, he said, and no bootlegging, and no fighting. He was discontinuing the *dop* system, which only made drunks of them, and would increase their salaries proportionately. (In the end he gave them a liter of wine on paydays.) If any of them had any complaints, they should come to him directly. If any of them were not satisfied with the conditions he had set, they were free to leave.

"They listened," Peggy continued. "I was watching from the house. But they didn't say a word. They didn't ask a question. I found it terrifying—their implacable silence. I didn't understand them. I had known only the Zulus, and they're completely different. They're silent, but they have dignity. I didn't know much Afrikaans then. Hugo said he expected the silence. He hadn't had much experience with the Coloureds, but he did speak Afrikaans. Even so, those first few months were frightening. The farm was so rundown, discipline was so poor, that Hugo didn't dare walk into the workers' area without his revolver, and never at night."

According to some of the other farmers, the Malans inherited a particularly unruly group of laborers. (There were nine families, about fifty-five *volk*, living on the farm at the time.) The previous owner had exploited them fiercely. He had paid them little and beat them savagely, and had never paid the bonuses he promised. He had closed his eyes to their bootlegging and to the violent fights that broke out almost weekly. Unlike the workers on some of the other farms, the Malans' workers were nearly all related to one another.

"Poor chap," Jack Freeling said, referring to Hugo. "He couldn't have inherited a more dissolute lot. Old Gustave Maree—he was the previous owner—had collected the scum of the valley. He never paid them anything. Hugo's got rid of the worst, and I must hand it to him, he's made the most of the others. His biggest problem is that they're all related. They're always jumping into each other's bed and knifing each other. For a while there wasn't a week that the police weren't hauling one or another to jail on a Saturday night. I suppose I was lucky. None of my workers were related. I'd have broken them up if I'd been Hugo. I'd have got rid of the whole bloody lot."

The relationship between the Malans and their workers improved slowly. At first the workers tried to take advantage of Hugo's inexperience. But he proved tougher than they expected. He kicked out the troublemakers and advanced the better workers. He took a fatherly liking to one young man, sent him off to a training course, and made him foreman.

"Frankly, I've been disappointed in Aubry," Hugo confided. He had just come in from inspecting the new trellises he was putting up in the south field, and he was listening to his wife's description of their first years on the farm. "He's a bright enough chap, but he doesn't seem to have the will. I told him when I made him foreman that he was going to have a rough time, that he was going to be challenged, and that he would find himself alone. I told him *that* was the cost of advancement, and that if he wanted to advance in life, he would have to bear it. He doesn't have it in him though."

"How can he expect to lead others," Peggy asked, "when his house is the messiest we have? Anna—his wife—is part of the problem. She's a tramp. She throws rubbish out the door. She neglects her children. She's been in bed with nearly every man on the farm."

"I'd like to tell Aubry to get rid of her, but I can't," Hugo said.

"Yes, that's the problem," Peggy continued. "You know what's best for them but you can't tell them. You feel you ought to, and you know you shouldn't. They have to make their own decisions. It's the specter of paternalism that haunts us."

Peggy went on to describe the fighting that took place on the farm during their first few years. She takes a certain scandalized delight in talking about it and about the sexual encounters of her *volk*. She is not unusual in this respect. The English farmers and, perhaps to a lesser extent, the Afrikaners often talk about the drinking, the fighting, and the promiscuity of their workers. They complain about it; they are horrified; and they are entertained. "It adds a bit of spice to their lives," Zachary van der Merwe says cynically. "Those superrespectable ladies know all the dirt that goes on a few hundred yards from their homes. They hear about it from their maids. That's as close as they ever get to it. That's as close as they want to get to it. They never ask themselves why their maids tell them who knifed whom or who's sleeping with whom."

"The fighting was terrible," Peggy Malan continued. "Every Saturday night we would lie awake and listen to them. At first it was frightening. I thought they'd attack us. Hugo slept with his revolver next to the bed even though he assured me they would never come to the house. I remember one night in particular. It was so dreadfully embarrassing. We had just fixed up the dining room and had friends over from Durban. The screaming and the howling began. I sent one of the maids to ask them to be quiet. They were for a few minutes. Then there was a most ghastly scream—and a banging at the kitchen door. Hugo got his revolver and went to see what it was all about. Aubry was standing there at the door, his hands covered with blood. He said that Tommie had stabbed Willie in the neck. Before he had had time to finish his story, two men dragged Willie into the kitchen. Fortunately, Aubry had had the sense to stick a rag into Willie's wound. It slowed down the bleeding. One of our guests was a doctor and was able to stop it. We called the police, and they took Willie to the hospital. They found Tommie at a neighbor's. The whole thing evidently started when Tommie called Anna a slut, and Willie—he's Aubry's brother—tried to defend Anna."

"The next morning I had a very serious talk with them," Hugo said. "I told them that I would not put up with any more fighting on the farm and that the next time anything like this happened I would kick them all out."

"Of course, we fired Tommie," Peggy said. "He was in jail for six months. Do you know that the day he was released, he waited at the café where he knew I shopped to ask for work! That's the way they are, these Coloureds. They're not like the Zulus. They've no sense of dignity."

"Or personal pride," Hugo added. "That's what I've been trying to develop in them: a sense of pride. They must take pride in their work. Then they'll develop a sense of their own worth."

There were other violent incidents on the Malan farm, but after the stabbing, there was a fundamental change, both Hugo and Peggy assured me, in their relationship with the workers.

"They began to come to us with every problem," Peggy said. "It became intolerable. They tried to get us to intervene in their family problems. Hugo refused. He said there would be no end to it. They came with their children at all hours. I remember Mary coming at five one morning because her daughter had a cough. It was nothing serious, a minor cough that could have been treated later if it had to be treated at all. She tapped at our bedroom window!"

"I asked her why she had come so early," Hugo said. "She said she thought her daughter was dying. I told her that she could not possibly have thought *that*. It was just a minor cough."

"She just stood there," Peggy added. "Not a word. I find their passivity so irritating. They're so dependent. They have no will. You tell them what to do. You explain why they should do it. They seem to understand. And they do what you say as long as you're there, but the minute you leave, they go back to their old ways. And then they hang their heads when you discover them. They've no self-respect. I suppose it's our fault. We give them little enough to respect in themselves."

"No," Hugo said. "It's not a question of giving them anything. It's a question of their learning to respect themselves. You can't give a man self-respect. You can only treat him with respect. And I will treat any man, whatever his color, with respect if he merits it. But I will never give any man my respect if he does not merit it."

Hugo was talking thickly through his moustache. He went on to proclaim the virtues of "meritocracy." "I don't believe a man or a woman should have a vote just for the asking. They should merit it. It's not a case of race. There are plenty of whites who have the vote and who don't deserve it. There are Blacks who should have the vote and others who shouldn't. If you have to work to achieve the vote, then you will respect it. Look, even in your country, in America, where everyone has the vote, how many actually vote? And how many of those who vote take it seriously? Why should we entrust the vote—our political welfare—to those who can't think? Why should one of my workers who can't read, who can't keep his house in order, have the same political power as I do or you do or any educated man does?"

"But it's not their fault," Peggy put in. "It's we who made them the way they are. We are responsible for their ignorance."

"No," Hugo said again. "It's not we who are at fault. We must accept the world as we find it and change it, rationally, and not emotionally. As I said, I can't give a man self-respect. I can only help him achieve self-respect. It's here that the government is at fault. They have created laws that prevent us from helping the other man achieve self-respect. They've blocked us, and *that* infuriates me."

"And so we try to do what we can here on the farm," Peggy said apologetically. "It takes so much time and so much patience. Just when you think you've accomplished something, it slips away. Carol Reid told me this morning that the Wentworths discovered one of their boys chopping down a tree in front of his house. Tom had ordered him out because he came to work drunk. When Tom asked him why he was chopping down the tree, he said he couldn't get the *bakkie* up to the door to carry away his furniture. They've no respect for anything. I've tried to get them to plant flowers in front of their houses, but with the exception of Elsie—she's my maid and likes to help me arrange flowers—none have. I've offered them seeds and cuttings."

The world of the Coloured, of drinking, fighting, and promiscuity as white South Africans depict it, is a sort of anti-world, contrasting with their own idealized one of gentility, respectability, and, as they say, Victorian morality. It may also refract their own drinking, fighting, and promiscuity or their fantasies of such drinking, fighting, and promiscuity.

There is a fascination with the anti-world—the world of, say, the exotic, the psychotic, or the criminal—so long as it remains distant and abstract: depicted. It is in many respects a mythological world. Whatever its basis in reality, its description seems always to step out of reality into the imaginary. Desire, less constrained by the demands of reality than by those of traditional idiomatic (mythic, archetypic) figures, plots, and symbols, is given extravagant play. Just as the native peoples of South Africa were often understood in demonic terms by the early settlers, so today, especially among the fundamentalists, there is a tendency to see the anti-world of the Coloured and the Black in demonic terms. The homelands are filled with witch doctors and sorcerers; the locations are filled with *tsotsis* and *skollies*—hooligans—who take on extrahuman proportion. (I am not denying the existence of the *tsotsis* and the *skollies* in the townships any more than I am denying the existence of the witch doctors and sorcerers in the tribal reserves. Undoubtedly they exist. I only wish to call attention to their symbolic role in the white South African's depiction of reality.)

In the valley, however, the anti-world is in fact neither distant nor abstract. The workers' quarters, the *premier lieu* of riot and fornication, is a few hundred yards from the farmhouse, the bastion of gentility, respectability, and propriety. It is a constant reminder that the anti-world is very much part of the world. Paradoxically, reality intrudes *here* into the mythic, rendering it frighteningly real. Talk of drinking, fighting, and promiscuity—talk that seems an attempt, under these circumstances, to make the anti-world less terrifying— in fact makes it more terrifying. In the valley, talk is constantly confirmed by actual occurrence. The white is caught in a circle from which he cannot escape.

Drinking, fighting, and promiscuity are, of course, only part of the "Coloured" world. Gentility, respectability, and propriety are also part of it. These are seldom mentioned by whites. Despite their anxiety, the farmers are slow to improve their workers' lives to the point of "respectability." (They can take out government improvement loans at one percent for twenty years.) But to dismiss their procrastination as "imperialist avariciousness" or "capitalist greed" may be to lose sight of the fact that they themselves are ensnared economically and psychologically in an exploitative symbiosis. Hugo Malan makes small improvements each year. Sometimes he says it is a question of economy. At other times he says that he improves his workers' quarters as they themselves improve. It is their reward for good behavior. He points to the "instant dilapidation" of the workers' quarters on several large farms, owned by Johannesburg corporations. "The managers were foolish enough to make improvements before their workers were ready for them."

The existence of this anti-world in *their* midst is particularly disturbing to the English farmers, who, unlike the Afrikaners, have not, *as yet*, got used to it. They are recent arrivals; they have come from other parts of the republic, where they lived in other circumstances and with other defenses and subterfuges. Here in Wyndal they cannot escape it. Some have built walls between their homes and those of their workers. Others have planted hedges or rows of trees. Still others, like Peggy Malan, have encouraged their workers to plant flower gardens. These are all magical strategies that in the end only emphasize the gap between the two populations.

The distance created by apartheid, understood not only in legal terms but as a frame of mind, enforces the predisposition to view the world of the Coloureds or, elsewhere, of Blacks as a grotesque anti-world, and to act according to their view. It is perhaps no accident that several English and Afrikaans office workers with whom I spoke agreed that they had become close to Coloured colleagues only after some violent argument in which each said what he thought of the other. Violence, at some level, may be the only way to break out of the circle—to enter into a relationship rather than to depict and exploit.

Hennie

"Now, very often these people are actually demon-possessed," Hennie said, referring to the members of some Coloured gangs in Cape Town. I had asked him about his experiences as a prison chaplain there. He had volunteered to be a chaplain but was not given permission until the prison psychologist called him in one day to treat a man, a European, who was thought to be demon-possessed. Hennie himself believes in demons and often, though inconsistently, interprets individual acts of violence and madness in terms of demons. He has performed exorcisms often—both in Rhodesia and in South Africa. Ever since his first charismatic experience, he has felt confident in treating the possessed. "I began to pray and suddenly I realized I was not alone. Christ was there with me. I knew I would be victorious. I know how to deal with Satan.

"These blokes are like puppets the demons use. When they are in this state, they are no longer human. They do such inhuman things. Three of them got together once and cut another bloke's throat with a razor blade. They belonged to one gang, and he belonged to another, and they had carried their feuds right into prison. They cut out his heart, chopped it into pieces, and made everyone in their cell eat it. There are usually about fifteen blokes in a cell, and they wanted to establish their authority. On another occasion some blokes slit open another bloke's stomach and played with his insides while he was still alive."

Hennie had not seen these prisoners, but he accepted the stories he had heard in prison uncritically. He occasionally talked about demonic possession in his sermons and at times recounted some of his prison experiences. His European parishioners were offended by the violence of his imagery, but his Coloured parishioners seemed to accept it quite naturally. "For them the chopper is a reality," he said when I asked him about it.

Several farmers in Wyndal have organized farm clubs to improve the lives of the Coloureds. Often these clubs are aimed at giving the laborers some distraction that will discourage them from drinking. One farmer has Saturday night film shows. Several others have cleared ground for soccer fields. (Coloureds are said to be good soccer players but poor rugby players.) And still others—those who claim they cannot afford to do it alone—have pooled their resources and fixed up a game room with a television set in their barns. Younger English- and Afrikaans-speaking women have begun women's clubs on their farms. Although they have had limited success, they have brought together English and Afrikaners in a common purpose and improved relations between them. Other clubs are church-run and as such limited to the Afrikaners. Hennie has not encouraged these organizations in his parish. He is not opposed to them *per se*, but they are not his priority. "They offer easy expiation, and little else," he said once.

Organizations to improve race relations are found throughout South Africa. Some, like the Black Sash, have manifest political goals. Others, like Kontakt, a *verligte** Afrikaner women's organization, are decidedly nonpolitical. "We are pragmatic in orientation, we do not want to give handouts," one member of Kontakt told me. "We want to improve relations between whites and non-whites. We want to get to know them, and we want them to get to know us. We recognize differences in our styles of life and in our cultures. We don't necessarily want to change them. We want each group to appreciate the other and to make only those changes *they* feel are necessary. We're neither social workers nor missionaries." Still other organizations, like the valley farm clubs, are rather more immediate responses to conditions seen as unbecoming by the whites. In all these organizations women dominate. They are, so to speak,

---

*Literally, "enlightened." The *verligtes*, like the present prime minister, Pieter W. Botha, have been described as "pragmatic centrists," who are opposed to the *verkramptes*, the ideological hardliners in the South African political spectrum. "*Verligte*" is sometimes incorrectly translated as "liberal."

a daytime activity, when men are away at work. Theirs is the realm
of economics and politics and not that of everyday social understanding and domestic welfare.

Margot Prinsloo

"We started a club for Coloured women on several neighboring
farms because we feel you can only reach families through the
women. We've made quite a lot of progress in two years. We had
cooperation from the Department of Coloured Affairs. They gave
us advice and some financial help, and told us which institutions
would send out experts to give courses. Many of them do. I was
surprised.

"We meet once a week from three to five or half past five to do
something constructive. Tomorrow, for example, we will be learning to crochet sweaters. They can either keep them or, if they are
good enough, they can sell them. We've made arrangements to sell
them at a women's cooperative in Bellville. It will give them a little
extra money. They've learned to arrange flowers—to beautify their
homes. You can see the results. They never knew how to arrange
flowers, and now when you enter their houses you will find a nice
little bowl of flowers. Or you'll find something else they've made.
They like to make pictures with flower petals. It gives them a
tremendous sense of pride because they have been creative. They
can show what they've made to their friends. We've also had courses
on cooking and nutrition, but these have not been as successful.
They are less concrete. It will take time.

"We're just scratching the surface. Four farms are involved in our
club, and there is one other club in the valley. Peggy Malan has
talked about starting one, and so has Diana Wentworth, but her
husband has been too sick for her to start anything. It's going to take
time. It's an educating process. Perhaps that sounds paternalistic,
but it's true. We've received help from one woman who has been
organizing clubs like ours for years and is making an in-depth study.
She told us that there are certain things we can expect to happen.
At first they will always be late for a meeting and surprised when
it ends. They have no sense of time. If she hadn't spoken to us about
this, I don't think we would have carried on. It was so discouraging.
We would arrive promptly at three, and none of them would appear

before three-thirty or four o'clock. They would straggle in, without an apology. Now most of them are on time. We have got over our first hurdle. Now we are working on getting them to run their own club. At first they just sat there and waited for us to tell them what to do. Now they have elected a chairman, a secretary, and a treasurer, and they make up their own agenda. We don't want them to think we are running the club. We have been disassociating ourselves slowly, but we are keeping an eye on it to make sure that things are going the way they should. We give them a few suggestions for courses at the end of each term, and they choose from amongst them. Then we look for the institutions that can give us help.

"We've been lucky in one important respect. The woman on the farms in our club are all very religious. This has helped tremendously, and their *dominee* has encouraged them. His wife helps us whenever she can. I think the whole experience has deepened their faith."

I talked to Margot a year later about the club. She was discouraged. The Coloured women were taking a less active role than she had expected. They appeared dutifully at the meetings, but they had lost some of the excitement they had had the previous year. Margot and the other white women in the group had also lost some of their enthusiasm. Margot could not account for the change. "Sometimes I despair at ever accomplishing anything with them. It would be a pity to drop it." Neither Peggy Malan nor Diana Wentworth had started clubs.

Dominee Pieter Kotze

"When I moved out here, I ran into many things I didn't understand. I had to keep an open mind," Dominee Pieter Kotze said. "Superstitions function in various important ways," Pieter Kotze continued. He is often didactic and speaks with a schoolboyish enthusiasm. "When I came out here, I saw them simply as superstitions. Only later did I come to appreciate their function. Funerals, for example, are very important events in the Coloured community. They are a means of getting rid of the dead in a psychological sense. They never take me less than two hours. There are three services: at the house of the deceased, in church, and at the grave. At the house, the coffin is open and everyone files past, touching the corpse and covering it with flowers, except for the face. I was revolted by the idea, but I had to get used to it. They were also in the habit of leaving the coffin open in front of the pulpit, but I put a stop to that. At the cemetary there is a lot of crying and hymn singing as the coffin is lowered into the grave. I drop soil on the coffin and then give the spade to the chief mourner. Each mourner follows, putting a spadeful of soil in the grave as the others sing. After the funeral there is a big party. I don't stay for that. It lasts all night, and everybody forgets about the dead.

"Then there is a lot of talk about *doekom,* black magic, among the Coloureds. You don't find the laborers themselves dabbling in it. It's always the Malays. I suppose it's similar to witchcraft in England.

"A laborer once told me about funny things in his house. He said he had been bewitched. Evil influences—*sleg goed*—had attacked his wife and three children. At first he didn't pay much attention to it, but finally he called me in. When I arrived at his house, I discovered that his wife and three children were cold to the touch. They had no pulse and were not breathing. Or, at least their breathing was very faint. These states of coldness alternated with states of extreme frenzy. The children would begin to shout and cry, first the youngest, then the middle boy, and finally the eldest, always in that order. They would chase animals, break whatever was in front of them. They had bad dreams and wet their beds.

"The Bantu people believe in a spirit called Togolosh: a little Black man, very old, hairy all over, with a long beard, who never wears shoes. He is a sort of poltergeist who makes strange noises and causes milk jugs to fall over. The middle boy—he is supposed to be clairvoyant, like some other members of his father's family—saw Togolosh. He does not call the 'little man' Togolosh, but it is clearly Togolosh he is seeing. He told me the little man forced him to run around wildly. In such cases, all you can do is to hold the boys' hands tightly and pray. They come back to consciousness after a while.

"And there were other cases, too. One boy was badly treated by his parents and also ran wild. He had terrible dreams. I prayed for him, and he seemed to get better. We moved him into a neighbor's house, and the moment we did, he stopped behaving wildly. He told me that a weird old lady had bewitched him. She was a drinker and had blotches on her skin.

"I find it scary to come across people with these strange ways. I've heard about other cases in the area. The Coloureds don't like talking to whites about these things. They call them *vuil goed*, filthy things. They also talk a lot about the slim man, the clever man. He's a sort of magician. If something unusual happens, they say it is the slim man from Stellenbosch or Kraaifontein. I make it clear that I don't want to have anything to do with the slim man. It is of course difficult because they are not going to take the advice of an 'ignorant' man.

"I try to play down these superstitions. I accept their vocabulary to such an extent that at times it conflicts with my own beliefs. I don't disbelieve in the things they talk about. I don't believe in them. I simply do not have any belief at all. I accept it in a kind of ad hoc fashion. In this way it poses no conflict."

I was not convinced. Pieter Kotze seems threatened by relativism. At times, during our many long talks, he accepted a relativist position and at other times he became dogmatic. His sermons were always very authoritarian in style, and when I made house calls with him, I had the impression that he distanced himself from his flock by means of his ministerial authority. Had I been a member of his congregation, I would have had great difficulty in confiding in him, though I would have trusted him completely.

"I don't want to give you a false impression. Most of my time is spent on practical activities. I am not a very practical man, and I was not prepared for the practical side of the ministry in my studies. But I find most of my time is spent on keeping accounts, filling out forms for my parishioners, and attending committee meetings. I have to play more than one role. I suppose I had a romantic notion of the ministry—a pastoral one really—but instead of leading the life of a 'parish priest,' I have to fight the school board! I have to pray for those who have been bewitched! I have to worry about children who drift around town in the middle of the day because their school can't accommodate them. They trample gardens, they steal fruit. I stole fruit when I was little. It was not considered particularly bad. It was just mischief. But now people appear to be harsher. They immediately call the police."

"Isn't that because the children who are stealing the fruit are Coloured?" I asked. "You are white."

"Yes, to a certain extent, you are right. It's hard to explain. Things have changed since I was a little boy. Now everything has a monetary value. I was talking to one old Coloured man. He's a mason. He was describing the village in the old days. He called it horse brown. Whites and Coloureds lived side by side. They were friends. They took care of each other. And then suddenly, about eighteen years ago, all the Coloureds were moved out of the village. Oh, there are one or two Coloured families that still live in the village. They pass for white, but everyone knows who they are. I can't explain why they were allowed to pass. Such are the mysteries of this country.

"They built a few good houses in the Coloured community. Most of the people who live in them do not work in the village. It's been hard to sell them because they are too expensive for the locals, and the community is not considered particularly desirable to the so-called better Coloureds. They prefer to live in bigger communities where there are more people like themselves.

"I do not really understand how most of the laborers live. Many of them earn only seven rand a week. There was one farmer who paid them only six rand. He committed suicide recently. And then there is Glen Ross in Wyndal. Have you met him? He's a brute of a man. Fortunately, there are not many like him. The laborers seem to have ways of supplementing their incomes. They steal. They fence. They sell *dagga* [marijuana]. And many of them *shibeen* [bootleg]. That's very profitable. They buy the cheapest white wine in twenty-liter jugs and sell it for twenty or thirty cents a liter. Most *shibeening* is done by Blacks. They're good businessmen. They never drink themselves. They all have bank accounts.

"The Coloureds never save a penny. Theirs is purely a hand-to-mouth existence. They drink a lot. Some of them suffer brain damage from drinking methylated spirits. They seem to develop an immunity to it. I don't think the majority of the Coloureds are alcoholics. They do not need a drink the way an alcoholic needs a drink. Drinking is part of their style of life. There are some who smell permanently of wine, even when they haven't had a drop in days. I try to help them as much as possible, but it is difficult. I have nearly two thousand in my congregation. There is a social worker who visits us when she has time, but she is very overworked. Some of the farmers help. They give 'anti-booze' to the drinkers on their farms. I've sent a few away to treatment centers, but often the farmers don't want to let them go.

"I sometimes think that Coloureds are about a generation behind whites in style of life and values. They want all the rights of the white man but they don't want to mix with Blacks. Of course, the Blacks consider the Coloureds to be bastards. Some marry Coloureds, but it is for purely practical reasons. If they marry a Coloured woman and have children by her, they may be classified as Coloured and remain without a pass. But the Coloureds don't like to marry Blacks. There is a class distinction among them. The lighter the skin, the higher the status. The most 'respectable' members of my congregation do not want to mix with Blacks, and they don't want to mix with whites either. Apartheid works both ways, you see . . .

"The Coloureds have learned one thing: to play dumb. They can accomplish great things this way. I don't really know them myself. I don't think it's possible. They talk to me, but there is always a wall between us—a point beyond which I have no understanding. I can know about them, but I can't know them."

"How do you think the members of your congregation see you?" I asked.

"I don't have the vaguest idea," Pieter Kotze answered. He was taken aback by the question. "It differs so much. In rural congregations the white minister is generally liked because he brings status to the congregation. There is a large part of my congregation that simply has no view whatsoever except in terms of my authority and their dislike of authority. Others find me wonderful and unreal. They would like me to preach in the abstract, with words that they don't understand. They don't want to know me. They want me to be the embodiment of the holy man—the white holy man. They like to think of their minister as outside the community: too holy to see the way things really are. There are some very good people in my congregation. They're so good that I can't talk to them. They have too much respect for their minister, any minister. Many of them have undergone dramatic conversions after a drinking bout. If the minister has helped them, they respond with idealized love and respect. And then there are those, by far the largest number, who are reserving judgment until they know me better. Coloured people do not like to decide about whites until they have known them for a very long time."

Knowledge about gives the illusion of *knowing*. Pieter Kotze despairs of ever knowing his congregation. He says he can know about them but he cannot know them. And yet he talks as though he knows them. He is caught up, inevitably, in the illusion. It is embedded in his idiom. Knowledge of the other is always a matter of convention. The conventions are taken for granted. I know when I know someone else. I also know the limits of my knowledge. They are too conventional. Both these conventions remain unchallenged, that is, until a "first" cross-cultural encounter. Then everything is brought into question. There are no conventions that operate between people of different cultures in this first, mythic encounter. They must be developed. Of course, such a first encounter never occurs in pure form, for there is no society that has not developed conventions for knowing the alien and the exotic. The ethnographer strives somewhat foolhardily to break these conventions—to encounter the other in ruthlessly naked terms. He fails, inevitably, but ideally he raises the question of knowing the other. The ordinary man who encounters practically the alien and exotic raises no such question. He accepts his society's conventions for knowledge of them. His encounter is governed by practical exigencies.

Everyone who visits South Africa is immediately given bits of knowledge about people of other races. They resemble the bits of knowledge with which one comes away from a museum of natural history or from having read an old-fashioned manners-and-customs ethnography. "A Zulu will never greet you first. You must greet him. He is not being impolite. He is being polite in terms of his own tradition." "Kaffirs don't think like whites." "Blacks have to learn a job step by step. They think serially. They have no sense of the whole." "There are no Black mathematicians." "Coloureds have no sense of time." "Coloureds can understand a job if you explain it to them. They can think globally." "Coloureds live from hand to mouth; Blacks save." "Coloureds are drunk." "Malays make good carpenters." "Indians are good merchants; they are all rich." "Afrikaners are pig-headed." "Afrikaners have a strong sense of family." "Afrikaners are materialistic." "Afrikaner students don't think. They learn by rote." "The English are hypocrites." "The English are toffee-nosed." "The English have one foot in South Africa and one foot in England." "Jews always know when to leave a sinking ship."

These bits of knowledge are passed on like folklore. Not only do they give the illusion that one knows the other (or, on occasion, that it is impossible to know the other) but they confirm the picture that one has of the other. They also confirm the picture one has of oneself. The Afrikaner who asserts that the English are hypocrites is implicitly declaring himself, the Afrikaner, a non-hypocrite. The white who says that Coloureds have no sense of time is saying that he has a sense of time. One's sense of self is always mediated by the image one has of the other. (I have asked myself at times whether a "superficial" knowledge of the other, in terms of some stereotype or other, is not a way of preserving a "superficial" image of oneself.) These bits of knowledge and the resultant images of the other create and preserve a distance between self and other that is at the root of those attitudes from which apartheid, legalized or not, arises.

In my experience the most extravagant bits of knowledge that whites pass on to one another concern Blacks. Whatever their basis in reality, these bits of knowledge create a particularly distant, an exotic, image of the Blacks, which, like all exoticisms, is at once fascinating and alienating. *Blacks* are a marvelous vehicle for the whites' fantasies. They carry all the ambivalence that the white feels toward the other. They can embody a savage dignity and command a very special respect or they can incarnate fear and demand flight or siege. They permit all the rhetorical play that enables the white South African to situate himself comfortably, but not too comfortably, in *his* Africa.

"It will be impossible for Blacks to understand our ways for another hundred years," a Dutch Reformed missionary, a man in his late thirties, who was visiting in the valley, told me. He had spent his entire life among the Xhosa. "When they ask a question, they don't see it our way. They never had a money system. They had only their cattle. How can we expect them to understand the overdraft system? What is a checkbook? They think of it as money. They don't understand the debt relationship. They don't even realize that a telephone costs money. They still practice *lobola* [bride-price] and initiations. You've seen them all covered with white clay. They may wear suits and dark glasses, but, believe me, they don't change . . .

"The Blacks are very confused now. They do not know where to go. They must decide on a new life—a life that they don't understand. They can't return to their old ways. They are very frustrated. You can see this in the Black Consciousness Movement and the Black Theology Movement. They are bothered by the fact that

Jesus Christ was white. They don't understand that it makes no difference. They can't abstract. There are big differences in their mentality. It is not a question of intelligence. There are different types of intelligence. Blacks do not think abstractly. They think two-dimensionally. They prefer repetition. If you ask them to make a report, they will prefer to copy an old report rather than write a new one. They prefer to imitate. Even doctors—they can make excellent doctors—cannot cope with crises that require independent thought. They do not do well in the sciences or with computers. They are better at law and religion. There is not one Black engineer in South Africa. And they do not make pilots. Even in Kenya they are only allowed to fly small planes.

"I remember once I tried to explain to them that malaria is carried by mosquitoes. They were less interested in that than in who sent the mosquitoes! They don't really believe in germs. They are more concerned with their ancestors and their witch doctors. They'll go to a witch doctor for all sorts of reasons: to pass an examination, to regain their health, to be strong in love.

"The Coloureds don't have the forefather problem the Blacks do. They don't care about their ancestors. They are very different from the Blacks. I would say that the Blacks have a stronger personality. They have more pride. They have their own culture. They say Coloureds have no sense of responsibility. Coloureds always want to be white. They are afraid of the Blacks. They don't like to marry Blacks. If they could, they would marry whites. But Coloureds have a wonderful sense of humor. Have you ever heard them imitate a white man? Blacks are poker-faced. They never show their feelings, though their emotions change rapidly. One minute they will be friendly, and the next minute angry . . .

"The Blacks' real problem is that their leaders are very different from the ordinary citizen. Their leaders have visited England, Holland, America. They come back confused and get frustrated because they want to change everything at once and they can't. And then, of course, they have their personal ambition. Our forefathers had long years of experience—an experience that has affected all aspects of our lives. What is the Black man's experience? Witch doctors! There are over three thousand Black churches in South Africa. They call themselves Christians! Oh, it is far too soon for one man one vote."

* * *

Several other Dutch Reformed missionaries I had occasion to know drew a more sympathetic picture of the Blacks with whom they lived and worked. They were moved by their experience with Blacks. They had greater respect for them and tended to romanticize their culture. One missionary whom I met at Pieter Kotze's told me that through his experience with the Xhosa his own Christianity was deepened. "In their simplicity, they understand Christ's message with a purity that is lost to those of us who have spent years reading theology." He added that they had taught him humility and patience. "I've spent long hours trying to convey a message to them. At first I became angry when they didn't understand (I still do at times), but slowly I came to understand that their failure to understand was in fact my failure. They may have seen a problem where I did not." He discouraged their belief in witch doctors, but he did not condemn it as the workings of the Devil as several other missionaries did. He saw it as a symptom of their innocence and their ignorance.

White South Africans frequently draw the same contrast between Blacks and Coloureds that the missionary to the Xhosa drew. The Black seems to engage the white in a way that the Coloured does not. English and Afrikaners in the valley who had experience with Blacks missed them intensely. They complained that they could never understand the Coloured. He was "slippery" they said. With the possible exception of the urban disenfranchised, the Black South African, unlike his American counterpart, has close and meaningful ties with a rich cultural heritage, however denigrated it may be by whites and those alienated Blacks who long to participate in the white man's culture. ("My people are so rude," one Xhosa woman told me. "We have to learn manners if we are to advance.") Like American Blacks, *Roots* notwithstanding, the Coloureds have no such vibrant cultural center. "Coloureds always want to be white." They participate in a culture to which they have only partial access. It is, for most Coloureds, the culture of the Afrikaners, a culture that is turned in on itself, vulnerable, fragile, without international pretension, restricted, without transcendent possibility.

The Coloured can, of course, mimic the white man. He can at times play the "white man" better than the white man plays himself. Even the most superficial look at upper-class Coloureds—doctors, lawyers, and accountants—in Cape Town reveals this. Or he can fantasize domination, usually sexual domination, of the white. I remember sitting through lunch with an important Coloured official and an American woman, a student on a summer internship in Cape Town. At first the official regaled us with "in" government gossip and then with the frustrations that he constantly feels. Finally, with terrorizing insistence, he argued that white women prefer Coloured lovers. He was, I felt, verbally raping the intern and destroying my own sexual privilege. It was impossible for us to change the subject until he had completed his symbolic assault.

Such "assaults" are familiar to any European or American who has spent any time in the colonial and postcolonial worlds. In South Africa, for the Coloured, partial participant in the white man's culture, there lurks behind these fantasies the Black man and his sexuality. The Coloured has no greater access to the Black man's culture than to the white man's. Indeed, he has even less access. "Marriage"—often a metaphor in South Africa for cultural mixture —is more likely to occur (were it legal) between Coloureds and whites than between Coloureds and Blacks, so the missionary tells me. Even those young radical Coloureds who identify with Blacks politically, who insist on being called Black, are as mystified by the ideologies around them as American Blacks who identify with Africans. The Coloured knows he is odd man out in white South Africa and at some level he knows that he will be odd man out in Black South Africa. The present South African government exploits this double entrapment fully. As part of a divide-and-rule policy, Coloureds were given membership in a President's Council, albeit with only advisory power and now in their own parliament; they are allowed to own homes, though not the land on which their homes are built; a limited franchise is dangled before them. Their privilege is made clear to the Blacks. For the outsider, the Coloured is in many respects the symbol of the South African of whatever color or culture.

RENEWAL

Andre Roussouw

"The Dutch Reformed Church is fast asleep. I myself was an elder in the church. I was raised in a very Christian household. We were more religious than most. I worked in a missionary station in Zululand. I taught Sunday school here until I left the church, and now I teach it in the Baptist church. The children I've taught are very sensitive to the Renewal. They are not satisfied with the Dutch Reformed Church. I was always bound in by the church. I couldn't teach the subjects I thought important. There was always a lot of stress on church history. I feel it is completely unimportant at that stage. Children in the Dutch Reformed Church see religion as just another school subject—impersonally. In the Dutch Reformed Church you have religion, but *we* have something more. All Christians believe in the Holy Spirit, in the power of the Lord, and in Christ's mercy, but in the Dutch Reformed Church we never experienced it. The Dutch Reformed Church acknowledges speaking in tongues, but they don't really believe it. People in the church are satisfied with life if they don't have to make any sacrifices. Many ministers are in it for prestige and money and not out of faith. The minister is the head of the town. Not even the mayor has his power. Ministers earn twelve hundred to thirteen hundred rand a month, and they also get a house and car.

"I myself was satisfied until I saw that there was something more. Then life gets a lift. I was never really converted. I've always been a Christian. What happened to me was like walking in one direction and then changing to another. Nothing dramatic. I just knew I wanted something more. Dominee Naude came here for the first time about four years ago. The banker's wife had told some of us about him and invited him to come to heal the sick. I saw how he healed someone with a bad back. My back was also bothering me. He made me sit down and picked up my legs. I looked down and saw that one of them was shorter than the other. I watched the *dominee* pray over me, and the shorter leg got longer! I've never had a back problem since then. He also cured a German of cancer. It was about this time too that Tamara had experienced the Holy Spirit, and I saw how her life had changed. I went to Piet van Rooyen. He's a Baptist—from the Free State. He's the one who has taught us that we can call all experience the power of the Lord if only we allow ourselves to. He's an extraordinary man—a man of tremendous spiritual power. Before he moved to Wyndal, we all thought that somebody like him would come to us one day.

"Anyway, I went to Piet and I asked him to pray for me. He put his hand on me. Nothing happened. I was very disappointed. I went home and about a week later I was praying when suddenly I felt the Spirit enter my body. I didn't need a confirmation. As Piet says, if you've been filled with the Spirit, you feel no envy of those who have prayed in tongues.

"Everything changed for me. I used to be worried. I was always concerned about debts, about the crops. Now I don't worry. I know the Lord will be with me. I don't have much money, but I know that as long as I have enough to eat, I will have no worries.

"I was always against getting baptized a second time, even after I was filled with the Holy Spirit. I thought I could get away with just my christening. Then I went away for a weekend with a friend. I don't believe you know him. He's a Baptist and has the power of healing. We talked late into the night. When I went to bed, I got a clear message that I had to do it, and the next morning it was confirmed when I opened the Bible and read about what my friend and I had been discussing the night before. I found that he had been right and I had been wrong."

"How did you get the message?" I asked Andre.

"I was lying awake. I don't really know. After I decided to get baptized, I was afraid to go back on my word. If He wants me to do it, I thought, I have to do it. In the morning, when I woke up, I was thinking about the Dutch Reformed Church. I'm very sentimental about it. I heard the church bells ringing. I thought, Oh, I'll never hear those bells again. In my church we don't have bells. Is what I've done all right? I asked myself. It was then that I looked into my Bible and saw my decision confirmed. Two weeks later I was baptized up in the mountains behind the Malans' farm. Nearly everyone in our Baptist church, the Afrikaans Baptist Church, was once a member of the Dutch Reformed Church. I had spoken to our *dominee.* He came to my house for an interview. He was quite upset but said that he had expected it."

"How did your parents feel?"

"My dad was especially upset. People in the village—well, they didn't say anything. They've been much cooler. I don't have as much time. And it doesn't mean the same thing to me. I'm more satisfied. Family life has become more important."

Andre started to tell me how his family life had changed after his baptism, when Tamara joined us unexpectedly. Andre could not continue. Many people in the village observed that Andre and Tamara had not been particularly happy since Tamara lost her first child. Some were worried about their marriage. After Tamara's baptism, she was put under a lot of pressure (as was customary among the Baptist initiates whom I observed) to convert her husband. Andre resisted for a long time. He was, as he says, very sentimental about the Dutch Reformed Church. To leave the church was to betray his tradition, to disappoint his parents, to risk ostracism from the community, and to abandon a hope he cherished of becoming a member of the town council. After he received the Spirit, he and Tamara prayed together every night, as did the other villagers in the Renewal. Every time they had to make an important decision or even a trivial one in which they were not in full accord, Andre and Tamara would ask for Christ's help and wait until one of them (usually Tamara) or both of them had received Christ's word. When Tamara spoke, she often referred to the Lord. For example, if Andre wanted to do something she did not approve of, she would say, "I don't think the Lord wants us to push Him so far." One of the important decisions they had yet to make, when I last saw them, concerned Andre's will. Neither Tamara nor Andre had received the Lord's decision, and Andre, after delaying as long as he reasonably could, made a new will without telling Tamara. Tamara was stunned when she learned about it and felt that Andre had pushed the Lord unduly. After praying together, they decided to leave Andre's new will as it was until they received further word from the Lord. The "Lord," "Christ," and the "Holy Spirit" came to mediate their relationship, as I believe they often did for other married couples in the village. (I was reminded of the mediating role of possessing spirits in the daily lives of the spirit-possessed with whom I had worked in Morocco.) Andre's decision to become a Baptist, whatever its origin, served to bring him closer to Tamara. It served also to distance him from his parents—the parents who looked down on Tamara and feared she would lead their son and grandchildren astray.

"Sometimes I preach in prison," Andre continued after I had greeted Tamara. "It used to take me about four or five hours to prepare a sermon, and I was always very nervous. I never saw a conversion. I always felt that I was getting no results. Now, since I've been filled with the Spirit, I no longer have to prepare a sermon. Last time I preached, I was in the shower fifteen minutes beforehand! I was totally unprepared. I got up. Words came out. They were not my own. The roughest convicts began to to cry and to give themselves up to the Lord . . .

"Once I discovered how to be filled with the Holy Spirit, I found that I also had the gift of healing. I often prayed for my son, who has asthma, but nothing ever happened. Now that I have come to know Christ, I pray for him and lay hands on him, and he recovers. He had a bad attack a few nights ago. Tamara and I were sure he was going to die. He couldn't breathe. I began to pray for him, and he got better.

"There are many things we don't understand. I have recently heard of a man in Indonesia who can turn water into wine. There is also a man who lives near Durban who has managed to raise people from the dead. He is a German missionary and works with the Zulu.

"When I lived in Zululand, on the mission station, I felt very close to the Lord. There, people are completely dependent on what the Lord provides. They have no luxuries. I found the Zulus very different from the Blacks I had seen in the mines in Jo'burg when I visited there. They live in a wild state. They know nothing about politics. They've never seen an airplane. They are what we say in

Afrikaans, *baar*, raw, uncivilized. We had to abandon a Land Rover that got stuck. When we returned, we found that the Zulus had smashed up everything that was shiny. They were afraid of it. They're not against whites. They'd do anything for you. They always walk behind you or circle around you in the veld.

"Many people have left the Dutch Reformed Church because it is involved in politics. The Baptists are opposed to so much political involvement. It is very difficult to justify apartheid from a religious point of view, but the Dutch Reformed Church insists on doing just that. I myself am against apartheid. My politics are very different from those of the government. You look in this area alone and you see that the Coloureds in the Mission Church are far more lively than we are. Of course, I'm for social apartheid, but that would come naturally. Whites are not going to associate with Coloureds and Blacks, and Blacks and Coloureds are not going to associate with whites. But our church remains open to all. Piet says, 'If a man is walking down the street and hears singing and feels inspiration in his heart, how can we stop him from entering our church?' But on my own I'd prefer not to go to a multiracial church. We're not used to the Coloureds on a higher level. When I think of Coloureds, I think of the boys on the farm. They're on a very low level. They're not educated. They drink. I'd find it difficult to pray with them. I think they'd take advantage of us. It would be different with Coloureds of a better class."

Andre was very nervous and kept contradicting himself. Finally, I asked him if he had ever prayed with a Coloured or a Black.

"I was at a prayer meeting, a gathering of brethren, last June. There were people of all races there. We had gathered to pray and fast for our country. It was during the heat of the riots on the anniversary of Soweto. That was the first time I worshiped with a Coloured person. He was filled with the Spirit, and I could feel it. We held hands. If they had taken a picture of us and put it in *Die Burger* [an Afrikaans newspaper], it would have caused a scandal. You realize it is possible to mix. You don't have to live in the same house or on the same street to be able to pray together.

"I think that if people had more love and the gift of the Spirit, our political reality would change. It would get rid of the hate of Blacks and Coloureds. It could snowball all over the country. We would have no problems."

* * *

Most of the villagers in the Renewal say that it is only through Christ's love that a peaceful solution to South Africa's problems will be found. They share Andre's distaste for multiracial worship, but they acknowledge that a church that closes its doors to anyone because of skin color, like the Dutch Reformed Church, is acting in an un-Christian way. They are bothered by the contradiction and prefer not to think about it. Although a few women in the village have begun to evangelize in the Coloured community, no Coloureds have been invited or have come to any of the prayer meetings or Bible study groups that the white villagers have held for themselves. (Several men, among them Piet van Rooyen, were very angry with their wives for visiting Coloured households, and Piet, for one, forbade his wife, Annemarie, from continuing her missionizing.)

Several younger members of the Renewal, including Barbara Endicott, a young woman who had studied psychology at the University of Cape Town and who is married to a road engineer temporarily headquartered in Wyndal, are politically more radical. Barbara worked full-time in a multiracial youth ministry run by the Anglican Church before marrying and moving to the valley. She says that she and her husband would like to move to one of the homelands and establish a multiracial Christian community there. She has told no one in the valley about her youth ministry or about her plans for the future. "They would take us for radicals," she says. "They wouldn't understand.

"It is easy to get in tune with the attitudes of the people around here," Barbara explains. "But Cape Town isn't that far, so when we want a more challenging political discussion, we can go there, or invite friends out here for the weekend. It prevents us from settling into complacency. Even with Christ's love, you have to keep challenging one another—in a caring way.

"You see, most of the villagers in the Renewal have never known that things can be different. All they know is what they hear on the radio, see on television, or read in the newspapers: propaganda. They are simple people. They have come to Christ only recently, and they are still being established in their faith. I think now isn't the right time to start talking politics to them. Once they are more mature in their faith, then it will be possible to talk to them. Now it could cause a division, and that is not good.

"Many of them would probably regard Black Christians as wonderful people, but they are not yet able to share power with Blacks.

Their image of people has been modified but within a certain frame —not as strongly as we would want it. They must become stronger in their faith."

The gas lamps hanging from the beams in the Roussouws' packing shed cast an incandescent light on about forty men and women who were seated expectantly in a semicircle around a large black projector that Andre had found in a secondhand shop in Cape Town and had managed to wire to his tractor's battery. It stood there in their midst like some inadvertent fetish. The light, and the shadows it threw, exaggerated the guests' expectations. They had come to hear Dominee Malherbe from Cape Town speak about the Illuminati and other worshipers of Satan.

Andre and Tamara had decided to clear out the packing shed after the last Friday study group. Dominee Naude, always a favorite, had come to heal the faithful. There had been so many villagers that the Roussouws' lounge had not been able to accommodate them all. Andre was pleased. The Renewal was spreading far more rapidly than he had thought possible. There were at least six villagers, including the chief of police and the head of the wine cooperative, who had come for the first time. There were also several strangers, and Caroline du Plessis was there. Everyone knew that all the women in her family died of cancer.

Andre had spent the morning stashing away boxes, bins, scales, measuring gauges, the long table with rollers, and the even longer one without rollers that Om Max had made when he took over the farm from his father almost fifty years before. They were pushed into the room in which Andre stored his packed fruit before carrying it down in his *bakkie* to the depot for inspection and shipment to Cape Town and on to England, Germany, and France. Andre had always wanted to convert the shed into a meeting place for the faithful. (He dreamed sometimes of turning the farm into a retreat for those Christians who wanted to lead a simple life of virtue.) The shed was in use for only a few months each year, and now that he had joined the new packing cooperative, it wouldn't be used at all, that is, if the cooperative actually worked.

Tamara had made sure that the shed was carefully scrubbed down. She had wanted to wax the floors, but Andre had said that they were rough and would eat up liters of wax. Wax was expensive, and they had more important expenses. They would have to run an electric line into the shed—the tractor battery was barely strong enough to run the projector, and Andre had his heart set on a video recorder to show the miracles that fellow Christians in America were working. (Piet van Rooyen had seen a tape of a woman who had been raised from the dead. She had died twenty minutes before her resurrection.) So Tamara had to be content with having one of her boys polish the third packing table. It was pushed against the wall, covered with two white lace tablecloths, and spread with paper cups and plates, trays of biscuits and buttered bread, and several gigantic white plastic thermoses of coffee and tea that the faithful had brought to share with their neighbors. Tamara was nowhere to be seen. She was in fact putting her children to bed, and little Maxie was insisting that she tell him a second bedtime story. He always did on Fridays when they had a meeting. Andre was waiting in front of the farmhouse for the *dominee.* He was at least fifteen minutes late. Andre was shocked when he drove up in a BMW. It was unbecoming for a minister of Christ to squander his money on such a luxury when there were so many needy. "I was glad it was dark," he told me the next afternoon. "Most of the Christians didn't see his BMW. He was quite upset when he left because one of my dogs scratched it."

Dominee Malherbe had made a study of the Illuminati and other Satanic churches and organizations. He was a short, yellowish man, with thin black hair, a lock of which fell across his brow as he spoke. He had dark-brown eyes and wore thick glasses. Usually he spoke in a slow monotone, rolling his *r*'s excessively, and pausing over-dramatically. When he wished to make a point, he would remove his glasses, peer around for an inordinately long time, and then burst out with it, so startling his audience that they could barely take in whatever it was he was trying to say. He spoke mostly in Afrikaans, punctuating his discourse with biblical quotations, but for the benefit of the few English speakers in the group, he would translate a phrase here and there into English. He seemed particularly suspicious of me. He was a mean sort of man who was not much liked by his audience.

Piet van Rooyen, the unofficial leader of the Renewal in Wyndal, and Andre had decided to invite him to speak to the group after another guest speaker had mentioned him three months earlier. This speaker, who had described in intimate detail his initiation into the church of Satan—it sounded like a shamanistic voyage to the nether world—and his, and Christ's, struggle to free him from the Devil's clutches, had deeply moved the villagers, who had gathered to hear him. They talked about his initiation and the spreading of evil throughout the world in their prayer groups and after committee meetings. They vowed to learn more about Satanic worship. As good Christians they had to know their enemy. Dominee Malherbe was so booked up that he could not make it to Wyndal for three months. In the meantime, Piet van Rooyen led an occasional study group on the Antichrist.

Piet and Annemarie van Rooyen had moved to Wyndal about three years before from the Free State, where Piet had had a hardware store. He bought old Hugo du Plessis's shop on Kerkstraat, and as soon as he and Annemarie got the feel of the village, they began to sell religious books and tapes—Dale Rogers and Shirley Boone were favorites—on the side as they had done in the Free State. Piet and Annemarie are Baptists not from birth but by dramatic conversion from the Dutch Reformed Church, and they are committed evangelists. "We had a successful business and a nice home, and the money was enough," Annemarie said with a tinge of regret. "We were nicely settled in a warm little nest, and everything was going along smoothly when the Lord just said to us that it was time to climb again—to climb higher and higher and closer and closer to the Lord. That is how we came here. It was a very hard decision. Financially, humanly, speaking, it was absolutely the wrong thing for a man with a big family to move to a small town with a mini hardware store that never really made a profit. We were scared. Were we doing the right thing? We had come down to the Cape to visit one of Piet's cousins, and he brought us to Wyndal to meet some friends. We met a woman with a desperate spiritual need —she had come to her end—and we prayed for her, and the Lord filled her with the Holy Spirit. We flew home, and we thought, 'Well, praise the Lord.' We came down for a holiday, and there in Wyndal, amidst all those beautiful mountains, we were able to save a poor soul. We felt there was a deep spiritual need here. The Lord began to nudge us. When He speaks to you, He speaks in a soft voice, and He spoke to Piet. And Piet asked me if I thought we should move here. We prayed together and we fasted and we waited upon the Lord, seeking His face, and He spoke to us in many ways. He gave us a wonderful Scripture. He said to us in Deuteronomy: God said to Moses, but we took it as the Lord speaking to us,

'You've tarried long enough on this mountain. Now you must move away on a journey that will take three days [sic].' And you know, it is exactly a three-day journey from our home in the Free State to Wyndal! And the very next day we got a letter from Piet's cousin's friends here saying that Hugo du Plessis wanted to sell his shop. We could no longer doubt the Lord."

Piet van Rooyen is a thin, angular man, fanatic, always at the edge of self-control, envious and suspicious of those who have more than he has and seem to lock him out of their lives if not their thoughts. He was very shy, Annemarie says, until he came to know Christ. "When we would walk into a room full of people, he would always push me in front of him and go all red in the face." He is now friendly, but his friendliness is forced and seems, in a way, premeditated. He is a penny pincher and worries about his financial future but not his spiritual one. Although he would probably deny it, were he asked directly, he believes himself to be one of the chosen: an emissary of the Lord come to liven those who have not known Him or forgotten Him to His presence. Piet has made a study, as Annemarie likes to say, of the Book of Revelation and looks about with an expectant satisfaction for signs of the Second Coming. He has made a study also of the Antichrist, Satanic worship, and the spread of evil throughout the world. "It's hard to accept the fact of the birth of the Antichrist, but you can't dismiss it offhand. It may well be true. We are fighting SWAPO in the South West. We capture their weapons and analyze them, but we don't demand the same considerations when we talk about the possibility of the Devil." Piet refers to members of any religious group—"sects" he calls them—of which he knows little, such as the Quakers or the Seventh Day Adventists, as Satan worshipers. He has close connections with several extremist Baptist groups in the United States and distributes to the villagers cassettes of Americans confessing membership in one Satanic organization or another. The speaker on one of these tapes, a recording from a Baptist church in southwestern Maryland, confessed to having been the head of 5,000 covens in the American Southwest, with 65,000 priests and priestesses. Unlike Andre and Tamara's commitment and that of most of the other villagers in the Renewal, whose dogged Christianity is essentially innocent, Piet's religious commitment (so, at any rate it appeared to me) is edged with hatred and bigotry.

Piet explained that when he and his family arrived in Wyndal, the village was in deep spiritual need. "The villagers were hungry," he said. "Their appetites had been whetted, and then they had forgotten the object of their hunger." Piet was referring to the wife of the bank manager, a Baptist, who had begun to proselytize in the village about two years before Piet and Annemarie arrived there. She was apparently quite successful, and several villagers, including Tamara Roussouw, were filled with the Holy Spirit. And then suddenly, quite unexpectedly, her husband was given a position in a bank in the eastern Cape. The villagers give many explanations for the bank manager's new position. Piet, who claims to have studied the issue carefully, suggests that the bank manager's wife was such a successful evangelist that Wyndal's *dominee*, a member of the Broederbond, used his influence to bring about the transfer. Others claim that the bank manager was transferred because he had lost the Dutch Reformed Church's account. (Given the small size of the account, this seems unlikely.) The bank manager headed an English bank that was entirely staffed by Afrikaners and had been Wyndal's only bank until the arrival of an Afrikaner bank shortly after the bank manager took office. Pressure was put on the Afrikaners in Wyndal, as elsewhere in South Africa where the bank opened a branch, to join the Afrikaner bank, but most of them refused to do so because they had long-standing credit with the English bank and felt as though they were betraying their friends who worked there. They were also infuriated by the new bank building, which was modern, cheaply constructed of glazed tile and glass, and designed without regard to Wyndal's traditional architecture. The English bankers had been careful to build their bank in the traditional Cape Dutch style and had made use of local builders. According to several villagers, the Broederbond, many of whose members had an interest in the Afrikaner bank, urged the local *dominee* to encourage his parishioners to transfer their accounts to the new bank as a sign of their commitment to the Afrikaner nation. He did, creating a serious rift in the community. Despite objections from several members of his church board, the *dominee* did move the church's account to the new bank at about the time that the English bank manager's wife was having her first successful conversions. Shortly after, much to the *dominee*'s relief, the bank manager was transferred. Still other villagers, including Hugo Malan, say that the bank manager was a very clever chap, far too clever for a small-town bank, and had been given a far more important position in the eastern Cape. Whatever the true story, most participants in the Renewal insist, like Piet van Rooyen, that the bank manager was transferred because of his wife's meddling in the spiritual welfare of members of the Dutch Reformed Church. They agree, too, that after the bank manager's wife left town, they no longer felt the presence of the Lord as intensely as they had, that is, until Piet and Annemarie arrived.

Most of the villagers who were attracted to the Renewal were in the Roussouws' packing shed the night Dominee Malherbe spoke. With the exception of Andre and Tamara, and Om Max and Beatrix, who disapproved of all this religious enthusiasm but attended anyway because the meeting was on their farm, none of the farmers were present. Staunch members of the Dutch Reformed Church or conservative Anglicans, forced by Hennie's presence to attend the Methodists' meetings if they attended any services at all, the farmers would have nothing to do with any group that sacrificed religious propriety for a somewhat dubious sensationalism. Most of the villagers in the Renewal were, like Andre and Tamara, in their thirties and forties, although there were a few elderly who came to be cured of the ills that beset them—backaches, arthritis, and more serious ailments—and to be rid of the boredom and loneliness that was particularly strong in the long rainy winter months, when the excitement of the picking season was over. Younger people, predominantly single women, attended some of the Pentecostal churches in neighboring villages, but in Wyndal, the Renewal people, as they were sometimes called, came to the meetings in the Roussouws' packing shed, and earlier to those in their lounge, as couples. (They went to prayer meetings alone, as these tend to be sexually segregated.) They were members of the middling middle class, people of limited possibility: shopkeepers, artisans, clerks, garage mechanics, employees in the Cooperative, and a farm manager or two. They had neither the financial wherewithal nor the intellectual endowment nor the connections to transcend their rootedness, their *enracinement*, in Wyndal, in South Africa. They could lay no international claim, as many of the English farmers did, nor did they have the privilege to deny such a claim, as many of the Afrikaners did. They were there, at home, worried, threatened, overwhelmed even, when they thought of their own personal future and the future of their children and grandchildren—thoughts that they preferred not to harbor, I believe, and that they deflected, as they could, in transcending dramas of apocalypse and salvation.

It was through these transcending dramas that preachers like Dominee Malherbe made their appeal. They presented a simplified picture of the world, one, however, of cosmic grandeur, in which the forces of good and evil, of Christ and Antichrist, of God and Satan, were in epic contest. Little men, the people of Wyndal, were, like Job, unwitting pawns in this battle. They had to be continuously on their guard against the seductions of the Devil. Temptation was everywhere. Only through Christ would they be able to resist these seductions and temptations and achieve salvation. Other preachers, like Dominee Naude, a gentler, more considerate man, appealed less to the villagers' fear of Satanic influence than to their frailty. He came often, got to know them and their problems, and spoke to them about Christ's great healing powers. He would take those who were in need of cure aside (backaches were his specialty) and pray over them. There was nothing spectacular about his cures. He performed no public miracles. He criticized revivalists like Oral Roberts for their arrogant show. He would explain to the ailing that cure rested on their faith in Christ. He remained always humble, despite his successes, and this humbleness appealed to the villagers, who saw it as a sign of a man of both great faith and wisdom.

The villagers in the Renewal were themselves less concerned with matters of faith—*that* they had—than with the development of a *wholly* new relationship with Christ. Several of them had had intensely personal encounters with Christ. They had spoken in tongues and had almost daily conversations (in prayer) with Him. They deferred every important decision to Him. Most of those who attended the Roussouw's meetings, however, had had no such personal experiences. Some had actively sought them, others were simply waiting, and still others, the majority, were curious but noncommittal. Afrikaners, they were still active members of the Dutch Reformed Church. They came to the Renewal meetings like truant schoolboys, for they knew that their *dominee* did not approve of the meetings and looked askance at any Christianity that sacrificed the intellect to emotion, reason to experience, and an institutional and ritual order to an anti-institutional personalism always at the edge of chaos. "There must be order in the church," the Reformed *dominee* said. "I would not enter another man's house without first asking his leave to do so. I would not take it upon myself to undermine the institutional and ritual supports of a man's faith." They knew, of course, that were they to undergo a second baptism, they would have to leave the Dutch Reformed Church and suffer the ostracism that comes with that. (Tamara, Piet, Annemarie, and several other Baptists converts put considerable pressure on those who had been filled with the Holy Spirit to be baptized anew.) The few English who went to the meetings were less threatened. Hennie encouraged his parisioners to attend, and those who were not Anglican had no local church affiliation. (They were not Methodists.) Most of them were married to Afrikaners. That their number was so small (about ten percent of the villagers in the Renewal) resulted less from indifference than from circumstance. There were very few English of the middling middle class in Wyndal, and most of those who were of this class attended the Roussouws' meetings. The charismatic movement is, as I have noted, very strong in the Anglican Church and in other churches in South Africa whose members are largely English.

The Renewal provided one of the few avenues for the English and Afrikaners to meet each other in any but the most perfunctory way. Not only did they come together at the Roussouws' meetings, but they met rather more informally at prayer meetings. During my first winter in Wyndal, when Dominee Malherbe spoke and when enthusiasm was at its height, there were prayer meetings—"spiritual banquets," as Andre likes to call them—nearly every day. Some of these were organized by the Dutch Reformed Church or by the Methodists but most of them were called by people in the Renewal. Women met rather more often than men. Not only did the participants pray together, but they discussed puzzling passages in the Bible and tried to relate them to their own personal experiences. There was among the women a willingness to talk about family and marital problems that was altogether absent from the men's prayer groups. The women seemed to enjoy an almost naughty clandestinity. They joked about their secrets and speculated playfully about what men said at their meetings. My wife was reminded of women talking about the goings-on at stag parties. Men never talked about the women's groups. Women would pray for one another, and it became clear that these group prayers and the resultant "mediation" of Christ played an important role in both the articulation of family and marital problems and in their resolution. By sharing their problems, the participants got to know one another intimately, but by understanding them in loosely theological terms, they avoided the embarrassment that would have come from a purely personal confession. There was, as one woman put it, a joy in sharing the pain you had experienced and were sure you would never be able to reveal. There was also, she added, pain in the joy of sharing the sufferings of others.

The villagers waiting for Dominee Malherbe's arrival seemed unusually stiff. They greeted one another formally and then sat quietly. There was none of the bustle and talk that preceded other meetings at the Roussouws'. The villagers were usually quite friendly and talkative. It was not that they were lost in themselves. They were not. They were self-conscious, but no more embarrassed by their presence in this "truant" gathering than usual. Still, they seemed to be asking themselves why they were there. They seemed impersonal, isolated even from their spouses. I wondered whether each, in his way, was worried about what Dominee Malherbe was going to reveal. They knew he would be talking about the Illuminati, the band of leaders, including Carter, Mao, Brezhnev, Rockefeller, Oppenheimer (South Africa's largest industrialist, who controls, among others, the Anglo-American Corporation), the Rothschilds, Waldheim, and Margaret Thatcher, who were plotting to take over the world. They knew he would be talking about the future—their future. Was the subject matter of Dominee Malherbe's as yet unspoken discourse too close to home?

I always had the impression that the villagers in the Renewal, and others too, preferred to keep their talk about the Antichrist, apocalypse, and salvation separate from their talk about everyday reality and their prospects for the future. They could not, would not, relate in Durkheimian fashion the religious picture they drew of the world to their social and political understanding of their situation. The two orders of reality were, so to speak, barred from each other. They would argue, if I pressed them (and I pressed a few), that what occurred in the everyday world was only a symptom of a far greater drama, in which the forces of good battled those of evil. To see the Antichrist as symbolic of Blacks or communists, the apocalypse of a Black takeover or a revolution, and salvation of an escape or an overcoming was to render a vital causal relationship into one of anemic allegory. ("Allegories are in the realm of thoughts, what ruins are in the realm of things," Walter Benjamin writes.[1]) It was to get one's priorities all wrong. It was the cosmic, the religious, drama that determined the worldly. There were times, frequent times in Dominee Malherbe's preaching, when people in the Renewal (and other white South Africans as well) referred to the communists, though never the Blacks, as incarnations of the Antichrist. But these references were taken, I believe, rhetorically. "Communists" in any case were treated abstractly—elements in another, an international, political idiom that was in its way as removed from the immediacy of everyday reality as the religious.

It is the reluctance if not the downright inability to cross the bar between the religious order of reality and that of everyday life that gives the religious idiom its power. The discourse of preachers like Dominee Malherbe is resonant because it can evoke the relationship, usually atomistically, without overwhelming the audience with a down-to-earth—an intimate—picture of the end of their everyday life. It can play on the most prosaic fears without actually evoking them. It offers audiences a scenario ("more real than reality itself") that must at times touch base with everyday reality to be truly efficacious. Such are the references to Satanic churches, communists, and personages out of a contemporary folklore like Rockefeller, Brezhnev, and Mao. Preachers like Dominee Malherbe are all in their own way distant and abstract—removed from the immediate world in which the villagers find themselves. In waiting, with an inkling of what Dominee Malherbe would speak about—the future, as yet unarticulated and, so, devoid of content—the villagers gathered in Andre and Tamara's packing shed were, perhaps, caught in an empty moment, at the *point mort*, as the French call the neutral position of an automobile transmission, in which they could shift, to strain the metaphor, into harrowing contemplation of their *real* destiny or into a verbally more harrowing but perhaps less real, certainly more remote, contemplation of cosmic destiny.

Andre rushed Dominee Malherbe into the packing shed, explaining that he hoped to make the shed into a meeting place for Christians in Wyndal. Dominee Malherbe nodded disinterestedly. He looked around, gauging his audience professionally, and walked to the makeshift lectern that Andre had constructed out of an old table and a few boxes. Andre introduced him to Piet, who presented him to the group. Piet explained that it was their custom to sing and pray before a speaker spoke. "The Spirit warms us," Piet said, giving the *dominee* a knowing glance, but the *dominee* ignored it. Piet looked slighted. It was clear that Andre had already taken a dislike to the preacher. He looked around for Tamara, who had not yet appeared.

She was still in the house with the children. They could wait no longer.

The lights were dimmed. Andre turned on the opaque projector. It flickered for a minute and then there appeared on the wall that served as a screen the words of the hymn that begins, "His name is higher than any other." Hymn followed hymn, some in English, some in Afrikaans, mostly American imports. Piet led the singing. Annemarie played the guitar. Andre worked the projector. Those in the group who had once been moved by the Spirit or desired to be so moved swayed back and forth as they sang, boldly raising their hands in praise. Others raised their hands with diffidence, and still others, including Dominee Malherbe, stood stiffly, mouthing the words of the projected hymns. Despite Piet and Annemarie's effort, the group's enthusiasm was not as high as it had been at some of the other meetings I attended. No one prayed in tongues. Tamara came in just as Piet began the second to last hymn, "Father, we love You, we praise You, we adore You," and began sobbing uncontrollably as the group repeated the chorus over and over again, "Jesus, we love You, Spirit, we love You." A woman sitting on Tamara's right hugged and caressed her and finally managed to calm her down. Andre pretended not to notice. Tamara then sang the last hymn with such fervor that several other singers stopped to listen to her. The hymn was from Isaiah.

> How lovely on the mountains are the feet of Him,
> Who brings good news, good news;
> Proclaiming peace, announcing news of happiness
> Our God reigns, Our God reigns.[2]

Piet asked Dominee Malherbe to lead them in prayer, but the *dominee* motioned back to Piet to lead the prayer himself. It was a long, wordy, improvised prayer, mostly in Afrikaans but with an occasional English word or phrase thrown in, in which Piet asked the Lord for forgiveness and for the strength to overcome the enemies who surround us, tempt us, and lead us astray. Dominee Malherbe stood up, peered at his audience for a long time, and then began to speak slowly, ever so slowly, about the enemies of Christ, the birth of the Antichrist, and the imminence of the Second Coming. His favored text was the Book of Revelation. ("I know where you live; it is the place where Satan has his throne. And yet you are holding fast to my cause."³) His theology rested less on the Gospels than on Paul's letters, but unlike other preachers in the Renewal, he paid less attention to Paul's dramatic conversion than to his insistence on faith.

Dominee Malherbe's understanding of the Bible was, like the understanding of most members of the Renewal, literal. He abominated all allegorical and symbolic readings of Scripture, corruptions they were, products of Satanic influence, designed to lead the innocent astray. "For my part, I give this warning to everyone who is listening to the words of prophecy of this book: Should anyone add to them, God will add to him the plagues described in this book; should anyone take away from the words of this book of prophecy, God will take away from him his share in the tree of life and the Holy City described in this book." In fact, Dominee Malherbe's readings were filled with innuendos, hidden agendas, and intimations of relevance. He insisted, much to the disappointment of his audience, on the abstract, the impersonal nature of the Antichrist— he named no names—and thereby suggested a host of unnamed possibilities. He played with the villagers' desire for names, the way the seducer plays with the desire of the innocent, and enthralled them, albeit momentarily, with an extraordinary paranoid vision of the world—a world beset with fornicators, with Jezebel and Abaddon, with the great dragon with seven heads and ten horns ready to devour the innocent child destined to rule all nations who was miraculously snatched up to God and His throne. But Dominee Malherbe knew better, so it seemed to me, than to hold too long to this vision of concrete incarnations of the Devil lest he lose his audience. He went on to speak about the impersonality of Satan and the terror of his abstract power—and then he returned to the ordinary world of humans and spoke about the Illuminati. Again, he mentioned no names but implied that he knew names. He talked about certain people who had in one way or another been involved with the Illuminati and had then seen them, praise the Lord, for what they were: power-hungry men who had sold themselves to the Devil.

Inadvertently, at least I believe it was inadvertently, Dominee Malherbe set his audience up for Piet van Rooyen's cassette of a man who claimed to have been one of the Illuminati. (It was he who claimed also to have headed 5,000 covens in the American Southwest.) The man said that he was descended from the witches of

Salem, that with the exception of one woman, a prostitute, all of the so-called witches were in fact Christians, and that the real witches were those who had condemned the so-called witches. He had been a Green Beret in Vietnam, had killed his lieutenant in Germany, was thrown in the brig, and then, suddenly, was honorably discharged in the presence of United States congressmen and a senator. When he went home to Ohio, he received a mysterious envelope containing 2,000 dollars in cash, a first-class plane ticket to New York, and a letter ordering him to meet the chairman of the department of anthropology at Columbia, who gave him instruction in witchcraft and Satanic conspiracy. (There was never, I should point out, anyone of the name he gave in Columbia's anthropology department.)

The speaker on Piet's cassette grew wilder, more confused, megalomaniacal, as he went on haranguing his Maryland audience. He named names. The Church of All Worlds, the National Council of Churches, Scientology, Charles Manson's Process Church, the Rastafarians, the Order of the Garter, B'nai Brith, the Odd Fellows, the Civil Liberties Union, and the Knights of Columbus were all Satanic. The Rothschilds, the Du Ponts, the Kennedys, Onassis, Queen Juliana, were all prominent Illuminati. Elton John and the Beatles actually sang in the secret language of witches. The banks of England and France, the Federal Reserve ("really a private corporation"), the Chase Manhattan Bank, the Bank of America, the Common Market, Montgomery Ward, Standard Oil, Shell Oil, Sears, Safeway, Federal Department Stores, were all controlled by the Illuminati. The Trilateral Commission was the American name of the Illuminati. It was aided by the Council on Foreign Relations. The pyramid on the dollar bill was the Illuminati's seal: The blocks of stone symbolized its organization. (Piet had enclosed a dollar bill with the cassette.) World takeover was imminent. December 1980 was a possible date. (The tape was not dated.) There would be no food, no electricity, no fuel. There would be strikes, riots, and genocide. Jews and Catholics would be rounded up and killed. Over a million people would die the first year. Charles Manson would be released from prison. He was put there to establish an armed prison army.

The speaker offered no resolution. His audience did not seem to expect one. He explained only how he had been saved. He had become a drug addict. He was at his end in San Antonio. "I was in a paranoid mess," he said! He went to the movies and saw *The Cross and the Switch Blade* and then went to a Baptist church, where 500 people prayed and fasted for him.

The villagers were fascinated by the tape. Many of those in the Renewal accepted it as truth. It turned out to be a principal source of Piet's study of the spread of evil. He had obtained it from an American engineer who was working in South Africa. Piet said that Dominee Malherbe had also studied it. (The two men had a long talk after the meeting.) Dr. Steyn heard about it. He often read grand conspiracy literature. Several English and Afrikaner farmers, even with university degrees, began to talk seriously about the Illuminati and their imminent takeover. They justified their position by referring to a Stellenbosch professor who often lectured on the subject. His lectures had become so "paranoid," one of his colleagues told me, that even the most conservative students in his class began to object. As a graduate of Columbia's anthropology department married to a member of the Council on Foreign Relations, I began to fear that my wife and I would be declared emissaries of the Devil if word of our affiliations got around. What frightened me was the ease with which the villagers in the Renewal accepted the ravings of the speaker. Their orientation was manifestly fundamentalist, and they carried their fundamentalism to whatever anyone said who deferred to Scripture or claimed to have been saved.

Despite Dominee Malherbe's refusal to name names, his preaching did have an extraordinary, historically specific, denouement. It was one of those moments that no one, including, I believe, the *dominee* himself, was prepared for that night. No one to whom I spoke afterward could adequately reconstruct it, nor did they care to remember it. As I recall, Dominee Malherbe was explaining the way in which the impersonal forces of the Antichrist become lodged in institutions and persons. He had been speaking for almost an hour and was tiring his audience. Suddenly, in total contradiction to what he had been saying all along about the impersonality of the Antichrist, he announced that according to certain reliable sources— sources whose information had been confirmed by the *dominee* himself through a careful reading of the Book of Revelations and the prophecies of Isaiah—the Antichrist was already born into the world. "Did anyone know when this birth had taken place?" he asked rhetorically. Much to everybody's surprise a young English woman named Celia, who was married to an Afrikaner shopkeeper, said as if to herself but loudly enough for everyone to hear, "February 6, 1962." The *dominee* stopped short, looked at Celia for a very long time, and finally said, "Yes, that is true. It is either February 6, 1962, or February 5, 1962." All eyes were on him. No one but the *dominee* dared look at Celia. He continued to peer at her, almost *hypnotically*. The silence seemed unbearable. "You must have had dealings with him or those under his power," he said at last, "for otherwise you would not have known." (The *dominee* and his audience were oblivious to his inadvertent self-confession!) Celia nodded embarrassedly and mumbled something that I could not make out. Dominee Malherbe said he would like to talk to her afterward and went on to discuss the youth of the Antichrist. As yet, he was too young to make his influence deeply felt, but, the *dominee* said, it was clearly only a matter of years. Unlike the speaker on Piet's Illuminati tape, Dominee Malherbe was not content to end his talk with a grim picture of the future and an attestation of his having been saved. He explained, quoting Paul's first epistle of the Thessalonians, that Christians, children of the light, were not destined "to the terrors of judgment but to the full attainment of salvation through our Lord Jesus Christ." What could not be determined, however, was when the children of light would be saved, whether before, during, or after the time of tribulation described in the Book of Revelations.

The question period was short. One man asked Dominee Malherbe if he could reveal the names of the Illuminati. "Should we not know our enemies?" He himself had heard that Harry Oppenheimer was a prominent member. Dominee Malherbe refused, insisting once again on the impersonality of the Antichrist. "We must not be blinded to his terrible power by one of his human incarnations," he said impatiently, and the audience echoed his impatience. No one looked at Celia, and Celia and her husband looked at no one. Andre gave the concluding prayer.

There was a good deal of unusually superficial chatter as the villagers drank coffee and tea and ate the biscuits and buttered bread that Tamara had laid out on her carefully polished table. It seemed to me that the villagers wanted to escape from what they had just heard into the ordinariness of daily life. Even someone as disapproving of the Renewal as Beatrix Roussouw admitted several days later that she found what Dominee Malherbe had said scary. "I'm afraid to say I didn't believe the *dominee*. Young people go into these

Satanic things more than people of my generation did. At least that's what Piet van Rooyen says. I don't dismiss it, but I'm skeptical. After all, the *dominee* had made a study of it, and he knows what he is talking about." Dominee Malherbe avoided Celia and disappeared as soon as possible into a side room with Piet. Celia seemed relieved. She had been watching him carefully. She and her husband, after dutifully drinking coffee to save face, slipped out of the shed without having said a word to anyone.

I was left talking to a young English woman, a friend of Celia's, who often prayed in tongues and took her prayers, and the prayers of others, as signs of divine election. She said that she was certain that Christ would save the true Christians during the time of tribulation. "None of us are so good as to be spared all suffering, but surely Christ will spare us—those who have met Him and have learned through Him to love even our enemies—the full suffering of the time of troubles." When I asked her what Celia had said to the *dominee*, she claimed not to have heard.

I tried on several occasions to visit Celia, but somehow she never seemed free to see me. When I asked Andre about her the next day, he said evasively that all he knew was what the *dominee* had said. She must have been involved in one of Satan's churches. Om Max, who was there, said that he had heard that she had once been associated with the Scientologists. Piet inferred, when I asked him about Celia, that she had been involved in a coven and with a spirit medium. I do not know whether or not the villagers treated Celia differently after the meeting. She received a second baptism, as did her husband, a few months later, in the spring, when the mountain waters, where the baptisms were performed, were warmer.

Margot and Tommy Prinsloo

Tommy Prinsloo, Irene's son, called Margot in when, at the end of my first winter in Wyndal, I asked him what he knew about the religious turmoil in the valley. After tea Margot had left us to tend to her daughter, who had just awakened from her afternoon nap. It was a cold, rainy afternoon, and we all sat close to the fire in the lounge of the old *junkerhuis*, which Tommy and Margot had restored. Tommy was interested in the Renewal, as were all the farmers (from a distance, to be sure). He saw it as primarily a women's phenomenon. Like Margot, he was deeply committed to the Dutch Reformed Church and hoped to become an elder in the near future. He encouraged his workers to attend church, sent those who had drinking problems to church-run clinics, and was friendly with Pieter Kotze. Tommy shared Pieter Kotze's liberal theology. They had been students together at Stellenbosch, where Tommy had studied agricultural engineering, and Pieter was, as Tommy once put it humorously, "the devil in the Angel Factory." Neither Tommy nor Margot, whose father was a well-known professor of philosophy in Pretoria, could accept a literal reading of the Bible, and they were troubled by the softmindedness of so much Renewal thinking. They represented, for me at least, the new Afrikaner, young (relatively), liberal (relatively), worldly, opposed to the conservative government, worried about the future and yet confident in their ability to remain in the country and share power with the Blacks.

After joking about Barbara Endicott's attempt to convert me (she had "worked on" me for over three hours the week before), Margot began to talk about a friend of hers who had joined the Renewal. "She's an extremely intelligent person and, well, she's had five kids in six years' time. She's a bit overwhelmed."

"I think that's an understatement," Tommy interrupted.

"One morning she phoned me. It was about two months ago. She said she couldn't make her class (she was a part-time teacher) and asked if I couldn't fill in for her. I'd done it in the past. She said something terrible had happened to her. I thought she had been raped or something. It sounded so horrible. But, no, she had received the Holy Ghost. I thought, Good gracious, is that so terrible!" Margot laughed. "But, this person, you know, you cannot talk to her anymore. It is impossible. This morning I saw her in a shop. I said, 'Louisa, why don't you come to tea. We're having a library meeting.' (She used to be active on the library committee.) 'Oh, no,' she said. 'Now that I'm a new person, I don't have time for that kind of thing.' She's always like that now. She doesn't teach anymore."

"All they have time to do now is talk religion," Tommy said.

"*Dominee* was away these last few weeks on holiday, and they were busy converting everybody . . ."

"Like a bunch of naughty school kids when the teacher leaves the room," Tommy added.

"Poor old *dominee*. When he returned, he saw that his flock had dispersed. He didn't know what had happened. Luckily it was Ascension Week, and there were prayer meetings and church services. He was able to bring a lot of people back to their senses. They have prayer meetings every day, and they preach about the Holy Ghost until it comes out of their ears. I think they're off their rockers. They leave the church or pull away from it. For what? I don't want to get too involved because I just get so cross about it."

"To a certain extent it's fashion," Tommy said. "And it comes from boredom. These women have nothing to do with their lives."

"But they could read. Louisa used to read. I read an article in the newspaper this morning about one of her ancestors. I asked her about it, and she answered that she didn't have time to read the papers anymore. Oh, you just can't communicate with these people!"

"It seems to be spreading throughout the country," I said.

"My dad told me a very interesting thing," Margot continued. "At the turn of the century in Paarl, at the time of Arnoldus Pannevis and the language movement, there was a lot of religious enthusiasm, people praying in tongues, falling to the ground and foaming at the mouth. Pannevis was disgusted by it and wrote a very strong letter to the local newspaper about it. It seems to me it's been going on for centuries."

"Do you think it is a reaction to the Dutch Reformed Church?" I asked.

"Yes," Margot answered, and Tommy echoed her.

"We were talking about it with Pieter Kotze the other day," Tommy continued. "He thinks that it is because people don't get the opportunity to take an active part in the services."

"Could it be a reaction to apartheid?" I asked.

"I don't think it has anything to do with apartheid," Margot answered. "Some of the most intolerant people in the valley are serious about the Renewal. Last week I had to leave the shop for a few hours to take one of our workers to the hospital, and I left a Coloured girl in charge. She's very reliable. When I got back, I discovered that one of these women in the Renewal, who's also part of our cooperative, was so upset that she had called a special meeting to discuss my absence—really, my leaving a Coloured girl in charge. She was raging."

"How do you feel about apartheid in the church?"

"I think it is terrible. Its opposite shouldn't be forced down people's throats either. We shouldn't say, 'Now you must come to our church.' If they want to have their own church, fine, but there must be no bars. I mean, if they want to come, why not?"

"I'm sure," Tommy added, "that if you say to the Coloureds here, Would you like to become part of the white church, they'd say, No, we've our own church."

"And the Blacks?" I asked.

"Well, I don't know the Blacks very well," Tommy answered. "Not too many of them are in the Dutch Reformed Church. They have their own Bantu churches. But I wouldn't refuse them entrance. The Christian church must be open to all."

"The problem in this country," Margot said, "is that the government is dominated by the Transvaalers. They're fanatical. Katrina, the woman who was so upset about the Coloured girl, is from the Transvaal. There is no talking to them. My dad says the same thing, and he knows them."

"Why do you think so many people in the valley are joining in the Renewal?" I asked.

"It's not politics. I'd say they have a lot of stress in their marriages. I can tell you that all the people I know who are in it are a bit unbalanced. They all have different reasons for being unbalanced. Louisa, for instance, has had too many kids in too short a time. She's gone from one extreme to another. She's a bit off her rocker. And then there's Celia. She too has gone from one extreme to another. Apparently, before she moved out here, she was already involved in some sect or other."

"They're not constructively busy," Tommy said. "They're bored, and that's the story. It's not as simple as that, but basically that's the cause."

"But what worries me," Margot continued, a bit impatient with Tommy, "is that they don't have time for their children or their husbands. Louisa said she has no time for her children anymore, and she is wrong. Of course, her husband is very strict with her. She must do everything herself. She must make the children's clothes. She must do all the cooking and mending and washing and what have you. For a while, until she began to teach, she wasn't even allowed to have a maid. She had to do everything, absolutely everything, herself. Of course, South African men are different from European ones. They're stricter. Tommy helps more than most, but he'll never wash a dish."

Tommy blushed, and Margot smiled flirtatiously at him.

"Vincent," Tommy said, changing the subject, "do you have the impression that the average sort of person you've been talking to is uncertain about the future of this country?"

14

THE
FUTURE

Hennie

"Now, I've told you about my dad and his attitude. He took up arms in defense of what he loved and believed in. At the same time he took a chance. He could have got himself shot. That was the chance he had to take. If you believe in something, you have to do whatever you can to defend it.

"I found that the Rhodesians who stood up most fully for the African were the first ones to leave. They left the African to stew in his juices. They didn't stay to help. The people who shouted most were the ones who cared least for their country."

Hennie and I were talking about South African liberals. He treated them with considerable scorn. They held "the right ideas." They opposed the government. They condemned apartheid. But they did little to change things. They were content to complain, to criticize, and to oppose. "Words, words, words," Hennie said at one point in disgust. They would be the first to leave the country in a crisis. (Like many other Afrikaners and English-speaking whites, Hennie was especially critical of liberal Jews, who "as they criticized the government, are taking full advantage of the situation the government has created. Their sons and daughters are already leaving the country.")

"The liberals talk themselves into a kind of panic," Hennie said.

"They paralyze themselves. They talk themselves out of doing anything.

"I find that when you keep looking at a problem, the problem eventually overwhelms you. When you're looking at a solution, you've got a completely different attitude. It's easy enough to run the government down. It's completely different to try to find a solution. That's the Progs' problem. They're an opposition party. They criticize the government, but they don't have any real solutions to our problems. They're caught up in their own opposition.

"And then, of course, people don't like to rock the boat. I found that in Rhodesia as well. I say that if the boat can't stand a bit of rocking, it isn't safe on the open sea. I firmly believe that you have to know how much the boat can be rocked before you can come up with a solution to its problems. You can always add a couple of stabilizers, but they offer no real solution.

"The government doesn't much like publicity either. See, criticizing the government gives the outside world a bad impression. And we must not let the world think we're not right. But this is false, and it's the easiest way of getting away with murder. Take the so-called Information Scandal. We never did find out what happened. I can't believe that the present prime minister knew nothing about it. Most of the money was directed through *his* defense department. But he says he knew nothing about it, and people just accept it. It's tragic. I'll take my hat off to the American system—to your Watergate investigations. People here call the Information Scandal South Africa's Watergate, but there is no comparison. Everything's left in secrecy here."

"Is there much corruption in the government?" I asked.

"I don't know. What worries me is that public funds are being used for party purposes . . . "

Hennie went on to discuss in greater detail the Information Scandal—"Muldergate," as the scandal came to be called after Cornelius P. Mulder, the minister of information. While individual corruption in government circles is apparently relatively infrequent, group patronage is not. As Heribert Adam notes: "Policy is made for the consolidation of the group as the highest priority to which other considerations must be bent and accommodated. The law itself represents a mere means to the end of enhancing ethnic patronage."[1]

"In the fight for survival," Adam quotes Mulder, "no rules apply."

I asked Hennie if he saw any possibility of a split in the National Party. During my stay in South Africa, particularly during the winter of 1981, there was a lot of talk about a split between the most conservative members of the National Party under the leadership of the Transvaaler Andries Treurnicht and the more liberal supporters of P. W. Botha. Most of the people I talked to in Wyndal, including Hennie, ruled out the possibility of a split. Some supporters of the Progressives, thought, magically, I believe, that a split could lead to a solution of many of South Africa's gravest problems by bringing about a realignment of party loyalties. The more liberal Nationalists and the Progressives would join forces, in the most millennial view, to defeat the conservatives from the Transvaal, who were leading the country to disaster. Together, they would be able to do away with apartheid and somehow (it was never specified how) solve the problem of the vote. South Africa would at last be free to develop into a great nation. Hennie's view was more cynical. He saw little chance of a split and in the event of a split—one did in fact take place in 1982—little real change.

"The Afrikaner is a traditionalist," Hennie explained on this occasion. "He'll sacrifice a lot to keep things the way they were. P. W. Botha doesn't have the courage to split the party. He's too weak. He'd be considered a traitor. And then again, it's to his advantage to keep Treurnicht in the government. That way, Treurnicht has to accept some of the responsibility for what the government does. It's a way of silencing him. If a change is made, he can't go and squeal and say he was never part of it . . .

"Now that the government has started the homeland policy, it can't get out of it. I must go back a bit into history. When the Africans were defeated, when Dingaan was defeated in 1838, they had only known how to live by might. When might was taken away from them, they became a lot of rabble. It was only when the government created apartheid and the homeland policy that the Africans became aware of their identity. It is only when someone tries to club you over the head that you realize that both you and your enemy are human, that you both have separate identities. Suddenly the Coloured man became aware that he was Coloured, when previously he was nothing. Suddenly the Zulu became aware of the fact that he was a Zulu and had a homeland and needed leaders. And he found leaders, and the government has had to accept these leaders. They had not foreseen this. Now the Venda have got their little country, and so have the Zulus and the Xhosa and every little tribe. Whether we like it or not, they're not going to give up their countries for the sake of a bigger South Africa. Certainly their leaders will not. They're not really interested in the welfare of their people but in achieving their own ends. It was the same in Rhodesia. I'm afraid we shall never be a Union again. The homelands policy had effectively done away with that. We will become something like the United States: some sort of federation. The problem is that the Coloureds do not have a homeland. Nor do the Indians. Somewhere along the line they will have to be accommodated with in the European setup."

"And what about the urban Blacks, in Soweto, for example?" I asked. Hennie seemed to have forgotten about them. There are in fact millions of Blacks, living in urban and rural slums, who have lost all but nominal ties with their "homelands." The government classifies them, nevertheless, according to their tribe of origin and would ideally make them into citizens of their "tribal homeland." As such, they would have no right to participate in the white South African political process and could be sent back to their homelands in accordance with immigration policy.

"Well, you see, in many ways they are completely detribalized. They can't really go back to their homelands. They have nothing in common with their people. This is the one thing that really needs urgent attention," Hennie said limply.

Even a man as open-minded as Hennie, I thought to myself, cannot bring himself to say simply that the Blacks should be given the vote and freedom of movement. Was Hennie's commitment to the Coloureds a way of avoiding the Black problem? He often seemed indifferent to the Blacks. Like other whites in the Cape, he claimed not to know them and could, therefore, safely ignore them. Hennie went on to talk about the horrors of apartheid, the breaking up of families through reclassification and immigration, and eventually—he seemed to talk himself into it—the legal status of the Blacks.

"Whether we like it or not, Soweto is a fact, and we need people there. We can't do without their labor. So somewhere along the line they've got to be given a legal existence and recognized. We've got to do something about it so that the people we draw from there are capable of doing what we need, what we want them to do. We have to train these people to be mechanics, electricians, and technicians. Unless we do that, we are going to go under. It's no use sitting with an Afrikaner nationalism, with an Afrikaner identity, and being swamped by the world.

"Our system is unacceptable. We offer no real alternative. If we don't make any significant changes, I'm scared that what is happening in the South West [Namibia] will happen in South Africa. It's a question of time. Once the problem in the South West is resolved, they'll start concentrating on the Republic. The government has to face facts. They must train a responsible leadership. They can't go on arresting, detaining, and banning every African leader who surfaces. Then you will have no one to negotiate with when the time to negotiate comes. And it will come."

A few days before I left Wyndal, I received a note from Jack Freeling with two editorials from the *Cape Times* discussing South Africa's political future. Jack wrote, "I think these two newspaper clippings just about sum up the present sorry situation. All we can do is to wait and see what is going to develop. Not a happy situation." I read the articles, which Jack had carefully pasted on a sheet of blue drawing paper, and found nothing particularly new or insightful in them. Insofar as they discussed the immediate future, both in fact proved to be wrong. Why then had Jack thought to send them to me? He had certainly read many such articles. I do not know, but I think it may have had something to do with preserving an image of the future, which I have tried to characterize as a waiting for something, anything, to happen. It is an often paralyzing image, in which time present is somehow sacrificed to time past in order to avoid the terrifying contingency of time future.

Anxious concern about the future is a dominant leitmotif in South African self-reflection. It is a constant preoccupation in the press, among South Africa's intellectuals, writers, and artists, and in the political discourse of both the Nationalists and the opposition. It dominates religious thought, deflected or not, in fantasies of Apocalypse and Second Comings. It governs the thoughts and reflections of ordinary people, like the whites of Wyndal, who are waiting, like Jack, for something to develop. It is a concern for the future that is centered on a problem or a set of problems that some whites, like Zachary van der Merwe, see as a national cancer. It is an image of some age now. "English statesmen have for more than fifty years been accustomed to say that of the Colonies of Great Britain none has given to the mother country so much disquiet and anxiety as

South Africa has done," James Bryce, onetime British ambassador to the United States and author of the popular *American Commonwealth*, wrote in 1897 in the conclusion to his *Impressions of South Africa*. He went on to observe that anyone in South Africa who looks sixty or eighty years forward suffers grave anxieties.

South Africa is, at least for its whites, and for overseas observers, a country whose identity is constituted by an image of a problematic future. "What do you think will happen?" is the first question I am asked by Americans and Europeans who learn that I have been doing research in South Africa. "How many years do you give the whites?" "When will the Blacks take over?" "Will there be a bloodbath?" "Do you think they will make it?" The very self-consciousness of "a future" is itself indicative of its peculiar rhetorical if not experiential role in the constitution of South Africa's identity.

For the anthropologist, to be cast as a prophet is to be cast in a strange role. Anthropology is popularly considered to be a salvage discipline. Anthropologists are thought of as archaeologists of waning humanity, desperately trying to create a heritage out of a few social and cultural shards. No one really questions the future of the people we typically study. Their extinction is written. It may be lamented, but that is all. The future of South African whites is another matter altogether, and yet, I suppose, as good a case can be made for their extinction as for that of the tribal people we study. I am not sure. The important point is that for well over a century now, white South Africans have seen their days numbered, and for well over a century, outside observers have also seen them numbered. This image of a problematic and limited future has certainly affected the way South African whites view themselves and their country. It has also affected the way outsiders think about the South African and his country.

There were many different answers the whites gave to my questions about their future, but they all assumed the reasonableness of the question itself. A few, like Hennie, insisted that one look not at the problems but at the solutions. Others, the majority, like Jack Freeling, were caught up in the problems themselves. And still others, like many members of the Renewal or for that matter Zachary van der Merwe in his Oriental mysticisms, deflected the mundane future into a transcendent one. Few of those I questioned— Tommy Prinsloo was an exception—began by talking of their ordinary plans for the future. They immediately launched into descrip-

tions of distant political and social scenarios. They spoke of time, of
being rushed, of the interference of friendly and hostile governments, the United States and, more abstractly, the communists, and
press provocation. They also spoke of the changes that had already
taken place in South Africa, those that had to be effected, and those
that would have to be resisted at all costs. I sometimes had the
impression that talk of change substituted for bringing about real
change. Curiously, many talked in far more blatantly racist terms
when they discussed their future than they did at other times. Most
of the answers to my questions about the future were expectably
filled with contradictions in both style and content. All of them gave
a privileged status to South Africa, which I am tempted to understand in Calvinist terms. There was often in the responses of even
the most secularized an implicit if not explicit assumption that they
(or South Africa) were somehow "chosen" whether by God or the
forces of history. In the most Calvinist versions South Africa was
seen as God's testing ground for a new social order.

For many Americans and some Europeans with whom I talked,
South Africa also represented the possibility of a new social order.
The questions I was asked about South Africa seemed to be inordinately invested with emotion and concern. It was as though the
future of South Africa played some symbolic role or other in the
cultural if not the psychological life of those who questioned me.
South Africa is a symbolic element in the discourse of the West, and
like all such symbolic elements, it has, as anthropologists now like
to say, a bipolar structure, representing at the ideological pole, to use
the jargon, esteemed moral and social values and at the orectic pole
less acceptable, often grossly physiological concerns.[2] Alan Pifer,
former president of the Carnegie Corporation, said recently in his
Commemoration Day Lecture at the University of Witwatersrand
that he found South Africa "endlessly absorbing as a microcosm of
the worldwide problem of how peoples of differing colors and
cultures are to live peacefully together."[3] There was certainly something of this in the symbolic investment I detected in the people who
questioned me about South Africa, but it would be a mistake, I
believe, to reduce their "absorption" to this concern. South Africa
also represents primordial and not particularly acceptable fears of
racial mix and cultural loss, of rushed time and the absence of
direction, of Apocalypse and perhaps even extinction. I myself find
the question of South Africa's future distressing. I am overcome by

both a magical desire for it all to work out and by the knowledge that it will not work out ideally, that there will indeed be bloodshed if not a bloodbath, that people will, as they always seem to, behave in extremely cruel and inhuman ways, and that, despite the pronouncements of racial equality and promises of universal franchise and the freedom to live where and with whom one wants, there will still be great injustice and suffering. I find that I cannot take easy refuge, as I look at South Africa, in the Western conviction that there are solutions to all problems. Hennie may insist that we look at solutions and not at problems, but he has yet to come up with a workable solution. "Solutions" are rhetorical figures in our particular cultural discourse that permit us from time to time to deny the overwhelmingness of social existence, to mask our impotence as individual actors, and to believe that the ideal can become the real.

Dominee Pieter Kotze

"Sometimes I am pessimistic and sometimes I am optimistic," Dominee Kotze said when I asked him about South Africa's future. Earlier in our conversation he and his wife had made it quite clear that they would not leave South Africa in the event of a Black takeover unless they were absolutely forced to leave.

"Fear is our biggest problem," the *dominee*'s wife said. "People are acting out of fear. You can feel it."

"Yes, fear is very unhealthy," the *dominee* added. "People do not open their eyes. They are afraid to. They prefer to remain stupidly blind and ignorant."

"They are convinced of their truth. They are not ignorant," the *dominee*'s wife corrected.

"Well, it is an ignorance without drive," the *dominee* conceded. "The liberals are always making plans. The Nats do too, for that matter. But there is never a meeting of people of different races."

"What about such multiracial organizations as Kontakt?" I asked.

"Oh, I suppose they are a step forward," Pieter Kotze said. "But, really, they are nothing more than the converted talking to the converted. Upper-class whites talking to upper-class Blacks and Coloureds. We're sitting on a time bomb with a short fuse."

"How long do you think it will be before something happens?" I asked.

"A couple of decades at the most. Not less."

"I felt a greater urgency in Johannesburg," I said.

"It's all smoothed over here," Pieter Kotze's wife said. "Everything in the Cape is always quieter. There is such a pretense to gentility."

"Cape Town people never believe anything will happen," her husband agreed.

"If you talk to the conservatives about change, they don't listen. They classify you as a liberal or even a communist, and then they dismiss you."

"What would your solution be?" I asked Pieter Kotze.

"I would split the country into open land and homelands. Seventy percent of the population would live in the open areas, but eighty percent of the area would be homelands. These would include a white homeland, mostly in the Karoo. None of the homelands would be economically independent. They could socially legislate, within limits of course, as they chose. In their homeland, the whites could have their silly paradise. I think people would flock to the homelands to live, but they would probably want to work in the open lands, which would be subject to different, more open rules. There would be strong deportation rules to keep the people in order. The federal government as a whole would handle foreign policy and trade and would ultimately be controlled by the open areas. Those who live in the open areas might have an extra vote. The Defence Forces would also be run by the federal government, with participating units from the homelands. Of course, I'm not sure how viable this is."

Pieter Kotze had clearly thought about his country's future. His solution reminded me of countless others I had heard from the people of Wyndal and read about in the newspapers.* Hugo Malan's "meritocracy" was even more fully elaborated. The most extreme

---

*The idea of a white homeland has been pushed, for example, by many Afrikaners, including members of the influential South African Bureau for Racial Affairs (SABRA). SABRA was planning in 1980 to take active steps to implement a white homeland to be called Orania or Oranika. SABRA's director, Dr. Chris Jooste, sees Orania as a place where "racially pure" whites would build up "with their own hands" their own homeland. In July 1980, Dr. Jooste said, "I don't see anything strange in this at all. This is probably the last country in the world where servants, for example, are Black. There is no reason why a white person should not be a servant—we can't all be masters" (*The Weekend Argus*, July 12, 1980).

was one in which every South African of whatever race would receive a vote, but each vote would be weighted according to the merit and race of the voter. An educated white's vote would weigh more than that of an uneducated white. It would also weigh more than that of an educated Black. The American federal system and the Swiss canton system, often misunderstood, were frequently invoked as models.

"We must maintain vital contact with people of different races," Pieter Kotze went on. "We must bring about a meeting. Yet a meeting does not mean a mixture. I am a Westerner. I am content with that. I will never be an African. I am very much part of the Western tradition. I can't really understand, that is, understand deeply and experientially, other traditions, Zen Buddhism or what have you. I am blocked that way. But then, they are blocked too."

It was not exactly clear who the *they* were, Buddhists or Blacks or all of those who did not share the *dominee*'s cultural tradition. It was, in any event, a massive they.

Zachary van der Merwe

"When I visited England I was startled by the autonomy of its future—a damned dismal one at that. We miss that autonomy here. We are still living on a frontier. Once it was Dark Africa with its wild animals, its cannibals and savages. Today it is politics and the big bad wolf—communism. It is really quite energizing, because one is participating in real history, raw, elemental history. The issues are very hard. Where light and space are clear, as here, contradictions stand out.

"There are always very direct and gross contradictions between one's private fantasies about unity and equality and the reality around one. And in this country, it's very hard to ignore them. It's like poverty in India. It's so great, so monumental, so overpowering, and so absolutely gross that one individual can't hope to effect a total change. So what does one put one's faith in? All my life I've seen evidence of man-made structures being totally insufficient. I hate to feel that I'm retreating into quasi-spiritual solutions to the world's problems, but I see a spiritual experience of life as the most practical experience. If I can extend, in my own consciousness, a blessing into a situation like Cross Roads,* where people are being thrown out of their homes, it will have its effect.

"When I look at my work, I realize that I have to accept my role as a resonator of tranquility and not simply join the theme song of this country, which is so discordant. No resolution to the situation in this country can develop without such tranquility. When I read about Cross Roads, I felt helpless, pained, and angry at the power of the government. I was particularly moved by a woman who had brought twelve of the homeless back to her house in one of the white suburbs and put them up in her garage. I thought I should be doing something too. (I used to be much more active.) But then, I realized that I couldn't allow myself to feel helpless, pained, and angered because then I'd just be one of the mob. There is nothing I can do that will actually help the situation. If one is unsure of oneself, then one is going to be swayed by the current of events. It's like the weather. If one is going to be affected by the weather, then who is one? The situation in Cross Roads is the result of the polarization of man's consciousness. It is only through finding unity in one's own consciousness that one can be effective in dealing with whatever comes up. Without a sense of wholeness and unity within oneself, one feels a sense of fracture and polarization and goes on dancing to the song of external happenings."

"But aren't you running away from your responsibilities here, in the everyday world, where perhaps you can help a bit?" I asked. Zachary seemed to be taking flight in a Hindu passivism. He was very defensive.

"I can accept that kind of criticism because I know where it is coming from—from a person dealing with the physical experience of reality. The Western world is evidence of the breakdown of that sense of reality. Western rationalism has been a very finely tuned

---

*Cross Roads is an "illegal" Black squatter community on the outskirts of Cape Town that has managed to survive repeated police raids. Periodically, the police tear down the shanties, and their inhabitants are fined and sent back to their homelands. These raids and razings make headlines in the English-language and, sometimes, the Afrikaans press, producing a scandal. They are the cause of shame and guilt among many whites, some of whom perform expiatory protests or contribute clothing and blankets. In the winter of 1981, at the time of one such raid, Black lawyers succeeded in clogging the courts, which had been handing out fines at the rate of ten to twelve per hour. The government eventually had to abandon their project of destroying the community.

development of a sense of man's apartness from his environment. It is a kind of apartheid—a more pervasive kind—because apartheid as it exists here is a particular syndrome of this rationalism. To change the situation here one has to embrace a very different stance. I remember moaning and groaning about the problems of South Africa to an Indian friend. Suddenly he banged his hand down and looked at me and said, 'If you give the problems of the waking state one jot of reality, one iota of reality, then you are lost.'

"I've been thinking about you and your particular work. You are very interested in scratching the surface for evidence of undercurrents of social feelings, customs, and habits and in trying to find some kind of coherent picture that reflects the surface. I would not necessarily try to interpret the undercurrents. It's a little like making a diagnosis or a prognosis of the state of a plant without actually knowing that it flowers and bears fruit.

"When I see people like my parents physically gathering in the poor and giving them some kind of solace, I say OK. There is also the Red Cross. They are concerned with the physical reality of the man sitting in his hut or in his Mercedes. They are lost in the waking state. I see beyond that, the mere physical. I am looking for causes. I can't simply believe that you get rid of a disease by clearing away a symptom. If you were to take the squatters near Cross Roads and put them into totally new buildings, they would say OK. But in a year those buildings would be slums again because you wouldn't be treating the cause but the symptom.

"You've seen the same thing in your country. Our problems may not be quite as subtle as elsewhere, but because they are institutionalized doesn't make them worse than those elsewhere. You've got the problems of migrant workers in Europe, which are as damaging to friendly relations as our problems are. South Africa just happens to be a fashionably contentious issue. Everyone points a finger at this country and singles it out as being a cancer. But there are cancers elsewhere too. They may not be fashionable, for the moment."

"You could argue that Blacks living in Soweto are physically no worse off than those living in Harlem," I said. "I'm not sure of that. But even if it were the case, there are still differences. The most important is that some Blacks in Harlem are able to get out. Here in South Africa they can't. And that is a reality—even if it is only a partial, an apparent, a waking reality!"

"I think it is a very temporary reality. I think it is changing. It's bound to change. There is no way it can't. It's only a matter of years. Whether or not it changes in my lifetime is of no real concern to me. Every time I go to the locations (I used to have a pass, but now I don't even bother with that), I have a sense of a community that is based on a lot of distortions. One of the distortions is the political one of having to live in a community like that. If they were to have a choice, I don't know whether or not they would live in a community like that or maintain that style of life. There is a lot of ignorance, and their aspirations are, you know, purely material. Their hearts are in the washing machine, the television, and the car.

"Whatever the African's future, he will have a very painful time because he has to evolve out of the elegance of his own innate culture, out of his fluency, his poetry, and the way he is locked into his landscape. His world has been totally disrupted. He has been thrust willy-nilly into the twentieth century. He has got to work through psychologically the Industrial Revolution, the Russian Revolution, into something like American democracy. He has to take these steps. He will not be able to skip over middle-class preoccupations and look to further horizons and meanings to gain a *new* and elegant relationship with his surroundings. For the moment he is faced with brute contrasts, and these brute contrasts awaken in him brute emotions, brute aspirations—reactions rather than creative actions. Reactions are what revolt is made up of. On the reactive level there can be no real creation. It is only when the reactive phase is over that real creation can take place.

"I see society as a sort of pool. There are various pretty boats floating on the water, but there's a whole lot of scum on that water, too. Rearranging the boats is not going to change the quality of the dirty water. To effect real change in a society and in the quality of people's lives, one has to look at the cause and see what real cause means. And real causes, for me, start with oneself. One can't point a finger at the world or any institution, no matter how tempting and easy it is, before looking at oneself. Take my friend, Manfred. He says he's a poet. He screams at the government and censorship and the puritanical nature of blah blah blah. I look at him as a person, and I see no difference in his life. He is still only reacting, though he thinks he is creating.

"I used to see my work as an effective means of making some kind of ripple. I took the ripples—they are easy to make, especially in this country—for signs of change, for change itself. I thought I was doing something! And all the time I was aware of the contradiction that I saw everywhere between people who produce beautiful works of art, theater, dance—images—and the very ugly images they make of their own lives. I had to bridge the gap. I could not live with the gap between my public self—my stage sets, my influence—and my private life. I had to make a clean sweep of it.

"I find people here, everywhere, to have bad breath. You might be dressed in an impeccable suit, but if you are going to talk to me with bad breath, I will not be comfortable near you. In the same way people talk about effecting change at the material level, but that talk doesn't change the cesspool of the mind. Equal opportunity doesn't make any difference to me anyway. There is only one opportunity, and that is life! To have equal opportunity in order to buy a house anywhere you want to is not the main issue. The main issue is when you've got the house, wherever it is, what are you going to do with your life? One can be effective in making life absolutely worthwhile in the slums of Calcutta or Soweto or in those of Constantia. The slums of Constantia are people's lives. Those of Soweto are people's houses. They are equally slums. Am I making myself clear?"

"Yes, I can understand your point and I even agree with some of it. But still I am haunted by the image of a Black woman in Wyndal, a maid, who sent her son to the Black school, a one-room hut, and discovered that he was learning nothing. So she now sends him hundreds of miles away to another school in her homeland, where she thinks he will learn something. She can have no influence over him. She has to sacrifice her motherhood to be a good mother."

"That is very difficult," Zachary said. "In a sense it's a very welcome thorn in the flesh of the would-be white ivory-tower liberal, because the thorn in one's flesh is a very real motivation to clear one's ethics."

I must have looked disgusted, because Zachary went on to say that he probably sounded very self-concerned and self-involved. "I don't see my role as effecting gross change on the gross level of making schools available for that woman because there are people doing that."

"Are there?" I asked.

"I can't do everything. I stick to my role as a subliminal rabble-rouser. Through the theater, through my person, I express nonverbally the experience of unity. I become a silent note in society's babble. Whatever its effect—I can't even look at its effect—but its effect is there, I know, because it is present in my experience. My experience of the world, of society, is an exact mirroring of my interaction and involvement in that world and society. I affect it through the quality of my intentions."

Tony Freeling

"The next generation is going to build up its own link," Jack Freeling said. We had been discussing the loss of ties with England since South Africa became a republic. Jack was proud that his permit to join the British army during World War II was signed by George VI. "They're going to have their own attachments."

"What do your friends think about the future?" I asked Tony, Jack's fourteen-year-old son, who had been listening.

"We talk a lot about it. And we feel that it's not going to be very long now until the Blacks take over. There are some who think it will be another fifty years. Some say it's going to happen in five years. Opinions are varied, really very varied. I personally think it's going to take quite a long time. We're not going to give in until we're sort of forced to hand things over.

"I think it will be another ten or fifteen years. And I'm going to stay. I'll stay until I feel threatened or I feel I'll be better off somewhere else. Then I'll leave. But before that I'll stay here. I mean, there's a . . . Life's a future for me. I'm sort of interested in becoming a certified accountant, and there's a demand for them. They need them. I've got to stay here . . . For my . . . the country. It's my country, you know."

"It's on a very poor street, just now," Jack said sympathetically. His son was determined and upset. Jack told me once that he had tried to talk to his children about the future but they simply got so upset and insecure that he and his wife had to stop it altogether. "They must find their own way," he had said. "They must find themselves. One can't influence." And yet it was Jack who encouraged Tony to study accounting. "He'll get a position in an international firm," he said on another occasion.

"I don't mind a Black government. I'll still get my salary. I can live where I like, and I'll be happy. And I'm set. But if they take my salary away and tell me where I have to live . . . "

"If they do to you what we do to them," Jack put in. Everyone laughed.

"Where would you go? Where do your friends say they would go if they had to leave?" I asked.

"Oh, some of them say they'll never leave. They'll join the commandoes and fight to the death. They're willing to take a bet. We'll crush the Blacks. That sort of thing. It's very sort of nasty. Yeah, there are a couple of strong believers who say that no matter what happens the white person will rule again. And then there are some who don't see any change happening. They think the Blacks are too stupid to do anything."

The Most Bigoted Man in the Valley

"You people from overseas are always putting pressure on us to change. You Americans and your President Carter. Waldheim! He's the worst of the lot. Look what he's doing in the South West: giving it to the communists. And the United Nations—it's a kaffir organization. All they want is power and big Mercedes. You all want us to change. You don't understand. We have lived with the kaffirs. We fought against them, taught them, take care of their health, educate them, and uplift them. We want to change too, and we are changing. Look at the bank clerks in Cape Town. They're Coloured. That's change. And the shopgirls. They're Coloured. We're trying to speed up evolution a bit, but you can't go too fast. That's what you people from overseas don't understand. You think you can change everything overnight. You can't. You have chaos—bloodshed, revolution, destruction. Everything my forebears built, and I myself built (I'm eighty-three this month), will be destroyed. I can't see it that way. We need time, if your President Carter and your Waldheim would let us handle our problems ourselves. We understand these Blacks. I was raised with them, in the Transvaal. I spoke their language. There is a man in the government—you may have heard about him—who said that the Black man thinks slowly. Everybody is upset about it. I think he's right. The kaffir is slow in his attitude toward change. He does not make quick decisions. If you ask one of the boys to make a decision, he says, 'Baas, give me some time to think it over.' They are closer to nature. The relationship between whites and Coloureds is very good. It's the press that distorts the relationship between whites and Blacks. They are really quite happy. The farmers treat them well. No farmer would treat his horse badly because he has to use it. It would be foolish. It's the same with the workers. It would be foolish to treat them badly. What good would they be?"

"You talk about giving one man one vote. It's nonsense. It didn't work for the Coloureds. They just played one party against the other. How can you give the vote to a bloke who can't even read the names of the candidates? He'll vote for anyone who promises him something. When will *you* have a Black American president?

"Now, you tell me, who will take advantage of this situation? The communists. They're our principal threat—not the Blacks, not the Coloureds. We *know* them and can handle them. It's the communists. Your President Carter should be worrying about them. And Waldheim too, but he's probably one of them. I can't understand why no one has assassinated him. I'd give the money myself. I've been up in the South West. It's a beautiful country, a hard country. And now this Waldheim wants to give it to the communists—and the Cubans. Look at what your President Kennedy did when the Russians put missiles in Cuba—in your backyard. And now you'd let the Russians do the same in our backyard! We're your only support in Africa. I think this man Reagan understands that. We're hoping he gets elected. He had a man here this winter to talk to our leaders. They say he understands our situation. It's all a question of understanding. You haven't been here that long. When you are, you'll understand. When my ancestors came over here from Holland in 1689, the kaffirs were wearing loincloths. Even the women were only wearing something between their legs. They had only the bow and arrow. Their way of life was simple. They lived in a simple hut: just a bunch of sticks piled up against one another. Look at them today. They're wearing clothes, just like you and me. That's change. And it's only been three hundred years. That's not very long to make a Black man into a white. Yes, I believe they should have the vote—when they're ready. It'll be in a thousand years, and, thank the Lord, I won't be there to see it."

Dr. Jakobus Steyn

"I think South Africa has a future. We'll have to come together as white men. And the ones who think there is no place for them here, the quicker they go the better. We should unite. British feeling should go. I think we should be like the American nation. To hell with the past, with where your parents came from, and all that. There are always a few leftists, who are very liberal, who would like to fight, to give their lives to the Black man. But these same types are now fleeing from Rhodesia. They're getting out of the mess they helped create. It just doesn't make sense. It is those whites who are militant. Most Blacks are not so militant-feeling as you people from overseas think. I'd say a big percentage of Blacks and Coloureds know that the white man has taught them everything they know. They know the white man is feeding them . . .

"Oh, we have problems, but I think we have a future. We are not a nation yet. I don't know if we are going to be a nation. Time is running out for the white man. If we don't take a stand together, then we'll go under. We have to take a very firm stand toward the Coloured and the Black. We must, however, explain why we do the things we do. We are prepared to share the country—territorial segregation, as we have done with the homelands. We're prepared to do that. I am even prepared to let them cut off the whole western Cape, to give it to the Coloureds, if that will solve the problems between the Coloureds and the whites. I'll make my sacrifices. But I'm not prepared to let my culture go by letting those people take over. Sorry. I'll be in South Africa until they take over. If they are going to take over, the majority, then I'll leave. I'll never be able to sit here and be ruled by the Black man."

"Where would you go?"

"I wouldn't know. Wherever there are no Blacks."

"That might be a difficult place to find."

Dr. Steyn ignored my comment. I asked him if he worried about his children's future. Some English critics of the National Party have said that the Afrikaners must have a secret hatred of their children because they are leading them to certain death.

"The children see things differently, fortunately, I suppose. They are much more brainwashed in the last few years. In my young days, it was never thought of—playing rugby with Coloureds or Blacks. Today it is done every day. The result is evolution. If you slowly give people a chance to get to know one another, I think then kids could be happy playing sports together. Later they might even go to school together. I see you are still having problems in America putting Blacks and whites together in school. I mean they are forced together, and that is bad. These things must be faced. But, of course, there are certain leaders who like to force things down another nation's throat . . ."

"Do you think there will be violence in this country?"

"I am sure there will be. There is violence at the moment, but I doubt if we will ever have a war. There are too many Coloureds and Blacks who are not militant. It is actually the extreme whites who are trying to push the Blacks into being militant. Look at South Africa. How few bombs explode here with so many Blacks. Look at how many bombs explode in London with only a handful of Blacks. If South African Blacks were really militant, they could blow this country to pieces in a week's time."

"But they don't have the bombs."

"Well, they have access to them—from across the border."

"How do you see the education of Blacks?"

"There are five million of them in school, and there are only a million whites in school. Who's paying for it? We are; we pay the taxes, and we are doing a good job."

"But are the schools any good?"

"Many of them are very nice schools. But we just can't keep ahead of them. These people are breeding like I don't know what. They have families of ten, twelve, thirteen children. And they're poor. Their children deserve it, but they're reproducing, and we can't cope. It's impossible."

"Do you see Black participation in the government as a possibility?"

"No, I'm sorry."

"And Coloured participation?"

"The Coloureds might. I think we could come to some agreement with them later on: a qualified franchise where the educated Coloureds would join the white man in certain respects."

"And the educated Black man?"

"Yes, if you have a qualified franchise, then it must be for everyone. But five percent of the whites would be disqualified, and five percent of the Blacks would be qualified. As things proceed and the revolution takes its course, the percentages would come closer. It will take time. We mustn't be rushed, and the world is rushing us. They need to preach to other people what they themselves should have done."

Piet van Rooyen

I

"David Wilkerson, the man who wrote *The Cross and the Switchblade*, had a vision and saw a mighty spiritual revival in South Africa. He felt it would begin in the Cape and spread like a flame ..."

II

"I'm optimistic about the future. We are a testing ground for a new society. If we have time, we will become a peaceful, integrated community. I think we will have social apartheid. I don't associate with Blacks, and I don't expect them to associate with me. But if a Black man did try to associate with me, and I liked him, I'd become his friend. I have no grudges against anybody. People ask what I would do if my daughter came home with a Black man, but *that* would never happen. I don't think so, except very rarely. I'm proud of my heritage and my nation, and I wouldn't like everything to be mixed up.

"The Christian point of view is that there can be no one tradition. We are in our different traditions all brothers in Christ. Of course, we all fear a sudden change. Our kids have fewer problems about racial relations than we. There is a generation gap. So many things have changed, and probably not all the changes have been noticed. There are still divisions in the post office and sports stadiums, but rugby is now mixed. Tobias plays for the Springboks, and we are proud of him. Of course, a lot is exaggerated in the media. They stress poverty. But take the Indians. They don't want to return to India. They'd rather stay here."

III

"The end of the world will be heralded in by the Antichrist. It will be a period of rapture. Remember Lot and Noah before the world was destroyed. So the Reborn Christians will be removed from the world before its destruction. The common position is that all humanity will go through the seven-year period of trouble and tribulation, and then the end will come. The charismatic-Pentecostal version is somewhat different. They believe in two periods of three and a half years each. Some say God will take the true believers away before the time of troubles. Then there will be the millennium. For the Dutch Reformed Church, the millennium is really in your heart. It is not literal. It began with Christ's crucifixion."

"And what do you think?"

"I am studying the issue. I think the true Christians will be saved before the destruction."

"Is it imminent?"

"There are those who say it is."

Andre Roussouw

"There was a big Renewal conference a few years ago, and five people had the same dream one night. They each came from a different province of South Africa, and one of them came from the South West. They dreamed of a map of South Africa. It was a pale color, and suddenly a black hand moved down across it from the north until it was all covered except for little spaces between the fingers. In these spaces there were little fires, and gradually these fires got bigger and bigger and began to burn the fingers. As they did, the hand moved back until you could see the map all clear again."

"What does the dream mean?"

"The map is South Africa. The black hand is Black power, not the Black people themselves. The fires are Christians praying. It is through their prayer that South Africa will be saved."

Tommy Prinsloo

"I can still remember, after my last lecture at Stellenbosch, the professor said, 'Look, you guys who are obtaining your degrees at the end of the year, just don't think of yourselves as farmers. There is a vast difference between theory and practice.' I never realized it, and when I took over the farm—we had a manager—I was in such a flap, trying to put four years of theoretical knowledge into practice. I got frustrated. Luckily we kept the manager on for a year, and I went through a year of what you might call practical training with manager. He was an old-timer, and I must say I learned a lot from him. He knew how to treat Coloureds, and that you can only learn from experience.

"But, you know, the old methods of farming are no longer viable.

Already in '71, when I graduated, some of the farmers were realizing that they were going to run into financial trouble. Farming is a business venture today. You need capital and you have to get a good return on your money. I want to place this farm on a viable economic footing. There is no future in peaches. A good estate-bottled wine is the only answer.

"We live in one of the choice wine areas of the Cape, and, let's face it, we produce a very mediocre wine. We could do better, and that's what I am trying to do. We've got the wine co-op, but there's no real control over the quality of the grapes. What I want to do is produce a really first-class wine on this farm. I've talked to experts at Stellenbosch and at the KWV,* the wine board, and they assure me it is possible. The problem is capital. I'm advertising for it now, and I've got a few interested parties from Jo'burg. One of them is coming down this week. It's not going to be easy because we're a small farm, about twenty-five hectares. We'd have a better chance if we were a bit bigger."

"Have you asked your neighbors to join?"

"Yes. At first they were both interested, and then when it came down to the actual cost accounting, they got cold feet. They'd probably rather sell, like most of the farmers here, that is, if they got their price."

"Do you think the English who have just moved in would want to sell?"

"That depends. Most of them have moved out here for a way of life. They're businessmen primarily, and they're living off that. Farming is secondary, but make no mistake—they're not going to neglect their farms. It's also an investment. It's just not so important as it is for the Afrikaners, because they have other means. Wentworth wants to sell, of course, for an absurd price. He'll never get it. He was just a speculator."

"Is farming just a business venture for you?"

"No, not at all. I'm a bit of a romantic. Farming is in my blood. I like working outside. The happiest days of my childhood were spent on my uncle's farm. I love the feeling after a season of hard work of seeing the grapes go off to the press. It's hard to describe. It's a feeling that's attached to this old house, to its gables, its thatched roof, its old oaks—the landscape. It all ties in with wine-making."

"How do you see your future here?"

*KWV is the Afrikaans abbreviation for Cooperative Wine Growers' Association.

"Well, if my project comes off, I'll stay. If something unforeseen happens, not being able to raise the money, being convinced I'm barking up the wrong tree, then I may have to go back to university."

"What would you study?"

"I don't know. I don't think I'd continue in wine. I was lucky to have the farm. There were four of us who graduated in wine, and I was the only one who found work immediately in it. No, I haven't really thought it through."

"How do you see the political future of South Africa?"

"It will be governed by economics. I think we could have a fantastic future. It's a question of settling the racial problems, and that can be done. You know there is a tremendous generation gap among the Afrikaners. The younger ones think differently. It's extraordinary when we all sit down to a bottle of wine. The older ones, and some of the younger ones too, talk only in terms of the existing political situation. Most of the younger ones want something to happen because they realize that if something doesn't happen to get the races together, there will be no hope. We can't talk anymore in terms of needing time. That can no longer be justified. We have to act now."

"When did you begin to feel this way?"

"At university. We'd get together in our rooms at midnight and talk most of the night through. It was then that I came to realize how important change was. Of course, Stellenbosch isn't the same today. I think it's more conservative. It has its peaks and dips. I was there at a peak. We were always questioning ourselves, our government, our future. Sometimes I'm afraid we created a storm in a teacup, but I think it was important—for me at least.

"We've got a Black problem, but we've got a white one as well. And the white one is perhaps our biggest problem. Talk to liberals, to intellectuals, even to educated conservatives. They will admit that change is necessary. But talk to the mine workers, the railway men, the farmers in the Transvaal and the Free State. They don't want to budge. They've got to be educated to change."

Dora Hertzog

"The world is moving so fast," Dora Hertzog said. Dora is the thirty-year-old daughter of one of the National Party leaders in the valley. Her husband manages his father's farm. "I am not afraid. I do not really know where I would go if I had to leave this country.

"The journalists in the United States do not understand the political situation here. They have got out of hand. You know that the journalists who accompanied the Lions [the English rugby team that visited South Africa in 1980] were not sports writers. They were political journalists, and the rioters knew this. Yes, the Bantus—they are clever—knew this, and so we had trouble. The same thing happened in Soweto in 1976. Vorster had gone to a big conference in Austria, and the day he arrived, the riots began. The agitators wanted to embarrass him. It was a half-war. Black people against Black people. They were afraid of one another. Workers who wanted to go to work had to walk behind police vans for protection. A friend of mine saw it. It is the *skollies* who cause all the trouble. It was the same in 1962. Then there were riots in Paarl and Wellington. The Coloureds were encouraged by white agitators."

"What were those riots about?"

"They just wanted to kill whites. They butchered a white girl, and then a lot of them were shot. And not by the police." Dora laughed.

"By whom?"

"By whites who sat on rooftops with guns. They wanted to get back at them for having killed the white girl. The Coloureds are a very emotional people, and you can't trust the Bantus. A farmer here asked his Bantu foreman once, 'Tell me, Johnny, would you shoot me?' 'No, *baas*, I wouldn't shoot you,' Johnny said. 'I'd go to the neighbor's place and shoot the *baas* there. And his man would shoot you.' No, I'm not afraid of the Coloureds when they are alone, but if the Coloureds in Wyndal—I don't know how many there are but they are more than we—were to organize they could cause trouble . . .

"The government is spending so much money on the homelands. They are independent now. They spend a lot of taxpayers' money on Soweto. Now they are going to give them electricity. If a farmer builds his own house, he knows it will cost him five to seven thousand rand to wire it, and he saves up for it. Now these Bantus wait for the government to give them electricity. You give a Bantu something, and you get nothing back. And our government is now giving money to the homelands to win their favor. They are our neighbors, but we shouldn't have to buy them . . .

"Whenever you go into the city, you see it is the Bantus who surround it. If they were organized, they could cut it off. If the people in Soweto wanted to, they could cut Johannesburg off from Pretoria. Last week, during the riots, Cape Town was cut off from the airport. The youth who are protesting are unable to decide anything for themselves. It's the communists. They say all they need is a child until he is five to make him a communist for life."

"Do you think the communists want to invade South Africa?"

"America wouldn't let it happen."

"But do you think they really want to invade?"

"They want to create psychological unrest. We have to be more aware. I am a member of the commandoes. There are only a few women in it. They tell us we must be prepared because there will be trouble. But they never tell us what the trouble will be. They don't want to panic us, but they should tell us."

EPILOGUE

Since *Waiting* was first published last April, the unrest that began in South Africa in August 1984 with protests against the new tricameral parliament has continued with an intensity that resists all of the National government's heavy-handed efforts to stop it. No previous protests have lasted so long or been so geographically widespread. None has required such prolonged government intervention—the state of emergency that P. W. Botha was forced to declare on July 27, 1985, still goes on—and none has caused so many deaths. As I write, more than a thousand South Africans, almost all of them Black, have died in the rioting. Thousands more have been arrested, detained, or banned. Surveillance is at a peak; censorship has increased. The press must receive special permission to enter restricted areas, and television coverage of the rioting has been outlawed. (It is the old story: the press incites people to riot; that is, when it is not the *skollies*, the *tsotsies*, the communists, or other subversives.) So far, most of the violence has taken place in Black locations, like Soweto, Sharpeville, and Langa in the Eastern Cape, where, on March 22, 1985, the police shot and killed twenty people, or in "intertribal" strife, between Zulu and Pondo or Pedi and Ndebele, but there have also been incidents in white areas. In the "locations," many of the victims are reported to be "system Blacks" —Black policemen and councillors who work for or with the white government.

No previous protests have produced such moral outrage and incurred such strong, worldwide condemnation. In the United States, South Africa has been in the news nearly every day. There have been daily demonstrations—and arrests—in front of the South African embassy and its consulates, and the move to divest has spread from campuses to local and state legislatures and then to Congress. A number of corporations doing business in South Africa have begun to weigh their involvement seriously. Even the Reagan administration, whose policy of "constructive engagement" has been generally supportive of the white government, has had to question the efficacy of its policy and to impose some minimal economic sanctions, such as making the sale of Krugerrands in the United States illegal. Rioting has certainly had its effect on the South African economy. The South African government was forced to declare a moratorium on international debts on August 27, 1985, and the rand, already at a low of fifty-two American cents at the time the state of emergency was declared a month earlier, dropped below thirty-three cents. (In the last week or so, with an increase in the price of gold, the rand has risen to almost forty-five cents—a rise that suggests how indifferent money and gold markets are to political and moral violations.) Inflation has been running at close to 17 percent, and the prime lending rate has been as high as 25 percent. Riot control is not without its costs, either. *The Economist** predicts that the National government will have to increase its budget not by the 13.6 percent it originally planned but by about 20 percent—largely to defray higher military and police costs. There has been the usual fighting and the usual bad faith in negotiating a settlement in Namibia. There have been sporadic bombings throughout the country, and, in particular, land mine explosions near the Zimbabwe border, for which the African National Congress has taken credit. To put a stop to the activity of ANC guerrillas in the countries on its borders, South Africa (among other things) invaded Botswana last year and blockaded Lesotho—so successfully that the government there fell and was replaced by one that threw the ANC out.

The strength of the protests, I believe, has come as a surprise to everyone, Black, white, Coloured, or Asian, in South Africa. It must certainly have surprised the government, which appears to have

*December 21, 1985, pp. 89–90.

been duped by its own conjurings into imagining that the creation of a parliament giving token representation to Coloureds and Asians would be taken as a sign of real change in apartheid rather than the continuation of a divide-and-rule policy further separating Coloureds and Asians from Blacks. (Other changes, like scrapping the law against interracial marriages that was once considered a cornerstone of apartheid, have been viewed as cosmetic by all but the most conservative Afrikaners, who regard them as obscene.) The protests must also have surprised the ANC, which has attempted to take the credit for them (if not control of them) but has been less successful than its leaders may have hoped. The ANC failure has less to do with the factionalism in the Black community—a factionalism the government has always encouraged in its attempt to convince everyone, white and Black, that Blacks cannot rule—than with the conditions of riot in a society that has been denied any *real* opposition leadership. This absence of leadership is another feature of the no-win situation in which Blacks, and other members of the opposition, find themselves. If people in the opposition attempt to negotiate with the government, they lose their constituencies. If they refuse to negotiate, they are precluded from leadership through arrest, detention, banning, or death. It is no accident that one looks for leaders among the imprisoned—like Nelson Mandela—or among the banned and exiled in the African National Congress. The other possible leaders have been forced into silence or have had to play on the privilege of international reputation or, in the cases of Bishop Desmond Tutu and Alan Boesak, on whatever clerical immunity they may have. Boesak's arrest last fall suggests that in the end this immunity is of little consequence. Of all the Black leaders, Winnie Mandela, Nelson's wife, has probably been most successful in confounding the government with her public resistance to banning orders and to the other restrictions on her. (She is, of course, a woman in a society that finds female leadership unthinkable.) As one South African said to me, "Winnie seems to be turning the government on its head. She is like a runaway horse leading its rider back home." Of course, the question is: Where is home?

It would be absurd to assume at this time that the South African government has lost control of the country, that South Africa is in the midst of a revolution, that a change of regime is immanent. Whites are still very much in charge in South Africa—despite the protests, the bombings, and the weakness of the South African economy, despite the nearly universal condemnation of apartheid, the economic sanctions, the threats of economic sanctions, and the growing support for the ANC, despite a more sophisticated and often multiracial opposition (the United Democratic Front, which played an important role in opposing the new parliament, the unions with their new federation, the Congress of South African Trade Unions, and parties like the barely legal, militantly Black Azanian People's Organization), and, finally, despite the split in the National Party and the obvious cynicism of its propaganda about "change."

Most South African whites, certainly those of Wyndal, have little direct experience of the rioting and the protests. They read about the protests in the newspapers (insofar as the papers can report them), and they are provided with the usual explanations about the *skollies*, the *tsotsies*, the communists, and now about interference from Western Europe and the United States. The Wyndal whites may note a new sullenness in their workers or complain about the cheekiness of the clerks in the hypermarket or the garage attendants in Cape Town, but, for the most part, they concern themselves with the details of everyday life, with their farms and their neighbors. They worry about the fall of the rand, the prices of peaches and pears, and the real estate market more, perhaps, than they worry—or at least articulate their worry—about the future of their country. I suspect that, like whites elsewhere in South Africa, many of them have moved further to the right and a few further to the left. Most probably remain as they were when I was living there—removed from South Africa's fevered politics.

I have not been back to South Africa since *Waiting* was published. I have received letters from South Africans I knew and South Africans I didn't know, and I have talked to South Africans who were visiting here and to Americans who had just visited South Africa. All of them seemed certain that something was happening there that had never happened before, but now, as I read what they write about it or listen to what they have to say, I am struck by the repetition of a story formulated long ago. Obviously, I am not talking about the Blacks, Coloureds, Asians, or those whites who have committed themselves to ending apartheid. Despite the increase of martyrs in their ranks and the increase of sadness (it is more than political necessity that so many protests take place at funerals), people committed to ending apartheid have, as they say wryly, plenty of time on their side. It is the other whites—now, from afar, as they lose their uniqueness for me—who seem like actors who have lost their director but who go on rehearsing irrelevant parts against an aging and unreal stage set. They seem as bewildered as the whites who watched, uncomprehending, from windows and *stoeps* last December while 20,000 Blacks filed by, grieving, on their way to Molly Blackburn's funeral. What they must have found particularly bewildering was that Molly Blackburn was a white. She was an activist, a member of the Black Sash, a brave and humble woman, and she was killed with another white activist in an automobile accident that was just an accident, and had nothing at all to do with politics.

A few months ago, I sent an American to visit one of the Black South African leaders I respect most—someone who avoids publicity. Later, the American told me about a dinner they had together. It was in one of those big neo-Tudor houses in a wealthy, white, liberal Johannesburg suburb. Most of the evening went by in small talk until, suddenly, the Black leader said that only after every white mother who had lost a child or contemplated the loss of a child recognized that Black mothers suffered the same despair when *their* children died—only then would South Africa begin to be able to solve its problems. Some of the guests were offended by what they considered the Black man's dinner-table indelicacy, but after he had left for his own home, in one of the sprawling Black "locations" that surround Johannesburg, the hostess, who was more in sympathy with him, told her American guest that he never would have said that sort of thing ten years ago, or even five years ago. "You see how things have evolved," she said, using "evolve" in that peculiarly passive, South African way. What had the Black man said? Some might call it a threat, some might call it a prediction. For me, it was a desperate cry for recognition—a recognition which may now take more than rhetorical violence to achieve.

New York
January 26, 1986

CHRONOLOGY

circa 300	Migration of African farmers across Limpopo River into what is today South Africa.
1488	Bartholomew Diaz discovers Cape of Good Hope.
1652	Dutch East India Company establishes refreshment station at Cape peninsula.
1657	First free burghers start to farm in Rondebosch.
1658	About 400 slaves imported from West Africa.
1688–1689	150 Huguenots arrive. Some settle in "Wyndal."
1700	Afrikaner population reaches 1,000 and occupies territory within fifty miles of Cape Town.
1778	Fish River becomes eastern boundary of Cape settlement.
1779–1877	Kaffir Wars—border clashes between whites and the Xhosa.
1795–1803	First British occupation of Cape.
1800	Afrikaner population reaches 20,000.
	Trekboers reach Orange River in the north and Fish River in the east.
1806	Second British occupation of Cape.
1812	Black Circuit.
1814	Holland cedes Cape to British.

1815   Slachter's Nek.

1820   Arrival of 5,000 British settlers.

1828   Zulu King Shaka is assassinated and his military kingdom
               begins to decline.

               English becomes official language.

               Free Coloureds in Cape placed on political level with
               whites.

1829   University of Cape Town opens.

1834   British Parliament emancipates slaves in colonial empire.

1836–1854   The Great Trek. Afrikaners from Cape founded repub-
               lics in Transvaal and Orange Free State.

1838   Massacre of Afrikaners under Retief by Zulu chief Ding-
               aan.

               Battle of Blood River. Sarel Cilliers's covenant.

1843   Natal becomes British colony.

1860–1911   Indentured Indian workers arrive to work Natal sugar
               estates.

1867   First diamond discovered near Hopetown.

1870   Kimberley diamond rush begins.

1877   British annex Transvaal.

1879   Britain occupies Zululand.

1880   First Anglo-Boer War.

1881   British withdraw from Transvaal.

1884   South West Africa becomes German protectorate.

1886   Opening of Witwatersrand gold fields.

1895   Cecil Rhodes's coup against Transvaal fails.

1898   Whites complete conquest of African population.

1899–1902   Second Anglo-Boer War. (Treaty of Vereeniging, May
               31, 1902.)

1904   Importation of Chinese laborers for Transvaal gold
               mines.

1907–1913   Mahatma Gandhi's *satyagraha* (truth- or soul-force) cam-
               paign.

1910   Cape, Transvaal, Orange Free State, and Natal join to
               form Union of South Africa—a self-governing British
               dominion.

1910–1919	Louis Botha is prime minister.
1912	African National Congress (ANC) founded.
1913	South Africa's Parliament limits African landownership to Reserves (reservations).
	March of Natal Indians into Transvaal.
1914	Hertzog forms National Party.
	South Africa enters World War I on side of Britain.
	Afrikaners rebel.
	Mahatma Gandhi leaves South Africa.
1914–1915	South West Africa campaign.
1918	Broederbond founded.
1919	Union granted mandate over South West Africa.
1919–1924	Jan Smuts is prime minister.
1920	40,000 African miners strike on Rand.
1921	South African Communist Party founded.
1922	General strike of white miners over decision to increase proportion of Black miners. Riots.
1924	J. B. M. Hertzog becomes prime minister. Legislation foreshadows apartheid.
1925	Afrikaans recognized as second official language.
1927	Immorality Act prohibits extramarital intercourse between Europeans and Africans.
1931	Statute of Westminster: Union given full legislative freedom.
1932	Union abandons gold standard.
1933	Coalition government of Hertzog's National Party and Smuts's South African Party. Hertzog is prime minister.
1938	Centenary celebration of Great Trek.
1939	South Africa enters World War II on side of Britain (80 votes in Parliament for, 67 contra).
1939–1948	Smuts is prime minister for second time.
1946	Asiatic Land Tenure and Indian Representation Act, so-called Ghetto Act, prevents Indians from acquiring new real estate. Repealed in 1948.
	60,000 African miners strike on Rand.

1948	General elections of May 26. National Party comes to power.
1948–1954	D. F. Malan is prime minister.
1949	Zulu riots against Indians in Durban.
	Prohibition of Mixed Marriages Act.
1950	Population Registration Act, cornerstone of apartheid; assigns every person to racial group that determines his or her rights and obligations.
	The Group Areas Act provides for separate group areas.
	Suppression of Communism Act gives extensive repressive powers to government.
	Appeal to Privy Council abolished.
1952	ANC launches passive resistance campaign.
1953	Reservation of Separate Amenities Act allows any person in control of public premises to reserve separate and unequal facilities for different racial groups and abolishes power of courts to nullify such actions.
	Bantu Education Act removes African education from mission control and rests it completely in government hands.
	Central African Federation of Rhodesia and Nyasaland formed.
1954	Malan retires.
1954–1958	J. G. Strijdom is prime minister.
1955–1956	Congress of People Campaign.
1956	Coloureds disenfranchised.
	Riotous Assemblies Act, limits public and private meetings.
1958–1966	H. F. Verwoerd is prime minister.
	Pan-Africanist Congress (PAC) founded.
	Progressive Party founded.
1959	Extension of University Education Act forbids nonwhites to attend white universities and provides for separate "university colleges" for each racial group.
	Bantu Self-Government Act provides for homelands.
1960	Police massacre of Sharpeville Rioting.

1960	Poqo, sabotage unit of PAC, founded.
	ANC and PAC banned.
	White representatives of African voters removed from Parliament.
1961	South Africa becomes republic and withdraws from Commonwealth.
	Umkhonto we Sizwe (Spear of the Nation), a sabotage unit of the ANC, founded.
1962	"Sabotage Act" greatly broadens arbitrary government powers by expanding concept of sabotage, by placing burden of proof of innocence on accused, by extending bannings of newspapers, organizations, and gatherings, and by permitting indefinite imprisonment without due process.
1963	General Law Amendment Act permits repeated detention of persons without legal counsel.
	Federation of Rhodesia and Nyasaland dissolved.
1964	Continuing sabotage trials.
	Bantu Law Amendment gives government legal power to remove any Black from any white area at any time.
1965	Rhodesian unilateral declaration of independence (UDI).
1966	Verwoerd assassinated.
	UN General Assembly terminates South Africa's mandate over Namibia.
	61,000 Coloureds evacuated from District Six in Cape Town.
1966–1978	B. J. Vorster is prime minister.
1967	Terrorism Act.
1968	White representatives of Coloureds removed from Parliament.
	Steve Biko founds all-Black South African Students' Organization (SASO).
	Prohibition of Political Interference Act bans racially mixed political parties.
1969	Ultraconservative Herstigte Nasionale Party (HNP) founded.
1970	World Council of Churches extends nonmilitary assistance to African guerrilla movements.

1971	World Court rules South Africa's administration of Namibia (South West Africa) illegal.
1973	U.N. General Assembly forms International Convention on Suppression and Punishment of the Crime of Apartheid.
1974	South African army engages in operations against Namibian guerrillas (SWAPO—South West Africa People's Organization).
1976	Internal Security Act greatly extends powers of Suppression of Communism Act.
	Transkei becomes "independent."
	Mozambique and Angola granted independence.
1976–1977	Riots in Soweto and elsewhere in South Africa.
1977	Steve Biko dies in police custody.
	U.N. Security Council imposes mandatory arms embargo on South Africa.
	Bophuthatswana becomes "independent."
	Soweto's Committee of Ten founds Soweto Civic Association, which opposes government-created Soweto Urban Bantu Council.
1978	Information Scandal.
	Vorster resigns as prime minister.
	P. W. Botha becomes prime minister.
	Venda becomes "independent."
1979	Azanian People's Organization (AZAPO) founded to develop Black political and social consciousness and to mobilize country's oppressed.
1979–present	Periodic strikes of Black workers.
1980	Riots in Cape Town.
	Coloured school boycott in Cape Province.
1980	Senate abolished and replaced by multiracial President's Council with no Black representatives.
	Zimbabwe becomes "independent."
1981	Ciskei becomes "independent."
	Squatter communities around Cape Town demolished.
1982	National Party splits over Coloured and Asian participation in government.

1982	A. Treurnicht and F. Hartzenburg form Conservative Party.

President's Council submits proposals for extensive government reorganization, giving Coloureds and Asians some participation and strengthening position of president.

ANC bombs Koeberg nuclear power station.

White union leader Neil Aggett is first white to die in police detention.

ANC blows up six fuel storage tanks in northern Transvaal.

1982–1983	South African raids against ANC bases in Lesotho, Swaziland, and Mozambique.

United Democratic Front (UDF) founded to oppose constitutional reforms.

1983	Institution of Coloured and Asian parliaments.

Blacks, and many other non-whites and whites, protest absence of Black parliamentary representation.

1984	Coloureds and Asians vote for parliamentary representatives. Many boycott elections.

Riots break out after the elections. Defense forces called in to quell rioting in Black locations.

1985	Riots continue. ANC plays active role. The government declares a state of emergency on July 27. Thousands of protesters arrested. Over 1,000, mostly black, die. Severe press and television restrictions. Black students boycott schools. Miners strike. Bombings in Durban and elsewhere. Landmines explode in northern Transvaal. Violent clashes between Zulu and Pondo and between Pedi and Ndebele.

Prohibition of Mixed Marriage Act suspended.

Formation of Congress of South African Trade Unions —a multi-racial confederation of unions.

South African government declares moratorium on payment of international debt.

NOTES

INTRODUCTION

1. Bakhtine, p. 87.
2. For more detailed statistics, see South African Institute of Race Relations, 1982, 1983; Study Commission; Thompson and Prior; Nedbank Group; Legum.
3. See *The Economist*, June 2–8, 1984, p. 67.
4. See Study Commission, pp. 49–100 for good summary discussion.
5. See *The Economist*, April 28, 1984, p. 60, and May 5, 1984, p. 52 for details.
6. See Karis for a discussion of the ANC and other Black movements.

1. THE VALLEY. No notes.

2. WAITING

1. Memmi; Mannoni.
2. Lefebvre.
3. Malinowski.
4. Bourdieu.
5. Wittgenstein.
6. Kramer, "Fall of a House," p. 14.
7. Gordimer, "Living in the Interregnum."
8. Coetzee, p. 97.
9. *Ibid.*, p. 35.
10. van Wyk Louw, *Berigte te Velde*.
11. van Wyk Louw, *Berigte te Velde*.
12. Patterson, p. 44.

13. Compare Jordaan.
14. Marais.
15. Patterson, p. 53.
16. van Wyk Louw, *Berigte te Velde*; quoted in Moodie, p. 41.
17. Moodie, pp. 42–43.
18. See also Schlemmer.
19. Opperman; quoted in Moodie, pp. 43–44.
20. Translated by Anthony Delius. Cope and Krige; quoted in Moodie, pp. 43–44.
21. Patterson, p. 55.
22. Jordaan.
23. Worrall, p. 194.
24. de Villiers, "Introduction," p. V.
25. Garson, p. 21 ff.
26. Kramer, "Fall of a House," p. 14.
27. Watts, p. 42.
28. Watts, p. 47 ff.
29. Watts; Garson, p. 19.
30. Garson, p. 20 ff.
31. Schlemmer, p. 97.
32. Compare van den Berghe.
33. Lever; Schlemmer, p. 103 ff.
34. Schlemmer, p. 102.
35. Crapanzano, *Tuhami: A Portrait of a Moroccan.*
36. de Klerk, p. 93.
37. Kierkegaard.
38. Heidegger, pp. 365–366.
39. Heidegger, p. 364.
40. Gordimer, "Living in the Interregnum."
41. Tournier; quoted in Gilles Deleuze's "Postscript," p. 260.

3. THE PAST
1. Pakenham, p. 607.
2. Quoted in Moodie, p. 1.
3. de Klerk, p. 32.
4. Barrow, vol. 1, pp. 80–81.
5. Schreiner.
6. Reitz, p. 92.
7. Quoted in de Klerk, p. 24.
8. Deut. 14:2.
9. Quoted in van Jaarsveld, p. 11.
10. Streak.
11. Quoted in Streak, p. 157.

4. HOME
1. Quoted in Streak, p. 155.
2. Grosskopf.
3. Watts, pp. 55–56.

4. Watts, p. 48.
5. de Kiewiet, p. 70.
6. Welsh, p. 223 ff.

5. UPBRINGING
 1. M'Carter, p. 143.
 2. Vatcher.
 3. Quoted in Vatcher, pp. 288–301.
 4. Moodie, *passim.*
 5. Loubser.
 6. Russell and Russell, p. 106.
 7. de Villiers, "Afrikaner Nationalism," p. 371.
 8. de Villiers, "Afrikaner Nationalism," p. 372.
 9. Giliomee and Elphick.
 10. Dupreez, pp. 97–98.
 11. Russell and Russell, pp. 109–140.
 12. Sachs.
 13. South Africa Institute of Race Relations, 1983, p. 460.
 14. Thompson and Prior, p. 113.
 15. South African Institute of Race Relations, 1982, pp. 197–198.
 16. South African Institute of Race Relations, 1982.
 17. *Ibid.*, 1983.
 18. *Ibid.*, p. 436.
 19. Thompson and Prior.
 20. South African Institute of Race Relations, 1982.

6. POLITICAL CONSCIOUSNESS
 1. Krüger, p. 62.
 2. Quoted in Moodie, p. 75.
 3. Wolheim, p. 31.
 4. de Villiers, "Afrikaner Nationalism," p. 389.
 5. Quoted in Moodie, p. 179.
 6. Moodie, p. 180.
 7. Quoted in Moodie, pp. 183–184.
 8. *Die Volksblad,* August 24, 1940.
 9. Moodie, p. 238.
 10. Vatcher, p. 138.
 11. Worrall, p. 200.
 12. Mansergh.

7. MARRIAGE. No notes.

8. RHODESIA
 1. Kramer, *The Last Cowboy,* chap. 2.
 2. Gann and Duignan.
 3. Lessing, p. 7.
 4. Gann and Duignan.
 5. Coetzee, p. 8.

9. OVERSEAS

   1. Junction Avenue Theatre Company, 1978, pp. 41–42.
   2. Pessoa, pp. 109–110.

10. CONVERSION

   1. Rom. 13:1–2.
   2. Kuper, pp. 191–215.
   3. Rom. 5:3–5.

11. VIOLENCE

   1. Gerhart, pp. 250–251.
   2. Gerhart, p. 253.
   3. Study Commission, pp. 173–175.
   4. Study Commission, p. 83.
   5. Geber and Newman, p. 40.
   6. *The Argus*, June 18, 1980.
   7. *The Cape Times*, June 19, 1980.
   8. *The Argus*, June 18, 1980.
   9. *Die Burger*, June 18, 1982.
   10. Arendt, pp. 4–5.
   11. Arendt, p. 7.
   12. Fussell, see especially chap. 6.

12. WORKERS

   1. de Villiers, personal communication.
   2. *The Star*, June 5, 1980, p. 7.

13. RENEWAL

   1. Benjamin, 1977, p. 178.
   2. Isaiah 52:7.
   3. Revelation 2:13.

14. THE FUTURE

   1. Adam, p. 71.
   2. Turner, chap. 1.
   3. Pifer.

BIBLIOGRAPHY

Adam, Heribert. "Ethnic Mobilization and the Politics of Patronage." In Heribert Adam and Hermann Giliomee, eds. *The Rise and Crisis of Afrikaner Power*. Cape Town: David Philip, 1979, pp. 61–82.

Arendt, Hannah. *On Violence*. New York: Harcourt Brace Jovanovich, 1969.

Barrow, John. *Travels into the Interior of Southern Africa in the years 1797 and 1798*, 2 vols. London: T. Cadell and W. Davies, 1801, 1804.

Bakhtine, Mikhail. *Esthétique et théorie du roman*. Paris: Gallimard, 1978.

Benjamin, Walter. *Illuminations*. New York: Schocken, 1969.

———. *The Origin of German Tragic Drama*. London: NLB, 1977.

———. *Reflections*. New York: Harcourt Brace Jovanovich, 1978.

Bourdieu, Pierre. *Leçon inaugurale*. Paris: Collège de France, 1982.

Bryce, James. *Impressions of South Africa*, 3rd ed. London: Macmillan, 1899.

Bunting, Brian. *The Rise of the South African Reich*. Harmondsworth, Middlesex: Penguin, 1964.

Coetzee, J. M. *In the Heart of the Country*. Johannesburg: Ravan Press, 1978.

———. *Waiting for the Barbarians*. Harmondsworth, Middlesex: Penguin, 1980.

Cope, Jack, and Uys Krige. *The Penguin Book of South African Verse*. Harmondsworth, Middlesex: Penguin, 1968.

Crapanzano, Vincent. *The Hamadsha: An Essay in Moroccan Ethnopsychiatry*. Berkeley: University of California Press, 1973.

———. *Tuhami: A Portrait of a Moroccan*. Chicago: University of Chicago Press, 1980.

Davenport, T. R. H. "The Consolidation of a New Society: The Cape Colony." In *The Oxford History of South Africa*, vol. 1. Monica Wilson and Leonard Thompson, eds. New York and Oxford: Oxford University Press, pp. 272–333.

de Kiewiet, C. W. *A History of South Africa: Social and Economic.* London: Oxford University Press, 1941.

de Klerk, Willem Abraham. *The Puritans in Africa: A Story of Afrikanerdom.* Harmondsworth, Middlesex: Penguin, 1975.

Deleuze, Gilles. "Postscript." In *Vendredi ou les Limbes du Pacifique.* Michel Tournier. Paris: Gallimard, 1972.

de Villiers, André. "Introduction." In *English-Speaking South Africa Today.* André de Villiers, ed. Cape Town: Oxford University Press, 1976, pp. V–VI.

———. "Afrikaner Nationalism." In *The Oxford History of South Africa,* vol. 2. Monica Wilson and Leonard Thompson, eds. New York and Oxford: Oxford University Press, 1971, pp. 365–423.

———. "The English Language Press." In *English-Speaking South Africa Today.* André de Villiers, ed. Cape Town: Oxford University Press, 1976.

Dupreez, A. B. *Inside the South African Crucible.* Cape Town and Pretoria: H.A.U.M., 1959.

Fredrickson, George M. *White Supremacy: A Comparative Study in American and Southern African History.* New York and Oxford: Oxford University Press, 1981.

Fugard, Athol. *Tsotsi.* New York: Random House, 1980.

———. *A Lesson from Aloes.* New York: Random House, 1981.

Fussell, Paul. *The Great War and Modern Memory.* London and New York: Oxford University Press, 1975.

Gann, L. H., and Peter Duignan. *White Settlers in Tropical Africa.* Harmondsworth, Middlesex: Penguin, 1962.

Garson, N. G. "English-Speaking South Africans and the British Connection: 1820–1961." In *English-Speaking South Africa Today.* André de Villiers, ed. Cape Town: Oxford University Press, 1976, pp. 17–39.

Geber, B. A., and S. P. Newman. *Soweto's Children: The Development of Attitudes.* New York: Academic Press, 1980.

Gerhart, Gail M. *Black Power in South Africa: The Evolution of an Ideology.* Berkeley: University of California Press, 1978.

Giliomee, Hermann, and Richard Elphick. "The Structure of European Domination at the Cape, 1652–1820." In *The Shaping of South African Society, 1652–1820.* Richard Elphick and Hermann Giliomee, eds. Cape Town: Longman Penguin Southern Africa, 1979.

Gordimer, Nadine. *July's People.* New York: Viking, 1981.

———. "Living in the Interregnum." *New York Review of Books* XXIX (1983): 21–29.

Grosskopf, Johann F. W. *Carnegie Commission of Investigation on the Poor White Question in South Africa.* Stellenbosch: Pro-ecclesia-drukkery, 1932.

Hattersley, Alan F. *The British Settlement of Natal: A Study in Imperial Migration.* Cambridge: Cambridge University Press, 1950.

Heidegger, Martin. "What Is Metaphysics." In *Existence and Being,* 2nd ed. London: Vision Press, 1956, pp. 353–390.

Hollenweger, W. J. *The Pentecostals: The Charismatic Movement in the Churches.* Minneapolis, Minnesota: Augsburg, 1972.

Jordaan, Ken. "The Origins of the Afrikaners and Their Language, 1652–1720: A Study in Miscegenation and Creole." *Race* XV (1974): 461–493.

Joubert, Elsa. *The Long Journey of Poppie Nongena.* Johannesburg: Jonathan Ball, 1980.

Junction Avenue Theatre Company. *The Fantastical History of a Useless Man.* Johannesburg: Raven Press, 1978.

Karis, Thomas G. "Revolution in the Making: Black Politics in South Africa," *Foreign Affairs* LXII (1983): 378–406.

Kierkegaard, Søren. *A Kierkegaard Anthology.* Princeton, N. J.: Princeton University Press, 1951.

Kramer, Jane. *The Last Cowboy.* New York: Harper & Row, 1977.

—— ("X"). "Fall of a House." *New York Review of Books.* XXVIII (1981): 14–18.

Krige, Uys. "The Coffin." In *The Dream and the Desert.* London: Collins, 1953, pp. 173–189.

Krüger, D. H. *South African Parties and Policies, 1910–1960.* Cape Town: Human and Rousseau, 1960.

Kuper, Leo. *An African Bourgeoisie.* New Haven: Yale University Press, 1965.

Lefebvre, Henri. *Everyday Life in the Modern World.* New York: Harper & Row, 1971.

Legum, Colin, ed. *Africa Contemporary Record: 1982–1983,* vol. 15. New York: Africana Publishing Company, 1984.

Lessing, Doris. *The Grass Is Singing.* New York: New American Library, 1950.

Lever, Henry. "Changes in Ethnic Attitudes in South Africa." Paper delivered at Second Congress of the Association for Sociology in Southern Africa, Lourenco Marquis, 1971.

Loubser, Jan. "Calvinism, Equality, and Inclusion: The Case of Afrikaner Calvinism." In *The Protestant Ethic and Modernization: A Comparative Study.* S. N. Eisenstadt, ed. New York: Basic Books, 1968, pp. 364–383.

M'Carter, John. *The Dutch Reformed Church in South Africa.* London: Inglis, 1869.

Malinowski, B. *Magic, Science, and Religion.* Garden City, N. Y.: Doubleday Anchor, 1948.

Mannoni, O. *Prospero and Caliban: The Psychology of Colonization.* New York: Frederick A. Praeger, 1964.

Marais, J. S. *The Cape Coloured People, 1652–1937.* London: Longmans, Green, 1939.

Mansergh, Nicholas. *South Africa, 1906–1961: The Price of Magnanimity.* London: George Allen and Unwin, 1962.

Memmi, Albert. *Portrait du colonisé.* Paris: Payot, 1973.

Moodie, T. Dunbar. *The Rise of Afrikanerdom: Power, Apartheid, and the Afrikaner Civil Religion.* Berkeley: University of California Press, 1975.

Naipaul, V. S. *Guerrillas.* New York: Knopf, 1975.

Nedbank Group. *South Africa: An Appraisal.* Johannesburg: Nedbank Group, 1983.

Opperman, D. J. *Groot Versbok.* Cape Town: Nasionale Pers, 1967.

Pakenham, Thomas. *The Boer War.* New York: Random House, 1979.

Patterson, Sheila. *The Last Trek: A Study of the Boer People and the Afrikaner Nation.* London: Routledge and Kegan Paul, 1957.

Pessoa, Fernando. *Selected Poems.* Peter Rickard, ed. and trans. Austin: University of Texas Press, 1971.

Pifer, Alan. *South African in the American Mind.* New York: Carnegie Corporation, 1981.

Reitz, F. W. *A Century of Wrong.* London: Review of Reviews, 1900.

Russell, Margo, and Martin Russell. *Afrikaners of the Kalahari: White Minority in a Black State.* Cambridge: Cambridge University Press, 1979.

Sachs, Albie. *Justice in South Africa.* Berkeley: University of California Press, 1973.

Sartre, Jean-Paul. *Being and Nothingness: An Essay in Phenomenological Ontology.* New York: Philosophical Library, 1956.

Schlemmer, Lawrence. "English-Speaking South Africans Today: Identity and Integration into the Broader National Community. In *English-Speaking South Africa Today.* André de Villiers, ed. Cape Town: Oxford University Press, 1976, pp. 91–135.

Schreiner, Olive. *The Story of an African Farm.* London: Collins, 1953.

Sepamla, Sipho. *A Ride on the Whirlwind.* Johannesburg: Donker, 1981.

Serfontein, J. H. P. *Brotherhood of Power.* London: Rex Collings, 1979.

Sharp, John S. "The Roots and Development of *Volkekunde* in South Africa." *Journal of Southern African Studies* VIII (1981): 16–36.

South African Institute of Race Relations. *Survey of Race Relations in South Africa*, vols. 35, 36, 37. Johannesburg: South African Institute of Race Relations, 1981, 1982, 1983.

Streak, Michael. *The Afrikaner as Viewed by the English, 1795–1854.* Cape Town: Struik, 1974.

Study Commission on U.S. Policy Toward South Africa. *South Africa: Time Running Out.* Berkeley: University of California Press, 1981.

Thompson, Leonard, and Andrew Prior. *South African Politics.* New Haven: Yale University Press, 1982.

Turner, Victor. *The Forest of Symbols: Aspects of Ndembu Ritual.* Ithaca, N.Y.: Cornell University Press, 1967.

van den Berghe, Pierre L. "Language and Nationalism in South Africa." *Race* IX (1967): 37–46.

van Jaarsveld, F. A. *The Afrikaner's Interpretation of South African History.* Cape Town: Simondium, 1964.

van Wyk Louw, N. P. *Berigte te Velde.* Cape Town: Nasionale Pers, 1959.
———. *Vernowing in die Prosa: Grepe vit ons Afrikaanse Ervaring.* Cape Town: Human and Rousseau, 1961.

Vatcher, William H., Jr. *White Laager: The Rise of Afrikaner Nationalism.* New York: Frederick A. Praeger, 1965.

Watts, H. L. "A Social and Demographic Portrait of English-Speaking

White South Africans." In *English-Speaking South Africa Today*. André de Villiers, ed. Cape Town: Oxford University Press, 1976, pp. 41–89.

Welsh, David. "English-Speaking Whites and the Racial Problem." In *English-Speaking South Africa Today*. André de Villiers, ed. Cape Town: Oxford University Press, 1976, pp. 217–239.

Wilkins, Ivor, and Hans Strydom. *The Super-Afrikaners: Inside the Afrikaner Broederbond*. Johannesburg: Jonathan Ball, 1978.

Wittgenstein, Ludwig. "Remarks on Frazer's 'Golden Bough.'" *The Human World* III (1971): 18–41.

Wolheim, O. D. "The Coloured People of South Africa." *Race* V (1963): 25–41.

Worrall, Denis. "English South Africa and the Political System." In *English-Speaking South Africa Today*. André de Villiers, ed. Cape Town: Oxford University Press, 1976, pp. 193–215.

INDEX

About the Author

VINCENT CRAPANZANO is professor of anthropology and comparative literature at Queens College and the Graduate Center of the City University of New York. In addition to *Waiting: The Whites of South Africa*, he is the author of *The Fifth World of Foster Bennett*, about the modern Navajo, and two books about the Moroccans, *The Hamadsha* and *Tuhami: A Portrait of a Moroccan*, as well as numerous articles. He lives in New York City with his wife, the writer Jane Kramer.